The Long American Revolution and Its Legacy

THE LONG AMERICAN REVOLUTION & ITS LEGACY

Lester D. Langley

The University of Georgia Press
Athens

Designed by Melissa Bugbee Buchanan
Set in Adobe Caslon Pro
Printed and bound by Sheridan Books, Inc.

The paper in this book meets the guidelines for permanence
and durability of the Committee on Production Guidelines for
Book Longevity of the Council on Library Resources.

Most University of Georgia Press titles are
available from popular e-book vendors.

Printed in the United States of America
19 20 21 22 23 P 5 4 3 2 1

Library of Congress Cataloging-in-Publication Data
Names: Langley, Lester D., author.
Title: The long American Revolution and its legacy /
Lester D. Langley.
Description: Athens : The University of Georgia Press, [2019] |
Includes bibliographical references and index.
Identifiers: LCCN 2019007396| ISBN 9780820355764
(hardback : alk. paper) | ISBN 9780820355740 (pbk. :
alk. paper) | ISBN 9780820355757 (e-book)
Subjects: LCSH: United States—History—Revolution, 1775–1783—
Influence. | Revolutions—America—History. | Democracy—United
States—History. | Racism—United States—History. | United
States—History. | America—History.
Classification: LCC E209 .L34 2019 | DDC   973.3/1—dc23
LC record available at https://lccn.loc.gov/2019007396

For

MY BROTHER, BILL LANGLEY (1928–2018),
who in his senior year in high school refused to take a
whipping from the principal and was denied the right to
graduate, who joined the U.S. Army and became a good
soldier, and who in his lifetime proved himself a great
husband, father, citizen, and friend.

========

MY GRANDSON LEO DANNY LANGLEY,
who combines a love of science, computers, and
reading with an infectious likability.

========

MY DAUGHTER-IN-LAW, RYOKO "LYNN" SUWA LANGLEY,
who combines social grace and friendliness with
a thoroughly American flair for shopping.

========

MY CLASSMATES FROM THE BORGER, TEXAS,
HIGH SCHOOL CLASS OF 1958,
who want to "fit in" but refuse to be "fitted in,"
who believe that the United States of America is
America, and who have accepted me as one of their own.

========

THE CONGREGATION AND PASTORS OF SIERRA VISTA
UNITED METHODIST CHURCH OF SAN ANGELO, TEXAS,
who believe in inclusiveness, mission, music,
evangelism, and community.

========

AND DAVID M. K. SHEININ,
who understands America in both its U.S. and
hemispheric identities and why Canadians sometimes
say, "We are not Americans," but who sense that they
are children of the long American Revolution and
know they have also been its victims.

CONTENTS

ACKNOWLEDGMENTS

MY THANKS TO THOSE WHO HAVE READ various drafts or portions of the manuscript and to those on whose work on specific events or topics I have depended. I could not have written this book without the excellent work they have done. My thanks also to two anonymous readers, one of whom read the manuscript twice. I have responded to both in a positive way by incorporating their suggestions. David M. K. Sheinin read and reread chapters, offering both encouragement and invaluable editorial commentary. Brian McKnight and Cynthia Bouton, who teach U.S. and French and Atlantic world history, respectively, read portions of an early draft.

Walter Biggins of the University of Georgia Press has been both advisor and ally in my efforts to justify my emphasis on a "long" American Revolution and its legacy for U.S. history and the age of revolution. Former colleagues at the University of Georgia, notably Laura Mason, David Roberts, William Stueck, Peter Hoffer, and Thom Whigham, whose expertise ranges from Italy and France to the United States and Latin America, have influenced my thinking about revolution and nation more than they know. And, as in my other books, Wanda Langley has reprised her much-appreciated role of supporter and reader.

A NOTE ON USAGE

IT WAS COMMON IN THE EIGHTEENTH CENTURY and into the nineteenth to use "America" to mean "the Americas" and also to mean the territories or colonies in the Americas that were British or Spanish and so on. We "Americans" have largely gotten away with our identity theft of the name, which is understandable, because this country was born without a name. I have been alert to those places in the narrative where the distinction is necessary for clarity. I have never met anyone who believes that the controversial issue of "American exceptionalism" refers to any country other than the United States. Dictionaries sometimes identify "American" as pertaining to the United States or North or South America. There are 150 definitions of "American"—all hyphenates—in the Library of Congress Authorities Division. In those places where there might be confusion between John Adams and his son John Quincy Adams, I have referred to the latter as "Quincy Adams."

I have not corrected Abigail Adams's grammar in the quoted material from her iconic "Remember the Ladies" letter to John for two reasons. First, there would be too many *sic*s and, second, as John admitted in his response, disagreeing with Abigail about the power of women was risky. Those men who have married or had a long relationship with an "Abigail Adams" know what I mean. You know you're married to "Abigail Adams" when you say, "I have no desire to change anyone but myself," and she responds, "Why don't you?" Abigail was an invaluable friend and advisor to John. He could not have accomplished what he did without her. John had Abigail. She took care of the family business while he spent a career being a politician and statesman. John remained a contrarian to the end of his life. His rival and revolutionary ally, Thomas Jefferson, wrote inspirational phrases about freedom and liberty yet sometimes violated these ideals in his exercise of power. Jefferson acquired a following of worshippers and wound up chiseled on Mount Rushmore, but Adams got the better deal. He knew that when Abigail signed her "Remember the Ladies" letter as "Your ever faithfull Friend."

INTRODUCTION

I HAVE BOTH A PERSONAL and a professional bond with the long American Revolution. I am descended from a long line of Kentuckians—the male line from my great-great-grandfather, who was born in the last year of the eighteenth century, to my father, who was born in the last year of the nineteenth. My mother was born in December 1898, a few days after the signing of the peace treaty ending the war with Spain. My parents were married in October 1916, when President Woodrow Wilson ran for reelection on a peace slogan that belied his pro-British sentiments in the Great War. I was born in 1940, their eighth and last child.

My father saw the world and history as the Revolution's "economic man," a creature of self-interest; my mother and my sisters, as a morality play. My father's communal bond, as did that of George Washington and other U.S. presidents, lay with the Masons. My mother's spiritual life was rooted in the church and her faith in scripture. My father was intelligent and but for the Great Depression might have become a successful banker. I have memories of trying to read his detective magazines before I was in the first grade, and I thought I was impressing my teacher when I proudly told her I knew how to spell "bludgeon," although I did not comprehend what it meant. When my mother found out, she bought a book of Bible stories and read them to me. I loved my mother and especially the younger of my two sisters, who was eight years older and took care of me. When I was a little boy, and my older brothers had already left home, my mother and my sister more than my father influenced and shaped how I looked at things.

In indirect but important ways, over the 150 years that serve as the chronological benchmark dates of this book, my eighteenth- and nineteenth-century ancestors were beneficiaries of a "long" American Revolution, its promise of opportunity validated by the thrust westward. From what I know about them, they were reflective of the racial priorities and sentiments of a country born with what has been called its original sin of slavery as well as the parallel promise of equality in the Declaration of Independence, a country that became more preoccupied and then obsessed with race as it became more democratic. The character and beliefs of my ancestors defy facile sociological or cultural categorization save for certain traits that have helped me to understand them as well as the American Revolution and its legacy—a deeply felt sense of national pride accompanied with equally strong beliefs in individualism, freedom, militancy, and the redemptive power of movement, however depressing the consequences.

I doubt if my great-great-great-grandfather who left his home in St. Mary's County in Maryland for the new state of Kentucky in the 1790s knew how precarious his future might be. In the decade of the 1790s, only one in four in the state acquired land. The promise of a more democratic society morphed into a racial and gendered hierarchy dominated by white men with money and power allied with poor white males. Their concerns lay with Indian attacks and land speculators. It was unsurprising that in another generation, settlers in the western country composed Andrew Jackson's constituency of *Herrenvolk*, the master race, at a time when the Second Great Awakening swept the region. In the early twentieth century, my grandfather moved the family from Kentucky to Hunt County in the rapidly growing region of eastern Texas, where farming and oil held out promises of a prosperous future. In those years, populist and even socialist ideas took hold, and the region's racial preferences were proudly displayed in Greenville's welcome banner: "The blackest land and the whitest people."[1]

I suspect that my grandfather (born in 1870), a good-natured, diminutive man who was an orphan at age ten and in 1892 married an imperious woman from a more socially prestigious Kentucky family, shared the views if not the experience that fired the "redneck revolt" of the 1890s, southern populism, and the Jim (and Jane) Crow laws of that era. I know my father did. In many ways, his was a world and way of looking at race and religion I wanted to get away from, and after leaving for college and then going to graduate school, I believed I could leave my past behind me by moving on and moving up. I did, and in what was for me a transformative and rewarding experience, I learned about interpretation and evidence and the danger of projecting the present on the past. In the process, my willingness to assess a movement or an event or a cause or a decision as a moral issue weakened.

What complicated matters for me and others entering graduate school in history (and other fields as well) in the early 1960s was the coincidence of a still-contentious debate about the political and social climate of the Cold War, years of decolonization, and a world undergoing rapid and uncertain change.

Liberals found themselves challenged between two schools of thought about the direction of the country and its role in the world. One occupied what Arthur Schlesinger Jr. called the "vital center," which at home moved uneasily and for some too slowly into remolding the Democratic Party, addressing the condition of black America, and laying out a development program in Africa, Latin America, and Asia in an era when the Soviet Union offered an alternative socialist model for economic growth and the role of the state in society.

The legacy and meaning of the American Revolution, as well as religion, played special roles in meeting the Soviet challenge. In his spirited inaugural address of January 20, 1961, President John F. Kennedy invoked the credos of the American Revolution in explaining what was at stake in U.S. foreign policy in confronting the socialist threat to U.S. political, economic, and even moral interests in the world. The "same revolutionary beliefs for which our forebears fought," Kennedy warned, "are still at issue—the belief that the rights of man come not from the generosity of the state but from the hand of God." His definition of the Cold War as a religious as much as a political or economic confrontation and his calculated but understandable strategy of convincing Protestant America of the necessity of allying with Catholic America in that war meshed neatly with the country's postwar ideology of choice—American exceptionalism, or modernization theory, endowed by God and social science.[2]

In many university history departments, an alternative account of our revolutionary tradition—often identified with William Appleman Williams's still-relevant *The Tragedy of American Diplomacy* (1959) and especially *The Contours of American History* (1961)—rebutted with the view that our revolutionary heritage had been betrayed by leaders who had consciously pursued expansion and empire in the name of progress and peace at home. The history of the United States was the history of capitalism and the linkage of property and search for markets to expansionism. Years before Karl Marx scribbled his indictment of capitalism, American revolutionary ideology incorporated the belief that the ownership of property constituted an essential measure of the worthiness of the person. The real villain in the piece was not communism but liberalism, which in the name of progress and the maintenance of order and peace had violated God's earthly domain by persuading the individual that empire and expansion guaranteed his or her freedom and prosperity. The effect turned out to be the destruction of community and betrayal of the common good. Somewhere, presumably in the course of the long American Revolution, the United States had gotten on the "wrong side of history," which meant that our Revolution had not resolved the "social question," and in the name of national security and a messianic arrogance we had denied others' right of self-determination to have the revolution of their choosing.

ADDRESSING THAT QUESTION and the often-contentious literature surrounding the long American Revolution is a central goal of this book, and I'll begin with a few general comments about revolutions. Unlike rebellions, David Armitage reminds us in *Civil Wars: A History in Ideas* (2017), revolutions are relatively new and are often presumed to be about progress and liberation. Civil wars date back to the classical era and stem from grievances or are about blood and belonging. We may believe that revolutions can lead to a better society, but they sometimes end with the militarization of society and are used as justification for maintaining an army for domestic pacification and dealing with those who feel left behind as well as those who refuse to get out of the way. Revolutions are conditional on time, space, and circumstance, and they are self-defining.

Revolutions can also take a long time to leave their lasting imprint on a society or a nation. In a classic account published in 1961, Raymond Williams defined a "long revolution" as a "tragic disorder" that shapes us and provides us with the necessary ideas to describe what is happening in our efforts to control it. At bottom, it is, or should be, a "human revolution," a complex whole in which relationships matter. In other words, it is not deterministic or mechanistic. It is the antithesis of communism, which is dehumanizing.[3]

There was a warning implicit in that description, and as someone who spent his career teaching and writing about revolution, I am still haunted by the one described by Hannah Arendt in *On Revolution* (1963): Whatever definition we may give the word, revolution usually means war. Either in victory or defeat, those who are seduced by a revolutionary message may have to be pacified. If you are someone who doesn't like to be pinned down with a definition of revolution, it's somewhere between "when a wheel goes around once," which was my answer to a doctoral prelims committee in October 1964, and "chaos and complexity," two theories I found useful in writing *The Americas in the Age of Revolution, 1750 to 1850* (1996).[4]

There's a lot of room between those parameters, but that "space" is vital for understanding the meaning and legacy of revolutions and especially the long

American Revolution. Revolutions are complicated phenomena, and of the four major revolutions in the Atlantic world in the half-century after 1775—the American, the French, the Haitian, and the Latin, principally Spanish, American—the most complicated was the American. My purpose here is to narrate how and why I believe that. The chronological benchmark dates are broad, the geographical contexts range from the local and national to the Atlantic world, and the historical perspective draws on a rich literature from the theoretical and scholarly to trade books for the general reader and, if you are someone who believes history is a morality play, to scripture.

I HAVE DIVIDED THE NARRATIVE into three broad themes. The first and most critical identifies the American Revolution as the longest war in our history, as a civil war, and as a war of multiple faces, one expansionist, domineering, and menacing, its promises and history scarred by slavery, racism, expansionism, and white supremacy, and the other idealist, humanitarian, and dedicated to self-determination, liberty, freedom, and equality. These contradictory experiences and beliefs are knotted together in its history. The Revolution and what it meant for the person and the nation—the rights and well-being of the first and the security of the second—have defined who we are and why we are still quarreling over what it means. It is the only war in our history we cannot afford to lose. The world of the late eighteenth century may seem distant and alien from our modern sensibilities, but in 1776 law, religion, power, and natural (or what we call human) rights were paramount concerns. They still are, or at least we believe they should be.

We do need a dialogue with our past. Yet when we look to the past, especially the ideas and beliefs of the Founders, in our search for the proverbial universal truths, we find that the Founders rarely agreed on anything. They had as much trouble reconciling the Declaration of Independence with the Constitution—the liberal belief that "valued [the] individual freedom, autonomy, and self-sufficiency" and the liberal pluralism that required the "power, stability, and the efficacy of the state"—as we do today. Our individualism gives us the right to fulfill our own interests, our pluralism, the capability to protect what we have.[5]

The second involves assessing the American Revolution not only as a transatlantic or world phenomenon but especially as a hemispheric war with links not only to the French but, just as important, to the Haitian and Latin, especially Spanish, American struggles, as well as to the Canadian experience in

the revolutionary age. We have a symbiotic relationship with these three revolutions. The generation that came of age after the American Revolution felt
its impact and influence on their lives at a time when the power of the federal
government was limited but political leaders sensed the importance of using
celebrations and cultural symbols to promote a sense of national identity, in
part to lessen the appeal of alternative revolutionary movements, especially in
Haiti and Spanish America. Over the course of the nineteenth century, critical issues identified with the revolutionary age began to look different from
a hemispheric perspective. The War of 1812 was not only a British-American
war but even more so a civil war between republican Americans and monarchical Americans that bore a disturbing if less violent comparison to the wars
in Spanish America. The transatlantic abolitionist struggle against slavery
was a moral and pacific crusade, at least for its white if not its black and colored leaders. In the Americas, slavery was ended in the aftermath of the wars
of independence by decree and in some cases compensation to slave owners
or by armed struggle in two places: French Saint-Domingue (Haiti) and the
United States.[6]

The third theme is a reminder about the relationship between the Revolution, the person, and nationhood: we are an *old* republic but a *young* nation. The bulk of the narrative encompasses the 132 years between either the
creation of the republic at the Constitutional Convention in 1787 or Washington's inaugural two years later—commonly accepted dates for ending the
Revolution—and the end of the Great War of 1914–18 and the failure of
President Woodrow Wilson to bring the United States into the League of
Nations coupled with the shock that the Mexican and Russian Revolutions
gave to liberal internationalism, capitalism, and Christianity.

The American Revolution bequeathed not one but three nations, each with
roots in the formative years of the revolutionary age. It is critical to remember
the *order* in which they took identifiable form: the Confederacy in 1861, with
slavery and white supremacy as much as states' rights as its guiding principles;
the United States in the Great War, with the maturation of the white republic
and the capacity if not always the use of the power of the federal government
over the still-divided and fractious country; and Canada, which became a dominion after the Civil War and a nation during the Great War.[7]

I HAVE ORGANIZED the narrative into two parts. Part 1, "The New World's
First Republic," begins with the French and Indian War in the Ohio coun-

try of New France in 1754 and ends with the election of Andrew Jackson seventy-five years later. In this formative era in the history of the Atlantic world and the United States, the colonial crisis in the British Empire escalated into a rebellion and a war of independence. That war became not only a critical dynamic in the Second Hundred Years' War between Great Britain and France and their respective allies but also the first of four major revolutions that transformed the Atlantic world: the American, the French, the Haitian, and the Latin, principally Spanish, American. In this formative era, the development and character of both the Revolution and the early republic became entangled by the divisions not only within the country but also within the larger war in the Atlantic world. The revolutions in France, in French Saint-Domingue, and in mainland Latin America intruded into the republic's international affairs and its political life and culture. These disruptive forces continued after the War of 1812 as the rise of Jacksonian democracy coupled with the issue of slavery and race as national issues challenged the leaders of the old republic. In the 1820s they fashioned political compromises over slavery's expansion and a major statement about our relationship to Europe and our role in the Americas. These mitigated rather than resolved the contradictions left by the Revolution. As Thomas Jefferson and John Adams surmised, there would be a reckoning.

Part 2, "The Reckoning," relates that story in three chapters, beginning about 1830 with a more militant abolitionist movement and the Texas Revolution and ending with the Great War of 1914–18. In this ninety-year era, the republic wrought by the long American Revolution—described by Alexis de Tocqueville in *Democracy in America* (1835) as the welcome alternative to the French model—experienced a technological and commercial revolution, the expansion of the territorial domain by one-third in the 1846–47 war with Mexico, the emergence of a slave-labor plantation system that reached from the South into the Caribbean and Brazil, and the birth of the first nation sired by the American Revolution, the Confederacy. For the second time, as in 1774–76, leaders confronted a challenge in 1860–61 that defied a peaceful settlement within the political structures and legal restraints imposed on them without alienating their respective constituencies.

The war that began in 1861 became something more encompassing, more destructive, and more chaotic, and in its violence it expressed another face of the long American Revolution. European leaders in the 1860s measured their own futures in the context of what the civil wars and political crises in Mexico, Canada, and especially the United States meant for democratic and republican movements in their own countries. Monarchical government survived in Europe, and, as I relate in the last chapter, the country followed yet another tangled and often violent path toward industrial might and empire, world power, and nationhood in the Great War. A generation looked to the lessons and legacy of the American Revolution and the early republic for guidance.

I HAVE APPENDED chapter-by-chapter time lines to assist the reader. For the most part, the chapter organization follows a traditional textbook pattern, but the exceptions warrant an explanation. The usual chapter break between the Federalist Era (chapter 3) and the Jeffersonian (chapter 4) is the election of 1800. I have made that break at the end of Jefferson's first administration in 1805 because it came in the aftermath of the Louisiana Purchase, the resumption of the European war, and the declaration of Haitian independence. I have begun the chapter on the Civil War in the mid-1850s because that coincided with "bloody Kansas," the birth of the Republican and American Parties and demise of the Whig Party, political crises in Mexico resulting in civil war, and the escalation of anti-immigrant and anti-Catholic sentiments. I have ended that chapter not with the traditional ending date for Reconstruction (1877) but ten years earlier, with the onset of what is called Congressional or Radical Republican Reconstruction, where chapter 8 begins, as historians now extend the Reconstruction era to the end of the nineteenth century.

The bibliographical essay provides an assessment of both the current and the older but still relevant literature on the revolutionary age in the Atlantic world but with an emphasis on those works pertaining to the long American Revolution.

PART I

The New World's First Republic

CHAPTER I

A War of Consequence

IN THE SPRING OF 1754 there commenced in the region at the forks of the Ohio River a series of skirmishes involving colonial Britons and French Canadian traders. The conflict escalated into a major war between the British and French and their allies in North America, Europe, India, and the Caribbean two years later. The war had its origin in the local competition between Pennsylvania's and Virginia's interests and settlers, giving the French and their Indian allies an opportunity to exploit local animosities and take control. Both colonies had land claims in the area, but the Virginians argued that the Quaker-dominated Pennsylvania Assembly had proved ineffective in checking the French intrusion. The conflict came to be known as the French and Indian War in the colonies and as the Seven Years' War in Europe and New France.

The incidental fighting in this sparsely inhabited but commercially important trading region was part of a multifaceted and more consequential story in the history of North America and Europe. It was also a continuation of the Second Hundred Years' War (1689–1815) between Britain and France and their respective allies, a war triggered by Parliament's deposing of King James II in 1688. In a more meaningful sense, the Seven Years' War was also the first world war or "people's war": it was led by men who sought popularity and affection among their people and who were committed to expanding the commerce and power of the state at home and abroad.[1]

For the German-born British monarch George II, the war offered an opportunity to strike a blow at the French enemy. George II would not be around for the triumphant finale of the Seven Years' War. He died of a stroke in 1760, and the crown passed to his grandson George III, the first Hanoverian born in London. A morally upright man who spoke without a German accent, the young king was disinclined to take up the sword but determined to prove himself. His task lay in reaffirming the Crown's authority over a

Parliament George deemed corrupt. The war that had erupted in the Ohio River backcountry, he believed, would give him that opportunity.[2]

For those who handled colonial affairs in Whitehall (the central offices of the British government in London) and for Britons in the Atlantic seaboard colonies, there were more immediate concerns. Colonial Britons, especially powerful Virginia speculators, and British leaders had a special interest in the region. When Virginia governor Robert Dinwiddie got news of French activity into an area coveted by some of his wealthy friends, he dispatched a unit of the Virginia militia to demand their withdrawal. Its commander was an ambitious twenty-two-year-old lieutenant, George Washington. In the ensuing two expeditions, Washington suffered his first defeats in battle. His redemption came in 1755, when he joined a larger British force under General George Braddock in another penetration into the Ohio country. In this campaign, Braddock lost his life, but Washington proved himself in victory at the Battle of Monongahela and emerged a hero on both sides of the Atlantic. From the beginning of the conflict, he became increasingly resentful and angry about his treatment from his British superiors, especially their persistent pigheadedness about the way they wanted to fight the war in the western country. He knew the importance of using Indian allies, and he chafed at the charge that he was personally to blame for starting a war in the "backwoods of America [that] set the world on fire."[3]

Viewed retrospectively, Washington's actions in the Ohio River country in 1754 constituted the first blows of the American Rebellion and the seedtime of the War of Independence and the American Revolution. Neither of these seemed imaginable when war broke out in Europe in May 1756. On the Continent, where Britain's ally Frederick the Great of Prussia carried most of the burden of fighting and won several initial victories, the war ground to a stalemate. In Senegal in West Africa and in Bengal in India, however, the British triumphed, creating a new colony in West Africa (Senegambia) and enabling Robert Clive to establish a commercial base for the East India Company in Bengal. The most impressive British victory came in September 1759 on the Plains of Abraham near Quebec City, where forces under the command of Major General James Wolfe defeated French defenders led by the marquis de Montcalm. Indirectly, the victory reinforced the growing colonial demand to be treated as equals in the British Empire, or the Crown would face the consequences.[4]

The French defeat jeopardized the impressive French commercial and even cultural network among the Indians of the Great Lakes region, known as the middle ground. French king Louis XV called for peace discussions, but when William Pitt (the Elder), the mastermind behind British strategy in the war, insisted on cession of New France and other commercial concessions, Louis invoked a pledge of assistance from another Bourbon monarch, King Carlos III of Spain, to come to France's assistance. The British declared war on Spain in January 1762. Two months later, a British amphibious force laid siege to Havana and imposed a six-month occupation.

An Imperial Family Quarrel

More than any of the previous conflicts in the 125-year history of the Second Hundred Years' War, the Seven Years' War altered the way participants viewed their experience. Militiamen from Massachusetts who served in the British occupation of Havana came home believing they were as good as any soldier in the regular British army. Spaniards remembered the experience as well, but for different reasons—the enthusiasm with which the occupiers plied their goods and wares at a time when smugglers were often the advance agents in the promotion of a consumer market. Carlos was an ambitious monarch and had already set about reorganizing and streamlining the jurisdiction of his American "kingdoms" in a plan to mold them into colonies, thus enhancing Spain's stature among the European states. In the final peace settlement of 1763, the Spanish lost Florida but secured the return of the more valuable Havana. Despite their alliance with the losing French, the Spanish also obtained New Orleans and that portion of French territory west of the Mississippi.

The British triumph changed everything. With the assistance of European, Indian, and colonial allies, the armies of the young king George III had acquired a vast territorial bounty east of the Mississippi in North America, established effective control of India and the Caribbean, and gained presumably insurmountable advantage in the rich Atlantic trade. By war's end, some sixty thousand colonial militiamen and another twelve thousand in the regular British military had served in the war. By a statistical if not a patriotic reckoning, their numbers constituted a higher proportion of the population than that of the home country. The usually prosaic Benjamin Franklin exulted in the expressions of pride by ordinary people: "What an Accession of Power to the British Empire by Sea as well as Land!"[5]

When Franklin spoke enthusiastically about the British future after 1763, he voiced a sentiment that at last British leaders would recognize and accept as equals those loyal and proud Britons of the Atlantic seaboard colonies who had played such an important role in winning the war. Where the territorial spoils of the trans-Appalachian West were at issue, however, the fundamental differences between these two entities became clear. The matter proved more complicated than the immediate consideration of a huge war debt of £137 million (or more than U.S.$25.5 billion today) and the need for the colonies to pay something of the cost of occupying and administering the vast territories acquired from the French. (Two-thirds of the French monarch's income went to paying interest on the debt incurred during the war.)[6]

Indians in the Ohio region and New York had been major players in the war, and they intended to continue that role, expecting the same deference and concessions that European state powers made to one another. The brutal style of Indian warfare terrified rural European settlers living under British authority. Colonial publicists and provincial leaders were able to sharpen their ongoing political debate with the British government by appealing to a collective sense of victimization among rural families united less by racial hatreds than by apprehensions about pan-Indianist alliance and war, even as settlers killed Indians and dispossessed Indian lands. The imagined nightmare scenario of British invasion, pan-Indian uprising, and slave rebellion persisted into the American Revolution and the early republic.[7]

A parallel concern was the impact of a generation of colonial leaders who sensed they could shape postwar imperial policy. Before the war, the British had begun to develop a new colonial policy to check the influence of colonial leaders and deal with the rapid demographic growth of both white and African slave populations and the parallel growth of colonial exports of raw materials to the home market. In a changing economic environment, the appointed governors came under increasing pressure from the colonial assemblies and from their superiors in Whitehall to reaffirm the authority of the king over his "plantations" in America. Too often, governors' influence diminished before the politicking of a generation of transatlantic colonial agents (Benjamin Franklin was one) who exercised their persuasive skills and rhetoric about English liberty on parliamentarians.[8]

British officials suspended their colonial policy during the war but abruptly revived it in the aftermath of the Peace of Paris in 1763, believing they had inherited an empire in the Great Lakes with a Native population now beholden to them and not the French. Indians continued to trade but largely ignored British laws and customs, and the land rush of squatters, settlers, and speculators into the region east of the Mississippi escalated. To address the problem, the British designed what proved to be one of the most controversial documents in the postwar era, the Proclamation of 1763, a measure designed to transform North American territories acquired from the French and Spanish into loyal settler colonies yet preserve the lucrative trading network of the trans-Appalachian region. Washington had correctly predicted the need for such a policy. As someone whose economic future was intimately tied to western development, he also sensed that the future of those living in the thirteen colonies east of the mountains lay in the western country.[9]

But Parliament and the Board of Trade had a more coherent agenda for the British Empire in the western country, and mapmakers had already commenced their labors, drawing up a more detailed scheme for land distribution and regulating economic development there. This meant bringing a halt to the migration of a generation of ambitious speculators and land-hungry colonial Britons, who perceived what was intended as a temporary measure to deal with the chaotic conditions in the western country as a permanent threat. The proclamation reduced New France to what is now the size of Quebec and Ontario and instituted English civil law. Yet the combined problems of a large French-speaking population with its own religious and legal traditions and the inability of the government to populate the province with a significant Anglo population prompted British officials to concede that Quebec would remain largely French, much to the displeasure of its minority Anglophone inhabitants.[10]

Plans for Florida were similarly ambitious in design but ultimately disappointing in results. The British divided Florida (which then extended westward to the Isle of Orleans and north into present-day Georgia and Alabama) into two distinct royal colonies, East and West, with the idea of turning them into successful settler, plantation, and trading entities. West Florida languished, but to the more vigorous East Florida came southern planters from Georgia (the last royal colony of the original thirteen) with their slaves. Within the span of a decade, the British began to curtail the vigorous Creek trade with the French and Spanish, and the white population expanded rapidly. In the process, southeastern Indians had been compelled to cede 5.5 million acres.[11]

More alarming to colonial Britons were London's efforts to reconfigure the trans-Appalachian region into an Indian reservation, which conflicted with the longtime plans of Virginia speculators to remake the Ohio Valley into a colonial version of an imperial outback. In the early stages of the war, the Iroquois struck a bargain with the British to break the French hold on the western country. In return for ceding back to the Indians certain lands, coupled with a pledge not to build more settlements west of the Allegheny Mountains, the Iroquois agreed to throw in with the British and persuade their Indian allies to follow their lead. Their help, particularly in logistics and intelligence, would be critical to the British victory. At the same time, the abrupt change of events not only struck a blow at Virginia's land speculators but also meant the end of Washington's efforts to obtain a commission in the regular British army. He had proved in his molding of rough-hewn Virginians into a fighting force superior to other colonial militia or even British regulars that both he and they were deserving of equal treatment. In what became in retrospect prophetic words, he noted, "We cannot conceive that because we are Americans, we should therefore be deprived of the Benefits Common to British subjects."[12]

Washington was not alone in predicting the chaotic aftermath of the war in the Great Lakes region and Pontiac's Rebellion, an Indian uprising response that represented something more than a war over control of the land. Indian leaders wanted to be treated with respect and dealt with as equals at a time when British officers were more interested in affirming their "imperial superiority" over Indians and the white intruders.

Ten thousand British troops stationed in the western country proved unable to contain what rapidly became a war with racial overtones. In December 1763 a vigilante group in western Pennsylvania, the Paxton Boys, attacked a settlement of peaceful Iroquoian-speaking Conestoga Indians, whose forebears had signed a peace treaty with the colony's founder, William Penn. Pontiac's forces attacked and seized eight British forts and laid siege to Detroit for a year. With the harsh winter, the Indian threat diminished, and the British changed tactics. In following the French example and befriending the Indians, the Crown's officers negotiated a useful alliance that later paid off when the colonies revolted. As Pontiac explained to the Indian superintendent, Sir William Johnson, "We tell you now [that] the French never conquered us. . . . [I]f you expect to keep these [military] Posts, we will expect to have proper returns from you."[13]

In a meeting at Niagara Falls in July 1764, Johnson signed two treaties with

Anishinaabeg chiefs in which he pledged to reserve specified lands for Indian occupation. Settlers and land speculators from the seaboard colonies largely ignored the promise. In truth, British policy in the trans-Appalachian region was intended to regulate and control trade, not guarantee Indian land titles or recognize Indian sovereignty. The stark reality confronted by both Spain and Britain in their unrealistic division of North America at the Mississippi was that neither had the power to police the Native populations in their respective regions. Adversaries in war, each had to rely on the Indians to maintain the peace. For patrolling Louisiana, the Spanish had five hundred soldiers. British officers in the western country experienced parallel frustrations. Thomas Gage, who became British commander in chief for North America in 1763, ruefully summed up the situation in a recommendation for abandoning the western country: "Let the savages enjoy their desarts in quiet."[14]

His comment unintentionally revealed an uncertainty about what the British were confronting in North America: an increasingly assertive population that expressed its collective anger through print or in the streets. Reaction to the Stamp Act was but one example of how quickly matters could get out of hand. Passed with an overwhelming majority in Parliament, the act imposed a tax on newspapers, legal documents, almanacs, and most forms of paper. It precipitated a constitutional confrontation between the colonies and Parliament in which several legislative assemblies correctly asserted that in British constitutional law, taxes were a "gift," and only elected representatives of the people of the thirteen colonies could impose such a tax. Local action groups, notably the Sons of Liberty, sprang up to resist the law. Colonials boycotted British goods. Those who refused to go along sometimes found themselves facing angry neighbors who retaliated with intimidating condemnation and personal slurs. Angry crowds smeared shops selling British goods in defiance of the boycott with a mix of feces and mud called "Hillsborough paint," a mocking reference to the king's minister for colonial affairs.

What brought Parliament to heel, however, was not so much the initial public violence and rioting over the tax but the ability of colonial leaders to channel the resistance in an orderly way, such as shutting down proceedings in the courts until Parliament reconsidered the error of its ways. On the local level, the disquiet of the imperial crisis had spawned a new kind of leader—a person skilled in channeling and articulating grievances who would play a critical role in the coming republican cause. Such men found their home in the Sons of Liberty; women, in the Daughters of Liberty. Although considered men's intellectual equals, women were expected to fulfill their political roles in the home and the family. Their venues were taverns, theaters, salons, and the street.[15]

In conceding defeat over the Stamp Act, Parliament passed the Declaratory Act of 1766, which reaffirmed that body's indisputable right to legislate for the colonies. William Knox, a subcabinet official in the British government, confirmed Parliament's sovereignty in a succinct statement: the colonies were part of the British community and subject to the power of Parliament, not the legislatures of their choosing. Thirteen years later, George III recalled the debate within his own cabinet over the Stamp Act and expressed his regret that he had acquiesced in his ministers' recommendation to repeal the law. That decision, he said, had been his greatest error as king. George's memory may have been a bit fuzzy about some of the details surrounding passage of the Stamp Act and his objections to it, but there was nothing ambiguous about the Declaratory Act as a legal defense of Parliament's sovereignty or uncertainty about what George would do to bring his increasingly defiant and rebellious subjects into submission. At the same time, the circumstances under which the act was passed conveyed ambiguity: Parliament would not execute the law, but it left open the possibility that it would pass laws without colonial consent.[16]

Rebellion, Civil War, or Revolution?

In other words, acts of Parliament carried the same authority throughout the British Empire. The fact that Parliament had backed down in the Stamp Act crisis was not an admission that it had no authority to pass the law for the Atlantic seaboard colonies. That position was clear enough for advocates of sovereign rights but not for a colonial Briton with eminent social and political standing trying to appease his outraged neighbors and constituents. Such colonists saw themselves as belonging to a "natural" aristocracy, as opposed to those with an inherited rank of birth or kings who claimed "divine rights" and were not subject to any earthly authority. The natural aristocrats of British North America had to maintain their social status and influence in a world of rapidly changing notions about everything from the meaning of life and "natural rights" to what was necessary for order and progress. Most of the issues ventilated in the political and philosophical debates from the late seventeenth to the end of the eighteenth century (the age of Enlightenment) antedated the war and, as we shall see, applied to the other three revolutions that followed the American, but they resonated differently in Britain and the Atlantic seaboard colonies in the years after 1763. The most important were slavery, race, migration, the wealth and power of the nation, changing beliefs about the rights of the person, and religion.

Before the age of revolution, ideas and beliefs about the role and place of African slaves and slavery in the history of the hemisphere and British North America underwent compelling and sometimes disruptive changes. Until about 1700, 90 percent of the immigrants to America came from Africa, most of them to Brazil and the West Indies. (Only 4 percent of African slaves went to what is now the United States.) After 1700, some 75,000 arrived annually. On the eve of the American Revolution, in a colonial population of 2.5 million, 500,000 African slaves labored in a surprising variety of occupations in industry, manufacturing, shipbuilding, and mining, but most of them worked on the tobacco plantations and inland corn and grain farms of the Chesapeake colonies of Maryland and Virginia, where they constituted 40 percent of the population, or in the rice fields of the Carolinas and Georgia.[17]

To some British observers of this migration, African slave labor and the slave trade explained the wealth generated for Europeans and European nations. For others, there were moral and social issues involved in measuring the presumed benefits of slavery and the slave trade. The decade before the American Revolution witnessed the emergence of the world's first organized movements against slavery and especially the slave trade, an effort that united groups in England and France with antislavery religious sects in British America. Enlightenment thinkers and even some religious sects offered conflicting views about slavery: the belief that enslavement of human beings threatened human progress and was degrading was opposed to the views that blacks were inherently inferior and that progress depended on their labor. Increasingly, especially in the British Atlantic colonies, economic and racial dimensions entered the escalating debate between king and Parliament. Those same dimensions affected the parallel, often troubling, relationship between colonial Britons and British America's social elites and political leaders, as well as the rapidly growing numbers of poor whites with aspirations for greater liberty and opportunity.[18]

In the sixteenth and early seventeenth centuries, colonial elites drew little distinction between ordinary English laborers, soldiers, or sailors and Indians and Africans. By the early eighteenth century, the elites' growing reliance on white settlers in the militias brought about subtle but noticeable changes in attitudes. By the eve of the Revolution, a sense of white racial solidarity had taken root, and with it came concessions of greater respect for the social status and political rights of poor whites. As the British had discovered, these poor whites were also people on the make, people for whom the protests of the age would be about more than the unalienable rights of being English or resentments of their presumed "social betters." A significant number of them formed the last great wave of immigration into Britain's Atlantic seaboard colonies, migrants driven from the Scottish Highlands and Ireland by land enclosures or indebtedness. (Among the Scots-Irish immigrants in 1765 was the family of Andrew Jackson Sr., who died two weeks before the birth of his third son and the future president on March 15, 1767.) In British America they transformed the social landscape of the Atlantic seaboard colonies, where in one generation a migrant could rise from indentured servant to property holder. With land in the western country, these newcomers developed a sense of collective power. Their cause would be about the land and their claim to it and the sense that with property a person could be somebody.[19]

In an age when the rights and privileges of monarchs and those of noble lineage still commanded powerful influence, the notion that the guiding and explanatory rules in the world did not lie in theology or some presumably un-shakable philosophical principle seemed downright heretical. The proverbial "rule of reason" had entered enlightened public discourse. Of course, there was a problem in arguing that humankind ought to be governed by secular definitions of reason—a concept intimately identified with being "modern"—rather than tradition or religious faith. For the enlightened person of the day, particularly if he or she were British, liberalism and republicanism sustained individual rights and autonomy and civic-mindedness, respectively, and obli-gated social and political leaders to set a standard for public behavior. In the British context, if not always in the Spanish or French, both reinforced the strong sense of freedom as well as the hierarchical class-based society and imperial nation that other western European monarchs envied and rightly feared.

This changed thinking about the person created a problem for those who held power. Imperial Britain symbolized the exercise of power at home and abroad, and from the mid-eighteenth century on, the idea of who was a free man constituted an integral faith of popular ideology. More and more, on both sides of the Atlantic, the word "liberty" became a rallying cry for the rebellious and the opponents of tyranny. A more radical interpretation of liberalism challenged the narrow view identified with republican thought that only "virtuous" people were capable of understanding freedom by defending the natural rights of women, the disenfranchised, or even slaves with the argument that no government should violate these rights. At the same time, people in the rural communities of New England lived their lives in accordance with what has been described as the "reformed Protestant" tradition and believed that community responsibility, not individual autonomy, was the best guarantor of freedom. Deviance from community standards would not be tolerated. As a veteran of the Revolutionary War explained to the young historian George Bancroft, who assumed the man had read John Locke and other Enlightenment philosophers as inspiration for joining up, "Never heard of 'em. . . . New Englanders had always managed their own affairs, and Britain tried to stop them, and so the war began."[20]

My great-great-great-grandfather who migrated to Kentucky after the Revolution probably carried his Bible and a rifle with him. He may have heard about Martin Luther, who more than Locke was the ideologue of individualism. In any event, for those who held power and were ambitious, some ideas resonated better than others, notably so if the context were political or secular and especially religious. Far-flung enterprises and settler colonies in the New World exhibited an ethnic and racial diversity unimaginable by Europeans. Some political thinkers, notably Edmund Burke, an occasional defender of colonial Britons' rights, remained persuaded that empire and civil society constituted a single entity. Through controlled trade within the empire, a shared sense of mutual benefit, and, particularly, a belief in what Burke called a sacred trust, government would have the loyalty of its diverse subjects. The sentiment could be summed up in a phrase: Enlightenment universalism. Yet not all Enlightenment thinkers were prepared to discard notions about the benefits of place and culture. In his "Dissertation on the Canon and Feudal Law" (1765), John Adams described North America and especially Massachusetts as distinctively blessed by Protestants who believed in the rule of law, liberty, and civility, a place that was not cursed by feudalism or popery and where someone who could not "read and write [was] as rare as a comet or earthquake."[21]

A decade later, Adams's beliefs about the intellectual capabilities of his countrymen had been tempered by concerns about what would be necessary to defend the colonial cause with Great Britain. For him and those who see the War of Independence and with it the American Revolution as an ideological struggle between power and liberty, or largely a dispute over the meaning of the British Constitution, the break with the mother country constituted not only a continuation of the British revolution but also the first war of the age of reason, whose promise of progress and achievement would perish in the carnage of the Great War of 1914–18. Or, conversely, the case can be made for looking at the American Revolution as a religious war within the realm of transatlantic Protestantism, with the Civil War of 1861–65 framed as an apocalyptic struggle or the Great War as a conflict that began within Christendom and ended with Christendom in the dock.[22]

In any event, for both the religious and the secular, taxation became a major issue. Justin Du Rivage isolates the issue of tax policy as pivotal to the debate within the empire carried out among three identifiable groups of Whigs in the colonies and in the mother country: wealthy Whigs who believed in the legality of taxation but disliked its use if it interfered with trade; Whig reformers more concerned with morality in government, patriotism, and acceptance of taxation if it meant a secure future; and, perhaps most important, radical Whigs who demanded frugality in government, a strong military presence in North America, and facing up to the French enemy that threatened the nation. This last group acknowledged the colonial obligation to empire but "refused to transform an empire founded on exchange into one based on extraction."[23]

In a related sense, we may consider the conflict within the British Empire as the first of several European monarchical struggles for dominion over their transatlantic domains that reignited the war between Britain and France and its ally, Spain. What would set the pre-Declaration years of 1774 and 1775 apart from the preceding decade would be the collective intensity of emotion and sentiment fired by evangelical religion and feelings of hatred or ambivalence toward an unelected government, as well as the determination of large numbers of colonial people "to take up arms against an unelected imperial government that no longer served the common good."[24]

For those who presumed to shape and direct the colonial cause, this insurgency would have to be contained and mobilized to sustain any call for independence. More than that, such a cause would still need allies, both absolutist European monarchs whose only interest lay in dealing a blow to the British

Empire and people, particularly poor whites and people of color, whose commitment to any republican agenda was unpredictable. That uncertainty would transform wars between empires into civil wars within each and then into revolutions in the Atlantic world. In 1775 words such as "empire" and "civil war" were not new, and people knew and often fought over what they meant. But "revolution" was new, and few sensed what it could mean.

George III perceived the colonial crisis not as a revolution but as a rebellion, and he had to prove he could deal with it. In the decade after the Stamp Act debacle, there seemed to be no way to persuade the colonies to accept the constitutional structure of the British Empire without the use of force. And with Frederick North as prime minister, the king was determined to crack down on what he perceived as an insurrection. Mistakenly, he believed a show of military power in New England would be enough to quiet his critics at home and demonstrate to his unruly subjects abroad that they couldn't win. In London the demands of rioters and protestors calling for political reform and condemning corrupt government mirrored those in the streets and public spaces in New York and Boston. George turned his wrath on a persistent government critic, John Wilkes, whose condemnation of the propertied and privileged and calls for universal suffrage made him popular and won him a seat in Parliament. Instead, he was thrown in jail. Finally permitted to take his seat in 1774, Wilkes renewed his call for universal suffrage, but Londoners did not respond. Unlike Boston and New York, and later Paris, London would not become a revolutionary city.[25]

These events offered an illustration of what the British were up against in the public demonstrations over heavy-handed government both at home and in British America. At the same time, despite the outcries from Whig critics in Parliament, the king pressed back with equal determination. With Lord North leading the assault, Parliament passed the Coercive Acts, which closed the port of Boston and instituted military government in the colony, and the Quebec Act, which granted Quebec control of the territory between the Ohio and Mississippi Rivers and permitted French Canadians to retain French laws and practice Roman Catholicism. The latter hit the interests of traders, speculators, and settlers and angered Protestants. Response in the colonies was predictable, but in Parliament North also came under fire from Edmund Burke, who called for a return to the pre-1763 measures for running the empire and an end to harsh legislation.[26]

A Call to Arms

The reaction to these measures was mixed: local intimidation and random violence combined with pleas for order. In 1770 there were riots in New York and Boston protesting the quartering of British soldiers. In Boston troops killed five in response in an event remembered as the Boston Massacre. In the aftermath of the December 1773 destruction of East India Company tea (the "Boston Tea Party"), tensions and protests escalated. In 1774 the First Continental Congress sanctioned the ad hoc political organizations and local committees that sprang up, yet it cautioned against violence. New Englanders were not cautious in April 1775 in defying British troops at the Battles of Lexington and Concord, and two months later they defeated a superior British force at Bunker Hill, the first formal battles of the Revolution. In the aftermath, George Washington took command of the Continental army. In the fall of 1775 came two invasions of Quebec, both of which failed to persuade the French Canadians to join the patriot cause. Thomas Paine's *Common Sense*, which appeared in January 1776 and sold 150,000 copies, denounced the evils of monarchy and advocated the necessity of a break with the mother country. Paine reminded his audience that the war had already begun and demystified a world that ordinary people thought was alien and mysterious. He changed the language of politics.[27]

Paine's call to action came at a time when colonial leaders believed themselves more British than their predecessors and yet appeared to be encouraging the unruly behavior of ordinary people who defied parliamentary legislation. In Virginia a presumptive natural aristocracy confronted challenges from evangelicals, particularly the Baptists, who unlike the colony's Anglican gentry accepted blacks as brothers and sisters. In the Carolinas country people formed their own police forces or quarreled with the colonial government over land titles. Elsewhere a generation of young professionals sensed the latent power in the urban crowds of sailors, laborers, migrants, and dispossessed and situated themselves politically to benefit. Small farmers would come late to the protest movement against a perceived arbitrary Parliament, but they would prove crucial to the cause. Throughout the escalating troubles after 1763 there remained a belief that colonial leaders could handle the challenge from below. Governor Horatio Sharpe of Maryland alluded to perhaps the most troublesome consequence of "riotous meetings" in 1765 when he noted that such events inspired colonials "to think they can by the same way accomplish anything their leaders may tell them they ought to do."[28]

In the troublesome decade after Parliament's revocation of the Stamp Act, the political and social forces let loose threatened the once powerful binding ties not only between the colonies and the motherland but between gentry and commoner. A people once viewed as holding the same rights and liberties and speaking the same language as their fellow Britons in the motherland now sensed they were treated as inferiors living in workshops or plantations in outposts of the British Empire and whose only purpose was to enhance the power and wealth of the motherland. Benjamin Franklin, who lived in London from the mid-1750s to the eve of the Revolution, expressed more than a twinge of bitterness when he read dismissive comments in newspapers describing colonists as a *"republican race,"* or a *"mixed rabble of Scotch, Irish, and foreign vagabonds, descendants of convicts,"* or worse.[29]

As Washington discovered, such scofflaws and other social marginals would prove reliable during the darkest days of the war that was coming. Urban riots and protests represented a larger social dynamic: the democratization of society or enforcement of community standards. Even the beleaguered governor of the Massachusetts colony, Thomas Hutchinson, acknowledged that riots and unruly crowd behavior acquired legitimacy if such behavior constituted the only way for the urban community to defend itself against perceived injustice in an era of growing inequalities of wealth, poverty, and a complex marketplace in which smuggling became an accepted practice to satisfy the growing demands of consumers. On other occasions, urban crowds exhibited a more distinctive class behavior, particularly if their intent was to ensure the provision of necessities or obligations to the poor by those who held power. One prominent colonial leader, Landon Carter of Virginia, feared such behavior might lead to independence and a "form of Government that, by being independent of rich men, every man would be able to do as he pleased."[30]

Both George Washington and John Adams had decided that after the Battles of Lexington and Concord in April 1775 there could be no reversal of course. When the Second Continental Congress convened in May, some delegates favored autonomy or reframing a federated empire. Franklin, who headed up the Pennsylvania delegation, proposed a coalition of English-speaking peoples that would include Ireland, Quebec, and East and West Florida, even as he fretted over the breach with the mother country. A formal declaration of independence lay dormant for another year, but the ensuing months were a time of frantic activity. The Continental Congress authorized the raising of an army of twenty thousand and named Washington as commander. Franklin proposed a confederation and perpetual union of thirteen colonies with many differences, but in his opinion they all possessed a common vision of society and government. In the 1750s and 1760s, as the agent of Pennsylvania and other colonies in London, he was an advocate of the empire as a federation of equal and sharing entities, each with its own legislative body yet united in commitment to the mother country. When it was clear the British ruling classes had a different view, Franklin began to express an imperial vision that meshed with the budding secessionist movement in the colonies.[31]

To measure the Battles of Lexington and Concord by the observations of some contemporaries, the act of British troops firing on colonial militias constituted a civil war within the British Empire, an entity greater in its domain than the Roman Empire at its height. In its edition of April 24, 1775, the *Newport Mercury* expressed the significance of what had happened: "Through the sanguinary Measures of a Wicked Ministry, and the Readiness of a standing Army to execute their Mandates, has commenced the *American Civil War.*"[32]

If civil war suggested a unity by each side, a common effort proved difficult to sustain. In the First Continental Congress, John Dickinson had expressed concerns about the alienation of New England from the other colonies, and with good reason. New Englanders prided themselves on their communitarian history, reinforced by four institutions: the county court, the town meeting, the church, and especially the militia. The last had its drawbacks, among them a reluctance to engage in battles for other colonies. As did British commanders, Washington preferred semiprofessional soldiers, men who received a bounty if they enlisted for a year, agreed to fight beyond their home colony, and followed strict military discipline. "To place any dependence upon militia," Washington observed, "is assuredly resting upon a broken reed."[33]

Yet there remained a New England bond with slavery and the plantation colonies in the Chesapeake and the Caribbean that would embarrass abolitionists. Leading New England families benefited by their domination of merchant networks that exported farm produce and fish to the Caribbean and imported slaves as household servants. Stories of slaves' experiences and suffering proved as compelling as the stories of bonded laborers in Virginia.

New Englanders combined "piety and protest" in a complicated experience of colonial encounters with slavery and slaves that later observers, among them Nathaniel Hawthorne, expunged from historical memory.[34]

In Pennsylvania and especially Virginia, conservatives expressed concerns about the social anarchy they identified with Boston. Virginia's planter elites were particularly ambivalent in their views about the crisis. As slave owners and social conservatives, they shared few of the egalitarian traditions cherished by Massachusetts councilmen but could be infuriatingly hostile to royal authority and by their own twisted logic were persuaded that they were as much "slaves" to a political and economic system as their slaves in the field. In the Virginia Assembly their rhetoric could be inflammatory, and the House of Commons considered a proposal urging the royal governor, Lord Dunmore (John Murray), to humble the Virginia aristocracy. In the uncertain days of April 1775, Dunmore took the precaution of moving the local powder supply to a British warship. The action so infuriated local patriots that they surrounded the capital, Williamsburg, which in turn prompted Dunmore, himself a slaveholder, to issue a warning that he would emancipate and arm the slaves, indentured servants, and those free to bear arms and burn Williamsburg. In the aftermath, the House of Commons' motion failed, but Dunmore's actions had alarmed slaveholding Virginians and given the more outspoken an opportunity to portray themselves as defenders of the white race. In the aftermath, slaves did respond to Dunmore's offer, forming the Ethiopian Regiment in the Chesapeake region. In August 1776 they evacuated to British-held New York City.[35]

By the mid-1770s Virginia's patricians had become uneasy about their democratic past and how it had reshaped not only the social fabric of the colony but its politics. In 1700 Virginia's enslaved numbered less than 10 percent of the colony's population, and African slaves and white indentured servants often labored together in the fields. Through imports and natural births, that percentage reached to more than 40 percent on the eve of the Revolution. With the Great Awakening of midcentury, a revivalist tone entered public life and political discourse. Baptists and evangelical Methodists interjected emotion into their sermons, preaching the equality of men and women and welcoming blacks into their churches. The number of Baptist churches in Virginia grew from six to sixty in the decade after 1765, and Methodist churches swelled almost as fast. The mingling of poor whites and enslaved on riverbanks or in forest clearings listening to sermons about individual and social regeneration shook the colonial squirearchy. Virginia's attorney general warned that the evangelical preachers were persuading their followers to "forsake their Church and the cheerful innocent society of the friends and families, and turn sour, gloomy, severe, and censorious."[36]

Although they were only a minority of the slave population of the Chesapeake region, the slaves who converted to Christianity were often skilled and literate. Some attended the schools established by the Society for the Propagation of the Gospel. But most joined the evangelical Protestant gatherings sweeping the region, drawn by their message that all were equal in God's eyes or by the sermons of disapproval of the riches and pretensions of the planter class. Over time, however, they began to form their own churches, where they heard sermons about the link between Christian piety *and* material improvement. And in these gatherings they could discuss the ongoing debate between disaffected white slaveholders protesting their "enslavement" to British overlords and ponder what the "tocsin of liberty" could mean for the slave.[37]

Even at that late date the slaveholding Jefferson felt confident to advocate in his 1774 pamphlet, *A Summary View of the Rights of British America*, an end to the slave trade and to predict the demise of slavery. Presumably, that task would come under white direction. By the time Jefferson wrote those words, however, enslaved Africans had already begun to construct their own perceptions of identity and community, based more on kinship, community, ethnicity, and evangelical Christianity than the presumed bonds of solidarity of color. In his call for arming slaves, Dunmore had appealed to them as a collective group, and they increasingly perceived themselves as part of a larger community of the African diaspora. Women and blacks would play a role in the war on both sides, but they had more trouble than the multitudes of white males in staking a claim in the benefits of the revolutionary cause. In Virginia and elsewhere in the early republic, their collective power and the racial and social dynamics that defined it became a persistently troublesome issue.[38]

But in the early years of the war, Washington had other worries. In the wake of the failed invasions of Quebec in the fall of 1775, he grew more and more concerned about the prospects for success. Both French and British residents of the "fourteenth colony" bristled at the hybrid character of the Quebec Act of 1774, which stipulated a mix of French civil and English criminal law but no elected assembly. In Quebec there was nothing similar to the network established by the committees of correspondence to organize resistance. Quebec merchants hesitated in joining the Continental Association—what Abraham Lincoln identified as the seedtime of nationhood—and its call for an embargo of British goods out of fears it would cost them in their fur- and wheat-trading businesses. Some Canadians did join up and fight during the campaign, but they remained a distinct minority. Despite Canadians' grievances with the British, the republican cause in the colonies to the south was not their war.[39]

There remained fleeting hopes of support from British radicals, but not even Burke denied the right of Parliament to govern the colonies. In May 1776 a frustrated Lord North tried to placate colonial leaders with an offer to lift trade restrictions and pardon colonial rebels in return for ceasing hostilities. By then, a coalition supporting independence had gained the upper hand in the Second Continental Congress. Their reasons did not neatly conform to what Tom Paine had pointed out in *Common Sense*, but they were conscious of the impact it had made. Independence constituted a claim for a sharing of sovereignty because it challenged the legal principle that the western European powers had agreed to in the Peace of Westphalia in 1648—territorial sovereignty—and confirmed a war that had commenced with the Battles of Lexington and Concord in April 1775. "By referring the matter from argument to arms," Paine had prophesied in *Common Sense*, "a new era for politics is struck—a new method of thinking hath arisen."[40]

Paine's stimulating message in *Common Sense* included a defense of women but was not a call for revolution. Indeed, he used the word only once in his iconic pamphlet and then as a reference not to the ongoing colonial quarrel with Parliament but to the Glorious Revolution of 1688 in England, when Parliament removed James II and installed a joint monarchy of his Protestant daughter Mary and her Dutch husband, William III. Nor did the signatories to the Declaration of Independence perceive what they had done as a call for revolution; instead, it was an indictment of the king, not Parliament, for betraying their rights. Paine framed colonial grievances in an egalitarian political and social language that appealed to the artisans and journeymen who were caught up in a rapidly changing environment where the moral economy weakened before laissez-faire economics and their work as wage earners—and, by implication, their persons—diminished in value. In compelling phrases aimed at colonial Protestants, Paine invoked scripture to explain how monarchy was alien to God's will and promoted idolatry. Twenty years later, in similarly evocative phrases in *The Age of Reason*, he condemned the Bible's authority.[41]

Abigail Adams stated what was a revolutionary position about the colonial debate as well as the expectations of women. Two weeks after the departure of British troops from Boston in mid-March 1776, as John Adams grappled with the issue of independence at the Second Continental Congress in Philadelphia, Abigail began laying out her thoughts about sundry matters in a rambling letter to her husband, with particular attention to the views of people in other colonial cities about British retaliation if they proved as defiant of the king and Parliament as Boston. Save for George Washington, she had doubts about the commitment of Virginia's "Gentery Lords" and "common people vassals," some of whom could be "very savage and even Blood thirsty."[42]

In a judgment that contemporaries on both sides of the Atlantic often voiced, she questioned whether slaveholders had as much "passion for liberty" as those Massachusetts men and women who had stood up to the arbitrary actions of Parliament. Independence and a new "code of laws" for governance were, in her mind, the only choices. She added an oft-quoted caveat about what should be included—"If particular care and attention is not paid to the Laidies we are determined to foment a Rebelion, and will not hold ourselves bound by any Laws in which we have no voice, or Representation"—and one not often quoted—"Regard us then as Beings placed by providence under your protection and in imitation of the Supreem Being make use of that power only for our happiness."[43]

John's response is largely remembered for its dismissive tone and complaint about "petticoat power," but in fact he had already delivered a militant speech to his colleagues calling for independence and a plan to confederate the colonies as well as seek foreign assistance. For all her insights, neither she nor John could have predicted the course of the next dozen years. The Declaration of Independence invoked liberty, freedom, and equality in a cause that unleashed a *rage militaire* among a people who turned a rebellion into a war against the mightiest empire of the world. Their commitment found allies that made victory possible. But that success did not prevent a civil conflict that culminated in a brokered independence and a confederated government that Abigail Adams and the like-minded found dangerously weak in containing the unruly democracy the war had unleashed.

The constitution framed in Philadelphia in the summer of 1787, contemporaries sometimes averred, served as correction and affirmation of the Revolution or, conversely, as the counterrevolution of those who intended to undermine the democratic forces it had unleashed. Unlike John, who shared many of her views, Abigail may have been naive about what was necessary to build a wartime coalition or what help was necessary to achieve victory. The fragile bond between Massachusetts and Virginia, as much as that between the rebellious colonies and monarchical France, would prove vital to winning the war. What became equally troubling was the belief that in Virginia, unlike in Massachusetts, the culture that took root reinforced rather than militated against hierarchical and inegalitarian views. Virginians such as Jefferson may have been more eloquent about articulating the credos of liberty and freedom, but the Virginian hegemonic conception of what the West meant for the future of the country has persisted.[44]

THE DECLARATION OF INDEPENDENCE proclaimed by the Second Continental Congress to a "candid world" on July 4, 1776, represented the triumph of a fragile but necessary alliance between Virginia and Massachusetts and what each represented. John Adams had played a critical role in forging that alliance, but he wasn't worried about the insurgency brewing in Boston and other towns that had played a major part in bringing about the decision for independence as much as explaining his behavior to Abigail. It was one thing to defy a Parliament and blame a king *in detail* in the same document but something else to come up against a woman who had the capability to make him money and at the same time to make him feel guilty about belaboring issues that seemed cut-and-dried to her but not to him. She followed her disapproving words about men with the assurance that she was his friend. John understood that men were not going to repeal their "Masculine systems" because they recognized they were the "subjects" in the gender equation and should be "fair" and move "softly" in dealing with women. Of all those defiant of government, Abigail was John's first "Intimation that another Tribe more numerous and powerful than all the rest were grown discontented."[45]

CHAPTER 2

The Beginning of the Long American Revolution

IN JULY 1783, WHEN THE independence of the United States seemed assured, George Washington identified the reason for victory in compelling if not detailed or analytical terms. The war had been won, he wrote, "by a concatenation of causes [that] in all probability at no time, or any Circumstance, will combine again."[1]

Explanations about the causes of the war and the decision for independence followed a similarly complicated scenario. In the two-year period from the onset of the First Continental Congress (September 1774) to the decision for independence in July 1776 by the Second Continental Congress, which convened in May 1775, both British ministers handling the imperial crisis and colonial delegates framing measures to respond to British actions misread or misinterpreted the decisions and actions of the other. British ministers looked upon the defensive proposals of the moderates in both congresses as no different in intent from the more aggressive measures advocated by their more radical colleagues. Presuming there was a unity among the delegates, the British worked harder to discourage presumably "loyalist" colonies such as New York from supporting what the delegates recommended. This tactic in turn strengthened feelings of a unified effort among delegates who might otherwise have disagreed with their colleagues on a more militant course of action. In the end, British obstinacy got the blame! As Robert Morris Jr., a moderate and signer of the Declaration of Independence, wrote in June 1776, "Great Britain may thank herself for this event."[2]

Why those who drew on a republican tradition to affirm their belief in a "natural aristocracy" chose to lead what was a rebellion against a specific government has been at the heart of debates and conjecture from the time the Revolution began. If the republican tradition, with its notion of rule by learned men with a grounding in the public interest, could be reconciled with the liberal belief in political liberty and opportunity for "men on the make," then the choice of independence was a rational one. The transition from monarchical to republican government could be brought about, and the latent fears of a social upheaval by the "lesser sorts" (or what some called "the herd") could be averted. Those who would lead this war reinforced their decision with a belief in their purity in a corrupt world and the rightness—if not the righteousness—of their cause. For victory, as James Madison wrote, they had to rely on the people to choose "men of virtue and wisdom." This was the "great republican principle," and if those who governed lacked virtue, then "no theoretical checks—no form of Government, can render us secure."[3]

More important, an enlightened paternalism offered a better way to bring about the political liberty and just rule that backcountry English Whig gentlemen were calling for in George III's government. As Paine had urged in *Common Sense*, the men who convened in Philadelphia had the opportunity not only to frame a bill of indictment against George III but to affirm the rightness of their actions. In doing so, they invoked a word as powerful an incitement to action as self-determination, liberty, or freedom: equality. Slavery, as the Virginian George Mason acknowledged, made men "lose that Idea of the Dignity of Man," but a commitment to equality spelled the end of slavery. White slave owners now reacted to criticism of their treatment of slaves by responding that the British government was attempting to enslave *them* by threatening to seize their property.[4]

There was a novelty to their actions that had few precedents. In *Common Sense* Paine identified the source and inspiration for independence to the Glorious Revolution of 1688. As part of a transatlantic civil war within the British Empire, the dispute within the empire after 1763 and the break of 1776 also constituted a stage in the three English Civil Wars from 1642 to 1651 that had led to the events of 1688. Jefferson and other colonial leaders looked at the empire in much the same way we see the modern British commonwealth, as independent communities linked to the Crown. This was a distortion of how the British perceived the empire on the eve of the American Revolution. The "Glorious Revolution" had bonded the king and Parliament and in that act had reduced the Crown's powers. Parliament was supreme throughout the empire, and to deny that supremacy meant being outside the empire. George III acknowledged parliamentary supremacy even as he complained about dealing with it. The Declaration of Independence was not a civil war over succession to the throne but a new form of secession by the assertion of the right of a people to "dissolve the Political Bonds, [and] to assume among the Powers of the Earth, the separate and equal Station to which the Laws of Nature and of Nature's God entitle them."[5]

But it is possible to understand how a movement that began with the purpose of restoring the British Constitution would end in a war for independence from that empire. In 1763, as Adams had noted, belonging to an empire served as a unifying ideal for colonial Britons. Through their experience in the imperial wars and in the commercial revolution of the eighteenth century, colonials had found a collective identity in their Britishness. After 1774 that unifying power reinforced their rebellious spirit, and with the Declaration of Independence the drafting of new state constitutions insisted on laws protecting individuals and communities against judges, legislatures, and executives and upholding freedom of religion, jury trial, freedom of the press, and the right of petition against grievances. The right to vote was the standard of citizenship, and elections protected the citizens' freedom. Over the course of a decade, the Revolution's leaders had employed the rhetoric of eighteenth-century Whig and turned a protest movement against the Crown and the "Court Party" into a document that evoked the "conspiratorial theories embedded in British culture in 1688."[6]

Those colonial leaders who called for reconciliation and peaceful appeals for understanding after the Coercive Acts had to deal with something more compelling than appeals to English political tradition or a common bond with the British Empire. The dismissive responses of George III to colonial petitions and appeals for redress of grievances were met with contempt, while the dispatch of fleets and armies to "awe us into submission" warranted a strong response. As Paine had written in *Common Sense*, they called for the severance of loyalty to a king "who can unfeelingly hear of the slaughter of his subjects and composedly sleep with their blood upon his soul."[7]

In retrospect, the fear of anarchy proved of less consequence than the war the colonial cause unleashed, a war with the mightiest nation on the globe, a war whose political and ideological reach extended across the Atlantic into Europe as far east as imperial Russia and into the Caribbean and mainland Portuguese and Spanish America. For Paine, the critical theater of the war was the North American continent, one-eighth of the globe, awaiting liberation by those who believed in an empire of liberty. Although he did not know it when he scribbled those inspirational words in *Common Sense*, in 1776 Russian intruders were laying waste to Aleut villages in Alaska; Spanish soldiers and priests were moving up from the Bajío of central Mexico (where another rebellion would erupt in 1810) into California as far north as San Francisco Bay; in the Black Hills of South Dakota, the Sioux were establishing their own nation, which would do battle with General George Armstrong Custer a hundred years later; the Comanches were establishing the bases of their even mightier empire, which would stretch from modern-day Kansas to northern Mexico; and in the Southeast, Creek Indians had already negotiated trading links with Spanish Cubans. Each of these portended future confrontations and war.[8]

WITH THE DECISION for independence came an obligation to bring about a revolution in government, a republic, which, as the more religious perceived, would be a fulfillment of the duty to God, as well as to posterity. The republic would be a confederation, something very different from what the Parliament had created in the Glorious Revolution of 1688, and each state in the confederation began reserving for itself rights and privileges that would complicate the relationship between the central and state governments for years to come. The people understood as much as Jefferson that they had to prove that the cause they had embarked on was one that successive generations must not only preserve but also die for. Ironically, Pauline Maier points out, the Declaration was rarely read at celebrations in the 1780s, and no state adopted the words "all men are created equal" in its declaration of independence.[9]

The Search for Allies

What kind of war was coming was not clear. In 1776 the British correctly recognized a conflict between conventional armies, but the military command failed to mount an aggressive campaign to crush the Continental army. In a calculated move, the British shifted operations from Boston to New York and New Jersey, drove Washington from New York City, and restored royal authority. As the *rage militaire* of patriot wrath diminished with the outbreak of local battles between loyalist and rebel, the British refused to press the issue. To the disappointment of the Continental Congress, Washington appeared determined to keep his army intact and not stake everything on a decisive battle in the European tradition of warfare. He was better versed in what would later be called military strategy than his British counterparts. One approach looked to avoid large engagements and fight a war of attrition; a second, rooted in antiquity, called for an aggressive campaign of destruction of the enemy in battle. British generals vacillated between the two.[10]

British miscalculations that colonial society replicated that of the mother country confirmed their notions that artisans, farmers, and the middling class would not wage war for the benefit of privileged colonial elites and most certainly not for Virginia patrician slaveholders. By the time British leaders recognized the nature of the conflict and shifted their concerns to the building of a loyalist British America, the character of the war and the international situation had changed. In October 1777 a force under the command of Horatio Gates won a decisive victory over the army of British general John Burgoyne at Saratoga. British plans to cut off New England with invasions from Canada and New York City had failed. The victory reinforced American resolve to reject any reconciliation from the British and, as a committee of the Second Continental Congress had recommended in June 1776, "to take the most effectual measures for forming Alliances."[11]

That was not an easy choice, and from the onset of the fighting, both Washington and the Congress acknowledged that victory required not only the mobilization of a fighting force at home but also support from abroad. Ten months before declaring independence, the Congress had set up a secret committee of correspondence to seek out aid from presumed friends in Britain, Ireland, and Europe. By the summer of 1777 prospects for assistance from radicals in England and Ireland had virtually disappeared. That left the historic enemy of the British Empire: monarchical Catholic France. Two years of war and flagging patriot morale prompted American leaders to revise their thinking about the French connection. When Benjamin Franklin arrived to join Silas Deane and Arthur Lee in the triumvirate of emissaries to France in late 1776, American plans had expanded to incorporate not only a greater military but a political commitment—an alliance. In return, the secret committee and its successor agency, the Committee of Foreign Affairs, pledged never to cease military operations without informing the French. After the Saratoga victory—but not precisely because of it—the cautious French foreign minister, Charles Gravier, comte de Vergennes, finally came around. Ironically, had the British acted on securing French and Spanish assistance to end the war after Washington had been driven from New York, the vital Franco-American alliance might not have been established. The issue of the French alliance offered yet another example of the degree to which external events and dislocations, not bickering, limited the choices the Continental Congress faced.[12]

At that time, however, the British were in no mood to share North America with either France or Spain. When London revived the notion, it was too late, and the French and Spanish saw an opportunity to avenge their humiliation of 1763. Their respective monarchs believed a weak and fractious republic clinging to survival in a hostile world would pose no threat. On February 6, 1778, a monarchical Frenchman joined his republican counterparts and signed two treaties: the Treaty of Amity and Commerce and the Treaty of Alliance. Predictably, it was the latter that proved to be first a blessing and ultimately a curse. Informally recognizing U.S. independence, the French court committed to the fight until victory was won. In return, the Americans pledged not to sign a peace treaty with Britain without consulting their French ally, as well as to commit the nation to the defense of French possessions in America. Both treaties came in the nick of time. The British withdrew their ambassador to France, and less than two weeks later, Parliament appointed the Earl of Carlisle to head a peace commission to end the war, effectively granting the thirteen colonies autonomy but refusing to withdraw British troops and grant independence. The Congress rejected the offer in late April, a week after a French fleet departed Toulon for New York.[13]

For those of 1776 who had been the true believers in the degradation of Europe and the evils of monarchy, the Treaty of Amity and Commerce was palatable, even welcome; the Treaty of Alliance, difficult to digest. But both were necessary. After Saratoga, Vergennes rightly feared that the Americans might make peace and launch an attack against the French and Spanish West Indies. There was a dual shock to the region in American commercial assaults against mercantilism and in the unsettling implications of revolutionary rhetoric. Vergennes tried but failed to persuade the Spanish to join the alliance, but the Spanish came into the war in 1779 and, although disdaining any notions of recognizing U.S. independence, provided aid through dummy European companies. Spain's military contribution consisted principally of committing its ships of the line to the French fleet; supplying support to American guerrilla forces on the Florida border; and capturing West Florida, three Caribbean dependencies (Tobago, Saint Christopher, and Saint Eustatius), and Minorca in the Mediterranean. In the following year, as the patriot cause became more desperate with the shift of British attention to the southern theater, the French dispatched a force of sixty-five hundred men and a naval force to reinforce the American cause.[14]

Both governments permitted clandestine aid to the patriot cause before the signing of the Declaration of Independence. French arms and volunteers arrived early on, and in the western theater, the Spanish provided much-needed munitions and supplies. All told, the two governments contributed aid valued at $30 billion today. The Spanish were calculating in their support, recognizing that an independent United States would prove as formidable a foe as the British, but they feared just as much British designs on Central America and in Mediterranean shipping.[15]

The War within the War

By 1778 the internal divisions over the war—what Carl Becker called the debate over not only "home rule but who would rule at home"—had become a concern.[16] The narrative of the Revolution told from "the bottom up" has given us sharply divergent accounts about those who were not in positions of power but who would play an important role in the outcome of the war. On the one hand, the physical and emotional support of diverse groups in the seaport towns in the "urban crucibles"—particularly artisans, laborers, women, free colored, and even slaves—sustained those who presumed to lead them and ultimately felt betrayed by a denial of the revolutionary promise. Their role and disaffection may explain why significant numbers served in the royalist cause. These were people who correctly sensed that the social base of republics if not nations in the making remained too narrow.[17]

On the other hand, there is an equally compelling story, also from the bottom up, about the experience of those who served in the Continental army and endured the harsh winter of Valley Forge (1777–78), suffering Washington himself alluded to in his pleas to the Continental Congress. Between the *rage militaire* and creativity of the early years (1774–76) and the British shift to a southern strategy, popular support for the war waned, and the Continental Congress and the states proved either unable or unwilling to sustain the army. At Valley Forge, Washington noted the condition of his shoeless, unpaid soldiers and predicted that without assistance his army would "starve, disperse, or dissolve." His men were not average soldiers from the "middling classes" but social marginals. Later, when victory seemed assured, he speculated that historians would have difficulty explaining how the mighty Great

Britain could be defeated by such men, who were "always in Rags, without pay, and experiencing, at times, every species of distress which human nature is capable of undergoing."[18]

As he had done during the French and Indian War, he maintained a stern discipline over them, and despite the social gulf between them, which Washington considered an "accurate reflection of the social hierarchy that God intended," there existed a "mutual admiration."[19] Ironically, the grimness of Valley Forge embodied not the egalitarian values of the Declaration of Independence but the Aristotelian hierarchy of one (Washington), a few (his officers), and the many. His soldiers were men who had no other place to go—they were indentured servants, immigrants, men who had been slaves, or sons who did not inherit land. Washington had no illusions about their motives for joining the fight: they were influenced not by principles but by "Interest" and would never look beyond that. Perhaps as much as anyone and more so than others who have gotten more credit, they constituted the essential core of the nation the Revolution would create, and Washington more than any of the Founders understood why they were fighting. "I do not mean to exclude altogether the Idea of Patriotism [as a motive for fighting]," he wrote a fellow Virginian and officer in the Virginia Militia, but it "must be aided by a prospect of Interest or some reward."[20]

Patriot leaders confronted other disturbing realities as well, as the universality of revolutionary ideology and wartime manpower necessities altered the question of using slaves and even free blacks in the campaign. Free blacks in the colonial militias fought at the Battles of Lexington and Concord and formed part of the Continental army at Cambridge. News of Lord Dunmore's November 1775 declaration granting freedom to slaves who took up arms against their masters spread rapidly in Virginia and in the eastern colonies. But the apprehensions over its impact did not persuade Continental army officers and the Congress to arm slaves. Washington grew uneasy about the decision, rightly fearing that both free blacks and slaves would rush to enlist under a royalist banner. After Lord Dunmore's proclamation, Congress permitted reenlistment of free black veterans who had served in the army at Cambridge.[21]

Washington's command was one of fourteen, as each state could set its own standards for the makeup of its militias. As the war wore on, the restrictive policies of the early days gave way to acceptance of both free blacks and slaves, particularly in the militias of the eastern states. After the loss of

Savannah in 1779, Henry Laurens of South Carolina, who served as president of the Continental Congress from November 1777 to December 1778, and his son John persuaded Congress to fund an army of three thousand slaves, with compensation to their owners and the promise of freedom, but a fearful South Carolina legislature rejected the plan. Five thousand African American slaves fought for their freedom under a patriot banner, many of them in the war at sea. In the state militias, they fought in integrated regiments. Fifteen thousand slaves joined the British army. In the hotly contested Chesapeake theater, Virginia slaves went into battle sporting sashes with "Liberty to Negroes" inscribed on them, a reminder that the words of the Declaration of Independence resonated with slaves as well as Virginia slaveholders.[22]

The arming of slaves and the reluctance of the southern states to go along with the proposal is sometimes pointed to as evidence that the ulterior purpose of the War of Independence and the Revolution was the preservation of slavery and the assurance of white supremacy. As early as 1775 patriot newspapers committed to unifying a fractious and divided people circulated stories of British plans to foment insurrection and atrocities among Indians, blacks, Catholics, and Canadians against the escalating colonial rebellion. These fears coincided with Lord Dunmore's proclamation and stories about the raising of an Indian army in the Ohio country. In the Declaration of Independence, George III is singled out as the villain of this conspiracy. Such stories proved less effective in the South, where newspaper coverage lagged behind that of the middle colonies. Sustaining a common cause, Robert Parkinson argues, called on individuals to fulfill the call of Providence to aid Protestants, neighbors to band together against their enemies, and colonial leaders to see their common interests in the imperial crisis. The outbreak of war and the creation of a republic required a new script, one that stressed the importance of choosing sides and changing legal, political, and social value systems. In a monarchy, all persons were subjects, theoretically equal, and social distinctions are linked to royal prerogative and birth. The American Revolution created a republic where status depended more on exercising the full benefits of citizenship as a member in the community and the power to exclude persons from those benefits was greater.[23]

The problem with such an argument, however, is that it did not neatly mesh with a more complicated reality, notably, the roles of African Americans, both slave and free, during the war and into the early republic or the persistence of white revolutionary ideals coexisting with white racial nationalism. Southern hostility to arming slaves in the patriot cause, even in the face of wartime needs, persisted. In an age when monarchs were using slaves and Indians in their armies, those who led republican causes had to make concessions. Alexander Hamilton recognized an uncomfortable reality. Writing to John Jay, president of the Continental Congress, Hamilton alluded to the "contempt we have been taught to entertain for the blacks" yet continued with a reminder that "if we do not make use of them, the enemy probably will ... [and we will] give them freedom with their muskets."[24]

For the Indians, no less than the white settlers, the American Revolution was both a war of liberation and a continuation of a long eighteenth-century struggle. Most Indians tried to remain neutral. They fought on both sides. In the South, Cherokees tried to defend lands now claimed by patriot invaders committed to creating a new settlement, Transylvania. In the fall of 1776 six thousand troops from Virginia and the Carolinas swept into Cherokee territory to raze their villages. In the frontier region of western New York, the Indians of the Iroquois Confederacy (the Six Nations) paid a severe price for allying with the British. In the summer of 1779 Washington sent a four-thousand-man force into the region under John Sullivan for the purpose of destroying the Iroquois Confederacy's rule by wiping out Indian settlements. By the end of the war, the lives of Indians had changed as dramatically as those of whites, but their future seemed less certain. In the mythmaking accounts of the Revolution, they would be stereotyped as "merciless savages." As had the French, the British built their empire on Indian trade. In 1783 the United States, Colin Calloway has noted, intended to build its North American empire on Indian lands, which meant Indian removal or worse. The Indians had other plans.[25]

A second uncertainty lay in the presence of an outspoken minority of loyalists (approximately 20 percent of the population) who had denounced the high-handedness of Parliament but retained their faith in the "mixed constitution" symbolized in the British monarchy. Most of them fled into the cities under British protection during the war. The largest group—a mix of well-to-do and middling whites, poor blacks and whites, and slaves—congregated in New York, willing to play a role in the war. But British commanders considered them unfit for military service. When General William Howe placed the city under military rule, the loyalists protested the move. At war's end, some sixty thousand spread to the far reaches of the British Empire. Of the forty-four thousand who went north, the majority (thirty-five thousand) settled in Nova Scotia (which was split into mainland Nova Scotia, Cape Breton Island, and New Brunswick) and Quebec, where in time their numbers and intensity of feeling overwhelmed the predominantly French population. Eight thousand whites and five thousand free blacks settled in Britain. Six thousand white southern loyalists took their slaves to Jamaica and Bermuda. Years later, approximately eleven hundred of the freed slaves left for the new British colony of Sierra Leone in Africa. Loyalists prevented from recouping their losses from the U.S. government found relief from a debt-ridden British treasury in the form of land grants, pensions, and compensation of more than £3 million. But the loyalists often confronted the contradictions of postwar British imperial policy: freedom for black loyalists but relocation of loyalist-owned slaves, land to their Mohawk allies in the North, abandonment of the Creeks in the South, and the joining of hierarchical rule with liberal rhetoric, a postrevolutionary vision that well suited the empire as a counter to the French Revolution.[26]

An equally complicated dynamic was the role of religion, which ranged from the evangelical style in patriot oratory—perhaps best exemplified by Patrick Henry—and the more controversial view that ordinary people required more than rational arguments for taking up arms. The cumulative impact of the Great Awakening of midcentury and the outrage over British violation of colonial rights helped to fuel the movement for the disestablishment of the Anglican Church, faith in God as the creator of human rights, and affirmed beliefs about sin, divine providence, and virtue. Protestant clergymen were not bystanders to the patriot cause. They articulated its purpose in words common people could understand, invoking such biblical themes as "chosen nation" and the Israelite Exodus from Egypt. The Continental Congress set aside days for prayer, thanksgiving, and fasting in the public calendar. Baptists responded to the populist spirit of the Revolution, protecting their "liberty of conscience" with attacks on New England's religious establishment. Protestants within the colonies, notably Congregationalists, Presbyterians, Anglicans, and Methodists, ranged from ardent republican to apolitical in their sentiments. Protestants in Britain and in Canada went in a different direction. Both John and Charles Wesley expressed hostile and disapproving opinions about republicanism, and John Wesley's *Calm Address to Our American Colonies* (1775) warned that republican governments would lead to despotism or anarchy.[27]

By the standard measure of military capabilities and strength, the British might have won this war. The army had thirty-four thousand men, more than the major cities of the colonies, and a navy, perhaps not equal to the combined French and Spanish fleets but certainly superior to anything its rebellious colonials could muster. Even with the French entry into the war and the adoption of the southern strategy, victory seemed within reach. True, the British ruling class divided over the war, but the divisions within colonial society in both town and countryside ran equally deep. As Washington discovered in the aftermath of the *rage militaire* of 1775 and 1776, his most dependable foot soldiers were not the vaunted militiamen or farmers but those who did not easily fit in with the imagined communities of revolutionary lore. Yet these were the men who made victory possible. Then there was Washington's strategy of keeping the Continental army together rather than engage the enemy, a choice that brought condemnation from the Congress and several of his generals but that his aide, Alexander Hamilton, correctly sensed was preferable to risking everything on "a single cast of the die."[28]

But the American War of Independence was a different kind of war for the British. In the early years, local patriots took control of assemblies, courts, and the press and tossed out royal officials. British military leaders lacked a clear strategy and a central command system, and they confronted problems in maintaining a supply line to sustain an overseas war. After 1778 the war became a global conflict, in the West Indies, Mediterranean, Africa, and India, where the last battle was fought. It was the only eighteenth-century war in which the British lacked naval supremacy. Failure came not from incompetence or blundering but from insufficient resources, the lack of sufficient loyalist support, and the war's popularity in the colonies. The British sent an army for conquest not because they had no plan for occupying the country. Their army won the big battles and lost the little ones.[29]

Of course, the British made mistakes, and costly ones. When they shifted their efforts to the South, where up-country people had long-standing grievances against Low Country merchants, particularly for the latter's domination of the institutions to guarantee civic order, protection of property, and an orderly marketplace, the British expected to do better. Instead, the presence of British troops served only to exacerbate matters. British officers were often taken aback by the savagery of the war in the South. Loyalists who became victims of the destruction of property or vendettas sometimes responded in kind. Neither the regular British or patriot soldiers or the militias proved capable of protecting civilian supporters from retaliation by guerrilla bands. Patriot ministers implored soldiers to wage holy war against the British enemy and their Hessian mercenaries. Neither side looked on the war in the South as favorable to its respective cause; both attempted to deal with the problem. The patriot army had the advantage because it could move in prorebel areas, but the British had to move everywhere. Their commander, Major General Lord Charles Cornwallis, was happy to rid himself of this kind of war in the march through the Carolinas to Virginia. By the time his troops encamped at Yorktown, a combined Franco-American force of seventeen thousand had cut off any retreat into the interior; a French naval force prevented any escape by sea. On October 19, as its band played "The World Turned Upside Down," British troops stacked up their arms.[30]

The Battle of Yorktown marked a low point in British public morale about the war. Britain fought alone against five enemies: the United States, France, Spain, the Dutch Republic, and the kingdom of Mysore in India, a foe of the British East India Company. As Paine had intended and Washington had acknowledged, a rebellion had become a world war. Over one hundred thousand French fought in the war, forty thousand of them in the revolutionary theater. Although there are no precise records, an equal number of Spaniards served, most of them in the campaign to take Gibraltar. In the guerrilla war in the western country and the Gulf campaign, Spanish aid and participation proved vital. Yet even after Yorktown George III vowed to fight on. Others came to a different conclusion, one that a French observer made in 1782: "The people of America might be conquered by well-disciplined European troops, [but] the country of America was unconquerable."[31]

In eight years the British had been unable to achieve by force colonial acceptance of the mixed constitution that governed the empire, but they avoided a revolution at home. In the prewar years, John Wilkes had been able to fashion a coalition with the London crowd to bring about parliamentary reforms. In the Gordon Riots of 1780, crowd assaults on property and threats against Catholics perceived as enemies of the people escalated into a destructive force that set thirty-six fires and damaged property at Newgate prison, a distillery, chapels, and townhouses, plus other low-level destruction, estimated at £30,000 ($75 million today), threatening the Bank of England. In the process, the old Wilkeite reformers (and Wilkes himself) came down on the side of order as the city's reformers found themselves threatened by what one called the "mania" of the crowd. During the 1780s the reformist movement in Britain waned but would be stimulated by the endeavors of the

Constitutional Convention in Philadelphia in the summer of 1787. British radicals would find their spiritual renewal with the French Revolution.[32]

Containing Democracy, Affirming Power

So, too, would some American radicals, but in the same decade the sense of unity that had inspired a revolutionary nationalism had weakened. The reality was a country of thirteen little republics and a renegade separatist movement in Vermont that constituted the disunited states. In the two years before the terms of a peace treaty could be hammered out, an irregular war of civilian massacres by loyalists and Indians flared up in western New York and Kentucky, and the civil war in the southern backcountry continued. In the convoluted peace negotiations in Paris after Yorktown, American negotiators successfully parlayed British suspicion of French motives and gained cession of the western country from the Appalachians to the Mississippi River. The war had encouraged the possibility of creating a permanent confederation, but differences among the states and the exigencies of war had weakened the bonds between them.[33]

A nagging problem involved the chaotic conditions in the western country. In 1779 there were two hundred settlers in Kentucky; six years later, during the economic downturn in the East, there were thirty thousand, many of them demanding credit and protection from Indians. Washington visited the region and returned with stories of angry and disenchanted people threatening to ally with those Americans who had gone north to Canada or submit themselves to Spanish rule. Spanish governors in New Orleans commenced an irregular and ultimately ineffective policy of keeping American interlopers into Florida (which the Spanish had regained as part of the peace settlement) at bay by inciting Indian attacks on Americans. On other occasions, they often intrigued with other Americans, notably, George Rogers Clarke and John Sevier, who were promoting independent frontier settlements. Washington pinpointed the problem. "To suffer a wide extended country to be over run with Land Jobbers, Speculators, Monopolizers, or even with scatter'd settlers," he warned, "was inconsistent with the wisdom and policy which our true interest dictates."[34]

If pressed, Washington was prepared to act, but not rashly. In early 1783 (January to March) the weak and financially distressed government survived what amounted to a military takeover from senior officers who had petitioned the Confederation Congress for their back pay and appeared ready to back up their case with action. And they had the power to do it. A year after the Battle of Yorktown, ten thousand officers and men of the Continental army—many of them poorly clothed, ill fed, and fearful of going home with nothing—drilled every day near Newburgh, New York. Hamilton persuaded Washington to do something, and in a move of no small consequence to the future of the republic, Washington called his own meeting of five hundred Continental army officers, expressed his sympathy for their situation, and then implored them not to follow any "man who wishes . . . to overturn the liberties of our Country and . . . open the flood gates of civil discord, and deluge our rising Empire in Blood."[35]

In those compelling phrases, which brought some officers to tears, the man who would become a "republican monarch" six years later vowed that he would not become another "Julius Caesar" or "Oliver Cromwell," the Lord Protector of England in the mid-seventeenth century. Yet he retained his expansive vision for the western country. In the June 1783 "Circular Letter to the States," he identified the country's citizens as "Sole Lords and Proprietors of a vast tract of Continent . . . [and] possessed of absolute freedom and Independency."[36]

Long before Jefferson credited himself with the vision, Washington recognized that the nation's future lay in the "New Empire," a place for disgruntled and land-hungry soldiers, who had to be fitted into postwar society. Theirs was a troublesome mustering-out. With the arrival of the provisional treaty ending the war, the Continental army was disbanded, and a government with no money sent its soldiers home with paper promises to pay them. Even this gesture roused New Englanders to denounce the Congress for its excesses. A band of three hundred rowdy Continental soldiers, with local approval, marched on the Pennsylvania State House, where the Continental Congress sat, and with their muskets threatened delegates. Hamilton grew so disconsolate over the matter that he retired to upstate New York and hoped that reason would prevail. The reputation of the Continental Congress sank further in the public estimation. When state authorities refused to protect it from the mutinous soldiers, the delegates fled Philadelphia for Princeton in June 1783, and in the following months, Benjamin Rush wrote, the Congress was "abused, laughed at, pitied & cursed in every Company."[37]

The democratic and leveling power of the American Revolution sometimes took unexpected turns. One of the most alarming threats to order occurred in Massachusetts, where farmers angry about foreclosures and debtors banded together under a revolutionary veteran, Daniel Shays, and defied state authority. Using the Riot Act (authored by Samuel Adams) and federal assistance, the state put down the rebellion. To garner white support, the leader of the state's black Masons, Prince Hall, offered the services of that organization. In the political aftermath, the dissidents had the satisfaction of electing delegates sympathetic to their cause.[38]

The Revolution left an ambiguous legacy for black Americans, particularly in Virginia. There the impact of the Great Awakening and efforts of evangelical Protestants encouraged blacks to join Baptist and Methodist churches and persuaded some leading white Virginians, notably Robert Carter of Nomini Hall, to imagine a Virginia without slavery. The wartime example of slaves serving in both armies strengthened a sense of both black and white collective identity and prompted the Virginia legislature to repeal the prohibition on slave manumission. In practice, however, the law encouraged individual improvement rather than reinforcing notions of a collective black identity. The spirit of the law was predicated on the revolutionary promise of freedom, but in the postwar years, white Virginians increasingly looked upon skin color as a sign of inferiority and a mark of servitude. In the evangelical churches, racial distinctions divided white and black congregants, and blacks began to create their own churches.[39]

There was a religious as well as a social dimension to the assault on privilege. The Revolution's invocation of a common cause, coupled with the republican ideal of virtue, provided both conservative Calvinists and evangelicals with a moral inspiration to believe that the war against monarchy was the cause of Christ. Early in the conflict the Anglican Church establishment in Virginia agreed to suspend the church tax and interference in marriage ceremonies of the dissenters. British leaders might have capitalized on these fissures, but they mistakenly believed that Anglicans were loyalists and dissenters were rebels. After Yorktown, the Anglican Church attempted to recover its prewar privileges, but with the help of Jefferson, who had expressed the view that no one should be compelled to pay a religious tax or suffer for his religious beliefs, helped the dissenters in winning the free exercise of their religion. In 1786 the Virginia legislature passed an act (written by Jefferson) separating church and state. Evangelicals were elated.[40]

The apprehensions among the leaders of the Revolution went beyond the violent behavior of debtors or embittered farmers or discontent over the weaknesses of the Articles of Confederation. What the postwar years had created was a new kind of political figure, the opportunist. For those who believed in the republican tradition of responsible and virtuous political leaders, James Madison wrote in the "Vices of the Political System of the United States," state legislatures now included too many men who had no conception of the good of the nation and pandered to the crowd and what Jefferson described as "the endless quibbles, chicaneries, perversions, vexations, and delays of lawyers and demi-lawyers." Today we refer to this style as popular politics, but to the Founders such behavior boded ill for the republic.[41]

The religious and ideological impact of the American Revolution reached into the sugar colonies of the West Indies, where it inspired prorepublican ideologues and local power struggles. The war had not only complicated the relationship between metropolitan European powers and their Caribbean slave-based economies but in the process inspired free colored and even slaves to increase their demands for civil rights, the right to vote, and even equality as compensation for their military service. The evangelical strain of American revolutionary ideology accelerated the conversion of black and free colored in the West Indies to Christianity. British abolitionists took notice, as did West Indian planters, who perceived these dual movements as a threat to white supremacy. The division of the vast prewar British Empire, which extended from Nova Scotia to Jamaica, meant that disgruntled West Indian planters could not unite with their kindred spirits in the southern United States in a common cause against transatlantic abolitionism. Some (John Adams among them) often spoke confidently that the "republican spirit" in the West Indies would propel them into the U.S. camp in the event of another war. But self-interest and dependence made white West Indians captive to the British Empire. Living with a "besieged mentality," outnumbered by a black and colored majority, and fearful of slave revolt, West Indian planters had nowhere else to go—except, perhaps, back to England.[42]

Others were disheartened by the diminished revolutionary spirit of the postwar years—for example, the lessening interest in punishing loyalists—or the noticeable materialism of the times. The war intensified the capitalist development of society. The spending of almost $500 million in paper money for goods and services brought a generation accustomed to trade and barter into a market economy. Such behavior was not unique to Americans. What was noteworthy, as the French immigrant J. Hector St. John de Crèvecoeur wrote in number 3 of his *Letters from an American Farmer* (1782), lay in the identity of the American as a "new man" living in the "most perfect society now existing in the world" and as "free as he ought to be." Ironically, his description of Americans and their society in other passages of his book came from his prewar experience living on a farm on Nantucket Island, off the Massachusetts coast. He thought the war unnecessary and deplored the materialism and individualism of the postwar era. He could not understand that ordinary Americans emerged from the Revolution with many of the same beliefs of their forebears about the centrality of individual self-interest and the family and their intent to live in a republic crafted on those values and not the classical republican tenets of civic virtue and self-denial. The South Carolina doctor David Ramsay, who wrote one of the earliest histories of the American Revolution, deplored the "licentiousness of the people" and expressed the hope that they would be able to benefit from the "blessings of freedom without the extravagancies that usually accompany it."[43]

What mattered more to the revolutionary band of brothers was the uncertainty of its survival at home. Unlike British West Indian planters, they did not have the option of exile. For these men, democracy and the hostility of the public to a national authority ingrained in the Articles of Confederation government were the problem. Theirs was a deeper fear that ordinary Americans, especially white males, had "bought into" revolutionary ideology and were staking their claim and exacting their due. Wartime dislocation, resentment over profiteering, and the postwar economic downturn had taken a toll on the collective feelings of ordinary people, certainly, but in the troublesome decade of the 1780s, many found themselves increasingly marginalized by another group. In the unsettled financial conditions in the postwar years, men of influence and wealth had formed a patriot coalition (which included some former Tories) to provide financial stability in governance.[44]

For the latter group, then, the future of the country rested not only on containing the power of the first but also in persuading the states to relinquish some of their power to create a government capable of surviving in a hostile monarchical world. More than these issues were at stake, however. The words and spirit of the Model Treaty, drafted by the Continental Congress, conveyed a belief that the "one people" identified in the Declaration of Independence deserved a national government representing a union that the powers of Europe would respect. At the same time, the disruptive and tangled history of the Revolution extended into West Africa, Indian villages, the Caribbean, and Spanish America. In their relations with some of these peoples, the inheritors of the Revolution extended feelings of respect and acceptance as equals. To others, particularly people of color, the interaction meant a diminished status as "stateless people" or dependency; thus, they were not entitled to or worthy of the benefits of citizenship.[45]

In the uncertainties of the 1780s, James Madison, this generation's greatest political theorist, became the driving force in the calling of the Constitutional Convention. Madison skillfully framed the argument that with a strong central government to protect the country against foreign enemies and to control the states it was possible for a republic to expand—to become an empire—yet protect individual liberties and avoid the despotic leader. Madison played a critical role in determining the selection of the president not by Congress, as some preferred, but by electors in the several states. He had deeply conflictive feelings about slavery, and in the debate over extending the slave trade he insisted that the word "slave" be omitted from the Constitution because it was "wrong to admit in the Constitution that there could be property in men."[46]

Coupled with the Bill of Rights, the Constitution represented not the completion of the Revolution but a reconfiguration of the revolutionary exchange and, by implication, a reminder that the central government had a greater responsibility than the states in the conduct of war and foreign relations. Creation of an executive branch and the office of the presidency, a Senate to give small and large states equality, and a House of Representatives to reflect population suggested balance and equilibrium. Unlike the prescriptions under the Articles of Confederation, the Congress now had power to control trade, levy taxes, and control the territories, which could be treated like "internal colonies" until reaching sufficient growth to be admitted as states, and the Senate retained the power to approve treaties (including treaties with Indian nations) with a two-thirds vote. In a narrow sense, the Constitution created neither a consolidated government nor a modern union but replaced a confederation of sovereign states with a union of sovereign states. Certainly, the spirit of state sovereignty expanded in the early republic and provided a unifying force for those states identified with slavery's defense.[47]

Voices suggesting a more forthright approach to what some believed was the moral anomaly of slavery in a country professing a commitment to freedom and liberty weakened before others who recognized that the choice was either counting slaves for purposes of electoral representation (which the southern states wanted) or not counting them at all (which the eastern states favored). In the end, each slave would be counted as three-fifths of a person. The Constitution and the Bill of Rights, often praised as an essential compromise about shared power, would provide in 1861 the political, intellectual, and moral foundation for two powerful entities: the Confederacy, the counterrevolution; and a militarized revolutionary nationalism bent on its destruction. Only the most cynical could have foreseen the carnage of that war. The framers may have had their doubts about the future, particularly the willingness of the states to move beyond their "confederation mentality" and accept a stronger central government. As did Jefferson, they believed that the Constitution was "like the ark of a covenant, too sacred to be touched."[48]

A more immediate consequence of this phase of the American Revolution lay elsewhere. In the Northwest Ordinances, the states conceded that congressional rule over the territories would be relinquished gradually by a form of "colonial" rule to deal with the persistent challenges of Indian uprisings, separatist movements, and defiance of laws by squatters. Slavery would be prohibited in the Northwest Territory (the Ohio country), a concession by the slave states and especially Virginia, which had retained claims to the region. That concession permitted the eastern states to apply the revolutionary credo of natural rights against slavery. Implicitly, it meant that slavery could be extended into what was then the Southwest. Ironically, as Peter Onuf explains, the Constitution, through the authority of Congress, reinforced rather than diminished the power of each state as a political entity to affirm its particular claims and sovereignty.[49]

There was a social and cultural price to be paid for this, however, and with Virginia's lead the southern states began to exact it. In incremental doses of rhetoric that would require another half century to reach their full impact, southern political and social leaders advanced a variant of republicanism that valued liberty and equality for whites but warned that granting equality to slaves would lead to savagery and barbarism. Among Virginia's patrician slaveholding families, the belief that white opportunity and freedom depended on black enslavement evoked unsettling memories of black slaves fighting for the British in the fiercely contested Chesapeake region. At the war's end, several thousand had left with the departing British, but a great many more remained. Uneasy white Virginians now presumed that because of the revolutionary promise of equality and freedom, slaves now constituted something more than a labor force. They were the enemy within.[50]

None of the Founders wrestled with the tensions and moral ambiguities about slavery more than Jefferson. It is ironic—indeed, compellingly so—that it is Jefferson whose name we identify so closely with the Declaration of Independence and its revolutionary word *equality*, the most powerful concept unleashed by that document. From one perspective, undeniably, the legitimizing power of the word referred to the right of the individual to play a role in government at every level and enjoy true *political* equality. In time, as Danielle Allen notes, the power attributed to *liberty* or *freedom* depended on the misguided belief that the ideal of equality weakened, instead of reinforced, the goals of preserving liberty and guaranteeing equality. In 1776, Pauline Maier points out, the phrase "all men are created equal" referred to "men in a state of nature," and the purpose of the Declaration of Independence lay in justifying the independence of the United States, not the moral affirmation and meaning of equality. Presumably, the redefining of the Declaration's place in the nation's goals and purpose could be achieved through politics.[51]

NOWADAYS, THE JUDGMENT on the Founders for their complicity in this alleged betrayal of the revolutionary promise is sometimes as harsh as that of the abolitionist William Lloyd Garrison in the *Liberator* four decades later. Far from setting aside the divisive issue of slavery in the interest of compromise and their expressed dislike of the institution, the legal historian Paul Finkleman argues, they crafted in the Constitution a "slaveholder's compact" that made the protection of slavery virtually unamendable. And in so doing they created a "tension between the professed ideals of America, as stated in the Declaration of Independence, and the reality of early national America."[52]

This is a harsh judgment, although other historians have confirmed it. But if we frame the issue within the long history of the American Revolution, it would be inaccurate to attribute the Constitution's indirect but no less authoritative protection of slavery as either a victory of the proslavery forces or a denial of the egalitarian promises of the Declaration of Independence. Those delegates to the Constitutional Convention who were determined to keep the federal government from interfering in their control of slavery by affirming that slaves were property failed. The three-fifths clause, which affected regional political power and development for decades; a fugitive slave clause that protected claims to runaways; and the protection given to slavery where it existed may strike us as victories, but the refusal to *legitimate* slavery or the idea of property in human beings would become the "Achilles' heel of proslavery politics," a weapon abolitionists and antislavery forces could use, and lead to secession, war, and emancipation. In this sense, Sean Wilentz writes, "there is more truth in saying that antislavery, rather than slavery, caused the Civil War."[53]

The revolutionary band of brothers did consider themselves a natural aristocracy and held views and ideals that varied starkly—and hypocritically—from their political and social behavior. Those who articulated the revolutionary cause may have been naive in believing they could "freeze" the English Constitution in claiming their rights or were really "closet royalists" whose goal was to restore the prerogative identified with the Stuart kings in order to shield themselves from arbitrary parliamentary power. (John Adams fits more neatly into this configuration than Thomas Jefferson.) The power accorded to the president in the Constitution equaled that which James II had exercised before his removal by Parliament in the Glorious Revolution. "You young men who have been born since the Revolution," the old Federalist Rufus King remarked to Thomas Hart Benton, "look with horror upon the name of a King, and upon all propositions for a strong government. It was not so with us."[54]

These and similar judgments about the revolutionary leaders can distract us from their view about what was at stake in taking on the greatest power in the world and after 1783 the difficulty of creating a political entity capable of binding together thirteen fractious states. To ascribe largely economic motives to their labors, as did a generation of twentieth-century historians inspired by Charles Beard's indictment, *An Economic Interpretation of the Constitution* (1913), is to trivialize what was for them a monumental political task. Their solution in the Constitution was a political judgment meant to address the immediate problem of a perceived dysfunctional Articles of Confederation. The addition of the Bill of Rights served to make certain the states complied. It may be a rhetorical "stretch" to state that they "rescued" the American Revolution, but neither did they "hijack" it. Indeed, they gave it— or tried to give it—a national identity, a unifying cause. In a larger and more important sense, their purpose in the Constitution was to alert the world to the republic's intent to fulfill its international responsibilities and to shield it from the politics and machinations of rival European empires.[55]

The war unleashed ideas and beliefs about the worth of human beings that in the aftermath of victory had to be dealt with—sooner or later. (We will return to this question, especially the place and role of women in the republic, in the following chapters.) The Founders imagined an end to slavery, but a biracial society lay beyond their intellectual and moral grasp. That judgment would reinforce notions about white supremacy in the postrevolutionary years that metamorphosed into the racism of later decades. Together with the rapid expanse of slavery and the long war against Indigenous people in the nineteenth century, such beliefs and practices would make a mockery of another myth about destiny that some political and social leaders of this generation found distasteful but others found useful and their successors would transform into a national creed.

In *Common Sense*, Paine invoked an almost spiritual appeal for colonial Britons "to make the world anew." After he had relocated to France in the heady atmosphere of a revolution that had not yet turned more radical, he followed up that blockbuster with another, *The Age of Reason*, a defense of the French Revolution. For our generation but not always for his, Paine may be a more compelling figure than another Founder, the physician, educator, and writer Benjamin Rush (1746–1813) of Pennsylvania, a fervent supporter of the Revolution who also opposed slavery. Rush's judgment about the Revolution strikes at the heart of the problem. After the war, Rush softened his views about the salient political and social issues of the day. On the eve of the Constitutional Convention he made an acute observation: "There is nothing more common than to confound the terms of the American Revolution with those of the late American war. The American War is over: but this is far from being the case with the American Revolution."[56]

We do not know if he intended his words to be prophetic. A more acute observation about the Constitution lay in the response attributed to Benjamin Franklin to a query from a woman he met on leaving Independence Hall on the final day of deliberation. "Well, Doctor, what have we got—a Republic or a Monarchy?" "A Republic," Franklin answered, "if you can keep it."[57]

CHAPTER 3

The Revolutionary Equation

IN MID-APRIL 1789, WHEN HE set out from Mount Vernon to the country's first capital in New York City to assume the duties of president, George Washington did not dwell on the "late American war" but on his persistent "anxious and painful sensations" on what lay before him and his doubts about meeting the people's expectations. The seven-day journey across terrain and through cities that had been contested in war and often deeply divided in their loyalties was now the scene of a triumphal procession of a former soldier who would be introduced on his arrival as "His Excellency." Though still a commanding figure, on taking the oath in the Federal Hall's Senate Chamber, Washington appeared to one observer, Senator William Maclay of Pennsylvania, as "agitated and embarrassed" by the ceremony, as if it were a duty and an obligation he preferred not to have.[1]

Despite comments about his "monarchical bearing," Vice President John Adams reassured Washington that he must comport himself in a royal manner, and in the early years of his administration, Washington traveled with servants in a carriage that befitted a king. Maclay was an early and persistent critic. On hearing Adams refer to Washington's inaugural speech as "gracious," Maclay demurred: "We have lately had a hard struggle for our liberty against kingly authority . . . [and] everything related to that species of government is odious to the people."[2]

In time, Maclay's belief that the public would disapprove of the royalist trappings and pageantry proved true, but in the beginning, at least, there was a sense of unity. What the framers of the Constitution believed they had achieved was the creation of a union of states and entities that would not collapse into anarchy or despotism—a federation of balanced political entities designed to perfect the "old empire" the British had tried to destroy in their misguided policies after 1763. For some within the president's first cabinet, notably Secretary of the Treasury Alexander Hamilton and Vice President John Adams, newly returned from the post of minister to the Court of St.

James's in London, this was the Anglophile imperial project, the old empire reborn as a new nation united under a central government with a distinct executive branch. Others, such as Congressman James Madison, who had drafted portions of the Constitution and with Hamilton and John Jay had written *The Federalist*, a series of essays aimed at countering political opposition in the state legislatures, praised the appearance of a republic in a monarchical world. Although Madison had initially opposed the Bill of Rights as unnecessary, he followed up on his pledge to protect individual liberties in his successful campaign in Virginia for Congress by sponsoring their addition to the Constitution. Unlike his fellow Virginian, Jefferson, Madison rarely let his personal feelings intrude sharply into his political life.[3]

The prospects for the young republic may have seemed daunting but not insurmountable. Within a few years—some identify Hamilton's 1791 financial proposal for a national bank as the precipitating factor—Jefferson's agenda, coupled with his ambition, inspired a countermovement that drew on another revolutionary tradition, an Anglophobic, republican, professedly "constitutional" project that foresaw and, indeed, almost preordained an expanding republic. Perhaps naively, Jefferson believed it would be sustained not by force but by an anti-imperialist faith in the possibilities of incorporating neighboring peoples into the republic, perhaps not always as full-fledged citizens but certainly not as "subjects," which would have been their status in a monarchy. After all, in keeping with the revolutionary hypocrisies, the American empire was an anti-imperial empire. This was the model for expansion embodied in the Northwest Ordinances of 1787—a commonwealth of equal state-republics with territories in preparation for joining the fraternity, not a restoration of a corrupt, monarchical state. Despite his self-acknowledged role as heir apparent of this futuristic vision, Jefferson joined the cabinet as secretary of state after service as the country's minister to France.[4]

Neither of these overarching designs for the young republic could easily accommodate the diverse peoples whose lives and expectations had been altered by the experience of war. Consistent with the egalitarian phrases of the Declaration of Independence and Tom Paine's professed beliefs about a revolution making the world anew, the New World's first republic held out limited promise for some presumably left behind in monarchical societies, particularly women, free African Americans, and even Indians who appeared willing to adapt. For women, the prewar protest movement and the war had loosened colonial patriarchal bonds, given women greater control over their domestic lives, and opened new opportunities in education, but these paled alongside the opportunities and expectations provided to men of property and even to propertyless white males. In these years, African Americans were made hopeful by antislave movements and legislation in the northeastern states but in the face of growing racial prejudices began to fashion an African identity that would serve as a response to the more virulent racism of the early nineteenth century and, particularly, to the post-1815 colonization schemes of white and some black advocates. Similarly, for Indians, the Federalist decade of the 1790s offered a fleeting hope of a settlement with the new federal government that would safeguard the Indian confederations east of the Mississippi, a plan that would collapse with the continuing uncertainties of British and Spanish designs in the western country and the separatist movements of their American collaborators.[5]

There were competing revolutionary traditions from the onset of Washington's first administration in 1789 to about 1805, the midway point of Jefferson's two-term presidency. In these fifteen tumultuous years, a government and a people inspired by the twin concepts of empire and nation confronted alternate and sometimes intruding challenges both at home and abroad—from monarchical American loyalists who had fled north; from French revolutionaries first welcomed, then scorned; and, in what would prove to be a perceived threat to a way of life, from a slave revolt in French Saint-Domingue that would culminate in the creation of the second independent state in the hemisphere, Haiti. Two other complicating factors were the creation of a loyalist exile community to the north and the continuing strife in the western country, which would remain contested ground in the 1790s. That conflict would provide opportunity for another child of the Revolution, Andrew Jackson, whose name came to represent a more democratic and, to the Founders, more disturbing force within a rapidly changing political culture. In the western country, the feral, evangelical, and racial character of American nationalism took root, flourished, and, seventy-five years after the constitutional summer of 1787, plunged the long American Revolution into its greatest crisis.

Continental Uncertainties

Of all the crises of these fifteen years, that in the western country proved to be the most complicated and the most important—a legacy of the Revolution that became intertwined with the international crises of the era. The history of the region was by experience if not definition transnational, and the affirmation of national sovereignty, Washington believed, required its pacification.

The American Revolution in the western country and especially on the Gulf coast from Florida to Louisiana was a different affair from that of the seaboard colonies. Chaos and uncertainty best described the region for two decades after Lord Dunmore's 1775 pledge to vanquish the Indians in an ongoing conflict during which settlers and squatters held parallel hatreds of Indians and land speculators. As conditions worsened in the 1780s, settlers began to develop their own sense of community and sovereignty, a view predicated on Indian killing, racism, and slavery coupled with an increasing support for creating separatist states that could negotiate with ambitious Spanish governors in New Orleans for special privileges in trade and commerce. Spanish, not patriot, forces had subdued the British in Florida, and in the aftermath Spanish governors spoke about restoring claims northward along both sides of the Mississippi. They wooed settlers with promises of protection on condition of disavowing their loyalties to the new republic or to the southern states retaining land claims in the western country.[6]

Few understood the challenge better than Washington, who was not only an advocate (and beneficiary) of western expansion but a believer that western access to the port of New Orleans was vital for maintaining the bond between the eastern and southern states. Settlers and land speculators were the advance guard in this undertaking. For them, the Indian nations of the western country constituted the enemy. The Northwest Ordinances guaranteed these nations security in their land and property, but these assurances rang hollow to migrants to the region who believed the territory to be part of their revolutionary inheritance. The framers of the Constitution viewed Indians as second class but dependent on the federal government as honest broker between them and the states. Washington believed white settlers would become citizens. Indians would be granted lands that whites had to respect. In time, they would be assimilated. Indian regions west of the Appalachians were a diverse world. New religion and ideas and different ways of living existed alongside traditional Indian social manners. Indian communities absorbed goods manufactured in European mills. Imperial rivalries divided Indian communities.[7]

Washington's experience with Indians both as allies and as enemies in war illustrated what was for him a painful ambivalence. He knew the value of Indian lands that speculators and settlers coveted, and his western ventures helped to make him rich, but he did not share their racial hatreds. He was determined to avoid Indian removal and assert federal power. That in turn required dealing with Alexander McGillivray, leader of the Creek nation, in New York to negotiate a settlement. In an earlier confrontation with Georgians over that state's claims to Indian lands reaching from western Georgia to the Mississippi River, McGillivray mobilized seven hundred men as a show of strength, as if he intended to renew the battle. (McGillivray had been pro-British during the Revolution.) With the concurrence of Secretary of War Henry Knox, Washington made McGillivray a general in the U.S. Army with an annual salary of $1,200. In the 1790 Treaty of New York, the Creeks received sovereign control over lands in western Georgia, northern Florida, southern Tennessee, and most of Alabama, coupled with the government's pledge to use federal troops to prevent white interlopers from Georgia violating the treaty. When Knox informed Washington that enforcing the treaty would require five thousand troops (the size of the regular army was half that number), Washington realized the commitment he had made to the Indians was a promise he could not keep. Yet he persisted in warning against a purchase of Indian lands even as he recognized that national expansion would come at the expense of the Indians.[8]

The discord and defiance of law in the Northwest and especially the Southwest Territory (created by the First Congress in May 1790 and admitted as the new state of Tennessee in June 1796) proved too complicated to resolve by a show of direct federal power, as Democratic-Republican Societies (local political organizations created between 1793 and 1795 to promote republicanism and democracy and oppose "monarchist" sentiments) and hostile newspapers denounced such actions as the arbitrary exercise of power. The situation reminded Washington of the apocalyptic language he had used in describing the perils if the Articles of Confederation were not amended. "I do not conceive we can long exist as a nation," he wrote, "without having lodged some power which will pervade the whole Union."[9]

In his second administration (1793–97) Washington chose a more suitable place and adversary to affirm the authority of the federal government: a military confrontation with a group of western Pennsylvanians who had persistently refused to pay the 1791 federal excise tax on the production of corn liquor. The tax had been imposed with Hamilton's economic program to help pay the debt incurred in the Revolution. In July 1794, coincidental with a military campaign against the Indians in the Northwest Territory, a confrontation between a federal marshal sent to serve writs against the distillers rapidly escalated into a political crisis reminiscent of the disputes surrounding Parliament's passage of the Stamp Act. Washington called on state governors to provide the federal government with militiamen, and he vowed to take personal command of the "Watermelon Army" of 12,500 to crush the rebellion. The inevitable triumph proved to be less a victory for the rule of law than further encouragement of factionalism and the belligerent rhetoric that nourished the Democratic-Republican Societies. If they were permitted to continue, Washington warned, "they will destroy the government of this country."[10]

The show of force in Pennsylvania and in the Northwest Territory had a sobering effect on white and African American migrants in Quebec and Nova Scotia. Half of the residents of Nova Scotia came from New England. Ten thousand loyalists settled in Quebec. Their views about religious toleration, participation in local politics, and slavery were so disruptive that in 1791 the British elected to create a new province (Upper Canada, now Ontario) to be governed with a separate elected assembly under familiar English laws and separated from the dominant French Canadian majority in Quebec. The decision reflected a concern that Canada might very well become a liability or a diplomatic "hostage" if its former American subjects looked north for more conquests. Ironically, the ambitions of those in power in Upper Canada also proved a problem. The province's first lieutenant governor, John Simcoe, vowed to avenge the loss of the thirteen colonies by creating a "New Britain" in Upper Canada. In 1794 he threatened to lead an invasion to crush the republic, but the American war against the Indians ended the threat, at least for the time being.[11]

By then, James Madison, a cofounder with Jefferson of the Democrat-Republican Party, was president; Louisiana (1812) would join Kentucky (1792) and Tennessee (1796) as the third state south of the Ohio River; and the political and military power broker in the western country was Andrew Jackson, a roughhewn child of the Revolution who had acquired his hatred of the British during his experience in the war in the South and in British captivity. With the creation of the Southwest Territory, North Carolina lost its western lands, and with the assistance of its new governor, William Blount, Jackson became attorney for the Mero District. He soon became a slave owner, land speculator, and mercantilist and had a law practice, all of which made him an up-and-coming man of means and influence in Nashville. With Tennessee's admission to the Union in 1796, Jackson became the state's first representative to Congress. He knew the West and its ways, and he knew how its people felt about Indians, Spaniards, the British, and especially the federal government.[12]

Presumably, an ambitious man like Jackson could be useful to a government with continental ambitions even if he could not be easily absorbed into its political culture. The French Revolution posed a different problem.

The Sister Revolution: France

In the 1780s the appeal of everything American—the Declaration of Independence; the images and personalities of American leaders, notably Franklin, Jefferson, and Thomas Paine; and a fascination with the American assault on despotism and power—swept French high society. Virtually everything about the new republic inspired those French weary of traditional ways in religion, politics, or society. In their estimation, the American Revolution represented "the hope and model of the human race."[13]

These were bittersweet words for Louis XVI, who now confronted his own economic and political problems. The principal issue was the staggering debt created by the cost of subsidizing the American cause and particularly the frustrations of depending on tax revenue, which fell most severely on country peasants and the urban poor, moneys collected not by government agencies but by wealthy entrepreneurs who limited the amount they sent to the royal treasury and resisted meaningful tax reforms. In the years after July 1788 the French endured an economic and political crisis during which the king's authority and prestige eroded. The National Assembly (June 1789–August 1791) claimed the sovereignty once absolutely his, as well as a parallel mission to write a constitution for the nation. Its power lay in the Third Estate—those French who were not of royal blood, or titled, or ordained by the clergy—and prevented Louis and his army from abolishing it. The storming of the Bastille on July 14, 1789, marked the climactic end of a month of almost daily crises. Unlike George III, who did not back off from dealing with defiant colonials, Louis retreated in the face of militant Parisians. This was no revolt, according to a legendary story, but a revolution.[14]

Would the French become a sister revolution to its American predecessor? In the early, reformist phases of the French Revolution—from June 1789 until October 1791 and the onset of France's war with Austria and Prussia—Louis reigned as a constitutional, not an absolute, monarch; real power lay with the National Assembly, and both professed a commitment to representative government based on the will of the people. Clauses in the Virginia Bill of Rights and the egalitarian tone of the Declaration of Independence served as inspiration for the French *Declaration of the Rights of Man and of the Citizen*. (Portions of the document were written in Jefferson's Paris apartment.) French leaders called for a new political order predicated on reason and natural rights, not privilege or the divine right of kings, and in the free circulation of ideas. Finally, there was the powerful emotional and ideological bond forged by the wartime alliance against the British Empire.[15]

But the justification for that Revolutionary War alliance arose from military necessity and commercial strategy, not any common ideological convictions with the French monarchy. Washington's sentiments about the leveling influences of revolutionary France approximated those of Edmund Burke, who in 1790 described events in France as a "monstrous tragic-comic scene" that evoked "alternate contempt and indignation; alternate laughter and tears; alternate scorn and horror."[16] His assault provoked an estimated forty-five responses, among them Thomas Paine's *Age of Reason* and Mary Wollstonecraft's *Vindication of the Rights of Men*, which ridiculed Burke's argument that tradition, privilege, and hierarchy sanctified freedom and civilization. In a sequel, *A Vindication of the Rights of Woman*, she took issue with the notion that women were weak, "merely sentient beings," and incapable of rational thinking.[17]

After his service as U.S. minister in France, Jefferson returned home in 1789 fully persuaded that the French Revolution would spread throughout Europe. It would have an impact similar to that of its American predecessor, he wrote, and "the liberty of the whole earth was depending on that contest, and was ever such a prize won with so little blood?"[18] Paine and naval war hero Paul Jones immigrated to Paris in time to join the first anniversary of the storming of the Bastille, and Paine gained a seat in the National Convention (September 1792–October 1795). At the time, Americans proudly sported the distinctive French tricolored cockades and sang revolutionary songs. When news reached the United States that the French had won a victory at Valmy in September 1792 against Austrian and Prussian forces bent on destroying the Revolution and had followed up by declaring France a republic, enthusiastic crowds celebrated throughout the winter with parades and festivals.[19]

Already, the impact and promise of a transformation of the country had taken hold, most noticeably in Paris, where monarchical structures were physically altered to express a new purpose. Revolutionary ideologues crafted a new language of politics in which nation, liberty, rights, and citizenship acquired an inspirational meaning for ordinary people and served as reminders of a continuing revolution. Disturbing signs of a growing schism with the political culture and society had already appeared. The country was torn apart when the clergy were required to take an oath to the civil constitution. Louis, a devout Catholic, was in fact responsible for starting the war in the mistaken belief that the monarchy would be restored. In August 1792 Louis was arrested, and a month later the National Convention voted to depose him and declared France a republic. In the ensuing crisis he lost not only his power but also, literally, his head. In what Mike Rapport has described as the "orgy of iconoclasm" that accompanied the "second revolution," frenzied crowds roamed Parisian streets, tearing down or ripping up physical symbols of monarchy.[20]

Not even the execution of Louis XVI in January 1793 or the seventeen thousand killed in the subsequent Reign of Terror (September 1793–July 1794) noticeably quelled the public enthusiasm for the French Revolution that many Americans were convinced their own had inspired. Belief in the French Revolution became a test of one's faith in the American Revolution. At the same time, as the Federalist New Yorker Gouverneur Morris wrote in 1792, there was a parallel hope that the French Revolution would transform the former despotic ally into a model constitutional republic that would extend the "blessings of freedom to the many millions of my fellow-men who groan in bondage on the Continent of Europe."[21]

Washington's cabinet remained divided, however. In Europe, French apprehensions about a counterrevolution precipitated a conflict between France and Austria and Prussia, which in turn prompted a French declaration of war against Britain in February 1793 and the creation of the first coalition against the revolutionary regime. As long as the United States remained neutral, Jefferson could take comfort that his sympathy for the French Revolution stemmed principally from his antimonarchical, anti-British feelings. He had no wish to be considered a Jacobin, nor did he share Paine's advocacy of the "discourse of radical publicity," in which ordinary citizens shared a role in governance. He did not subscribe to Paine's notions of economic equality. His Francophilia was inspired less by emotion than by a genuine desire to free the young republic from continuing British domination and control.[22]

Washington's declaration of U.S. neutrality should have eased public uncertainties about the administration's course in the war, but the activities of the new French minister, Edmond-Charles Genet, created a political firestorm. An impolitic, dedicated revolutionary disciple, Genet did not limit his mission to securing permission to outfit French privateers in U.S. ports—then legal under U.S. law and consistent with the 1778 Treaty of Alliance—but zealously set about organizing filibustering expeditions against Spanish Florida and British possessions and appealed to French Canadians to rebel. Even Jefferson, who had looked upon the execution of Louis XVI as revolutionary justice, was taken aback by the negative impact Genet's activities were having on republican interests and his own political future. For John Adams, the Genet mission and its accompanying political agitation portended something far more ominous. Writing twenty years after the event, Adams may have exaggerated when he wrote that "ten thousand people in the Streets of Philadelphia, day after day, threatened to drag Washington out of his House and effect a Revolution in the Government, or compel it to declare war in favour of the French Revolution, and against England," but there was a palpable fear in this decade about the impact of events in France on the early republic.[23]

During the Terror (1793–94), conservative political and religious leaders began to demonize the French and especially their revolution in Gothic language—dead bodies lining the streets, murders, drownings, unimaginable cruelties, all committed in the name of liberty, a calamity threatening the young republic. In the name of the revolution, one cleric wrote, the French had become devils, depraved persons who had degenerated into beasts in their disregard for the restraints of law and religion. Noah Webster, the educator and Federalist theorist and an early supporter of the French Revolution, began publishing a series of anti-Jacobin pamphlets predicting that the French were becoming so cruel and violent that no government could contain them. In Quebec, Catholic priests expelled from revolutionary France supported the monarchical and antirepublican order, but the first Catholic bishop of the United States, John Carroll, praised George Washington for maintaining order, morality, and leadership and for making the country the "refuge of true liberty."[24]

Comparisons made by looking at similarities rather than the obverse almost always miss something. Of course, the Federalist critique of the French Revolution distorted reality, but then so did the enthusiasts who were blinded by the appeal of what was happening in France and who expressed their feelings by singing stanzas of "La Marseillaise," as if such expressions and toasts proved their own patriotism and the monarchical perfidy of their Federalist enemies. Parisians' experience during the Terror framed against that of New Yorkers during the *rage militaire* of 1775–76 and the British occupation that followed brought into sharp relief the divergence between the American and French Revolutions. Despite the economic severity of the 1780s, New Yorkers had more peaceful times to adjust and get on with rebuilding their lives. (Life on the frontier was a different matter.) Paris was the locus of the French Revolution, and from 1793 on the country remained at war with its enemies within and without and on the high seas. And in this uncertain and violent context, the repressiveness and executions of the Terror could be deemed necessary if unconstitutional ways to maintain the survival of the republic. As Robespierre, one of the revolution's victims, remarked: "The terror is nothing but justice, prompt, severe, inflexible; it is thus an emanation of virtue."[25]

Neither Jefferson nor Madison nor even the conservative Adams required a religious test to judge the French Revolution. Once Jefferson departed the cabinet, however, he distanced himself from the French upheaval and focused more on the British threat to the republic. For Adams, who had come to admire the British political tradition during his years as minister to the Court of St. James's, the only realistic choice lay in avoiding another war with Britain. It is one of the numerous ironies of this turbulent decade that these revolutionary allies of a kind followed such different political courses for the early republic, and the choice each made would culminate in a war. The growth of anti-Jacobin sentiment and the implication that Jacobin influence lay behind the creation of the Democratic-Republican Societies was not only a matter of immediate concern but also an indicator of the way religious teachings, whether apocalyptic or evangelical, were entering a foreign policy debate and, more important, how Americans perceived their revolution in comparative perspective. The domestic Jacobinism inspired by the French Revolution and manifested in the Democratic-Republican Societies, the English pamphleteer William Cobbett warned, was "familiarizing [Americans] to insurrection and blood."[26]

A more frightening and more complicated variation of the French Revolution occurred in French Saint-Domingue, the prosperous plantation colony in the western third of the island of Hispaniola. Events in France had prompted French planters and slaveholders to press for autonomy and free trade within the empire. Poor whites (clerks, artisans, and seamen, among others), whose numbers in the colony had increased since midcentury, launched their own democratic movement, directing their anger mostly at those free colored who had acquired wealth and social standing in the colony, largely in coffee production. In France the free colored won their case for equality, but in Saint-Domingue they met resistance and took to arms in a revolt in which both sides mobilized armed slaves.

Then, without warning, in August 1791 the slaves of North Province revolted. The uprising precipitated a civil war that altered the course of the French Revolution and the wartime strategies of the British, Spanish, and French governments. In June 1793 the slaves demonstrated their power by reducing the colony's most important city, Cap-Français (now Cap-Haïtien), to rubble. When news of the destruction reached Paris, the National Convention in two decrees endorsed emancipation and declared slavery a violation of human rights. Fearful white planters in the French West Indies (Guadeloupe, Martinique, and Saint-Domingue) had agreed to British occupation for their protection.[27]

White refugees from the colony had already begun seeking exile in the United States, warning of the horrors and excesses committed in the slave insurrection. Some abolitionists were heartened by news of the French decrees abolishing slavery in Saint-Domingue, but in the South and particularly in South Carolina the reaction was different. A few political leaders called for expulsion of slaves brought from the French West Indies, but that choice prompted objections that such an act constituted seizure of private property. Others blamed French revolutionary politics for an egalitarian rhetoric that transcended the racial divide. That discussion in turn prompted reconsideration of similar phrases from the Declaration of Independence. Then, as if swept by the incendiary winds from Saint-Domingue, a series of fires in cities over the next few years from Savannah, Georgia, to Albany, New York, heightened suspicions that "French Negroes" were responsible. As local authorities in Charleston complained after a series of blazes in June 1796, blacks from the island intended "to make a St. Doming[ue]" of the city.[28]

The emigration of white slaveholders from the island posed a problem for Congress. A proposal requiring them to renounce any claim to nobility as a condition of citizenship, as the naturalization laws required, passed. Another asking them to renounce their rights as property owners in human beings failed. The planters took delight in Federalist denunciation of French revolutionary excesses and found reassurance when Republicans reaffirmed the laws upholding slavery and property rights. At the same time, reaction to the Saint-Dominguan slave rebellion was not uniformly one of fear of a similar uprising in the United States. On the island, slaves revolted because they worked under horrid conditions; in the United States, it was commonly assumed, such brutality was virtually absent. Neither judgment could withstand close scrutiny; both were believed. As Ashli White has shown, a generation of Americans with unsettling memories of slaves in British uniforms during the Revolution managed to delude themselves that they were immune from such horrors.[29]

Antislavery religious leaders such as the Presbyterian minister David Rice often used vivid descriptions to portray the rising of the slaves as a heroic effort. Slavery was an institution of violence; in their bloodletting, the slaves were exacting their righteous vengeance against their oppressive French masters. By implication, some abolitionists expressed sympathy about the notion of slave uprising in the United States. Yet they recognized the danger in employing such incendiary words, particularly the graphic descriptions of slave rebellion as the onset of an apocalyptic struggle to redeem a degenerate society, lest they arouse among southern slaveholders and their northeastern allies an equally fearful retaliation.[30]

The French Crisis and the Haitian Revolution

In any event, for Washington the most pressing concern lay not in a domestic slave insurrection but in the persistent British violations of neutral rights and the British military presence in the Old Northwest. When British ships began seizing U.S. vessels trading with the French West Indies, Congress threatened to enact retaliatory legislation. To both governments, the prospect of a war over neutral rights was unsettling, and the crisis was resolved by the signing of a treaty that made possible what has been aptly called the "First Rapprochement" between the two governments. By its terms, the British agreed to turn over command of the Northwest forts and conceded a limited trade with the British West Indies. To the public, the terms were galling, and the Republican press excoriated John Jay, who had negotiated the settlement. Implicitly, the treaty violated liberal neutral rights and the 1778 defensive alliance with France. Success in gaining concessions from Spanish officials over free navigation of the Mississippi to New Orleans and willingness to resolve a persistent boundary dispute, however, did little to alleviate the administration's political problems at home or abroad.

The fact that the European war brought prosperity to the country's farmers and shippers or that the 1795 Treaty of Amity, Commerce, and Navigation, known as the Jay Treaty, made the country a major customer for British goods did little to dispel the factionalism and bitterness over the 1793 Declaration of Neutrality and Federalists' hostility toward the French Revolution and their sharp critiques of the Democratic-Republican Societies. In this increasingly poisonous atmosphere, Washington drew on his experience and sought advice, notably from Hamilton, to produce a classic statement about the importance and fragility of the Union and its republican experiment. What threatened the republic, he wrote in his September 1796 farewell address, was the undermining of the spirit of community and unity of the Revolution by partisan politics. The most memorable phrases of the address called for "good faith and justice toward all nations," followed by warnings about "passionate attachment to one nation," words that resonated with later generations as "entangling alliances."[31]

Washington may have exaggerated the impact of French revolutionary ideas on the Democratic-Republican clubs and their undeniably factious politics. More critical to understanding the public outcries over Washington's policies were the political passions fueled by the American Revolution, notably, its spirit of defiance of central authority and an anti-British animus that erupted in the debates over the Jay Treaty and lingered for generations. The French had created a nation and national institutions to contain the passions and behavior of such groups. Beginning with the Directory's assumption of power in 1795 and especially Napoleon's November 1799 coup, the official end of the French Revolution, the legacy would be a powerful central authority at home, the revival of empire in Saint-Domingue, and total war in Europe.[32]

The person who reaped the whirlwind generated by the bitter disputes of the 1790s was Washington's vice president and presumably kindred Federalist spirit, John Adams, chosen after an electoral balloting in which Jefferson wound up with the second highest tally of votes and by the constitutional rules of the day became vice president. The political convulsions of the next decade would sever their friendship and test their convictions, but each would understand the difference a revolution makes.[33]

The French had broken the first coalition against them in 1795, and despite the easing of tensions between the British and U.S. governments and the weakening of Jacobin control in the revolutionary government, French influence intensified on both sides of the Atlantic. British industrial workers were inspired by revolutionary slogans, as were Irish discontents, who launched a rebellion in 1798. As the French army under Napoleon swept across central Europe, it became a transformative force, introducing new laws and political institutions, deposing princes, altering social systems, and unintentionally inspiring latent nationalist sentiments. British leaders slept uneasily in fear of a French invasion.

In the Caribbean, with the considerable assistance of their black and colored forces under Toussaint Louverture (born Bréda), the French compelled the Spanish to cede the eastern two-thirds of Hispaniola. Three years later Louverture negotiated the withdrawal of the British army, which fearful white plantation owners had welcomed in 1793. Already, thousands of whites had abandoned the island, some to other British islands, others to Cuba, where they would invigorate the sugar industry, and to the United States, where white plantation owners were welcome but not the black and colored peoples who accompanied them. Nine thousand settled in New Orleans, already becoming a bustling Spanish, French, and American enclave. In Philadelphia, despite the city's reputation for its antislavery system, three thousand free colored immigrants from Saint-Domingue were treated with caution and reserve.[34]

The two foreign crises were intimately related. How Adams dealt with each probably cost him the presidency in the election of 1800. Jefferson responded to French seizures of U.S. shipping with militant rhetoric and calls for national defense. Federalists in Congress, some of them determined to undermine Jefferson's political constituency, pushed through two measures (the Alien and Sedition Acts) that lengthened the required time for residency (and the right to vote) from five to fourteen years and punished those who made or wrote "false, scandalous or malicious" statements about the nation or the president. Congress's intention in the Alien Act was to delay voting privileges in federal elections for immigrants who had flocked to Republican candidates. Of greater concern to Jefferson and his growing coterie of Republican associates was the Sedition Act, which undeniably violated the First Amendment and implicitly rebuked the notion that public opinion served as a safeguard of a free society. The public outrage over his anti-French course did not lessen Adams's resolve. Unintentionally, the French abetted his cause when it was aired in public that French negotiators had solicited bribes and loans from U.S. emissaries as conditions for resolving the disputes between the two governments.

Some orthodox ministers circulated stories alleging French designs on the country, including a plot by French Masonic Illuminati to employ Jacobin societies to spread social disorder and destroy religion in the Christian world. According to one account, the alleged conspiracy reached back to the 1770s and involved Mirabeau and Talleyrand as well as several Enlightenment philosophes, among them Voltaire. As the French crisis deepened, the prominent minister Jedidiah Morse warned in his sermons of the Illuminati's plans to instigate riots and even massacres within the country. Others would spread the secular message of French revolutionary thought with the intent of undermining religious belief.[35]

Although there were fears of a French invasion and apprehension over the presence of some twenty-five thousand French in the country, there was no formal declaration of war. Under Hamilton's prodding, the Federalist-dominated Congress called for creating a strong and permanent land and naval force to safeguard the republic. To forestall Hamilton's politicking, Adams named Washington as commander of a provisional army of ten thousand with the understanding that Hamilton would be second in command. Fears of war bred other rumors. Hamilton advanced the fanciful notion of aiding the Venezuelan Francisco de Miranda in the liberation of Spanish America, with Hamilton commanding the invading army. Hamilton did not get the larger role he believed would catapult him to center stage in the troubled politics of the decade. In his final year in the presidency, Adams became more conciliatory in his handling of the French war, successfully ending the treaty of alliance that had proved vital in the war for independence and so problematical for the country's neutrality in the struggle between Britain and France.[36]

The French were not deterred in their ambitious plans in the Caribbean and the Gulf. In a larger and more ominous way, Napoleon Bonaparte threatened the American Revolution. On November 19, 1799, he ousted the Directory in a coup that broke the Jacobin grip on revolutionary politics but not the French threat to monarchism and the conservative political order of Europe. The French Revolution had not yet remade the map of Europe, but it had begun to transform France, its administrative units, its society, and its culture. Napoleon nourished parallel imperial ambitions in the Caribbean, despite the setbacks in Saint-Domingue. If he were to restore French control over that autonomous colony, he needed a supply base in the region, and there was one logical choice: Louisiana and the Isle of Orleans. Within twenty-four hours of terminating the alliance with the United States, Napoleon compelled the Spanish to cede Louisiana to France. That was easy. Now he had to find a way to bring Toussaint Louverture to heel.

That meant confrontation with the United States. After his victory over a mulatto rival (André Rigaud) in a civil war, Louverture persuaded some former white plantation owners to return to the colony and sought help from the United States in dealing with the bands of guerrillas who recruited runaways from the harsh work on the revived sugar estates. Both Adams and the Federalists in Congress were responsive, invoking what became known as "Toussaint's Clause" in the sundry pieces of legislation dealing with retaliation against trade with the French colonies. Some of Louverture's former generals had acquired plantations and amassed fortunes. French reports sometimes described the colony as ravaged, ruled by inept and murderous antiwhite savages, yet in a special report of 1798 the U.S. emissary to Saint-Domingue portrayed the Dominguan leader as moderate in his dealings with former adversaries and deserving of U.S. assistance. Jefferson was suspicious of what expanded trade with the island portended. He wrote Madison that "we may expect therefore black crews and supercargoes and missionaries thence into our Southern states. . . . If this combustion can be introduced among us under any veil whatever, we have to fear it."[37]

Despite these warnings about dealing with Louverture, Adams moved ahead, assured by his antislavery secretary of state, Timothy Pickering, that Napoleon was secretly planning to restore slavery and white rule in the colony. If Louverture were brought down, Pickering reasoned, Napoleon could use Saint-Domingue as a base not only for strikes against U.S. shipping but also, more ominously, for an invasion of Jamaica and the U.S. South. "If the French should be so mad" as to carry out such a plan, Washington warned, "there could be no doubt of their arming our own Negroes against us."[38]

Most Republicans and even some Federalists were incredulous about the course Adams now followed—a union founded on political and military expediency between a New Englander and a former slave, an "African Bonaparte." Louverture pledged not to use his troops to incite slave unrest beyond the island and banned French privateers from using Dominguan ports. In return, he got much-needed U.S. trade. Although his professions of loyalty to France remained strong, his stated preference for an autonomous government with himself as governor outraged Napoleon as a challenge to his power and the honor and dignity of France. The rebellious blacks must be taught a lesson. Napoleon was sending his brother-in-law, Charles-Victor-Emmanuel Leclerc, to become magistrate of the island. He would have twenty-five thousand troops and Louverture's old mulatto demon, André Rigaud, to back him up. French engineer and colonel Charles-Humbert-Marie de Vincent tried to persuade Napoleon that Louverture was loyal and that an invasion would be doomed, but when he realized there was not stopping the determined first Consul, he sent a reassuring letter to Louverture of Napoleon's good intentions![39]

Leclerc did not arrive until January 1802. By then Napoleon had concluded peace pacts with all his European enemies save the British and the Dutch, and they would follow suit in late March. Jefferson was nearing the end of the first year of his presidency, the victor over Adams in a bruising election and a victory made possible, Federalists erroneously claimed, by the power of the three-fifths clause in the Constitution and the assumption that it gave slave states a preponderance in the electoral college. His inaugural remarks, crafted in lilting phrases designed to appease Federalists he had once mocked, incorporated phrases of reconciliation ("We are all Republicans, we are all Federalists"), but few of the losers were placated. It was Jefferson's way of lowering expectations about his revolutionary mission, but Pickering was so upset that he privately acknowledged that the only recourse was secession. As for French Saint-Domingue, Jefferson had no intention of pursuing Adams's dealings with Louverture. When the French chargé had inquired about his plans, the president had offered encouraging words: "Nothing would be more simple than to furnish your army and your fleet with everything and to starve out Toussaint."[40]

With such assurances, with sufficient troops, with Dominguan allies at his command, and with Louisiana serving as the supplier of a revived colonial empire in the Caribbean, Napoleon reasoned, slavery and white rule would be restored in Saint-Domingue. The civil war on the island resumed. Too late, Louverture realized that the only way to achieve autonomy for the colony lay in armed struggle. He called on his revolutionary brothers Henri Christophe and Jean-Jacques Dessalines for aid. But they had little commitment to the man who had stood in their way of profiting from the spoils of a long war. In a sequence of events worthy of a Grecian tragedy, Christophe and Dessalines persuaded Leclerc that the removal of Louverture would end the resistance and betrayed him. Napoleon's duplicity in his plans for Saint-Domingue soon became apparent and made possible the famous agreement ("Oath of the Ancestors") between Dessalines and Alexandre Pétion uniting black and mulatto forces in the final struggle to end French rule over the island.

The bond meant there would be no distinction between loyal or disloyal, slave or former mulatto slave owner, and the war against the invader would be one between an invading army bent on restoring slavery and an equally determined force united against it. In the savagery of the fighting, the war became racial, with atrocities on both sides. It ended with the expulsion of white slaveholders and the execution of those who refused to leave. The Haitian victory in 1804 represented an act of vengeance against the slave regime and a military triumph by black and colored insurgents over a succession of British, Spanish, and French invaders since the slave uprising of August 1791. Not until the Union victory of 1865 would the world witness such human sacrifice in the cause of bringing down a slave regime and a slave society.[41]

Jefferson the presidential aspirant had certainly expressed fears about slave rebellion inspired by the Haitian example, but the Haitian victory *indirectly* made possible the purchase of the vast Louisiana Territory and the creation of Jefferson the president's "empire of liberty," what the president's Federalist critics denounced as a "howling wilderness." (Ironically, in 1801, Jefferson's understanding of Napoleon's intentions in Saint-Domingue were secondary to his fears that the Haitian revolution would inspire slave rebellion in the southern United States.) The Haitian revolutionary impact on Atlantic world politics and the abolitionist movement is more difficult to measure. Clearly, the example of a free state created by former slaves inspired both slaves and free people of color about what could be accomplished in a hemisphere in which slavery and the plantation economy were so pervasive. Just as certain was the likelihood that nowhere else would slave uprisings replicate what the Haitians accomplished, because the demographics that worked in Saint-Domingue rarely favored slaves elsewhere. Slavery and the slave trade survived in French Guadeloupe and Martinique, and slavery and the slave plantation model became more entrenched in Brazil, mainland Spanish America, Spanish Cuba, and the U.S. South. Despite the proclamation by Haiti's first leaders that they did not intend to export their revolution, prohibitions against the movement of free blacks and closer supervision of slaves increased throughout the slave regions of the Caribbean. Apprehensions about French intentions to restore slavery in its former colony lingered for two decades.[42]

Stories of what the Haitians had done persisted, and for another half-century, the mere mention of the revolution prompted a momentary pause in every conversation about the inhumanity and moral perfidy of slavery and the worthiness of the abolitionist cause when measured against the prospect of "another Haiti." For those who lived in the slave states, the reminders of the Haitian slave rebellion caused a more fearful reaction. In 1800 interrogation of the defendants in Gabriel's Conspiracy in Virginia indicated that the conspirators were mindful of events in Saint-Domingue. They were even more inspired by the rhetoric of "New Light" Baptist preachers, who had appeared in prerevolutionary Virginia, welcomed converts regardless of color, and hoped to capitalize on the declining demand for slave labor as planters shifted from tobacco to grain production. The New Lights had preached the equality of all men before God and the right to resort to armed struggle, an inspirational message carried by boatmen in the carrying trade on Virginia's rivers. One of the conspirators defiantly declared that the slaves had "as much right to fight for our liberty as any man," and another compared himself to George Washington in his defiance of unlawful authority.[43]

Two years later, Jefferson referred to the revolt and to the ensuing discussions that slaves found guilty of insurgency might be relocated to places outside the United States, perhaps Africa. The Virginia Assembly elected to step up controls over the slave population and place limits on voluntary manumission. Slaves emancipated after 1806 were required to leave the state. Much like the Virginia revolts of Nat Turner in 1831–32, the two revolts of 1800 and 1802 brought Virginia's political elites closer to considering the end of slavery out of fear of the violent consequences if they did not act. "Tell us not of principles," the *Virginia Argus* of Richmond commented. "Those principles have been annihilated by the existence of slavery among us."[44]

The Revolutionary Legacy and the Empire of Liberty

Haitian slaves had achieved a social revolution within a revolution that in France represented class war but in Saint-Domingue became a racial and ethnic war. Those who presumed to lead the slaves ultimately had to recognize their determination to rid themselves of slavery, the plantation economy, and white supremacy, whatever the cost. Perhaps three hundred thousand died between 1790 and 1796, amounting to 60 percent of the 1789 population. Further physical damage occurred during the "scorched-earth" policy of the British occupation, when the occupiers suffered losses of fifteen thousand men to desertion or death and the British reconciled themselves to depending more on black regiments. Those who questioned their commitment or their capability as fighters paid a heavy price, none more so than the French, who lost a prized economy in a disastrous two-year war during which their best troops fell short in battles against slaves singing the militant hymns of revolutionary France. The Haitian Revolution, Franklin Knight reminds us in his magisterial survey of Caribbean history, was the "first complete social revolution in modern history," and every group and government that attempted to control, manipulate, or subdue the slaves underestimated what they were willing to do to gain and keep their freedom.[45]

A rebellion begun by slaves in 1791 had made possible the second independent state in the hemisphere and, indirectly, Jefferson's proudest moment, the Louisiana Purchase and the expansion of the empire of liberty. By his own assessment and that of his followers, he had redeemed the revolutionary promise in the spirit of limiting central authority and assuring a continental future for an expanding republic. With Jefferson's election in 1800, the symbiotic alliance forged with John Adams in 1776 seemed irretrievably broken. For Adams, the Revolution's legacy was republicanism, which required a strong executive, a constitutional government, and the rule of law, not the passions and uncertainties of public opinion. In other words, the Federalist model served best for a country that was a work in progress. For Jefferson, his erstwhile ally, democracy—a frightening word to Washington and Adams— constituted the greatest achievement of the Revolution. Adams's social rank depended on his place and role in government; Jefferson's did not. Adams was a Calvinist, a contrarian; Jefferson, an American version of antimonarchical Enlightenment thinking. The key to understanding their relationship lay in their commitment to the survival of the republic.[46]

Although riddled by continued partisan politicking and the blot of slavery, Jefferson's America resounded with confidence, purpose, a deep-seated sense of its own superiority, and revolutionary credos drawn from the natural rights philosophy of English thought and sanctioned by some of the more radical beliefs of French philosophes. In an era when several prominent European thinkers avowed that the peoples of the New World were innately inferior and incapable of creating nations or a civilization equaling that of Europe, the first generation of Americans coming of age in an independent country proudly asserted their superiority and accomplishments. They believed, writes Joyce Appleby in her social profile of them, that the legacy of their revolution was a distinctive society, one that "honored individual initiative, institutional restraint, and popular political participation." Such views appeared to validate the axiom that "might makes right" and in the example of trans-Appalachian settlement would lead to the creation of eleven new states by 1821.[47]

In Jefferson Americans saw a reformer who separated social and political power, proclaimed a universality of thought about liberty and equality while restricting their benefits to white people, expanded the franchise to include white males without property, assigned to women a social role as wives and mothers, emasculated Hamilton's fiscal design, cut taxes and the civil service, and conceded powers to the states and the people that perverted some of the revolutionary principles that he avowed. Ironically, the counterrevolutionary idea that social order was more important than extending the revolutionary ideal of liberty to slaves or even free blacks had inspired a countermovement in the free black community. Its leaders rejected armed struggle, colonization of manumitted slaves to Africa, and notions of black inferiority, calling instead for respect for the law, cleanliness, and justice for freed men sold into slavery as the most effective way of restoring the promises of the American Revolution.[48]

Women of the early republic were not yet poised to wage the kind of battle for equal treatment Abigail Adams had warned John about in her iconic "Remember the Ladies" letter of 1776. Despite the differences women made during the War of Independence—nursing, cleaning, and cooking for men, keeping farms and mills going, protecting property, and more—the men who wrote the laws and the Constitution and the Bill of Rights persisted in denying women's centrality in the political culture. Their commitment remained questionable. "Patriotism in the female sex," Abigail scribbled in a letter to John near the end of the war, "is the most disinterested of all virtues. . . . Deprived of a voice in Legislation, obliged to submit to those Laws which are imposed on us, is it not sufficient to make us indifferent to the publick Welfare?" An egalitarian democracy of men, it was believed, depended on the deference of women.[49]

In 1800 even the woman educated in the academies had not much more opportunity to control her future than her grandmother in 1750. She could teach school before marriage or not marry, and she could rear her children by republican principles. But in realistic terms she could not leave what was defined as the "feminine sphere." The war and the presumably continuing revolution it inspired had broken down some barriers for women, but women still had to channel their activities outside the home under male supervision or an appeal to a man. Even the independent Abigail Adams directed her solutions for liberating women to her husband with the reminder, do something or else. Despite the sharply defined roles for women in the early republic, Mary Beth Norton concludes, the "egalitarian rhetoric of the Revolution provided the women's rights movement with its earliest vocabulary and the republican academies its first leaders."[50]

By Abigail Adams's standards, Jefferson was out of step with the agenda of liberty's daughters but not with his followers. Passing through Philadelphia in February 1801, as her husband's presidency was in its final days, she wrote him about the "Democratic rejoicing" over Jefferson's election and the terror among others, "least their Swineish Herd should rise in rebellion and Seize upon their property & share the plunder amongst them."[51]

Although the Louisiana purchase lay more than two years in the future, Jefferson already had in mind how he would reward some of that "herd" who cheered his victory. He alienated many Federalists with the Louisiana Purchase, but his actions pleased a generation of land-hungry people who shared his apprehensions about the reversal of the country's future through continuing Spanish and British ambitions and separatist movements in the contested trans-Appalachian region, where Indians and settlers held competing notions about land use. In his mind, Louisiana's acquisition strengthened national security because it assured that the land west of the Mississippi would be settled by "our own brethren and children [and not] strangers of another family." That was his way of stating that the western territory was meant for white people. He subscribed to a belief in what subsequent generations called "American exceptionalism" and a parallel faith in a mythical American nation, the source of national legitimacy. The formal American state, which ultimately decided the contest between Indian and newcomer in the western country, might acknowledge regional and local differences. Louisiana fell into that category. In organizing its territorial government in 1805, Congress used the Northwest Ordinances as a guide but in the act accommodated local laws reflecting French and Spanish practices.[52]

Jefferson had the support of Adams's son, John Quincy, whose belief in a continental destiny for the republic ran as deep as Jefferson's. The younger Adams did not share the depth of the president's apprehensions about slave revolt and the place of people of color in the republic, but at this stage of his political life he held to the notion (as did Jefferson) that slavery would perish a natural death, and until then preservation of the Union required compromises about the matter. At the same time, an increasing number of political and social leaders of Jefferson's America, including some who opposed slavery, were arguing that colonization of manumitted slaves offered the most realistic solution to preserving the Union. In the Revolution, antislavery advocates had articulated beliefs that differences between whites and blacks were largely explained by environmental conditions and that both possessed an essential humanity. Some who held that view, notably James Otis, believed that coexistence between whites and blacks in the republic would be difficult. By the time Jefferson became president, the conservative view of race had strengthened its hold, particularly in the South. Fears of slave revolt and the growing assertiveness of free people of color to stake their claim in the new nation reinforced belief in a racial hierarchy. Acceptance of that myth was an important step toward the more rigid theories undergirding scientific racism.[53]

IN THE 1790S Jefferson had been the acknowledged leader of those who yearned for a more open, democratic society, but they had begun to draw a sharper color line, as he did. Successive naturalization laws of the decade had privileged white immigrants, and these had flocked to the republican clubs that so infuriated Washington and Adams. Both had mobilized these people during their presidencies, yet they continued to believe that the revolutionary promise was a republic led by the enlightened and educated and not the kind of democracy Tom Paine advocated or what Adams called a "mobocracy." Jefferson had benefited from their loyalty in his quest for the presidency. In power, however, he confronted not only their antagonism to his use of military power in the Louisiana Territory but also a dilemma that would befuddle his successors: the growing political division over the expansion of slavery and slave power and, equally important, a parallel uncertainty about the place and role of people of color in the republic. Some clung to the hope, as Jefferson himself believed, that slavery would not survive. As poor white resentment of manumitted slaves and free people of color heightened, Jefferson and almost every president who followed him believed in their colonization in Africa or Haiti or even in Central America. Jefferson sensed the impracticability of the plan but had no alternative. Abraham Lincoln shared his doubts, but he discarded them after the Emancipation Proclamation of January 1, 1863, and after black troops had demonstrated their willingness to fight and die for the Union.

Jefferson, a slave owner and a child of the Enlightenment as well as the Revolution, certainly did not harbor the fierce racial attitudes of ordinary southern white males. In some respects, he expressed views about slavery, the slave trade, and blacks that were similar to those held by such liberal West Indians as Bryan Edwards of Jamaica and Moreau de Saint-Méry of Martinique. Each wrote a book similar in intent to Jefferson's *Notes on Virginia*, each owned a plantation and slaves, and each was a man of influence in society and politics. As did Jefferson, both men condemned the Saint-Domingue slave uprising. Unlike Jefferson, the two West Indians accepted the interracial society in which they lived. They never thought of deporting blacks somewhere else. They did not see blacks as inferior, nor did they believe the West Indies would ever be a white man's country. But they were reconciled to West Indian conditions because they could leave.[54]

In the revisionist literature, Jefferson often stands accused of opposing federal power, as he did with the Alien and Sedition Acts, but remaining mute when it was politically inconvenient to speak out or, conversely, "capable of ruthlessness in the exercise of power."[55] As one of his critical biographers reminds us, principles enforced with actions can complicate matters. Jefferson believed the exercise of federal power constituted a denial of revolutionary principles. He wanted to rid the country and especially his beloved Virginia of slavery. But slavery was a denial of revolutionary principles. There seemed no practical way to deal with the removal of slaves until the Louisiana Purchase provided him with an opportunity to exercise his power as president in planning for development of the territory: first, as in the Northwest Territory, prohibit slavery; second, create a special fund out of land sales to compensate slave owners willing to free their slaves; third, resettle freed slaves in the new territory. The first and even the second might have passed muster with Congress, but not the third. Jefferson himself denied that possibility by inserting "white" before "inhabitants" in the purchase treaty's clause about the "inhabitants of the ceded territory." The other practical solution, which rapidly gained traction after the War of 1812, was the expatriation of freed slaves *outside* the United States and the territories it acquired in North America.[56]

As a southerner, Jefferson could not easily reconcile his revolutionary sensibilities with the uncomfortable political and social realities of his times. Republics, like monarchies, had their own hierarchical order, and they could be less inclusive. His once-transparent Francophilia diminished in the face of Napoleon's self-elevation to emperor in 1804, in his growing awareness that the office of president of the United States is less about intellect than character, and in the inner turmoil he experienced trying to reconcile his democratic instincts with his duty to keep order in a country that seemed well on its way to becoming, as some had feared, both slave and free. In the process he became less European, particularly when he thought in hemispheric rather than transatlantic terms. Both he and his longtime revolutionary ally and political nemesis John Adams would live long enough to witness how the "western question"—a phrase European leaders used to identify the problems posed by civil war and rebellion in Spanish America and the unsettled questions of North America—would precipitate a great debate about the meaning of the American Revolution and the republic it had created.

CHAPTER 4

The Republic in Peril

THOMAS JEFFERSON SPOKE THE LANGUAGE of nationhood. He believed that the United States could be an exemplar but not a crusader nation. It was exceptional because it possessed certain characteristics and opportunities that could serve those who came to the country to partake of its benefits. The United States was "acting for all mankind; that circumstances denied to others, but indulged to us, have imposed on us the duty of proving what is the degree of freedom and self-government in which a society may venture to leave its individual citizens."[1]

Use of the adjective "individual" offered an insight that J. Hector St. John de Crèvecoeur had invoked in his collection *Letters from an American Farmer* (1782) to describe the "American" of the prerevolutionary era—the European who left behind old prejudices and manners and with interaction and intermarriage with others of different ethnicities had become a new person who was individualistic, nonideological, pragmatic, hardworking, a "western pilgrim." John Adams never subscribed to American exceptionalism on commonsensical grounds because the notion implied uniqueness, made comparisons difficult, and imposed a way of thinking best described as an intellectual "trap," the secular equivalent of the religious "leap of faith." Some found solace in religion—Calvinist, traditional, or evangelical—to explain why the country had gone astray. Jefferson lived long enough to realize that the republican society he had imagined had become a democracy he deprecated for its excesses.[2]

Although his Virginia identity remained distinct, Washington had provided a symbolic role as national leader. Jefferson confronted a similar challenge of framing a national spirit out of the collective energies that had sustained the American Revolution in its darkest hours but had dissipated in the fractious political culture of the 1790s. One possibility lay in using public celebrations and rituals—some of them drawn from English traditions and publicized in the press—that had proved useful in mitigating the feuds among political elites. Nationalistic rituals provided a means to overcome a persistent localism by forging an identity with mass appeal and inspiring persons to identify not as New Englanders or Virginians and so on but as Americans, thus easing social tensions. As Jefferson acknowledged, nourishing a shared national identity encountered problems for some and benefits for others when it meant nurturing a political coalition predicated on white supremacy between plain republicans of the North and southern slaveholders or a political leader dedicated to bringing down a rival party.[3]

For Jefferson, there was the West and its allure, which had almost doubled the size of the country. Washington thought of the West in economic terms. Jefferson was a spiritual believer in its power "to nourish the present with news of the future," which called for people who were hardworking and committed to building communities and a diversified economy and who would not be prone to joining rebellions. To that end, federal land policy dictated managed growth with land sold at reasonable cost and clear land titles. With this "empire of liberty" the country could avoid Europe's problem of overcrowding and social conflict. As Joseph Ellis (a critical biographer) acknowledges, Jefferson recognized that "the United States was not just integrating the West into the union; the West was actually integrating the older United States into an ever-changing version of America."[4]

For the Federalist minority and even some in Jefferson's own Democratic-Republican Party, what Jefferson called the "Revolution of 1800" was not the "Revolution of 1776." Most of the old revolutionaries despaired of the future of a country that in their minds had become too democratic in its politics, too crass in its business life, and too evangelical in its religion. A splinter group, known as the Quids or Old Republicans, wanted liberty from government and freedom for the individual. Persuaded that agriculture offered the only secure basis for an economy, they deplored the damage that Jefferson's economic retaliation against both Great Britain and France did to the southern export market. Jefferson visualized the West as the country's salvation. His critics considered it a backwater populated by debtors, land speculators, opportunists, plotters, and proselytizers. To Federalists like the Bostonian Josiah Quincy, Louisiana and especially New Orleans—more Catholic, Caribbean, French, and Spanish in its culture, racial sensibilities, mixed-race population, and distinctive local politics—suggested "Babylon," not "Athens," and certainly not New England's vaunted "City on a Hill." The push for Louisiana statehood constituted a plot of the slave power, Quincy believed, and when the Federalist minority in Congress failed to prevent it, he morosely commented that it meant the end of the Union.[5]

Madison and Jefferson, too, had their moments of despondency. In the crises over the Alien and Sedition Acts in the late 1790s, both had invigorated the "Spirit of 1776" with warnings about a Federalist central government in collusion with British commercial interests threatening their uncorrupted republican dream. In power, they found themselves on the defensive, not only from Federalists but also from "old Republicans" denouncing a federal government as despotic as the one they had opposed in 1776. Frustrated, Jefferson began to think and behave in ways that have puzzled some modern biographers, either trying to "republicanize" New Englanders or demonizing them as enemies to be expelled from the Union. Increasingly, race and slavery became an obsession. Africans were a captive people, and he viewed their manumission and then colonization—an issue he dealt with in his *Notes on the State of Virginia* (1785)—as the only solution for both white and black people. That failing, northerners had to understand why southern whites feared slave insurrection and supported the spread of slavery into the western territories as a means of diffusing slave numbers. The survival of the Union and what the republic represented to the world hung in the balance.[6]

At the outset of Jefferson's second term (March 4, 1805), there were lingering fears about the uncertain international crisis. In Europe, Napoleon escalated his war of Continental political and economic domination. His decision to bring the recalcitrant Spanish and Portuguese firmly under French control would precipitate civil wars in Spain and in Spanish America and expand the transatlantic war with the British on the high seas. The United States now found itself ensnared in the transatlantic war between Britain and France and in the Spanish American crisis in ways that imperiled the economy, deepened the political divisions at home, and led to a declared war with Britain that took the form of a civil war in North America on the northern border and a guerrilla war on the southern frontier.

The intertwined domestic and international crises reopened old wounds from the revolutionary years. To a generation often wary of the meaning of the Haitian Revolution for the republic, the eruption of civil war and revolution in Spanish America awakened among some feelings of identity and solidarity with the stirrings of independence movements in the "other America." For Republican leaders, those sentiments posed a challenge different from the Federalist demurral to their policies or that symbolized by

Americans who had migrated to Canada—an alternative revolution in the hemisphere, one more open to mixed-race people and with less harsh slave regimes.

With their legitimacy at stake, a generation of Republican leaders now took on the formidable task of proving they were the true heirs of the Revolution by pursuing a course they anticipated would not only lead to war but also weaken their political enemies at home. In their self-appointed mission of defining the revolutionary legacy, they had raised expectations. Jefferson and his heir apparent, James Madison, learned that there was a price to pay for this choice. At war's end and despite the nationalist spirit identified with Andrew Jackson's victory at the Battle of New Orleans in January 1815, they had to acknowledge that the Revolution had bequeathed a dual legacy.

One lay in the prerevolutionary debate between republican and monarchical governance, symbolized in the estrangement between those monarchical British Americans who had migrated north and no longer called themselves Americans and their republican cousins who had remained behind in the states. More troubling was the second legacy of the Revolution: a republic more democratic but without a strong central authority and whose politics, economy, and society increasingly reverberated from the divisive dynamics of slavery, race, and war against Indians. A fundamental dilemma remained: Could they reconcile the first with the second without a war?

Crises Foreign and Domestic

In power, Jefferson often constrained the democratic changes of the times. Among the most persistent of these were movements to abolish the slave trade (which was finally approved in 1807), for the equal treatment for free blacks, and for the abolition of slavery. In Virginia and in the eastern states, the first had widespread support, but the second and third were becoming increasingly more controversial. The first well-organized movement, the Pennsylvania Abolition Society, emerged after the Revolution. Dominated by white social elites who favored gradualist approaches to abolition, the society used newspapers, pamphlets, and lectures and emphasized the inhumanity of slavery in its appeal. In the interest of maintaining national unity, it sought to reassure slaveholders of their property interests. African Americans, largely excluded from official membership in these early antislave organizations, focused more on maintaining their rights in the face of growing racial prejudice and opposing colonization, which gained wide support in the Upper South after 1815.

Although grateful for the support of white abolitionists, African Americans were becoming increasingly frustrated with whites' reminders of "patience" in pressing African Americans' claims. In the face of these formidable obstacles, free African Americans persisted and drew closer collectively, sensing that emancipation would be a long struggle dominated by four fundamental principles: "the centrality of black people, the commitment to universal freedom, the necessity of racial equality, and the ubiquity of violence."[7]

If those words expressed the Declaration of Independence in an African dialect, white Americans feared a different reference was in play. As former slaves began to develop their own sense of identity and create institutions to sustain it, they were increasingly confronted with white hostility coupled with reminders of their inferiority. Even those slaveholders who bemoaned the institution harbored fears that the emancipated slave would seek revenge and that slave rebellion was about "avenging America." Southern and even northern proslavers now had Bryan Edwards's 1797 book, *An Historical Survey of the French Colony in the Island of St. Domingo*, which placed the blame for the island's slave rebellion squarely on the activities of the Société des Amis des Noirs in Paris.

The Virginian St. George Tucker argued that republicanism and slavery were incompatible and that freedmen could not be incorporated into white society and should be colonized in the West. Almost two decades before, Jefferson had expressed a harsher judgment. In postrevolutionary Virginia, the number of whites exceeded that of slaves by only twenty-five thousand. In *Notes on the State of Virginia*, Jefferson happily noted that the first legislature of the state approved legislation ending the importation of slaves. "This will in some measure stop the increase of this great political and moral evil," he concluded, "while the minds of our citizens may be ripening for a complete emancipation of human nature."[8]

That made sense to white Virginians but was not that relevant elsewhere. To Jefferson, that portion of the Louisiana Territory in New Orleans and the Mississippi River Delta was an alien culture of people accustomed to authoritarian rule. They had their own legal traditions, which they had incorporated into a federated union where English common law prevailed. Most of Louisiana's residents preferred U.S. to French rule, but they objected to their situation with an undeniably undemocratic territorial government under W. C. C.

Claiborne, a Virginia native. Free blacks, Indians, and slaves joined white Creoles in staking their place in the new polity.

More than a collision of different cultures was at stake. New Light Baptist missionaries preached social equality of white, black, and colored. In the aftermath of the takeover, white planters from the southeastern states joined slave-owning French refugees from the Haitian Revolution. Louisiana experienced rapid economic development. Planters who had once relied on tobacco and indigo as their principal crops moved into Louisiana and shifted to cotton and sugar, both heavily dependent on slave labor. In time, these crops would connect Louisiana and its Deep South neighbors more closely to the textile mills of Great Britain and the U.S. Northeast. The internal slave trade—largely trafficking from Maryland and Virginia to the dynamic Mississippi delta region of the Deep South and (after 1808) an illegal slave trade from Spanish Cuba, Florida, and Texas—escalated. The security of the region remained a troublesome matter for slaveholders.[9]

In Virginia, militias and even informal bands of local white males maintained order, but the plantation empire coming into being in the parishes of the delta proved more volatile, providing opportunities for the politically ambitious. One was former vice president Aaron Burr. His reputation sullied after he killed Alexander Hamilton in their July 1804 duel, Burr departed Washington, D.C., at the end of his term and headed west, where, according to a warning Jefferson received, he plotted with other conspirators, perhaps the British, to overthrow the government. In 1806 he joined with his old friend General James Wilkinson, a Spanish spy, in a bizarre project for Louisiana's independence from the United States and, with the presumed support of both Britain and France, the seizure of Spanish Texas.

Separatist movements in the western country were nothing new, but this one struck directly at the power of the federal government, particularly at Jefferson. Concluding that the plan would not work, Wilkinson betrayed Burr and began arresting his followers. Jefferson formally denounced Burr as the leader of a conspiracy and stated that his guilt was unquestionable. Burr surrendered, and with the president's blessing the government charged Burr with treason. But he was acquitted largely because of Chief Justice John Marshall's charge to the jury that treason required stronger evidence than the prosecution had provided. Burr lived long enough to learn of the Texas rebellion and the creation of an independent republic. "I was only thirty years too soon," he told a friend. "What was treason thirty years ago is patriotism now."[10]

The Burr conspiracy coincided with another challenge of more ominous portent. In the spring of 1804 a fourteen-month peace in the war between Britain and France abruptly ended. What had been for the British a conflict over Jacobinism now became a war to the death, the final calamitous decade of the Second Hundred Years' War. Spain joined the coalition against Napoleon, and Lord Nelson's 1805 victory at Trafalgar effectively ended Napoleon's ambitious plan to invade the home island. On the Continent, however, the rejuvenated French army acquitted itself well, triumphing at Austerlitz in 1805. Because of its success and the ambitions of its leader and now emperor, France's "Grand Empire" had already commenced the transformation of the Old Europe with stronger and modern central governments, public works projects, a civil code, written constitutions, secularization of church property, religious toleration, civil rights for Jews, equality before the law, and abolition of privilege, corporate bodies, and tithes, as well as feudal dues. There was a democratic, revolutionary spirit in Napoleon's grand design, but it did not break the bond between monarchy and aristocracy. Napoleon considered himself a child of the French Revolution and as emperor ruled France as a virtual dictator. In the United States, the Constitution made the people the constituent power. When he became emperor in 1804, Napoleon declared: "I am the constituent power." Jefferson was not surprised. After the Louisiana Purchase, however, he deemed France a lesser threat than Britain, and he now had the confidence to believe he could deal with European leaders on an equal level.[11]

Jefferson's long affair with France was coming to an end. His animosity toward Britain remained; the acquired Anglophobia of his followers intensified. More than once the strategy of playing these two powers off one another had worked—during the early years of the War of Independence and again in the uncertain months of negotiating a settlement. In the 1790s the price for maintaining an uneasy balance between the two had been high. With the onset of Jefferson's second term, the stakes got even higher. In the aftermath of Trafalgar and Austerlitz, the battle between the two giants turned to economic warfare, which hit directly at the neutral shipping of the United States. In two decrees in November and December 1807, Napoleon established the Continental System, forbidding French allies and neutrals from trading with the British. The British responded with new orders in council reaffirming their right to search all neutral ships and to impress British subjects who had deserted to join the rapidly expanding U.S. merchant trade.

Napoleon in turn threatened to seize any U.S. merchant ship that docked in Britain. The most provocative incident occurred in June 1807, when the captain of a British warship fired a broadside into the USS *Chesapeake* after its captain refused a boarding in search of deserters. Under British law, any British subject obligated to serve in wartime who renounced his citizenship to escape service was a traitor.

Jefferson now faced a transatlantic crisis on the high seas. The Republican-dominated Congress sought to avoid war by passing the Embargo Act of 1807, which idled U.S. maritime commerce but which Jefferson predicted would bring the belligerents to their senses. As his Federalist critics and even John Quincy Adams (who reluctantly supported the measure) warned, the Embargo Act did far more damage to the U.S. economy by encouraging rampant smuggling on the northern border. Federal efforts to put an end to the illicit trade with militia met with violence. "I had rather encounter war itself," lamented Secretary of the Treasury Albert Gallatin, "than to display our impotence to enforce our laws."[12]

Despite Napoleon's ambitions and his acknowledgment that the embargo played into Napoleon's favor, Jefferson believed French domination of Europe offered a form of security to the United States. Some of Jefferson's French correspondents tried to persuade him that in time the kind of society emerging in France would be a model of Jefferson's America. That was a far-fetched notion, as was Jefferson's belief that he could use the embargo as a weapon to compel both Britain and France to respect U.S. power and rescind their retaliatory decrees. Jefferson privately acknowledged that the French suffered less from the measure. Britain depended on food imports; hence, it would be the first to capitulate. After the Louisiana Purchase and the resumption of the European war, Jefferson deduced that he could exploit the British-French rivalry. Governor Claiborne recommended seizure of both East and West Florida. Jefferson focused on a settlement of the West Florida issue—the strip of land between the Perdido and Pearl Rivers—on the specious argument that it formed part of the Louisiana Purchase.[13]

In the end, Jefferson miscalculated, and badly. The embargo made the United States a de facto French ally. Jefferson gained nothing in Florida. At home he became widely unpopular, and not only in Federalist New England. Even Timothy Pickering, who had little success in tarring Jefferson as the "Negro president" or for his opposition to the Louisiana Purchase, found momentary popularity because of his attacks on Jefferson's arbitrary use of executive power to enforce the law, such as unjustified search and warrant seizures and prosecutions for treason that in some cases were dismissed by Republican judges. Jefferson defended the embargo as a symbol of an agrarian South against a mercantile Northeast. He called for a march on Canada after the *Chesapeake* affair, but Gallatin warned him that the country lacked the men, money, and arms to undertake such a venture.[14]

Five years later, after the War of 1812 had commenced, the United States did undertake another invasion of Canada, and the result was a disaster. Congress repealed the embargo on Jefferson's last day in office. In the end, the real damage came to U.S. agriculture and commerce, as well as Jefferson's reputation. One notable victim of Pickering's relentless assault was John Quincy Adams, who lost his seat in the Senate. He was too vital to the Republican cause to discard, so Madison appointed him U.S. minister to St. Petersburg, where he would serve until 1814. In the citadel of tsarist Russia, he would find the order worthy of his intellect if not his conscience.

Revolution and Civil War in the Spanish World

By then, Jefferson had already become alert to stories of discontent over monarchical rule in Spanish America. Unlike the elder Adams, he was fascinated by the distinctiveness of "America" and believed that "the human race would begin anew" in the New World. The idea of the liberation of the southern continent from Spanish rule appealed to Jefferson, although in 1813 he expressed reservations about the capacity of a "priest-ridden people" to maintain "a free civil government." Yet he affirmed that such governments would be "*American* governments" set apart from the "never-ceasing broils of Europe" and their different interests. Predictably ambivalent, he expressed a belief in hemispheric solidarity and a parallel belief that in time the empire of liberty would "cover the whole northern, if not the southern continent."[15]

The seeds of Spanish American disaffection and even rebellion sprang up almost simultaneously with those in British North America after 1763. Carlos III became king in 1759, a year before George III assumed the throne. Unlike George, he possessed absolute power and a more enlightened view about modernizing Spain and his far-flung kingdoms in America. There were potential ominous problems, which indirectly complicated Jefferson's assessment of things. Discontented American Spaniards (Creoles) looked at the motherland, perceived its debility, but were fearful to act lest they unleash something frightening like the Haitian slave rebellion, which sent a death chill among white Venezuelan slaveholders in the 1790s, or the Túpac Amaru II uprising against Spanish rule in Peru in 1780, led by a mestizo who claimed Inca lineage. There white Creoles were initially heartened by the economic grievances of Peru's indigenous population but then became alarmed when the rebellion became a race war and, with the timely help of the Catholic Church, crushed it.[16]

From the mid-eighteenth century on, there were fewer destructive rebellions that bound people along ethnic and racial lines and suggested class warfare. More ominously, in the direction of their anger, the rebels made no distinction between American and European Spaniards. In such ominous circumstances, alienated Creoles who absorbed Enlightenment ideas about ridding themselves of the Spanish yoke became more hesitant to act. Their sense of Americanness and a desire for liberty or a "consciousness of national personality" persisted.[17]

Jefferson's concern lay with the United States' relationship with Spain and Spanish America, particularly on the southern frontier, and the impact of Spanish American rebellion on U.S. political culture and society. As the confirmed antimonarchist ideologue, he agreed with the sentiments expressed by a group of Philadelphia Republicans who welcomed news of Spanish American rebellion with approval: "May their noble exertions to emancipate their country from the shackles of *despotism* and *superstition* be crowned with complete success."[18]

The implications of such encouragement were a different and often unsettling matter. In late 1805 Jefferson and Secretary of State Madison were momentarily distracted by the plans of the fifty-five-year-old Venezuelan Francisco de Miranda (who had taken part in the 1781 Spanish assault on Pensacola) to liberate not only his native land but also the entire continent of South America. In their sense of being worse off than their slaves, Venezuela's white slave owners bore some resemblance to discontented Virginian Tidewater aristocrats in 1776. Carlos III's economic and social policies—such as the easing of restrictions on mulattoes (*pardos*)—particularly annoyed them, but in a society where one in five was white, they had been reluctant to emulate revolutionary Virginians. Miranda was unafraid. Denied help by the British, he found 180 willing recruits in the New York area—one of them the grandson of John Adams, who dropped out of college to join up—and in early 1806 set sail for the Venezuelan coast. But the expedition came to no good end. Among some Americans, the entire affair discredited those who championed the independence of Spanish America and revealed how little ordinary Americans knew about the region.[19]

That changed after 1810, when Spain and Spanish America from Buenos Aires to Mexico collapsed in civil war and revolution that in turn became entangled in the Continental war between Britain and France, as well as the political crisis between Britain and the United States. The triggering event of the first was Napoleon's decision to alter the political stakes in the European war by removing the pro-British Portuguese king, Dom João VI, which required permission from the weak and pliable Spanish monarch, Carlos IV, to allow passage of French troops through national territory. The British spoiled the plan by spiriting the Portuguese king and his retinue to Brazil.

The Spanish and Spanish American experiences proved far more complicated. Napoleon lured Spanish king Carlos IV and his anti-French son Fernando to Bayonne and forced them to renounce the Spanish throne in favor of Napoleon's brother Joseph. In the ensuing two years, 1808 and 1809— Jefferson's last and Madison's first year as president—Spanish resistance escalated into guerrilla war, prompting Napoleon to dispatch a two-hundred-thousand-man army into the country. Professing its loyalty to Fernando, the weak and demoralized patriot Central Junta fled to the port city of Cádiz, where it lingered under the protection of British warships.

Over the next two years, against the backdrop of a persistent guerrilla war, Napoleon and Joseph (now José I) commenced the transformation of Spain and Spanish America in the legal and secular spirit of the French Revolution. The nation, not the king, was the symbol of unity. Sovereignty resided with the people, and the ancient legislative body, the Cortes, included representation from all parts of the empire. By 1812 the Cortes had drawn up a liberal constitution, a remarkably modern document that loosely followed the 1791 French Constitution, substituting a constitutional monarchy for its absolutist predecessor and reaffirming the unity of Spain and America under a central, unicameral government. With some important qualifications, plans for a similar relationship between Britain and British America had been advanced after 1763 but had not survived popular protest.[20]

But the British-sustained Peninsular War had already begun in Spain, and in Spanish America, from Buenos Aires to Mexico, localized civil wars between American and European Spaniards had erupted in the aftermath of disputes in the open forums (*cabildos abiertos*) over those loyal to the deposed

Fernando, or those who favored autonomy, and others who called for independence. As in the thirteen colonies, the internal wars that ensued took different form from place to place, often with far bloodier consequences. In northern South America, the civil war unfolded as a conflict between provinces, particularly in Nueva Granada (modern Colombia and Panama), or between cities, as in Venezuela. There, Simón Bolívar insinuated himself into local politics, and in defiance of his orders as a member of a delegation dispatched to London seeking British assistance, he made possible Miranda's return to the province. Active in the Patriotic Society, Miranda and his followers spearheaded Venezuela's declaration of independence (July 5, 1811) and the creation of a federalist government modeled closely on that of the United States. Miranda was specific about his revolutionary choices. "Two great examples lie before our eyes, the American and the French revolutions," he affirmed in a letter to Pedro Gual, a Venezuelan rebel. "Let us discreetly imitate the first; let us carefully avoid the disastrous effects of the second."[21]

There would be no republican miracle in Venezuela. One year after its birth, the republic collapsed from the weakness of a central authority, financial difficulties, and a ferocious royalist counterrevolution in which slave and mixed-race troops from the Venezuelan plains waged a race war, the most savage and destructive conflict in Spanish America's wars of independence.

The Mexican scenario followed still another course. In the name of good government, the abolition of slavery, and the return of Indian lands, Miguel Hidalgo, a priest facing punishment for conspiracy, raised an army of mestizos, Indians, and blacks in a cause that terrified both peninsular and American Spaniards. A campaign that promised social revolution soon collapsed into a race war that united whites in their quest for equality between American and European Spaniards and a guerrilla war in the countryside.[22]

All three of its predecessors—the American, French, and Haitian Revolutions—impacted the Spanish American upheaval, but measuring their influence can be tricky. Modern assessments and the U.S. posture toward them often follow different trajectories. In contrast to what occurred in British America, these were not anticolonial struggles or, as in France, sharp breaks with the past; instead, they represented part of a revolution within the Spanish world. This experience sharpened the distinction with the U.S. War of Independence. A variation emphasizes how white Spanish American patriot leaders proved more accepting of nonwhite people in their cause than their

British American counterparts, thus expanding the definition of "American" in their conception of inclusivity.

As the civil war in Spanish America intensified, the lofty notion about expanding U.S. influence and commerce within rebellious Spanish America withered before the reality that the Madison administration possessed no option to match the bolder and more successful British political adjustments to the war within the Spanish world. In Spain, Britain was the enemy of Napoleon and the friend of monarchy, yet British traders enjoyed commercial arrangements with Spanish American patriot groups, especially with Portuguese Brazil after the Braganza monarch moved there. After receiving a copy of the Venezuelan Declaration of Independence, a special committee in the U.S. Congress resolved in late 1811 that when Spanish American patriot groups created representative independent governments, the Congress would join with the executive branch in welcoming them into the community of new states. The statement was a recognition that the intent of the patriot cause was to fill the void left by the removal of the Spanish monarch. At the same time, as Arthur Whitaker alertly noted, it represented a muted call for hemispheric solidarity.[23]

Among Federalists and even some Republican leaders, this was an idea whose time had not yet come. For one thing, Jefferson and then Madison faced the difficulty of trying to balance the fragile but sorely needed economic ties to Spain, persevere in demanding respect for their neutral rights from the British, and fend off continuing Federalist assaults on their foreign policy. Public opinion about South American patriots remained strong, however, particularly at Fourth of July celebrations, at which revelers toasted the South American cause as one emulating their own. Expatriates and agitators from the various war zones came to the United States to obtain loans, weapons, and ships and even to press for recognition. (By the mid-1820s some two hundred had arrived.) Venezuelans and New Granadans settled mostly in Philadelphia. Those from Mexico and the Caribbean went principally to New Orleans and the Gulf Coast. Spanish American patriot leaders were familiar with Paine's *Common Sense*, and they responded well to those U.S. editors and publicists who perceived the anticolonial struggle in South America as a variation of their own. As a Baltimore editor scribbled on the eve of U.S. entry into war with Britain, "When independence is the cause, South and North America have but one cause."[24]

The Civil War of 1812

The sentiment persisted, although it would subside with the realization that North and South America did not have a common enemy. On June 18, 1812, a frustrated Congress declared war on the British Empire. For two years the British and particularly the French government had been playing a game of deception in dealing with the United States. In this diplomatic scenario, Madison would commit to relieving the French from U.S. commercial restrictions and impose them on the British if Napoleon would rescind his decrees. The French emperor appeared to comply but failed to follow through, leaving Madison and the Republicans in Congress embarrassed. Throughout, the apparent weakness of the administration in dealing with Napoleon elicited scoffing from New England Federalists and even a few Republicans. When it became clear that peaceful coercion had proved ineffective and that a war with France was unthinkable but a war with Britain was conceivable, then no British concession—such as the suspension of some of their restrictive orders on U.S. commerce—that did not address impressment would make a difference.

The War of 1812 is often identified as a second war of independence because of the patriotic fervor it inspired. For contemporaries, the war also brought back memories of old revolutionary grievances, as well as new ones the Republican majority in Congress had compiled against the British: impressment of American seamen, many of them Irish who had escaped the hard labor of the British navy; plundering and harassment of U.S. neutral commerce on the high seas; encouragement of "Indian savagery" in the western country; and more. All were attributed to a British government whose practices demeaned U.S. sovereignty and citizenship. Although the wartime agenda differed sharply from the complaints of Spanish Americans in 1810, there was that critical similarity: a demand for equality and respect from the former motherland coupled with uncertainties about loyalties within the country.

In the Revolution, regional differences had mattered. They still did in 1812. The "War Hawks" from the western country called the loudest for war but lacked the votes to make the difference. New England Federalists, already suffering from federal crackdowns on violations of trade restrictions, were lukewarm or even hostile to the notion of a war with Britain. A prominent Democratic-Republican, Representative Joseph Barnum of Massachusetts, accused the Federalist opposition of doing "everything in their power, to subvert the principles of our happy government and to establish a Monarchy on its ruins."[25]

As in the *rage militaire* of the early years of the Revolution, feelings of pride, determination, and self-image became knotted with other calculations, such as the political benefits that can accrue to a party and a movement—in this case, the Democratic-Republican Party and the brand of republican beliefs Jefferson's name gave to it. (It was not uncommon to read or hear references to the "Republican Party" to mean "Democratic-Republican Party.") In the wartime political culture, those who identified with the Democratic-Republican Party and accepted Jefferson's brand of republican ideology and belief, which justified a stronger central government, had leaders with enough oral firepower and arrogance to affirm that the party of Jefferson *was* the nation.

Therein lay the problem of unanticipated consequences from a war that divided as much as it united. It put the old Federalist Party in its death throes, but it also invigorated a democratic political movement that Jefferson had founded and, a decade after the last shots were fired, that Andrew Jackson would make his own. Both Jackson and Jefferson welcomed the war. Jackson blamed the British for inciting Indian attacks in the western country. For Jefferson, the opportunity of driving the British from North America meant "indemnity for the past, security for the future, and emancipation from Anglomany, Gallomany, and all the manias of demoralized Europe."[26]

"Mr. Madison's War," as Federalist critics called it, was both an anti-British and anti-Federalist conflict. Devoted Democratic-Republican newspapers, such as the *Baltimore American* and Philadelphia's *Democratic Press*, waged editorial assaults on the Federalist minorities in their respective cities. On hearing the news that war had been declared, a Baltimore mob destroyed the press of the *Federal Republican*, whose editor had characterized Democratic-Republican leaders as pawns of Napoleon, democracy as foolhardy, and immigrants as ignoramuses who should be rounded up and deported. Federalist critics now perceived the wartime spirit as a force pushing the republic more and more toward despotism. In response, Jefferson approvingly recalled stories of mob violence against loyalists during the Revolution and in that militant spirit suggested that the country's outspokenly antiwar Federalists should be hanged for treason and their property confiscated. A hastily called Federalist convention in New York called for a policy of obstructionism because Republicans condemned their opposition to the war as treasonous. Jefferson claimed a higher calling for the charges against the Federalists. "I will not say our *party*, the term is false and degrading, but our *nation* will be undone. For the Republicans are the nation."[27]

More than security was at stake in the call for ridding North America of the British presence. In the Jay Treaty, Washington had infuriated the Democratic-Republican editorialists, who saw the document as a betrayal of the Revolution. In the years afterward, large numbers of Americans—dubbed "Late Loyalists"—began migrating north into Upper Canada, attracted by low taxes and other incentives and not a sense of commitment to the British Empire. Their numbers propelled Upper Canada's population from fourteen thousand in 1791 to seventy-five thousand (roughly three-fifths of the province's population) in 1812. Some British officials welcomed them as "loyal peasants" showing their gratitude to the king. Others were suspicious of their motives. A particularly harsh critic referred to them as "a nest of vipers in the bosom that now so incautiously fosters them."[28]

Presumably, these were people who could be counted on to welcome incorporation into the republic. In this instance, however, Federalist warnings about the futility of waging a war of conquest with a weak and inadequately funded military turned out to be true. Republicans wanted to drive the British from Canada but had no precise plan for what to do with the province if the campaign proved successful. The invading soldiers, many of them poorly disciplined and poorly trained, seemed more intent on looting than on engaging a foe with Indian allies who battled with a ferocity American militias and soldiers had encountered in the trans-Appalachian campaigns against Indians in the prewar years. (Britain's Indian allies, more than the militias, proved critical in defeating the American invaders in 1812 and 1813.) The latent belief in creating a white republic persisted. Confronted with a need to replenish the army, the Republican Congress persistently balked at enlisting free black men in the belief that whites would refuse to serve alongside them. (Black recruits did serve in the naval service.)[29]

Although there was little thought among Americans in the United States about restoring a monarchy—George Washington, after all, had comported himself as a "republican monarch"—the War of 1812 in the northern theater was a civil war between Americans committed to the republicanism inspired by the Revolution and those Americans in Upper Canada who had fled the Revolution and remained committed to empire and monarchy. The domestic civil war was that between Republicans and Federalists. Indians fought in both the northern and southern theaters, but in the North even their British allies became disturbed about the way the Indians waged war. In the war on the northern frontier, Tecumseh and his warriors and the soldiers led by an able British general, Sir Isaac Brock, turned back the U.S. invaders of Upper Canada in 1812.

American-born residents of the province mocked the American proclamations condemning the tyranny of British rule. Incensed that the population did not rally behind them, Americans in the second invasion of Upper Canada in 1813 plundered and burned towns on the north coast of Lake Erie and torched public buildings in the small provincial capital of York (now Toronto). In the ensuing battles, much of Lake Erie's north shore became a devastated war zone. Incompetent leadership cost the invading Americans in the campaign against Montreal, only thirty miles from the U.S. border.[30]

On the southern frontier, the war deteriorated into a racial conflict between Indians who were inspired by the fiery rhetoric of Tecumseh and white settlers whose loyalty to the national government rested principally on assurances that they, not the Indians, were the rightful heirs to the Revolution's "promise" of land. After the covert U.S. occupation of West Florida from the left bank of the Mississippi to the Perdido River in 1810, the U.S. Congress passed the No Transfer Resolution, opposing the transfer of territory in the Western Hemisphere from one European power to another. Congress approved the failed invasion of East Florida by Georgia patriots in 1812 but expressed less enthusiasm about an invasion of filibusters into Spanish Texas (the Gutiérrez-Magee Expedition) in the same year. Frankly, the administration's support, given to local people living in the area who were initially enthusiastic and then tentative when the raids encountered resistance, offered yet another indicator of the determination of borderlands people to bring Spanish Florida under U.S. control. When the irregulars in the Patriot Army became bogged down and had no Spanish enemy to confront, they took to looting and pillaging the plantations and farms along the St. Johns River.[31]

It was in this volatile region and among these people that Andrew Jackson made his mark. The young Jackson had fought British regulars during the Revolutionary War in the South and despised the loyalists. He condemned the British for their encouragement of Indian raids against white settlers. From mid-1813 until the spring of 1814, he led a volunteer force of Tennesseans, Kentuckians, and Indian allies for the singular purpose of making the Southwest safe for white settlers and, in his words, to provide a "bulwark against foreign invasion" and the "introduction of foreign influence."[32] Jackson's behavior inspired both admiration and concern in his superiors in Washington, D.C. In a war of few victories, he won battles, but too often his notorious temper and single-minded judgment raised concerns. When the Spanish began to reinforce Pensacola in response to the occupation of West Florida, Jackson openly spoke of war with Spain until he received direct orders to be quiet about such notions. His superiors were convinced Spain would not go to war over Florida.

A prospective British invasion of the Gulf coast, possibly at Mobile but more likely in the lower Mississippi delta and New Orleans, was altogether different. Already Jackson was getting warnings about the vulnerability of the city and the surrounding plantation districts, where free blacks and slaves outnumbered whites twenty-five to one. In New Orleans, Jackson encountered Spanish and French Creoles, some of them refugees from the Haitian Revolution, free people of color, slaves, Acadians ("Cajuns") expelled from Nova Scotia following one of the colonial wars of the previous century, and Americans of English descent. Jackson's army reflected this heterogeneous ethnic and racial diversity of colored, white, Indian, and slave. Warned by the local slaveholders that arming slaves and free people of color might be risky, as had been the case during the Haitian upheaval, Jackson curtly responded that such men were deserving of equal treatment: "They must be for, or against us—distrust them, and you make them your enemies. [P]lace confidence in them, and you engage them by every clear and honorable tie to the interest of the country who extends to them equal rights and privileges with white men."[33]

Such expressions of solidarity rang hollow among local slaveholders who remembered the slave revolt in January 1811 on the sugar plantations of French planters outside New Orleans. The local sugar economy had thrived after the French defeat in Haiti, and newcomers flocked to New Orleans to make their fortunes alongside the French planters, who were equally determined to preserve their power and social standing. In 1809 and 1810, when ten thousand white refugees and their slaves had migrated from Haiti to Cuba and later sought entry into the United States, Governor Claiborne had initially invoked Congress's prohibition on admitting slaves from the Caribbean, as did other southern governors. Under pressure, Congress exempted Louisiana from the ban, and white immigrants brought three thousand slaves to New

Orleans. As they had in the 1790s, Americans had to deal with large numbers of refugees in a place undergoing rapid change and slaves with memories of the Haitian upheaval. Although estimates of the numbers of slaves involved vary greatly, the insurrection struck fear among whites. Only two whites were killed, largely because slaves anticipating a reward had alerted the planters to the revolt. After a decisive battle between the slaves and the white militia, thirty of the slaves were executed. The decapitated heads of some were impaled on spikes as an example to other slaves. In the aftermath, Claiborne, a Jefferson appointee disliked by locals, exploited planter fears to hasten Louisiana's admission into the Union.[34]

When the country went to war in June 1812, the seeming invincibility of the French army had already begun to falter. In Iberia, the British under the Duke of Wellington went on the offensive, driving the French first out of Portugal and then from Spain the following year. An even greater disaster came in the wake of the invasion of Russia, where in retreat a mighty army of six hundred thousand was reduced to only thirty thousand. By early 1814 it was clear that the nation wanted peace. Recruiting became a problem. Taxes went unpaid. Napoleon's marshals turned on him. His once-compliant Senate voted to depose him, and the allies invited Louis XVIII to assume power under a liberal charter. On April 6 Napoleon abdicated, and a week later the allies granted him safe haven with a generous pension on the island of Elba.

The victors gathered in Vienna to create an international system to deal with the myriad issues left in the wake of the French Revolution and, more important, to prevent another from rising in its wake in Europe. Although it would have a mixed legacy, the Concert System of Europe they crafted was based on the willingness of its participants to compromise about threats to peace in the international order. Designed for a Europe devastated by the wars of the French Revolution and Napoleon, the system proved ill-suited to settle the wars in the Americas.[35]

With the defeat of Napoleon's army in Europe in the spring of 1814 came fears that a vengeful British ministry would step up the campaign in North America. In August the British landed a force in the Chesapeake and pushed on to Washington, D.C. In retaliation for the destruction of government buildings in the invasion of Canada, the invaders, many of them war-weary veterans of the Peninsular War, set fire to public buildings in the city, including the Capitol and the Executive Mansion. Most government employees fled the city. One who stayed behind to safeguard some of the mansion's culinary and art treasures, the story goes, was President James Madison's engaging and flirtatious spouse, Dolley.

As in 1775, there were fears that the invaders might arm local slaves. Both free and slave African Americans had already formed military units under the command of General William Hull for the defense of Canada. In the Chesapeake campaign, stories circulated about slaves setting fires to attract British patrols, and in some instances British officers offered freedom to slaves who would surrender to them. (The third verse of Francis Scott Key's wartime poem that was renamed "The Star Spangled Banner" referred disparagingly to blacks marching under a British banner.) Participation of African Americans in the defense of the country was not inconsiderable. The socially and racially diverse troops Jackson led into New Orleans at the end of the war contained the largest number of African American soldiers in a U.S. military unit until the Civil War.[36]

The Chesapeake invasion strengthened British resolve both in North America and in the peace negotiations that got under way at Ghent, Belgium, in August 1814. In its initial offering to the five-member U.S. delegation, the British delegation proposed a discussion of the legality of impressment of naturalized U.S. citizens who had been British subjects, sought greater restrictions on U.S. fishing in Canadian waters, and proposed the strengthening of Canada's defense with an Indian buffer zone on the northern frontier.

John Quincy Adams, who had departed from his diplomatic post in St. Petersburg to head up the five-member U.S. delegation, noted in his memoirs that over the following months the British position appeared to stiffen, while divisions among the Americans became more apparent. In a move that infuriated the Kentuckian Henry Clay's western sensibilities, the British proposed that in exchange for extending access to the Newfoundland and Labrador fishing grounds the Americans in turn grant British rights of navigation on the Mississippi. Albert Gallatin defused the tensions and created a unity among the group by saying that the East was willing to sacrifice the West, and the West would do the same to the East. To Adams, access to the fisheries was a paramount objective, but he assured Clay that if the British were unwilling to grant it, he would join Clay in denying their access to the Mississippi. Clay responded that such a move would probably mean the loss of both.[37]

When news of these demands reached war-weary New Englanders, Federalist critics of the war convened at Hartford, Connecticut, to discuss their options. A minority spoke openly of secession. (In 1811 arguments over Louisiana's admission as a state had prompted some of the first calls for secession.) From the Treasury came a warning of an impending financial crisis and the inability of the federal government to sustain the war. After three weeks of discussion, the representatives issued a report limiting the federal power to impose embargoes, declare war, and, more ominously, reduce southern power in Congress by removing the proviso that slaves would no longer be counted in determining representation. Unlike the Second Continental Congress, where those determined on independence had prevailed, the secessionists at Hartford were unable to sway their colleagues. The somber mood reminded some of them of the Revolution's darkest hours, prompting one army officer to comment that "a war to try men's souls ... can alone save this Government and this Nation from disunion & disgrace."[38]

What the nation received was a reprieve. The delegates in Vienna suddenly confronted the prospect of a renewal of the war. The French had agreed to the restoration of the monarchy and accepted Louis XVIII with the implied promise that there would be no reversal of the revolutionary laws on land and property. There were rumors that returning members of the aristocracy and the church would regain their properties. With that threat, Lord Liverpool instructed his peace commissioners at Ghent to settle for more lenient peace terms. In a stroke, as they had done at the end of the Revolutionary War in 1783 and again during the crisis on the western frontier in 1794, the British abandoned their Indian allies but demurred to the U.S. request never to use them in a future North American conflict. The presumptive end of the war effectively made the impressment issue of little import. Related questions over boundaries and navigation of the Mississippi remained for settlement. Henry Clay described the Peace of Christmas Eve in sobering words: "We lose no territory, I think no honor."[39] This was a sobering assessment from a war hawk from the western country who had taken to heart President James Madison's indictment of the British for their punishment of Irish seamen who joined "our political family" and for "let[ting] loose the [Indian] savages" in order "to dismember our confederated Republic."[40]

For Europeans and especially the French, 1815 began in uncertainty when in February Napoleon escaped from Elba, rebuilt a military force, and in March gloriously entered Paris to proclaim the restoration of the empire. It lasted for a hundred days, until the battle in mid-June at Waterloo in the

Belgian countryside. A second exile followed, this time to the South Atlantic island of Saint Helena. There the man who had changed the face of Europe wrote his memoirs, a recording of events that inspired the myth or "Gospel of St. Helena," which continues to inspire the French and befuddle serious scholars.

Undeniably, Napoleon had consolidated many of the reforms of the French Revolution and introduced them into the empire and vassal states, but he had done so by betraying some of the fundamental principles of the *Declaration of the Rights of Man and of the Citizen*. He was not the herald of liberal or nationalist causes, yet for different reasons he inspired both. He may have been the enemy of the true French Revolution, but more than anyone he was responsible for making it a universal phenomenon.[41]

The year 1815 was also pivotal in the long American Revolution. In the United States, the victory of Andrew Jackson's ragtag army over six thousand British regulars at New Orleans in early January provided a divided people with a sense of vindication and national pride. Jackson's popularity surged in the country but not among some of his troops. When the fighting ended, the opposition of local leaders and his ambitions persuaded him not to follow through with his pledge of compensation to his black and colored soldiers. He dutifully returned slaves to their owners and solicited the British to do the same with those runaways who had sought refuge in their ranks. Ever conscious of the political implications of the victory, Jackson's boosters later boasted that the victory had prevented a reversal of the peace settlement.

That was not likely, as Britain and Spain had never recognized the validity of Napoleon's sale of Louisiana to a third power when France acquired the territory. There was concern that the British might return Spanish sites taken during the war. In the end, the meaning of Jackson's triumph became obscured in national mythology. Contrastingly, a popular song of the times glorified the frontier militiamen and their victory over British professionals. In their victory, writes Daniel Walker Howe, these warriors had defeated the past and assured the nation of a prosperous future.[42]

That judgment, as contemporaries soon discovered, had to be measured against what the people had inherited from the Revolution and what could be discarded without losing the benefits and promises of the republican society Jefferson had extolled. The wartime victory, some Republicans averred, lay in the humiliation of New England Federalists and their "monarchical spirit." Republican anger at them was palpable. True to form, Jackson viewed the actions of New Englanders at the Hartford Convention as akin to treason during a time of national peril: "These kind of men, although called Federalist, are really monarchist, and traitors to the constituted Government."[43]

The Union had survived, but the sectional and ideological divide remained, an indicator of a reckoning for a future generation. Technology, immigration, and economic development accelerated after 1815 and transformed the nation into two mighty inland empires, one in the Deep South built on plantation slavery, where the meaning of the Revolution followed one pattern, and another in a northern industrial empire, centered in those states carved out of the Northwest Ordinances, where a divergent revolutionary tradition had taken root and would flourish.

JEFFERSON DID NOT live to see the maturation of those two empires and how they would clash—he and Adams died on the same day, July 4, 1826— but he did live long enough to follow the often contentious and to Jefferson troubling national debate over slavery, race, democracy, and the security of the country. Both bore witness as well to the intensity of feeling and questions about how the place of women, slaves, free persons of color, and white males in the more democratic society of the postwar era would become intertwined with two other hemispheric revolutions: those in Haiti and in Spanish America, where the war of independence became a continental struggle. The latter's impact on postwar Europe and the United States would be profound.[44]

In the last decade of his life, Jefferson learned a lesson about the meaning of the American Revolution in a world swept by a revolution not only in ideas and politics but also in religion. For someone with a deep-seated belief in the secular legacy of the American Revolution and the transformative power of the West in national development, Jefferson had difficulty understanding the religious nationalism of a region dominated by Baptist and especially Methodist revivalism, which suited the unruly character of frontier people.

The power of this evangelical religious nationalism not only shook Jefferson's republican secular sensibilities but also troubled conservative New England Federalists and their finely tuned Protestant patriotism, which had strong roots in the Revolution. To check the chaos they believed was engulfing the western country, the latter turned to missionaries and moral improvement societies to carry out their project of incorporating the frontier people, including the Indians, into their conception of a united country.

Andrew Jackson, who emerged from the war a hero with political ambitions, represented people who had a different agenda. He, too, was a child of the American Revolution.[45]

John Adams and Thomas Jefferson had been revolutionary allies and political foes whose differences often mirrored those of the political culture of the early republic. By the onset of the War of 1812 they had renewed their correspondence and found a degree of commonality that comes with age. Jefferson stopped being a European; Adams never ceased to be a New Englander.

But it was Jefferson, not Adams, who lent his name to the creation of the country's first political system, whose fundamental purpose was less the safeguarding of the revolutionary promise than the regulation and control of a generation who saw few contradictions between the compatibility of democracy and slavery, freedom and white supremacy, and an empire *for* rather than *of* liberty. Jefferson's Federalist critics were essentially correct in their insistence that his election in 1800 meant the triumph not of democracy but of slavery and its locus of power within the South. Northern Republicans had played a distinctive role in the 1790s in developing the conditions that made Jefferson's victory possible. Equality for white males remained a goal of both the southern and northern wings of the Democratic-Republican Party. For significant numbers of nonslaveholders in the North, slavery remained distant, geographically and ideologically, despite their connections to it, and they took pride in their promotion of democracy even with the conflicting reality of slavery.[46]

With such distortions of both morality and reasoning, a generation believed that the American Revolution and the political system it had bequeathed provided a model for avoiding the political and social dilemmas confronting Europe's monarchical governments. The final decade of the wars of independence in Spanish America bespoke a different kind of challenge—not only how to define a foreign policy for a democracy but also how to deal with slavery and the place of people of color in both a national and a hemispheric context and what that meant for understanding the meaning of the American Revolution.

CHAPTER 5

The Western Question

THE WESTERN QUESTION REFERRED TO the continuing war within the Spanish Empire that in the mid-1820s ended with the final victory of Spanish American patriot forces in royalist Peru. In the fifteen years commencing with Jackson's victory at New Orleans and the final Battle of Waterloo, European leaders resolved to prevent another French Revolution on the Continent, Spain undertook a fierce counterrevolution in Spanish America, the Spanish American revolution and civil wars became a continent-wide struggle for independence, and the United States experienced some of the most troublesome times in the history of the early republic.

These fifteen years brought to the fore old issues stemming from the revolutionary years and the early republic: slavery and the color question, democracy and the political system, relations with Europe and especially Great Britain, the continental vision and project the Founders had articulated, the hemispheric "place" and role of the United States, and the relationship between the central government and the states.

The wars for independence in Spanish America prompted a generation of ordinary North Americans to see these conflicts as complementary to their own War of Independence against a monarchical government. They followed the campaigns of two Spanish American revolutionary leaders, the Venezuelan Simón Bolívar and the Argentine José de San Martín, who transformed the war into a continental struggle. Both mobilized significant numbers of slave and free colored soldiers. The breakup of the Spanish Empire presented the United States with problems similar to those experienced by the Founders in the 1780s and 1790s: the challenge of revolutions in the hemispheric neighborhood that required a stronger union between the states and a more creative national policy to meet that challenge. As Americans became "less British," they sensed and expressed a revolutionary kinship with the "other Americans" also struggling to break with a colonial past. In this way, North America, too, formed a significant portion of the Western Question.

In the decade after 1815, the idea of hemispheric solidarity and the faith in the ability of the political system to reconcile potentially divisive issues weakened under intertwined domestic and international tensions. The support of republican Haiti given to Simón Bolívar and the role of slaves in the patriot armies in Spanish America became embroiled in several parallel debates: the acquisition of Spanish Florida, the U.S. response to European and especially British and French efforts to restore Spanish rule on the Spanish American mainland, and the expansion of slavery and the role of free people of color within the United States. The last complicated the volatile political climate occasioned by the admission of Missouri as a slave state. As newly independent states came into being in Latin America in the early 1820s and the British government refused to support a French-led restoration of Spanish rule, the challenge to the administration of President James Monroe became one of containing British influence *without* conveying to the public that U.S. interests *depended* on British power. The U.S. response came in President Monroe's December 1823 statement—drafted principally by Secretary of State John Quincy Adams—opposing future European colonization in the Americas.

The revolutionary canon that ultimately became known as the Monroe Doctrine portended a departure from a reactive to a more assertive and more aggressive role for the United States in the Americas. Beyond its implications for U.S. foreign relations, Monroe's statement addressed the disturbing political divisions within the United States associated with the democratization of politics, symbolized by the rise of Andrew Jackson, and the persistent political quarrels about the relationship between the central government and the states and the powers accorded to each. In the spirit of the Declaration of Independence, the Monroe Doctrine represented a democratic statement to a monarchical Europe and a manifestation of the United States' nationalist sentiments. The last hurrah of the old republic was the presidency of John Quincy Adams. Its successor—fittingly identified with the surging popularity of Andrew Jackson and the political revolution that appropriated his name—was more democratic, more assertive, and more self-assured than the republic crafted by the revolutionary generation. Beneath that democratic façade and conceit lay an unmistakable apprehension that without control from the center, slavery and the parallel racial sensibilities identified with that institution threatened to rend the political and social fabric.

Postwar Prospects and Challenges

How and why this shift came about seems clearer to us than it did to contemporaries. The immediate postwar issue for European leaders was controlling the latent revolutionary forces in society and their challenge to stability. At Vienna in 1814 they had created a more complicated "system of peace" to replace the balance-of-power formula emanating from the Treaty of Utrecht (1713), which Napoleon had virtually destroyed. They recognized that Europe would probably not survive another revolution of the scale the French had dealt the world.[1]

John Quincy Adams had another fear. Writing to his father from his post in London in early August 1816, he expressed an uneasy feeling about what lay before the nation. "The conduct and issue of the late war has undoubtedly raised our national character in the consideration of the world," he wrote, "but we ought also to be aware that it has multiplied and embittered our enemies. This nation [England] is far more inveterate against us than it ever was before. All the restored governments of Europe are deeply hostile to us. The Royalists everywhere detest and despise us as Republicans."[2]

President Madison, derided in the Federalist press and even by some Republicans for his leadership failures during the war, sounded a jubilant tone about the United States' prospects. To identify the party of Jefferson with a more nationalist agenda, the name was now changed to the National Republicans, whose leaders molded an alliance between southern and western leaders such as Henry Clay. One of the more outspoken war hawks, Clay latched his postwar political future to promoting the American System, which called for a higher tariff, responsible sale of public lands, internal improvements, and the revival of a national bank to promote development and ease the money shortage in the western country. The changes in the national mood were palpable. Manufacturing expanded. A generation of entrepreneurial managers took advantage of the newfound opportunities and became more beholden to the economic program Clay and Madison were promoting. Southerners and westerners who fell into step with the very un-Jeffersonian belief in the central government as a director of broad economic guidelines now considered themselves more American.[3]

Old grievances persisted, and new fissures in the political culture appeared. Diehard republicans like the writer and Virginia politician known as John

Taylor of Caroline vilified the new economic policies as little more than attacks on individual property owners, particularly on their ownership of slaves. His sentiments were a portent of a more aggressive proslavery defense in the making. At the same time, as northern states took steps to eliminate slavery and northern political leaders began to question the expansion of slavery into the territories, the north-south sectional ties weakened. In response, others looked to reinforce the power and influence of the slaveholding states and the character of a republic dominated by whites.[4]

For the first time since the Revolution, questions about slavery and the role of people of color in the economy, politics, society, and even foreign policy of the country called for a hemispheric as well as a transatlantic assessment. What was happening in the Caribbean and on the mainland of Spanish America now seemed more critical not only for the security of the United States but also relative to the ongoing debate over slavery as a national issue.

Slavery and colonialism had survived, but the Haitian Revolution had liberated five hundred thousand slaves, dealt irreparable damage to the plantation economy, and left in its wake two seemingly irreconcilable entities, Emperor Henri Christophe's kingdom of coerced laborers in the North and Alexandre Pétion's colored republic in the South. Elsewhere the numbers of slaves had declined very little, but with fears of slave revolt, abolitionist pressures, self-purchase, and freedom granted for wartime service, their conditions had improved. At least, there was hope, despite the persistent Haitian fears of another French invasion. "If an end to slavery was hardly in sight in 1815," David Geggus has observed, "its elimination by either violent or peaceful means was much easier to imagine than it had been a quarter-century earlier."[5]

The Haitian Revolution had its most noticeable impact on Spanish Cuba, where slavery and the plantation economy rapidly expanded but where the social and cultural shock of a successful black revolution nearby was palpable. White Cubans had supported the 1801 French invasion, yet the Haitian victory had benefited Cuban plantation owners with an expanding market and the skills of refugee Haitian laborers. In the crisis of 1808 and then the uprisings on the mainland in 1810, the Spanish had held dissident white Cubans in check with promises to maintain slavery. Maintaining order in a volatile environment required soldiers or militias, which ordinarily included black and colored troops, some of them from the Haitian kingdom of Henri

Christophe. Independence for Spanish Cuba posed more of a threat than an opportunity for the United States, as either independence or any move for annexation to the United States would precipitate British intervention and exacerbate the debate over slavery's expansion and the role of free people of color in politics and society.[6]

In Mexico, a royalist force led by Agustín de Iturbide defeated the insurgency led by José María Morelos, who had resurrected the rebellion by disdaining Miguel Hidalgo's race war and calling for a constitution and democratic government. Restored to power in Spain, Fernando VII had turned his back on Spanish liberals, abrogated the 1812 Constitution, and resolved to crush the insurgency in his kingdoms. An expeditionary force of sixty thousand men, officially an army of pacification, departed in sixty ships for America. Their presumed destination was the Río de la Plata, where royalist forces had failed to defeat the insurgents, but the Spanish commander, Pablo Morillo, chose to disembark with his army in New Granada and Venezuela. The invasion would bring on a continental war of liberation and renew what had been one of the most destructive and savage campaigns in the revolutionary age of the Americas—in Simón Bolívar's native Venezuela.

In different ways, the Latin American wars of independence, especially in the Bolivarian theater, both inspired and frightened a generation of Americans who had identified that cause with their own Revolution and self-affirming second war of independence. Such feelings distorted realities of a commonality of hemispheric civil wars, and the discussion was often highly partisan. Federalist editors dismissed any notion of inter-American community or harmony. Contrastingly, during the war Republican editors looked southward and perceived powerful anticolonial movements that were poised to divest Spain and Portugal of their colonial possessions. The real enemy of hemispheric harmony and U.S. interests, other Republican editors warned, was Great Britain, whose leaders calculated that independent but politically weak and commercially vulnerable states could be easily transformed into protectorates.[7]

Quincy Adams clearly agreed with that evaluation, but episodes and issues of the struggle in Latin America sometimes complicated discussions not only about U.S. policy but also about the attendant domestic debates over republican governance, the economy, and slavery and the role of people of color in the country. Everywhere, it seemed, the name Bolívar and the way he was fighting the war intruded into the discussion. His name inspired Americans to name towns or their male offspring in his honor. Bolívar became a revered name in the United States before he acquired that exalted status among Venezuelans. To a generation of editorialists who placed their emphasis on the universality of republican ideals rather than on racial differences, Bolívar's eloquent appeal for British and U.S. aid in his iconic Jamaica Letter of 1815 and, that failing, his willingness to seek aid from Haiti's Alexandre Pétion in return for enlisting slaves in the cause, providing for gradual abolition of slavery, or his acceptance of people of color in the affairs of state confirmed in some minds the notion of racial equality and the belief that it would bring about a more harmonious society. Ironically, though not necessarily inevitably, in New Granada (modern Colombia and Panama) this radical belief coexisted with a rising racism in the new republic, prompting charges and fears of a race war.[8]

This was a simplistic assessment, because these editors often failed to consider what these matters could mean for the debate over similar issues in the United States. In the decade commencing in 1817, Bolívar, more than any other Spanish American patriot leader, not only changed the character of the war but also remade himself from the Venezuelan rebel into the American revolutionary. Both the war and the man prompted North Americans to take another look at who they were and what they stood for.[9]

Slavery, Statehood, and the Color Question

When Quincy Adams returned from his post in Great Britain to become secretary of state (1817–25) in the Monroe administration, the war in Spanish America became an early concern. Convinced that the conflict was at bottom a civil war, he was troubled over violations of the country's admittedly weak neutrality laws by Spanish American agents in purchasing and outfitting ships, obtaining financial support, buying arms, and recruiting sailors. Certainly, he was not alone in his reaction to Bolívar's decree that freed those slaves who took up arms in the patriot army, and in late 1817 Adams expressed doubts that the "cause of Venezuela is precisely the same as ours."[10]

Details about Bolívar's role in the two failed republics after the country's declaration of independence in July 1811 disturbed some in the Congress. Bolívar's explanation about the fall of the first in the summer of 1812—the weakness of the federal model of governance and the royalist counterrevolution—proved less unsettling than decisions he made after he launched the military campaign to retake power. The first was the controversial "War to the Death Decree," a pardon to Spaniards and Canary Islanders who joined the patriot cause but death if they were neutral and immunity to Americans (Creoles) regardless of their loyalties. The second was the institution of a dictatorship in the second republic, necessitated, he argued, by the killing of whites by the royalist "Legions of Hell" from the Venezuelan plains.

The savagery of that race war sent Bolívar into exile again, but it persuaded him (as it would his Argentine contemporary, José de San Martín) that victory would require the mobilization of the continent's overwhelming numbers of mixed-race people and even slaves. Despite his persistent doubts about the motives and reliability of slave soldiers and the place of people of color in public affairs and civil society, Bolívar adopted that strategy. Their presence and that of the foreign mercenaries who joined in the campaign made the difference. But Venezuela would be left a wasteland.[11]

North Americans would not experience such devastation until the Civil War. For Quincy Adams there was a more important distraction. In the spring of 1818 Andrew Jackson reprised his role as pacifier of Spanish Florida in the First Seminole War, capturing Pensacola, stirring fears of war with Spain, and creating a diplomatic crisis with the British for his execution of two British subjects deemed guilty of abetting Indian attacks. There were parallel rumors that Jackson intended to invade Spanish Cuba, coordinating the move with a slave uprising on the island. Although Adams and Jackson were opposites in almost every respect save two—a fervent belief that Spanish rule in Florida had virtually collapsed and a parallel determination not to show weakness—Adams defended Jackson in a testy cabinet session.

Coincidentally, Jackson's raid occurred while Congress debated the country's posture toward the Spanish American cause. How Bolívar was now fighting the war came under fire. When one southern congressman alluded to the "War to the Death" decree, Henry Clay, a convert to the justness of the patriot cause, responded: "Could it be believed if the slaves had been let loose upon us in the south [during the American Revolution] that General Washington would not have resorted to retribution?"[12]

This was an apt retort for those who remembered how Lord Dunmore's 1775 threat to arm slaves to confront defiant Virginians had served to accelerate the movement for independence. Washington's dilemma was different from Bolívar's. Washington commanded people from a different social class he did not "know," but most were white. Confronting dwindling numbers in the Continental army, Washington did comment that a war in defense of slavery gave the Crown an advantage. Bolívar commanded people who were of mixed race, black, mestizo, and from all regions of the social spectrum, but he had to have them in order to win.

Slavery and the place of black and colored people and Indians were import-ant factors in the U.S. War of Independence, but the racial dynamic in that conflict never reached the unsettling levels experienced in the Caribbean or in the Spanish American theaters. In the Venezuelan war, Bolívar ordered the execution of a black officer accused of insubordination and inciting a race war. A white officer guilty of a similar infraction but apologetic escaped punish-ment, a signal to white Creoles that Bolívar was willing to draw a color line.

Mindful of his promise to Pétion, Bolívar pledged not only an end to slav-ery but justice for the slaves willing to fight for their freedom, but he retained his suspicions of their motives for fighting. In the end, he feared, they would demand something for their efforts in achieving independence, and that might be not just equality but absolute equality. If slaves were not brought into the struggle, they would survive and the whites would die. Then there was in his mind the terrifying apocalyptic finale: Haiti, where in victory the slaves had killed their masters.[13]

By another measure, of course, the Spanish American willingness to mo-bilize slaves in the cause and give people of color a place in the new republics contrasted sharply with the U.S. experience. As did others of his generation of political leaders, Clay considered the people of Spanish America unpre-pared for taking on the responsibility for a free government, yet he empha-sized their capabilities and prospects for doing so if given the opportunity. In his March 1818 speech, "The Emancipation of South America," he alluded to the observations of Alexander von Humboldt and others about Spanish Americans' "great quickness, genius, and particular aptitude" for the exact sciences and noted the existence of nine universities.[14]

A year later, Bolívar himself would echo Clay's indictment of Spain for stifling the cause of liberty in Spanish America in his address to the Na-tional Congress of Venezuela in Angostura (now Ciudad Bolívar), in the Guyana region of eastern Venezuela. In a passage praising the United States for its ability to preserve unity with a federal system, Bolívar followed with an explanation of why the federal form of government was unsuitable for Venezuela. Later in the year, following the liberation of New Granada, the National Congress created the Republic of Colombia, comprising Venezuela, New Granada, and Quito (modern Ecuador), which joined later. Bolívar was passionate about the need for unity and made a point about referring to what some Americans (among them Jefferson) dismissed as societies plagued by miscegenation. "Unity, unity, unity," Bolívar emphasized, "must be our motto in all things. The blood of our citizens is varied: let it be mixed for the sake of unity."[15]

Clay had another approach to achieving unity, and slavery and the place of unfree labor in the economy lay at the heart of his plan. Its degree of inclusivity fell far short of that Bolívar had identified. Clay's American System, a centerpiece of the new National Republican Party, called for a stronger military and navy, public works, a tariff, a national bank, and federally funded colonization of manumitted slaves. Many old-line Federalists could identify with the project and its emphasis on projecting strength abroad in an uncertain postwar economy. And they were instinctively suspicious and fearful of the political culture cobbled together in the creation of Colombia. As a writer in the prestigious *North American Review* argued, unity in a republic required a "free and unmingled race of men." Ironically, as the union of disparate states forming Colombia took shape, Bolívar expressed a similar sentiment when he wrote that the localism and racial diversity of the new entity would remain a debilitating impediment. In truth, he feared *pardocracia*, rule by people of color.[16]

The dimension of the American System that called for incorporating the country's fractured regions conflicted with deep-seated traditions and posed other problems. A growing number of eastern political and economic leaders were becoming more vocal about the "Virginia dynasty" in the presidency, slavery, and the slave trade. Their critique rested less on opposition to slavery where it existed and even less on compassion for the slave and more on their belief that dependence on unfree labor and even on the labor of free blacks hampered the nation's capabilities for competing in the global economy. Clay was particularly concerned about his native state of Kentucky, whose backwardness he attributed to slavery's deprivation of education and incentives for African Americans as well as the state's unwillingness to implement a manumission program. Clay was a proverbial mover and shaker in the American Colonization Society, formed in 1816 for the purpose of relocating manumitted slaves and free blacks outside the United States. Publicly, the society reaffirmed the sanctity of slave property. Privately, some of its prominent members called for the colonization of all African American labor, slave or free, outside the country. Jefferson shared their sentiments and their hypocrisy, and his patrician Virginia contemporaries understood his: they knew about but rarely discussed his longtime relationship with Sally Hemings, his mulatto slave and mistress whose father was Jefferson's father-in-law. As he explained to a young Virginia slave owner thinking about emancipating his slaves, removal of ex-slaves was imperative because "their amalgamation with the other color [white] produces a degradation to which no lover of his country, no lover of excellence in the human character, can innocently consent."[17]

Deep South political leaders perceived the American Colonization Society as a challenge to a way of life, and abolitionists and free blacks condemned it as racist. The reality of the grip of slavery and the revolutionary promise was far more complicated. Despite the antislavery rhetoric that accompanied the Revolution in the eastern states and the prohibition of slavery in the Northwest Ordinances, slavery remained a national institution. (Illinois entered the Union in 1818 with a constitution permitting "de facto slavery.") Just as Bolívar's promise to make the liberation of a continent a movement for liberating the slaves had fallen short, so too had the antislave movement in the eastern states. From 1780 to 1804 the laws of Pennsylvania, Rhode Island, Connecticut, New York, and New Jersey contained emancipation statutes *but* freed only the children of slaves once they reached a certain age. Manumission by private owners in the Chesapeake region and Upper South increased the number of free blacks (others bought their freedom) but did not lessen the growing concerns about the "slave power" and the expansion of slavery within the continental empire.

Since the Revolution the idea of continental empire had become a staple of both political leaders and economic forecasters. After all, land for a growing population was part of the revolutionary heritage. There was an imperial dimension to this belief, one intimately linked to notions of the nation's place among the powers of the world. And though few of the Founders would have stressed the matter in their public comments, the West served as a dumping ground for Abigail Adams's troublesome white males. Quincy Adams privately railed against the slave power, accusing it of wanting Texas because it would become another slave state, yet where continental empire and national security were at stake, he could be firm.

His negotiation of the Transcontinental Treaty of 1819 with the Spanish, which not only secured Florida but also marked out the boundary between

U.S. and Spanish territories all the way to the Pacific, exemplified his skills. It took another two years to gain approval, largely because of Spanish wariness over U.S. policy toward the Spanish American independence movement. Although Quincy Adams considered the U.S. claim to Texas as weak, in 1820 he came under pressure from western congressmen to set the treaty aside, recognize the independence of the Spanish American states, and "insist on the Rio del Norte [Rio Grande] as the western boundary." He was both blunt and prophetic in his rejection of such a course: the United States had no just claim to Florida and was obtaining the province, and to push a weak claim to Texas would disturb the precarious balance between the states.[18]

There were also equally critical political, economic, cultural, and, increasingly, racial dynamics in play in the matter of Missouri statehood. Alabama (1819) and Mississippi (1817) had entered the Union as slave states, and it was generally understood that slavery would be allowed in Florida. Alabama represented largely the spoils from Jackson's war with the Creek nation, and the urgency of Florida's acquisition stemmed largely from fears of British ambitions in what was a maritime province lying on important trade routes and in Spanish Cuba.

To those who believed the western lands should be reserved for white settlers who would create solid communities and strengthen a diversifying economy, the notion of a slave state of white masters and slaves producing commodities for a shrinking market defied logic in a world of instability and uncertainty—food riots, failed industries, financial crises, unstable empires in Spanish America and in the Near East. As the editor of *Niles' Weekly Register* noted in the spring of 1820, "The civilized world . . . is so unsettled, that there is no such thing as telling to-day what the morrow may bring forth, and the opinion is generally entertained, that the '*age of revolution*' is not over."[19]

He wrote these words as the economy slipped further into one of its gravest economic crises of the postwar years, a downturn precipitated by a variety of factors but particularly by the irresponsibility of state banks in printing paper money and making loans. The ill effects hit the cities first, then the countryside. In the ensuing presidential campaign, there emerged no real alternative to Monroe, who was not ideological and perhaps best symbolized both the values of the revolutionary generation and the spirit of the modern nationalists. The caucus system persisted in politics, but in twenty-one of twenty-four states the separation of property holding and the right to vote was rapidly becoming the law for both whites and blacks. At the same time, five states had begun to impose sharp restrictions against black suffrage, which affected the pace of democratic reform and frustrated both whites and blacks.[20]

For the old-line Federalists in the eastern states, particularly Senator Rufus King of New York, nothing rankled as much as the three-fifths clause in the Constitution, which gave the slave states so much power. In 1820 King decided to take his conscience and his eloquent voice into the battle over statehood for Missouri. The political crisis that ensued involved more than the future of the U.S. economy or the assurance that the western country would be inhabited by white community-spirited farmers and laborers rather than white masters and black slaves. The introduction of an antislavery amendment to the application for statehood by Representative James Tallmadge of New York touched off a bitter dispute in the House, but the amendment passed, only to die in the Senate. With a request for statehood by Maine, the Senate agreed to admit Maine as a free and Missouri as a slave state. There followed another amendment permitting slavery in Missouri but forbidding it north of latitude 36°30' (Missouri's southern border) in the rest of the Louisiana Territory. Henry Clay rightly took the credit for working out the details.[21]

Both constitutional and moral issues intruded into the debate. Proslavery advocates contended that to deny a prospective state the right to sanction slavery was tantamount to denying its right to equal treatment under the Constitution. Their critics responded that the immorality of the institution of slavery constituted a denial of republican government. The matter might very well have been easily resolved had not the Missouri constitutional convention given the legislature the right to exclude free blacks and mulattos, which set off another round of complaints by mostly northern congressmen. With Clay leading the movement, Congress secured a pledge from Missouri that the state would never enact any law violating the U.S. Constitution.

The Missouri crisis raised issues that went beyond the extension of slavery or the economic future of the country. Running throughout the debate were two variants of the meaning of freedom on a collision course; sooner or later, the government would have to resolve the dispute. In a letter to John Adams, Jefferson confirmed his sympathies for the states "afflicted with this unfortunate population," which now confronted the unsettling choice of giving their slaves "freedom and a dagger" if Congress compelled them to do so. And in more memorable lines, Jefferson commented that "this momentous question, like a fire bell in the night, awakened and filled me with terror."[22]

Jefferson approved the Florida acquisition and that of Texas as well, in large part out of fear of a unified antislavery North that might get control of the federal government. Quincy Adams agreed that the compromise preserved the Union but then surmised that a preferable course might have been to press the issue, which in turn might have led to a revision of the Constitution and the creation of a union of free states "unpolluted by slavery" that would inspire the slave states to emancipate their slaves: "If the Union must be dissolved, slavery is precisely the question upon which it ought to break."[23] Not even Quincy Adams or Congressman James Talmadge Jr., who spoke in similarly apocalyptic phrases—"If blood is necessary to extinguish any fire which I have assisted to kindle," he acknowledged, "while I regret the necessity, I shall not forbear to contribute my mite [to it]"—could have imagined the enormity and carnage of the war that did come.[24]

The experience of this contentious debate served to reinforce the growing divide within the United States over slavery and the role of people of color. Perhaps the most portentous words came from Senator King, who declared in tones that shocked even the constitutionalist mind of former president Madison and southern political leaders that laws permitting slavery were "absolutely void, because [they are] contrary to the laws of nature, which is the law of God, by which he makes his way known to man and is paramount to all human control."[25]

As if those warnings were insufficient, the South Carolina Low Country experienced a slave revolt in June 1822 that some attributed to King's fiery language during the Missouri statehood debate. The putative leader of the revolt was a former slave named Telemaque, who had the good fortune of winning the lottery and with the money purchased his freedom. In an urban venue where slaves and free colored more easily intermingled, Telemaque, who took the name of Denmark Vesey, interacted freely with other skilled slaves, free blacks, sailors, artisans, and even criminals. Among the slaves and in the African Methodist Episcopal Church (founded in 1816), Vesey preached equality and defiance of white authority. According to a story told by a slave to his master, when Vesey learned of the Missouri statehood debate, he talked about King's speech and spoke more defiantly about the liberation of Charleston's slaves. Local newspapers carried ads placed by the Haitian government inviting free blacks to migrate to the island. Vesey had lived in Haiti when he was a boy, and his plan called for an escape from Charleston and a return to the island.[26]

Urban areas provided special opportunities for a well-organized slave re-volt. But Vesey's plan went awry when another slave betrayed him, and the governor dispatched troops to Charleston. Suspects were rounded up. Some of them told of a planned uprising of nine thousand slaves and free blacks, seizure of the arsenal, slaughter of the city's white males, and ravaging of white women. The first hanged were Vesey and five associates. Another thirty followed them to the gallows before the judges decided to call a halt to the executions. Stories about the revolt struck fear into white society. At one extreme in this rhetorical squabble stood the Charlestonian Edwin Holland, who called the Negroes "*Jacobins*" and "*Anarchists*," the "*Domestic* Enemy" and "the *common enemy of civilized society*, and the *barbarians* who *would if they could, become the destroyers of our race*." At another was the African American minister and educator William Watkins, who informed a group of free blacks in 1825 that the example of Haiti offered "an irrefutable argument to prove that the descendants of Africa were never designed by their creator to sustain an inferiority, or even a mediocrity in the chain of being."[27]

Watkins's profession of faith that history was on the side of the abolitionists directly refuted a tenet of the secular Enlightenment that identified a lasting breach between a person's inferiority or subordination, on the one hand, and spiritual freedom, on the other. Western culture had arrived at such a position on the eve of the American Revolution, but antislavery books, pamphlets, sermons, and plays had not prompted slave owners to free their slaves. By the early 1820s, a half-century of war and revolution had demonstrated the weakness and vulnerability of slavery. Most newspaper editors believed that Spanish Americans who were establishing republican governments could learn from the United States. Where the issue was gradual emancipation of slaves, the Quaker abolitionist Benjamin Lundy argued that U.S. leaders could learn from Colombia's emancipation law. In mid-1822 Lundy confidently predicted in the periodical the *Genius of Universal Emancipation* that "the fiend of slavery in North America is surrounded ... [by] the free states of this Union on the east, the north, and the west [and] Hayti and Colombia, on the south."[28]

Hemispheric Bonds, Hemispheric Differences

Lundy wrote these words in the same year that the United States recognized Colombia—the political union of Venezuela, New Granada, and Quito. The decision marked a small but significant shift in U.S. policy toward the war in Spanish America and with it the way U.S. political leaders and ordinary North Americans viewed that war. On July 4, 1821, Quincy Adams delivered a major address in the House of Representatives that spoke to twin alternatives about how the United States should position itself in a troublesome world to meet the threat of the Holy Alliance toward reform and liberty in Europe and, presumably, in Spanish America. (The Holy Alliance had its provenance at the Congress of Vienna when Prince Alexander I of Russia called for an organization of Europe's sovereigns to commit themselves to governing according to Christian principles. The intent was to preserve the status quo and, later, to come to the aid of Fernando VII.) One suggestion called for joining with the British in an Anglo-American statement concerning the likelihood of Spanish America's independence, which the editor of the *Edinburgh Review* had proposed, or a "sort of counterpoise to the Holy Alliance ... in the two Americas in favor of national independence and liberty," which Henry Clay advocated.[29]

In phrases both George Washington and his father would have approved, Quincy Adams dismissed the first alternative as a dangerous departure from the first president's warning about involving the country in Europe's troubles and the second as too presumptive about creating a political union between the two Americas. The better route was a middle course—a warning to Europe and the defenders of colonialism to heed the "sound of the trumpet upon Zion" and to reject the European belief that recognition of a belligerent during hostilities was a violation of neutrality. The U.S. War of Independence had demonstrated otherwise, proving its cause was both just and legal. So, too, was that of Spanish Americans. An ideological if not a political bond united the two Americas, he said, but there should be no U.S. intervention in foreign wars between power and right, "even wars for freedom[, lest such action] change the very foundation of our own government from *liberty* to *power*."[30]

Successive generations of twentieth-century political leaders and foreign policy thinkers have quoted that speech when discussing U.S. intervention in foreign civil wars or undertaking wars of liberation. Quincy Adams had those in mind, certainly, but a presidential election was looming, and to succeed he had to chart a perilous course between seemingly irreconcilable positions about the hemispheric wars to the south. One represented New England wisdom, perhaps best though ignobly expressed by Edward Everett, editor of the prestigious *North American Review*. In a piece entitled "South America,"

Everett described involvement in those struggles as a "highly anti-republican" turn. In even harsher sentiments, he added: "We have no concern with South America. . . . Not all the treaties we could make, nor the commissioners we could send out, nor the money we could lend them, would transform . . . their Bolívars into Washingtons."[31]

There had always been a counterpoise to such views among those who had a role in shaping policy or had influence with those men who acknowledged the diversity of the continent, the desire of its people to be released from European control, and their capabilities for self-governance. But those who held such views oftentimes expressed an opinion that the United States should not enter a war on behalf of Spanish American wars of independence. If those countries elected monarchy, as did Brazil, so be it. Some writers, such as Henry Marie Brackenridge, a congressman from Pennsylvania, expressed little support for the visionary idea of a hemispheric congress of nations but considered cooperation desirable. Other North Americans, influenced by Humboldt or the American Philosophical Society, developed inter-American scientific and cultural exchanges with like-minded counterparts in Spanish America and became more vocal in their support as the armies of San Martín and Bolívar converged pincer-like on the last stronghold of Spanish royal power in Peru. When San Martín and Bolívar parted ways in the summer of 1822, their supporters' obsession with the Venezuelan and what his revolution meant for whites and especially for slaves and free colored intensified.[32]

Increasingly, events in the Caribbean and in Spanish America began to intrude more tellingly in discussions of policy, and they weighed on Quincy Adams. In September 1822 a group representing dissident Cuban slaveholders, persuaded that the pliable Spanish king would yield to abolitionist pressures to end slavery on the island, appealed to President Monroe to annex the island as a preliminary step toward statehood. Monroe was already under pressure to recognize Haitian independence, as Haiti had become the preferred choice of emigration for manumitted African Americans. (Some eight thousand manumitted African American slaves and free colored people migrated there in the 1820s at the invitation of President Jean-Pierre Boyer, who desperately needed U.S. recognition.) Secretary of War John C. Calhoun, citing the example of Louisiana statehood, voiced approval of the Cuban appeal, but Quincy Adams demurred, noting that such a move could bring on a conflict and maybe another war with Britain, and the island would be "revolutionized by negroes."[33]

Less than a year later, Quincy Adams scribbled his thoughts about the irrevocability of Spain's loss of Puerto Rico and Cuba, their importance as "natural appendages" of the United States, and a prediction of Cuba's inevitable "gravitation" to the United States. The occasion for the remark was the 1823 French invasion of Spain and the toppling of a liberal regime (installed after a military coup in 1820) that had taken a radical turn. Approved by the last formal meeting of the Quintuple Alliance (Great Britain, France, Russia, Austria, and Prussia) at Verona the previous November, the French action restored Fernando VII to absolute authority and permitted him to again renounce the liberal 1812 Constitution.

British policies on the question of recognition of independence that resulted from a revolutionary movement had already begun to change, and in 1817 and 1818 Monroe and Adams had discussed the desirability of further isolating the British from their European allies on the question of Spanish American independence. The British foreign secretary, Viscount Castlereagh (Robert Stewart), remained aloof from any formal cooperation with the U.S. government, but he refused to sanction the intervention in Spain or in Greece. After his death in August 1822, his successor, George Canning, who believed in cultivating public opinion on such questions, called for recognition of the new Spanish American states.[34]

News of what had occurred at Verona prompted Bolívar to resurrect his plan for a confederation or a defensive league among Spain's former colonies against any European monarchical alliance determined to restore royal authority. In a commanding position, he threatened to take his army of slaves, mulattos, and fierce plainsmen into the last bastion of royal power—Peru—and compel an arrogant Spanish monarch to negotiate. The British would be participants, but they would not be in a dominating position. Although popular sentiment in the United States remained strong for the Spanish American cause, Bolívar remained ambivalent and even suspicious of U.S. involvement. For the United States, and especially for Quincy Adams, the French invasion signaled a warning of a wider war, perhaps not to the extreme of destroying the republican institutions of the United States as described in the *National Gazette* in August 1821, but more likely a threat of the Holy Alliance to reverse the course of the wars of independence in Spanish America and sufficiently alarming to call for a response and a statement about the foreign policy of a democracy.[35]

In time, that response would become known as the Monroe Doctrine, the most remembered portion of the president's December 1823 annual message to Congress. The salient issues—the Greek struggle for independence, Russian penetration on the Northwest Coast, and apprehensions over a combined French–Holy Alliance movement to reverse the course of the Spanish American wars of independence—provoked a running debate within Monroe's cabinet. Three other issues further complicated the discussion: the proposal by British foreign minister George Canning for a joint statement disavowing any interest in acquiring Spanish colonial possessions and opposing any European assistance to Spain in recovering its colonies in the New World; the knowledge that four cabinet members (John Quincy Adams, William H. Crawford, John C. Calhoun, and Smith Thompson) had political ambitions to be Monroe's successor, as did Henry Clay, Speaker of the House of Representatives; and the uncertain prospects about the political threat posed by Andrew Jackson. By his own accounting of the preliminary discussions about the crisis, Quincy Adams laid out a worst-case scenario: if the European allies restored the Spanish to power, they might follow up by recolonizing a portion of the continent, with the Russians taking California, the French installing a Bourbon prince in Mexico and perhaps in Buenos Aires, and the British, on record in favor of Latin America, deciding to enter the search for spoils by seizing Cuba.[36]

Monroe's final draft did not read so ominously. Its first principle—U.S. opposition to further European colonization in the New World—was aimed principally at Russian ambitions in the Far Northwest. The second—a statement opposing European interference in the New World—resulted from apprehensions that the Holy Alliance, particularly France, which had dispatched troops to Spain to restore Fernando VII's absolute rule, would embark on yet another effort to alter the course of the Spanish American war and restore monarchical rule. The third principle pledged U.S. noninterference in strictly European conflicts, which had specific implications for those U.S. political leaders such as Daniel Webster who had strong feelings about assisting the Greeks in their war against Ottoman rule. One sentence in the message—"It is impossible that the allied powers should extend their political system to any portion of either continent without endangering our peace and happiness"—prompted concerns about war with Britain. Quincy Adams agreed, then added that such a conflict would put "high interests of different portions of the Union in conflict with each other, and [thus endanger] the Union itself."[37]

Democracy and the Revolutionary Legacy

By implication, Monroe's statement left open and, indeed, encouraged what later generations would identify as Manifest Destiny or, conversely, imperialism—the further expansion of population and new territories as the best means of reconciling the differences among the states. In a departure from the dispiriting views of most of his generation of Founders, Monroe compared the condition of the country in 1783 with that of 1823 and confidently concluded that "the history of the world furnishe[d] no example of a progress in improvement in all the important circumstances which constitute the happiness of a nation which bears any resemblance to it."[38]

As had Washington's farewell address, Monroe's December 1823 message had a dual purpose: to reaffirm in the public mind a sense of confidence that the country had weathered a dangerous international crisis with its honor and security intact and, just as important, to ensure that Quincy Adams, whose father had benefited from Washington's memorable words, could translate his role in that crisis into the presidency. It was no easy task. Jackson gained the most electoral votes in the 1824 presidential election, but without a majority, the decision was thrown into the House of Representatives, where Henry Clay threw his support to Adams and, in what some Jacksonian supporters called a "corrupt bargain," was rewarded with the position of secretary of state. Yet the prospects for a hemispheric bonding in the revolutionary cause seemed brighter than ever. As Lundy had suggested at the time of the Missouri crisis and the first issues of the *Genius of Universal Emancipation*, Haiti, Buenos Aires, Chile, and Colombia had joined antislavery ranks, but the United States, "who has pompously and ostentatiously styled her domain 'the cradle of liberty' and 'an asylum for the oppressed of all nations,' appears likely to be 'last on the list' of those who practically support the genuine principle of rational liberty, which they were the first to profess!"[39]

Lundy was ahead of his time in calling for a fulfillment of the Declaration's promise of equality to all. Those white Americans who toasted Latin American independence remained principally interested in the antimonarchical examples (Brazil excepted) and republican purpose in the wars to the south. Free African Americans perceived abolition and equality as fundamental to those struggles. In any event, Quincy Adams's concerns about Latin America focused on other matters. By the time he took the oath, mainland Latin America had independent governments, and Simón Bolívar's international popularity soared, particularly in the African American community in the United States. The Liberator was toasted as the Spanish American "George Washington" even as warnings about his use of executive power in Peru and Colombia escalated. Alexander Everett, U.S. minister to Spain, put the matter bluntly in early 1827: "The [possible] establishment of a military despotism in Colombia and Peru" might encourage Bolívar to carry out an assault on Spanish Cuba. "A military despot of talent and experience at the head of a black army," he continued, "is certainly not the sort of neighbor we should naturally wish ... to place on our Southern frontier."[40]

Quincy Adams's attitudes about people of color, especially if they were citizens, had changed appreciably during the Missouri crisis, but he could understand Everett's way of thinking. (Edward Everett, Alexander's brother, was Quincy Adams's brother-in-law.) Proslavery southerners would identify him as the archenemy of slavery, but he was not an abolitionist, and, like Lincoln, he fought slavery on its flanks by opposing its expansion. His presidency (1825–29) proved to be the twilight years of the old revolutionary order in the United States, a political era symbolized by the political battles of two men, John Quincy Adams and Andrew Jackson, both nationalists and children of the revolutionary tradition but with distinctive notions about what the Revolution meant, particularly for the role of central government and the use of power in governance and development.

Quincy Adams detested party politics and party loyalty yet was intensely partisan in a religious sense. He subscribed to the postmillennial teaching that Providence called for the uplifting and moral improvement of humankind, where economic development, political liberalism, and Protestant Christianity united to combat the intolerant Catholic autocracies that ruled Europe. Postmillennial thinking combined a belief in progress with revivals—in steam engines and in biblical prophecy. In that spirit, the president pursued an ambitious economic program of building roads and canals, favored the creation of a national university (as had Washington), promoted the creation of a naval academy, and, with Clay's enthusiastic blessing, recommended sending representatives to a special conference of former colonies of Spain to Panama to discuss defensive measures. The Congress of Panama had been the brainchild of Bolívar, who originally had excluded the Haitians, the Brazilians, and the United States but who did invite the British (his vice president had overridden him). Such an ambitious commitment required time and money and would probably raise public opposition, the president explained, but he urged Congress to push ahead so as not to convey to other governments the notion that "we are palsied by the will of our constituents."[41]

The recommendations and the tone of that remark sparked a firestorm in the Congress. There were objections to making commitments to other hemispheric governments or having U.S. delegates participate in formal gatherings with people of color or that were based on the misuse and arrogance of federal power. Once dismissive of the capabilities of Spanish Americans for self-government, Quincy Adams now accepted the older unionist beliefs of the Founders to make the case for a federal presence in Panama as a means of strengthening the frayed bonds between the states. He sensed that the Spanish American revolutions, which had excited ordinary North Americans, presented a challenge to fulfilling the Revolution's goal in ways reminiscent of the challenges confronted by the Founders in the 1780s and 1790s.[42]

Critics within the Congress derided the measure as another example of federal intrusion into the rights of the states and a quixotic attempt to promote equality among the independent states of the hemisphere. At a time when abolitionists in the North and especially in Britain were becoming more outspoken, the Congress of Panama occasioned an opportunity for southern members of the Senate to revisit the language of the Declaration of Independence, particularly its universalist phrases about equality, inalienable rights, and self-determination, and to offer a demurral. The reality of inequality, not the abstraction of equality, should be the guiding directive for the nation. As the acerbic John Randolph put the matter, "No rational man ever did govern himself by abstractions and universals."[43]

In a larger and more meaningful sense, Quincy Adams appeared to represent a revolutionary tradition that seemed formal and secular, indifferent if not always hostile to the democratic and religious sea changes in a country shaped by the rise and power of the common man, community spirit, and the revivalism that would impress Alexis de Tocqueville in the 1830s and disgust British travelers. At the same time, the professed belief by the surviving members of the Revolution's natural aristocracy that the nation on July 4, 1826—the date on which both John Adams and Thomas Jefferson died— stood in control of its own destiny had to be measured against the reality of a continuing British imperial, economic, and even cultural presence.[44]

These and other indicators were reminders also that revolutions do not follow a linear pattern and that those who serve a revolution, as Bolívar lamented in a private letter in 1829, "plow the sea." By then, most of his radical social changes identified with his idealism and grand designs for the new republics had collapsed. His once faithful Venezuelan allies rebuked him for his interference in their plans to reward the victors. He was vilified in Peru and even in Bolivia, whose creation out of Upper Peru he had blessed with a constitution that any British Tory would have admired. Out of the Congress of Panama he had managed to salvage a design for Andean unity, but that, too, was collapsing. He had reached too far. Part of the problem was Bolívar's authoritarian style. His presumption that the old urban social elite could recover from the ravages of war and resume its rightful place in governance proved to be a fantasy. His rural and mixed-race troops did not share his judgments or sympathies.[45]

In the final two years of his life, Bolívar assumed dictatorial power to save Colombia from chaos and squabbled with his old Venezuelan comrade, José Antonio Páez, over dispensing land and other privileges to veterans of the war. Meddling in Colombian political squabbles by the U.S. minister, William Henry Harrison, so angered Bolívar that it was a factor in his comment about the United States "plaguing America with miseries," although he may have intended to include the other American states as well in his indictment.[46]

Ironically, Bolívar's once-lofty vision of combining a war of liberation with a campaign against slavery continued to resonate strongly among African Americans in the United States. In the late 1820s, at a time when proslavery thought was gaining strength in the country, the first black-owned newspaper, *Freedom's Journal*, regularly identified South America and Haiti as places where people of color could achieve dignity and equality in a multiracial society. Lundy's *Genius of Universal Emancipation*, the country's most prominent antislavery newspaper, regularly pointed to Latin America as an inspiration for achieving racial equality within the country. Among free black and colored advocates in the United States, the gradualist approach to ending slavery and especially the paternalism and program of the American Colonization Society had already fallen out of favor.[47]

Saddled with the 150-million-franc indemnity to the French, Haiti offered little prospect for free African Americans looking for an alternative future, although the Haitian Revolution as a symbol of slave liberation remained strong. In 1829 David Walker published his fiery *Appeal to the Coloured Citizens of the World*, which called for immediate emancipation and slave rebellion in the South. Walker had lived in Charleston and knew about Vesey, and the *Appeal* conveyed Vesey's militancy and uncompromising rhetoric. In response, white abolitionists in the United States, notably William Lloyd Garrison, and their counterparts in Britain began calling for immediate emancipation.[48]

FEW REALIZED HOW long it would take. A half-century of war and the three major hemispheric revolutions had left a mixed legacy that was at once both reassuring and disturbing, particularly in the United States. Racial slavery in 1775 was legal from Quebec to the southernmost regions of the Americas, but slavery had been overturned in Haiti in 1804 and in Upper Canada (Ontario), Central America, and Mexico by 1830, and it had ended or been weakened through manumission in the eastern and northern states of the United States and in mainland Spanish America. Except for Haiti, which in 1830 included the eastern portion of Hispaniola, slave labor still existed in the European West Indies, but the slave population had declined. Through treaties and laws, the United States, Great Britain, and four European states (France, Spain, Portugal, and Holland) had outlawed the once-thriving legal slave commerce on the Atlantic. All this had happened for different reasons: the power of such revolutionary ideals as equality, liberty, and freedom, inspired by secular ideology, evangelical passion, or the necessity of arming slaves with promises of freedom.[49]

Not only had slavery thrived, but the slave population had grown, either by natural reproduction or by the illegal slave trade, in Brazil, the southern United States, and Spanish Cuba. In the United States and Latin America, slaves who had won their freedom either through manumission or as a reward for their service often found themselves in legal limbo. They grew increasingly frustrated over perceived unequal treatment or were forced back into slavery. There were other parallels in the revolutionary legacy in the Americas. Independence in Spanish America had ended such burdens as Indian tribute and the caste system, but efforts to integrate the Indian into republican society had fallen short. The imposition of a liberal capitalist system often meant the loss of Indian lands, as in the United States. Liberal rhetoric about fundamental human freedom, constitutional government, and opposition to military rule and church privilege did little to assuage the condition of a people suddenly dumped into a new political and economic system that promised so much but offered so little. In the United States, the use of legal pressures and even military force to dispossess Indians of their lands proved more severe.[50]

Racial prejudice existed widely in independent Latin America. What proved to be strikingly different in the United States, Robert Cottrol has noted, was the inherent conflict between the institution of slavery—human bondage—and a revolutionary ideology of egalitarianism and freedom, a contradiction that was identified in the Declaration of Independence and that would grow with the extension of democratic rights, access to land, education, and other improvements to the lives of white males. Laws and social practices protecting the rights of free colored people proved to be weaker than the law of slavery and the racism that accompanied it. Racism persisted in Latin America, to be sure, but in the nineteenth-century United States there was little or no racial etiquette, no subtle distinctions either in racial designation or in the perception of race as a continuum rather than a binary condition that for some made it imperative to draw a color line. In a nation coexisting with slavery and an egalitarian revolutionary ideology, there would be a reckoning.[51]

Keeping the peace between these presumably irreconcilable forces required a political system that could adapt to the realities of a republic where older republican sensibilities of deference and dependency among white males had given way to a belief that prosperity and peace required tolerance and acceptance of authority. The grand design of the Founders—a republic of citizens whose values and habits were molded from above—had been made irrelevant, and the natural aristocrats of the old republic had become victims of a revolution they could no longer contain. In the future those who led had to prove themselves capable through coalition building of managing the new democratic forces that could not easily be placated in a reconfigured and more democratic political system that now incorporated anti-Masons, working-class urban laborers, evangelicals, antiliquor reformers, suffragettes, anti-immigrant blocs, and especially abolitionists. In this volatile political culture, where slavery and the Union lay at the heart of the matter, some looked to the Constitution or a vigorous continentalism or even armed struggle. Such was the uncertainty of the revolutionary legacy.

It was a hemispheric concern as well. After a half-century of global conflict, the presumption that viable nation-states in the New World would follow in the wake of wars between European empires proved to be a fantasy. Instead, revolution had produced civil wars within empires, not conflicts between them. The legacy was independent states that were in turn riven by social and political discord. In the world and particularly in Europe, the French Revolution had unleashed an upheaval so powerful that its defeat required an unprecedented coalition of powers, but in its ideological and political wake it transformed the meaning of revolution and France and made that country a nation. With all the power at his bidding, Napoleon Bonaparte could not defeat the revolution in French Saint-Domingue and the creation of the New World's second independent state, Haiti. In the aftermath of independence, Haiti plunged into civil war between black and colored factions, and even in achieving unity under Jean-Pierre Boyer in the 1820s it survived only by subjecting its governments to onerous loans from its former French rulers. In 1825 the Venezuelan Simón Bolívar was the darling of the Atlantic world; five years later, he described the condition of independent Spanish America in words as condemnatory as those he had earlier ascribed to Spain. The mobilizer of black and colored troops and the unifying leader in wartime joined the conservative backlash of peacetime.[52]

Presumably, the United States and imperial Brazil were the hemispheric exceptions to this grim postrevolutionary condition. With the Missouri Compromise and especially with the Monroe Doctrine, the United States had configured a plan for its expanding federation and at the fiftieth anniversary of the Declaration of Independence provided its citizens and the world with a statement of where it stood and what it stood for: independence, self-determination, nonintervention in distinctly European affairs, freedom of the seas, and anticolonialism. It was the self-chosen protector of those hemispheric states too weak or too incompetent to fulfill the goals of a civil society. In an oft-quoted July 4, 1821, address, John Quincy Adams had employed gendered language, imagining the United States as a "woman" who was restrained from going abroad to destroy monsters but the defender and vindicator of liberty at home. By implication, Adams expressed the concerns of white males over the role of women in the public sphere, as well as men's doubts about the abilities of Spanish Americans to sustain democratic governments in the wake of the savagery and chaos of their wars of independence.[53]

Not even Jefferson's warning of a "fire bell in the night" had conveyed something so apocalyptic for the United States. But other modern judgments about the comparative postindependence experiences of the United States and the independent states of Latin, particularly Spanish, America can be misleading. Felipe Fernández Armesto, I believe, exaggerates by describing the wars of independence in the Americas as "the making of the United States and the ruin of the rest of the Americas." Undeniably, the colonial experiences of mainland Spanish America and imperial Brazil (and nineteenth-century Spain) contrasted sharply with those of the United States, where the passage from rule by a constitutional monarchy to a republic seemed less hazardous and easier to accomplish than that experienced by Spanish Americans. There was no concurrent civil war in Britain between 1775 and 1783 to compare in severity with that in Spain from 1810 to 1815, and the economic prospects of the United States in the Atlantic economy after 1783, as well as its domestic political condition, offered similarly disproportionate advantages to what Latin America (excepting Brazil and conservative Chile) confronted. Louisiana offered an example of the U.S. capability of assimilating an alien and European frontier region that Latin Americans might have envied. It may have remained legally, demographically, and especially culturally different for years after statehood in 1812, but the sense of uncertainty about its incorporation into the nation declined because its leaders could largely agree on white supremacy, socially and politically, and its economy was connected to the East and increasingly to the South.[54]

But the postindependence history of the Articles of Confederation and the Old Republic was fraught with political strife and uncertainty. Undeniably, the United States avoided the militarization of society in its War of Independence, and it had allies whose support was of greater consequence in achieving independence. After the unity of the *rage militaire* of 1775–76, the divisions within the patriot cause and between the colonies spilled over into the postindependence era. There were moments when the political and economic prospects for the republic brightened, but former allies now became adversaries, and the international situation that had been so favorable during the war years became more problematic. The civil war of the revolutionary years lingered, as did the apprehension of the reversal of history and the end of the republic. Not even the Peace of Christmas Eve 1814 would dispel that fear.

Nor would the reassurances of the Missouri Compromise and the victory of Jackson, presumably a staunch ally, erase the lingering apprehensions of slaveholders that *their* empire of liberty would remain unthreatened from a slave insurrection that had allies among abolitionists in the United States and Great Britain, sanctuaries in Canada and in Mexico, and inspiration from the Caribbean and the example of the Haitian Revolution and what it had achieved, however precarious the future of the independent state of

Haiti. Bolívar had confirmed what could be accomplished by arming slaves to achieve victory, and in the last years of his life he bemoaned the *pardocracia*—rule by people of color—that came in the wake of independence.[55]

In a larger sense, Adams framed the American Revolution as a struggle within the British Empire that had become a world war and in independence had proved its worthiness as an independent republic that had not succumbed to dictatorship or monarchy. It had exercised imperial ambitions in North America on the specious grounds that it was defending liberty and advancing democracy. It had become more democratic in its politics, but its racial dynamics and acceptance of slavery mocked the revolutionary promise. Such contradictions bespoke one of the conditions of nationhood: the willingness to overlook these and other flaws in the name of unity or security.

That entity would become the first nation crafted from the long American Revolution—the Confederacy. And the war its defiance precipitated would be the kind of war Bolívar had experienced. As a New Englander and the son of two revolutionary icons, Quincy Adams remained uncomfortable with the role he had played in continental expansion and became an outspoken critic of the militant, democratic, proslavery, and race-obsessed democracy he identified with Andrew Jackson and the slave power. In his career as a U.S. congressman after his presidency, he found redemption, if few political successes, in changing the course of the country's history.

For someone who wrestled with his own racial identity, Bolívar, more than his North American contemporaries, understood that revolutions, particularly the civil wars they can precipitate, complicate rather than resolve the racial dynamic, especially for those who see history as a morality play. Unlike John Quincy Adams, he did not grasp the import of what that had meant for his life until it was too late and his pursuit of glory had racked his body and destroyed his soul.[56]

PART 2

The Reckoning

CHAPTER 6

The American Democracy

THE QUARTER CENTURY BEGINNING ABOUT 1830 was a defining period in the history of the long American Revolution. A generation experienced a transformation in communications and social relations and a vigorous market economy. Women's rights, temperance, and peace movements took root, along with reforms in educational and penal institutions, changes in religious practices, and the springing up of utopian societies. Some of the hundred or so of these societies founded in the nineteenth century were created to alleviate the economic despair from business failures or job layoffs. Others sprang from the Judeo-Christian belief in a "New Jerusalem" or the Enlightenment faith that every social problem had a solution. Few of these societies survived the Civil War.[1]

Entitlement to "equality" now had multiple requirements dependent on gender and color, among other qualifications. The government and society that Alexis de Tocqueville cataloged in his two-volume *Democracy in America* defined equality as the elimination of privilege, which connoted aristocracy, and exalted equality and democracy, which meant ending political and economic barriers to the common man's persistent quest for personal freedom and happiness, particularly material comfort. White males were entitled to equality, but women and free people of color continued to exist under both legal and social restraints. Communities on occasion collapsed in localized violence against those deemed a threat, such as abolitionists and Latter-day Saints. Retaining the sanctity of private property, ordinary people began to abandon their notion that there must be a balance between those who believed power rested on property and those who identified power with numbers. The goal of society was individual self-improvement, but increasingly, as white males claimed equal rights, those of free blacks and women lessened.[2]

By comparison with Europe, the prospects for political and social improvement in the United States looked much better. Hopes for a political revolution in France with the July 1830 revolt ended not in the creation of a republic but with the passage of power to Louis-Philippe, the end of the monarchical alliance with the Catholic Church, and hereditary appointments to the Chamber of Peers. The Russian tsar crushed a Polish uprising and incorporated Poland into his empire; popular revolts in Italy and the German kingdoms failed. In Spain, Fernando VII still held power, unrepentant and absolute, and after his death in 1833, the country experienced forty years of civil conflict (the Carlist Wars) between those who favored a secular, liberal future for the nation and those who wanted to continue the rule of absolute monarchy and the Catholic Church. Elsewhere, there were victories for popular movements: the Belgians declared their independence from the Netherlands, and the Greeks finally wrested themselves from the Ottoman grip. In Great Britain, the death of Charles IV, the accession of William IV, and the appointment of Charles Grey, 2nd Earl Grey, as prime minister accelerated the long-dormant movement for parliamentary reform in 1832, which ended the notorious rotten boroughs and gave greater representation to urban areas. But the working and lower middle classes still did not get the vote.

The Age of Jackson in the United States reflected the beliefs of the man who was a disciple of the militant American Revolution. Where his predecessor had equated liberty with power, Jackson viewed his election as a contest over liberty and power, with farmers and artisans arrayed against a country where technological change, economic growth, and political power lay in the cities, in commerce, and in industry—a triad of interests threatening rural America and urban laborers, who resented controls over their personal lives and feared the manufacturing economy that denied them equal status with their bosses. A nationalist and constitutionalist by profession, Jackson had opposed the expansion of federal power in the 1820s but was a fervent defender of union, confirming that "without union our independence and liberty would never have been achieved [and] without union they can never be maintained."[3]

At the same time, his conception of nation reflected the values of the people of the western country, a region sprinkled with squatters and impoverished settlers, land speculators, and opportunists. The landless squatters were scarcely representative of what Crèvecoeur had in mind when he described his "new American" of the prerevolutionary years, and federal land laws were designed to discourage their migration. By the 1830s and 1840s they constituted perhaps 35 percent of the southwestern states and figured significantly in the political culture of Jacksonian America. The political battles of the era—a legacy of the revolutionary tension between a still-infant capitalist economy and republican liberty and equality—became the foundation of the two major political parties of the era, Democratic and Whig.[4]

In retrospect, the violence of the era was an omen of what lay ahead for the next generation. The problem, as Abraham Lincoln sensed, was the decline in respect for the law that accompanied the increasing violence. Mob protest on behalf of liberty in 1775 served a noble purpose, Lincoln believed, but mobs that committed outrages by burning churches or printing presses or by hanging people constituted a threat to liberty and government. Unlike Jackson, another frontier lawyer, Lincoln articulated his respect for the law in the revolutionary tradition, not in a democratic expression of the people's anger. "Let every American, every lover of liberty, every well-wisher to his posterity," he declared in a Springfield talk in 1838, "swear by the blood of the Revolution never to violate in the least particular the laws of the country."[5]

The age reverberated with the bellicose rhetoric of the Revolution and demands for fulfilling the continental dominion Jefferson had described as an "empire of liberty," which Jackson understood as an "empire *for* liberty." A Jackson disciple, President James K. Polk (1845–49) would fulfill that goal in his one-term presidency, but at the cost of a confrontation with two European powers (Britain and France) and war with Mexico. What some contemporaries called a "wicked war" sharpened the contrast between the two Americas. "Young America" was arrogant, defiant, materialistic, increasingly racist, beholden to a professedly nationalist slave South, and imperial. Its most dynamic regions were the agrocapitalist empire of plantation slavery of the Mississippi delta and the states carved out of the Old Northwest and Far West. By the 1840s the wealth and power of the first inspired a vigorously proslavery expansionism that looked southward to the Gulf of Mexico, the Caribbean, and even Latin America for new territories and promoted free trade in the search for global markets, more land for white slave owners, and more steamboats to ply the mighty Mississippi.[6]

Young America's obverse face was transnational America, a federation of disparate political and social groups that were ambivalent about immigration and racial equality, increasingly fearful of the power of the slave states in the national government, and uncertain about the survival of the republic in a political system that strained under the tensions between the two. In the great debates of the era—over abolitionism, the economic and political power of the slave states, and expansionism, among others—there remained a fleeting hope that the republic created out of the American Revolution and the War of Independence would follow the course of neither the French Revolution nor that of the other hemispheric states whose postindependence politics struck some U.S. observers (and Tocqueville) as troublesome and fractured.

The Texas Revolution

Westward expansion, it was sometimes argued, would reinforce the symbiotic relationship between these two Americas. As Robert Walker, secretary of the treasury in the Polk administration, wrote in December 1847 as victory in the war with Mexico seemed imminent, "A higher than any earthly power still guards and directs our destiny, impels us onward and has selected our great and happy country as a model and ultimate centre of attraction for all the nations of the world."[7]

In the early 1830s Tocqueville grasped the power of both sentiments when he wrote about American migration into Texas: "They purchase land, they produce the commodities of the country, and supplant the original population [and] if Mexico takes no steps to check this change . . . Texas will shortly cease to belong to that government."[8] For those who dreamed of incorporation of western ports to further the nation's commercial future on the Pacific, Texas was less important than Alta California, certainly, but an independent Texas dominated by American settlers yet free of federal authority and susceptible to British and French influence posed a strategic risk and a particular concern for Mexico. Since the American Revolution, the Spanish and then the Mexican hold on the vast expanse of northern Mexico had weakened under persistent raiding by a formidable nonstate actor, the Comanches. At their height, the Comanches (and their Kiowa allies) dominated an expanse stretching from north of present-day Oklahoma southward into northern Mexico and from western New Mexico eastward almost to the Mississippi. Their scorched-earth tactics were carried out with a ferocity and brutality that plagued the Mexican government. Presumably, immigrants from the United States would mitigate the problem.[9]

To that end, the Mexican government permitted Stephen F. Austin to settle families in the province with generous land allotments, but the settlers were required to convert to Catholicism and become Mexican citizens, and they were prohibited from owning slaves. Within a few years, the number of immigrants exceeded that of Mexicans, and the Mexican government ended legal settlement. But illegal entry continued, and, as before, Americans brought their slaves with them. As concerns of eastern and northern political leaders about the "arc of slave empire" from Spanish Cuba to Texas collided with equally vigorous defenses of slavery among southern political leaders, the matter of Texas's annexation became an explosive political issue.

By 1834 the American population in the province numbered nineteen thousand (including two thousand slaves), which dwarfed the Tejano population of fewer than four thousand. In 1833 Antonio López de Santa Anna became president and commenced to deal with the recalcitrant states of northern Mexico. His measures provoked a rebellion in Texas and Alta California, and in the ensuing war he lost Texas. Most Tejanos were fiercely anticentralist and thus sympathized with the demands for autonomy within the Mexican state. In the end, the Tejanos, as well as the Californios, wound up as losers—hated by their countrymen for their disloyalty to the mother country and ultimately driven from power and influence by the Anglo immigrant onslaught. As Pío Pico, the last Mexican governor of California, lamented, "We find ourselves threatened by hordes of Yankee immigrants who have already begun to flock into the country and whose progress we cannot resist."[10]

To see the support for annexation and this conflict as part of a U.S. drive to continental domination glosses over a few complicating matters. The momentary alliance of American immigrants with dissident Tejanos depended in part on a common interest in the rapidly expanding cotton economy in the region northeast of San Antonio after 1820. Mexican law forbade slavery, but Austin and his Tejano allies were able to weaken application of the law. Santa Anna's determination to bring the defiant northern province under the control of central authority accelerated the independence movement, a decision explained not only by the desire to preserve slavery but by a "complex tangle of cotton, slavery, and Mexican federalism."[11]

Undeniably, there were powerful ethnic and cultural dynamics fueling the Texas rebellion. The settlers who arrived with Austin and even Austin himself saw themselves less as agents of U.S. expansionism and more as variants of the American revolutionary tradition, people who no longer fitted in or saw opportunity or owed money or were simply moving on to escape problems or to move up in society. Sam Houston, dispatched to Texas by Jackson to assess the numbers of Comanches and Pawnees in the province, fell into several of those categories but after the war remained persistently proannexationist.

Austin himself became a convert to the rebellion when he was unable to secure Mexican statehood for Texas, describing Texans as "the alien subjects of a people to whom they deliberately believed themselves morally, intellectually, and politically superior."[12]

From October 1835 to the early months of 1836, the rebels successfully held off their Mexican adversary and dispatched agents to New Orleans and other towns in the southwestern United States to get recruits for the cause, promising generous land grants to join the fight. The newcomers proved even more defiantly anti-Mexican, and the rebellion became a revolution with the Texas Declaration of Independence on March 2. Although the fall of the Alamo to Santa Anna's forces on March 6 dampened Texan spirits, six weeks later, Sam Houston's forces overwhelmed Santa Anna's army at San Jacinto. For the victors, the choices seemed clear: annexation to the United States or, that failing, U.S. recognition of Texas independence. Jackson determined that speedy annexation "would be seen around the world as a gross violation of the law of nations."[13]

Recognition of the Texas republic was a given. In doing so, Jackson underestimated both the anger of Mexican leaders about the U.S. role in the Texas rebellion and the resolve of Texans to embark on their own course of settling affairs with Mexico. In 1836 they could not replicate the Louisiana route to entering the Union. In Louisiana the United States had encountered angry refugees from the Haitian Revolution, but they had lacked an imperial urge. Texans constituted a different branch of the American Revolution. Their rebellious spirit drew its strength and its vitality from its egalitarian, liberal, and imperial ideologies. The spirit and tone of the Texas Declaration of Independence (March 2, 1836) expressed the defiance of the U.S. declaration of July 4, 1776, but with an evangelical addendum: a refusal to submit to the "combined despotism of the sword and priesthood" and the condemnation of a Mexican government for inciting the "merciless savage" on them. For former president and now congressman John Quincy Adams, the war in Texas was "not a servile war but a war between slavery and emancipation, and every possible effort has been made to drive us into the war, on the side of slavery."[14]

In other words, Texans should be denied statehood. It was a "moral question" in the mind of someone who had been an enabler of expansionism for strategic and political reasons but who had now found a higher and nobler cause. Texans had their own agenda, which they believed God had sanctioned. As residents of a republic set geographically in a pivotal place on the

North American continent, they could play the game of international politics. They could continue their war with Mexico and fulfill their own imperial mission. They were responsible for the war that erupted in 1846 as much as James K. Polk was.

Tocqueville's America

Tocqueville framed his account of Texas in *Democracy in America* in the context of the "empire of their own language and manners," providing yet another example of the qualities and strengths of the United States and a reminder of the British heritage in the Anglo-American character. He conceded there might be roadblocks in the way of this inevitable preponderance of the country's destiny. The "dismemberment of the Union ..., the abolition of republican institutions and the tyrannical government that might succeed [it]," he wrote, "may retard this impulse, but they cannot prevent the people from ultimately fulfilling their destinies."[15]

Tocqueville the sociologist surveyed the country's multilayered and intersecting governmental structures—federal, state, and local—as well as its political parties, lawyers, and what he saw as a preoccupation with the rule of law. Tocqueville the moralist provided a warning about the "tyranny of the majority" and the dangers of a despot or popular dictator who professed to be a leader of the people but on gaining power violated their rights. The redemptive grace of the American but not the French revolutionary experience was its definition of equality or the equality of status, which meant that no white man was any other white man's inferior. Tocqueville anticipated that this secular spiritual faith might spread throughout Europe and the world because of its implied acknowledgment of the *right* of the *individual* to affirm his or her own identity. In this way, the desire for equality would lessen before the stronger impulse of individual wants and desires. At the same time, Tocqueville noted that Americans were joiners, creating associations committed to such social causes as temperance and abolition. Individuals took public pledges in support of these causes.[16]

Of course, there would be people left out or left behind in such a democracy, certainly the Indian and the slave. Tocqueville viewed the degradation of the first and slavery as the country's two sins. Tocqueville and his companion Gustave de Beaumont arrived in the United States a year after passage of the Indian Removal Act of 1830, which reversed Washington and

Jefferson's policy of permitting Indians who had adapted to an agricultural society to remain on lands east of the Mississippi. But the state of Georgia contended that in 1802 the federal government had promised it would purchase lands belonging to the Five Civilized Tribes (Chickasaw, Choctaw, Muscogee-Creek, Seminole, and Original Cherokee Nations) in a reasonable time. As pressures against them escalated, the Cherokees of North Georgia, some of whom had adopted the dress and living style of the state's white residents, became more defiant and in 1827 declared themselves an independent republic, just as the discovery of gold unleashed an invasion of white squatters and miners into the region. In vain, northern missionaries protested the illegality and immorality of Jackson's decision to remove federal troops protecting the Cherokees.[17]

Jackson saw removal as the only way to shield the Indians from white retaliation. The Cherokees fought the Georgia law in federal courts and won their case in the Supreme Court in a presumably deciding judgment by Chief Justice John Marshall. The decision struck down the Georgia law, not the Indian Removal Act, thus making improbable any validity to stories that Jackson responded with the remark that Marshall could not enforce the decision because there was nothing to enforce. The Cherokee leader John Ross understood that the real threat to the Five Civilized Tribes was the federal government and the president. Using tactics he had employed in Florida fifteen years before, Jackson compelled the Cherokees to sign a treaty agreeing to vacate their lands and move west.

In effect, the decision meant removal of the other tribes as well, although some, mostly Seminoles, joined fugitive slaves and fought back from their hiding place in the South Florida swamps. As did slavery, Indian removal revealed the inhumane face of Jacksonian America and played out in two theaters: the Second Seminole War (1835–42) in the Florida swamps, which cost three thousand lives, and the tragic Trail of Tears exodus, which commenced in 1838 and during which thousands of Indians succumbed to disease, exhaustion, and starvation. By a perverse logic, Jackson explained Indian removal as a humane act: "What good man would prefer a country covered with forests and ranged by a few thousand savages to our extensive republic . . . and filled with all the blessings of liberty, civilization, and religion?"[18]

Slaves and slavery were different matters. Tocqueville's arrival in the United States in 1831 virtually coincided with the founding of William Lloyd Garrison's defiant abolitionist newspaper, the *Liberator*, and Nat Turner's brief but deadly slave revolt in Southampton County, Virginia. Coincidentally, British abolitionists stepped up their call for an immediate end to slavery in the British West Indies, and at the end of the year Jamaica erupted in a series of slave revolts known collectively as the Christmas or Baptist Revolt. The cause of Turner's revolt remains uncertain—an uprising inspired by the incendiary writing of Garrison or Walker, as many southern whites believed, or a murderous rampage in a remote Virginia county against white families directed by a literate, messianic fanatic. In response, the governor mobilized three thousand soldiers, militiamen, and vigilantes against fifty to sixty blacks in a pursuit in which more than a hundred suspected insurrectionists were killed. Fears of race war gripped Virginia, and southern states rushed to pass laws making it a crime to teach slaves to read.[19]

In contrast to what happened in the United States, where slave emancipation became linked to the even more volatile issue of racial equality, the Christmas Revolt in Jamaica accelerated the drive toward emancipation in the British West Indies. The appeal of the abolitionist movement did grow stronger in the United States in the 1830s, particularly among women active in reform movements. To southerners, Turner's revolt reinforced fears of murderous slaves bent on revenge for their years of suffering. The British West Indies had a tradition of slave revolt—in Barbados in 1816 and in Demerara in 1823. In Jamaica, particularly, Baptist and Methodist religious sects built a following among African Creoles and gained headway in their long crusade in Parliament to end slavery. Turner's force numbered sixty slaves. Sam Sharpe, leader of the Christmas Revolt, preached the equality of men in his quest for freedom and mobilized sixty thousand followers, among them blacksmiths, carpenters, drivers, masons, and other leaders of the slave community. A few southern observers of the Christmas Revolt predicted a massive slave insurrection in the South, but after 1831 and the Turner revolt until the Civil War the only slave revolt of consequence was the Seminole War in the early 1840s.[20]

Abolitionists in the United States as well as missionaries in the British West Indies opposed violence even as Jamaican planters and legislators predicted that emancipation measures would provoke more and bloodier uprisings. In the aftermath of the Christmas Revolt, sentiments in Parliament shifted rapidly to accept emancipation, perhaps out of resignation that the political clout of the West Indies lobby had declined along with the economic importance of the region. In 1834 Parliament approved the abolition of slavery in the British West Indies, an act that freed eight hundred thousand slaves but consigned most to an apprenticeship system. When the system was abolished in 1838, Parliament provided compensation of £20 million (or almost $22 billion in 2016) to forty-six thousand slaveholders both in the West Indies and in the home islands. Production dropped rapidly, but the British had demonstrated that it was possible to avoid "another Haiti."[21]

Abolitionists objected to violence, but they justified slave rebellion, which prompted a harsh reaction not only from southerners but even from antislave northerners, who were offended by the abolitionists' transnational alliance with their British counterparts and their ambiguous views about the Union. Slave emancipation in the United States was linked to sharp racial antipathies and fears that freed blacks would displace white workers. Christian revivalists of the day might argue fervently that the United States as a Christian nation must overcome the sin of slavery by accepting an "immediatist" solution, but such views served to incite even stronger opposition to their cause. As Garrison discovered, the political and social order as well as the economy of Jacksonian America depended on slavery in fundamental ways, through consumption of slave-produced foods or links to slave-produced commodities in the export market. Tests of Christian sincerity about slavery strained the relationship between the Presbyterian, Baptist, and Methodist churches that served as vital social and cultural links between North and South. Slavery was becoming a moral issue: the United States could not be the "new hope of mankind," a more perfect society, as the Declaration of Independence promised, if its power were built on coerced labor.[22]

As much as he admired the British imprint on American democracy, Tocqueville's judgments about American slavery largely reflected those expressed by the leaders of the American Colonization Society. Slave labor proved economically debilitating because the slave had no incentive to improve his lot. Emancipation offered no solution, as the slave would be unable to compete, and the presence of the freed man would further intensify white racism. Tocqueville's occasional apocalyptic passages evoked reminders of Bolívar's fears of *pardocracia*, a democracy of mixed-race people, with its suggestion of race war. "Wherever the whites have been the most powerful, they have held the blacks in degradation and in slavery," Tocqueville wrote, "[but] wherever the Negroes have been strongest, they have destroyed the whites."[23]

He may have been thinking about Jean-Jacques Dessalines's "final solution" for the white planters who refused to leave Haiti in 1804. With the immeasurable help of former president and now representative John Quincy Adams, abolitionists did achieve one stellar victory during the decade in the

Amistad case, which had profound political as well as legal implications. The case involved fifty-three kidnapped African slaves taken to Spanish Cuba in 1839 and then declared native Cuban slaves, which permitted their sale. (Importation of slaves into Cuba was illegal under an 1817 British-Spanish treaty.) En route to their new destination in eastern Cuba, the slaves took over the ship *Amistad*; killed the captain, cook, and several of the crew; and for sixty-three days followed a zigzag course until the *Amistad* ran aground off Long Island, where both the slaves and the cargo were seized by federal authorities. Had their disposition been left to President Martin Van Buren, then facing a reelection battle, and the Spanish consul, the slaves would have been sent back to Cuba to stand trial. But abolitionists came to their defense, and in the ensuing court battle, which reached the Supreme Court, Adams appealed to the Declaration of Independence and the right of revolution in his successful defense of their claim to be returned to Africa.[24]

In an era of democratization and heightening racial tensions and fears of rebellion, such victories were rare. In this regard, the U.S. experience resembled more closely that of postwar mainland Latin America than the lingering influence of transatlantic abolitionism. There, the reliance on slave and free black support by both royalist and patriot forces was much greater than in the American Revolution, but the status of *libertos* (freedmen) and even free blacks and mulattos remained ambiguous. Chile, the Central American Federation, and Mexico decreed emancipation with compensation to owners in the 1820s. Elsewhere, slaveholding and conservative interests pushed through laws that delayed the "womb law" rules, the granting of freedom to a child born of a slave mother, which led to full emancipation. Free blacks and mulattos complained of the unwillingness of whites to extend the full benefits of citizenship and equality. Liberals especially felt constrained because they needed the support of former slaves and free blacks but were also dependent on placating slaveholders and the propertied class. Increasingly, the North American and Brazilian models of revolution—independence without emancipation—seemed preferable to the French.[25]

American Continentalism

On that point, Tocqueville would have agreed, if only because the French revolutionary experience had led to centralization and the despotism of Napoleon. Domingo Sarmiento and the "Generation of '37" in Argentina, who bemoaned the "barbarism" of the countryside and suffered the tyranny of the caudillo Juan Manuel de Rosas, would have seconded Tocqueville's positive appraisal of American democracy. But Argentinian liberals were much more Europeanized in their beliefs about the virtue of the city and lived far enough from the United States that they need not fear U.S. territorial expansion. Indeed, in the 1820s and 1830s two ideologically different Argentine governments unsuccessfully called on the United States to enforce President Monroe's December 1823 warning against further European encroachment in the hemisphere.[26]

Such a benign perspective glosses over the cost of American continentalism. A project aimed at securing the Union and furthering the democratic promise of the Revolution ultimately led to sectionalism, disunion, and the undermining of the dream of a yeoman republic destroyed by its commitment to empire in the name of security and its tolerance of slavery in the cause of progress and social peace. Viewed retrospectively, then, of the two most powerful inspirations of the Revolution—a demand for equality or autonomy, on the one hand, and access to western lands or empire, on the other—the second proved stronger, with tragic results.[27]

For this generation, there remained uncertainties, particularly about a lingering British threat. Preoccupations and apprehensions about the British presence assumed various forms, from the probably exaggerated notion that the British imprint continued to permeate American high culture or controlled the national banking system to the belief that the British ruling class assumed that the republic would not survive. On the northern border there were fears that local conflicts would escalate or apprehensions that in the Texas republic the British and the French would prevent Texas's annexation as a state. British abolition of slavery in the British West Indies and a justifiable apprehension about British pressure on Spain heightened U.S. suspicions about the "Africanization of Cuba," which would include the abolition of slavery and the substitution of free labor, which slaveholders viewed as a threat. In one sense, U.S. expansion in North America replicated the British imperial project in North America but without the apparatus of imperial administration, instead espousing state power in the project of economic development. As fears of an "empire of slavery" took root, northern Whigs and then Republicans began to articulate a version of anti-imperialism in which a mobilized nation would bond the state-directed economic program with the cause of liberty, equality, and union to battle a slave-based empire.[28]

The perceived British threat on the northern border reflected the strains in a relationship with a country not yet precisely defined and a people not yet reconciled with the American Revolution. In the fifteen years after the Peace of Ghent, the United States and Great Britain signed agreements providing for the neutrality of the Great Lakes and joint occupation of the Oregon Territory, which included the present-day states of Oregon and Washington and the Canadian province of British Columbia, as well as parts of Idaho, Wyoming, and Montana. In the 1830s Jacksonian democracy, a populist legacy of the American Revolution, exerted a powerful and divisive impact on both French Lower Canada and Anglophone Upper Canada. In the former, Louis-Joseph Papineau, a popular figure in the Legislative Assembly, looked to rectify the grievances of the French-speaking inhabitants against the Anglophone ruling oligarchy through annexation by the United States. The firebrand in Upper Canada was William Lyon Mackenzie, who had strong antislavery convictions but saw in the vigorous young republic to the south a model of economic progress and republican institutions.[29]

The situation was further complicated by resentments of the children of Americans who had migrated to the region after the Revolution and claimed full rights as loyal subjects. The rebellion that ensued in 1837 had the support of John L. O'Sullivan of the *Democratic Review*. O'Sullivan, who coined the inspirational phrase "Manifest Destiny," applauded what Papineau and Mackenzie were doing. But neither President Van Buren nor Sir George Arthur, lieutenant governor of Upper Canada, wanted a war. When Papineau and Mackenzie and their followers took refuge on U.S. soil, created a provisional government in the Niagara District, and commenced to send raiding parties across the border, Canadian militias retaliated. Van Buren in turn sent General Winfield Scott (who as a young officer in the War of 1812 had led U.S. troops in the Niagara District) to restore order as a pacifier. Mackenzie was arrested for violating U.S. neutrality laws. In the aftermath, Mackenzie accused the Americans of betraying his cause, and Upper Canadians declared a victory.

The British now decided that Canada might not be worth a war, but tensions with the United States had to be eased, and in 1840 Upper and Lower Canada were united in the Province of Canada, although usage of Canada West and Canada East persisted until 1867. Two years later, with the Anglophile Daniel Webster in charge, Britain and the United States settled a lumber war along the troubled Maine–New Brunswick border and clarified the border from Lake Superior to the Lake of the Woods in the Webster-Ashburton Treaty. Although calls for absorbing British Canada persisted throughout the nineteenth century, the settlement and attendant compromises meant that the United States no longer feared living with a monarchical government on its northern border and that Canadians were willing to abide a republican neighbor on their southern, at least for the time being.[30]

In the 1840s plans and ambitions for the peaceful fulfillment of the dream of continental empire collapsed. Westward expansion as a grand project for democratic institutions, community, farmers, and free labor now seemed threatened by multiple forces, notably a British government seemingly bent on containing the United States and a proslavery power with western as well as Caribbean ambitions. Jackson sensed that Texas lay at the epicenter of this danger: Texas was, he wrote in 1844, "the important key to our future safety—take and lock the door against all foreign influence."[31]

Since the birth of the republic, Texas's leaders had been preoccupied with security from both Mexicans and Indians, particularly the Comanches and Kiowas, whose raids plagued not only Texas settlements but also those in northern Mexico. Sam Houston, Texas's first president, looked to U.S. annexation as the best security for the republic. His successor, Mirabeau B. Lamar, opposed annexation, pursued an aggressive Indian policy, and promoted Texas's claim of a boundary southward and westward to the Río Bravo (Rio Grande), an area encompassing half of present-day New Mexico, the Oklahoma panhandle, and portions of Colorado, Kansas, and Wyoming. In 1842, during Houston's second term, Texas militias raided Matamoros and Santa Fe. Both were repulsed.

But the republic proved more successful in another, more important sense. As the Spanish and then Mexican leaders had recognized, the Rio Grande held the key to development of the region and control of both the Santa Fe–Chihuahua and Matamoros–Saltillo trade. In advancing the republic's interests in this endeavor, the Texans made good use of two groups among the heterogeneous mix of immigrants: lawyers and merchants. The first understood well the weakness of Spanish and Mexican land laws in the Anglo-American judicial system; the second played an equally critical role in the rapidly changing social and cultural milieu of the republic. South of the Nueces River, prominent Anglo and Mexican families sometimes formed business and social alliances or even intermarried. In the traditional area of Texas, which lay north of the Nueces, land-hungry and ambitious newcomers engulfed Mexican settlements, and the old Spanish families of historic San Antonio were pushed aside. Even Juan Seguín, a hero at the Battle of San Jacinto and mayor of San Antonio, had to flee.[32]

By the 1844 election, then, uncertainties about the Oregon, California, and Texas issues had become ensnarled in both domestic and international politics. Losers in 1840, Democrats entered the campaign divided over Texas's annexation and slavery's expansion into the territories. Mexican political leaders, divided between centralists and federalists (the ideological and political equivalent of antifederalists in the United States), were nonetheless united in opposing U.S. annexation of Texas and increasingly receptive to a British proposal to broker Texas independence. Texas, more than Oregon, aggravated the sectionalism that Calhoun and other southern leaders had been pushing from the early days of the Jackson administration. The latent and powerful opposition to creating another slave state—one that might very well divide into several slave states—came as a blow to the northern wing of the Democratic Party, whose success depended on harmony between the sections. Once the northern Democrats began to relinquish ground to their southern allies, the instinctively ambivalent Whigs affirmed their claim to the mantle of a truly egalitarian party committed to the ordinary American. Henry Clay expressed a Whig belief in "intensive" rather than "extensive" development when he wrote that the country should "unite, harmonize, and improve what we have than attempt to acquire more."[33]

The intertwined issues of slavery, westward expansion, and democracy now served as pivotal flash points marking the country's future. A rueful John Quincy Adams viewed the shifting political winds as the degradation of the republican ideal of the Founders. Adams sensed the dangers in the more complicated forms of democracy that took root in the 1830s and 1840s—the democracy that absorbed and justified a belief in a master race with its parallel conviction that equality and liberty for whites meant enslavement or colonization or at least a second-class status for blacks. The American Board of Commissioners for Foreign Missions, which had been active in the Cherokee Nation, found itself at odds with the taking of Cherokee land for white settlers and the policy of Cherokee relocation. In the North, particularly, anger over the growing numbers of Irish, German, and French Canadian immigrants was a portent of the anti-immigrant movement of the 1850s.[34]

There was a gendered as well as a cultural and an ethnic dimension to this equation. Ordinary Americans who passed the bar of acceptance as the heirs of the revolutionary promise did not have to be propertied or literate or native-born to qualify, but the white male occupied an important place in the republic. Even that distinction became more complicated if one compared a Protestant whose familial roots went back to the colonial era and a Catholic Irish man only recently arrived in the country. Democratic republics required a pecking order of acceptance and rank different from that of the republic of Federalist or even Jeffersonian America, but leaders had to pretend that all were equal and that the nation was not only right but righteous in its quest for continental dominion.

That task required not only a purposeful leader at the helm but a citizen-soldier. O'Sullivan believed that Manifest Destiny would be a peaceful process spread by families seeking a better life in the western country, missionaries, and agents of commerce. That was one version of imperial destiny, perhaps, but there was another that required planning, strategy, power, and muscle, the last supplied from men and women who were sufficiently accustomed to violence in their lives that they could be relied on in the pursuit of empire. Few understood this better than Jacksonian Democrat James K. Polk of Tennessee, former Speaker of the House of Representatives and former governor of his home state, who narrowly defeated Whig Henry Clay for the presidency in the 1844 election by his frank stand on Texas as well as his ability to cut into the immigrant vote in key northern states.

Polk was boastful, ambitious, and purposeful. His inaugural address, which came shortly after the Congress had approved Texas's admission to the Union as a state by the unusual route of joint resolution, mixed familiar refrains of the genre with reassurances for those who had cause to worry. It was a re-affirmation of commitment to union and the sovereignty of the states and a rebuke of those who threatened political harmony with discord, a bold statement of the equality of all citizens, a reminder to the world that the United States did not threaten with its "military ambition," and a reaffirmation that the acquisition of Texas was justifiable because it was "once our own" and necessary to reassure a generation that feared a British challenge to Texas's rightful role in North America. Adams had come to a different judgment about Texas before Polk took the oath of office. "The annexation of Texas to this Union," Adams recorded in his diary in June 1844, "is the first step to the conquest of all Mexico, of the West India islands, of a maritime, colonizing, slave-tainted monarchy, and of extinguished freedom."[35]

Polk professed an alternative vision. He put a proverbial spin on British interference in the annexation of Texas by invoking Monroe's 1823 message as a justifiable precedent to declare U.S. opposition to European colonization or dominion on the North American continent without U.S. permission. As if to deny culpability in what critics perceived as a Machiavellian move by Democrats and proslavery expansionists, Polk proudly noted that Texas's admission to the Union "has been a bloodless achievement. . . . We have not sought to extend our territorial possessions by conquest, or our republican institutions over a reluctant people."[36]

The claim of a "clear and unquestionable" title to the Oregon territory (which would have incorporated present-day British Columbia) was similarly flimsy. Had Polk stuck to it, the British government stood ready to go to war. It was one thing for London to accept Texas's annexation and statehood as a rebuke to its brokering of Mexican acceptance in Texas's independence or even U.S. determination to acquire a California port, but the British were *not* going to be denied access to a Pacific port. Neither the martial slogan of northern Democrats—"Fifty-four forty or fight!" (referring to the southern boundary of Russian America)—nor Polk's invocation of the Monroe Doctrine as denial of European interference in U.S. continental expansion scared them. No Mexican leader could acquiesce in Texas's loss or the sale of California and New Mexico and survive. Polk would accept no less, and he began to soften his position on the Oregon question. In the Oregon treaty (June 1846), the two governments agreed on the forty-ninth parallel as the boundary between Canada and the United States from the Lake of the Woods to the Pacific.[37]

War with Mexico had already commenced with a skirmish between General Zachary Taylor's dragoons and Mexican troops near present-day Brownsville on the north bank of the Rio Grande. The fighting claimed two American lives and permitted Polk to confirm that American blood had been shed on U.S. soil, a statement more reflective of his duplicity than his reputed cunning. In their tone, congressional debates over the declaration of war replicated familiar themes. Representative Joshua Giddings of Ohio condemned the war "against an unoffending people" and as a "violation of the Constitution . . . and the precepts of the religion we profess." In a response in which he equated such remarks with "treason," Representative Stephen Douglas of Illinois invoked the Declaration of Independence of 1776 and its justification of self-defense in the name of liberty and freedom as confirmation of the right of the country "to repel invasion by a brutal and perfidious enemy."[38]

The United States fought the war with three armies: one under Taylor for the campaign in northern Mexico; a second dispatched to occupy New Mexico and California, where a group of American settlers had overturned the local government, proclaimed an independent republic, and waited for reinforcements; and a third led by Winfield Scott to drive inland from Veracruz and occupy Mexico City. Mexico had thirty thousand soldiers, many of them Indian conscripts who were poorly trained and had outmoded artillery; the United States had five thousand regulars who were reinforced by volunteers and much better equipped.

Yet victory proved more difficult than Polk had imagined. He had counted on a quick end to the war as well as Mexican compliance with U.S. territorial claims in return for much-needed cash to satisfy the country's debt. When the resistance proved more formidable, Polk decided on sending Scott to take the war into the Mexican capital. Taylor took Monterey in September 1846 and would have continued his campaign, but Polk ordered him to hold his position and transfer his best troops to Scott. After a narrow and costly victory at Buena Vista, which earned him widespread coverage in U.S. newspapers, Taylor drove Santa Anna from northern Mexico. Scott laid siege to Veracruz and, following a series of victories in his inland march, occupied Mexico City in September 1847. Victory seemed confirmed.

For "Young Hickory" there was little satisfaction. His two most successful generals, Taylor and Scott, were prominent Whigs, and they were reaping praise in the press and in Congress that the president thought was rightfully his. Some in his cabinet (notably Robert Walker) and at times even Polk himself wanted to seize all Mexico as indemnity. John C. Calhoun opposed such a course beyond sufficient territory for defensive measures because it would add an undesirable racial mix to the general population. "Ours . . . is the government of the white man," Calhoun protested, "[a]nd yet it is professed and talked about to erect these Mexicans into a territorial government, and place them on an equality with the people of the United States." Protestant religious groups concurred but for different reasons: an antipathy to the war and the parallel fears of expanding slavery, as well as a revulsion to the corruption of Mexican culture.[39]

What had begun as a regular war between two armies had become a guerrilla war on the Santa Fe Trail and in Alta California as Indians unleashed attacks against Mexicans, other Indians, and Americans. In California the army confronted an uprising against Mexican authorities by rebellious Americans (the Bear Flag Revolt in June and July 1846) who had encouragement from U.S. Army officer John Charles Frémont. They followed the Texas example and declared a free republic. Unlike earlier American settlers who had integrated into California society, the newcomers regarded Mexicans as their racial inferiors. Once news of the official beginning of the war arrived and marines and sailors from U.S. ships began subduing coastal towns, Frémont and the Bear Flaggers fell into line, yet Mexican resistance persisted. In northern Mexico, the invading troops, initially welcomed, turned to pillaging, raping, looting, and even murder.[40]

The invasion of central Mexico and the occupation of Mexico City dramatically altered the context of the war, especially for Mexicans, who now perceived the conflict as a struggle between two nations. Mexicans banded together in resistance, fired by a popular nationalism that drew its strength from a need to defend national independence and their Catholic faith, with its promise of eternal life, and to protect Mexican women from assault. Perceived as racially inferior by the invaders, Mexicans became convinced that with U.S. rule they would be turned into slaves, as had people of color in the northern republic. Anti-Catholic rhetoric, both supporting and condemning the war, swept a country where some Protestant religious leaders, notably the evangelist Lyman Beecher, synthesized political, expansionist, and religious sentiments into a frame for understanding the future of the United States and for understanding Mexicans. Thus, incorporation of Catholic Mexicans into the Union inspired some to warn of decline and others to speak of opportunity to settle new lands in the name of God and freedom.[41]

In the uncertainties of the course of the war and especially the resistance to the invader, Polk became increasingly frustrated. His Mexican counterpart, Antonio López de Santa Anna, was similarly perplexed. His government found itself confronting two enemies: the U.S. invaders and a resurgence of revolts by country people against landowners that spread throughout the country. As a Whig-controlled House balked at funding the war, in Mexico state governors and legislatures resisted new tax impositions from the central government and inspired church-led revolts. As Polk's territorial demands escalated, so did the criticism of his conduct of the war, yet the challenge confronting the Mexican Creole elite was similarly precarious. The guerrilla war in the countryside, aggravated by the U.S. invasion, suggested race war but involved access to the land and reminded Creoles of the 1810 Hidalgo Revolt. As much as anything, fear of a civil war and its danger to the social structure largely explained why at the end the surrendering of half the country to the United States seemed more palatable than facing the wrath of a vengeful mestizo nation and barbarian Comanches in the North. In the circumstances, the U.S. Army began to sell arms and ammunitions to Mexican state militaries to enable them to suppress the rebellions. They were greater threats than the U.S. invaders. Yet the "war of a thousand deserts" reinforced a view in subsequent Mexican narratives that the invading Americans had incited the Indians.[42]

What Polk really wanted was a compliant Mexican delegation suing for peace in Washington, D.C. What he got was a treaty satisfying virtually every original U.S. goal but in circumstances—a special emissary he tried to recall but who had defied him by negotiating it—that failed to soothe the president's overwrought ego. Polk had no choice but to send the Treaty of Guadalupe Hidalgo to the Senate, where his Whig detractors held their noses and joined their Democratic colleagues to approve it. In the end, he got virtually everything he wanted and the expansionists demanded. A humiliated and defeated Mexican government received U.S. $15 million and ceded more than 50 percent of its national domain to the United States but received assurances that the United States would police the Indian tribes raiding into Mexican territory and return cattle they had stolen. Those Mexican nationals who remained in the United States were assured of protection of their civil and property rights. In approving the treaty, the Senate struck the provision about honoring Mexican land grants. Disputes over land grants persisted well into the twentieth century, and in the 1960s and 1970s leaders of the Chicano movement often invoked the treaty in their protests about the denial of rights to Mexican Americans.[43]

Among some there remained a troubling feeling that the outcome of the war spelled trouble for the Union and distorted the meaning of the revolutionary promise. In the United States and in Mexico, the literature of the war often revealed more apprehension about the nation rather than patriotic assurance. Over time, contrastingly, Mexicans began to use the narrative of defeat to affirm the heroism and rightness of their cause, while North Americans began to erase from their memories the ugliness and "wickedness" of the war. Lincoln got it morally right when he decried Polk's deception about the beginnings of the war: "As a nation *should* not, and the Almighty *will* not, be evaded, so let him [Polk] attempt no evasion, [for he must know that] the blood of this war, like the blood of Abel, is crying to Heaven against him."[44]

Young America

In the postwar years, Lincoln's condemnation had little effect on the true believers of the Young America movement, who were absorbed by two distinct
legacies of the American Revolution. The first was the belief that despite the
inequities of wealth between the propertied, the opportunity to acquire property in sizes large and small would be the great social leveler, an alternative
for the propertyless to move up by moving on, a way of creating new communities in new territories that would become new states. A second, equally
powerful belief held that each generation would be more prosperous, enjoy
greater liberties and freedom, and possess a strong commitment to family,
community, and the nation.

Young America—a phrase borrowed from Giuseppe Mazzini's Young Italy
movement—spoke to this idealism and to parallel movements outside the
United States, particularly to the republican movements in Germany, Ireland,
France, and Poland. The United States would be an asylum nation for those
suffering from the repression of European governments. In North America,
the United States had a duty to expand the empire of liberty and its universal
values of conscience, trade, person, and equality. On the eve of the war with
Mexico, O'Sullivan wrote of the "right of our manifest destiny to overspread
and to possess the whole of the continent which Providence has given us for
the . . . great experiment of liberty."[45]

Such biblical exaltations of a war that to some had begun as a defensive and
just cause in 1846, increased the national domain by a third, and reminded the
British and the French of the country's determination not to be contained in
its westward march offered little reassurance to those persuaded that Mexico
was the victim in this "wicked war." More than these, the Mexican-American
War exposed the dual face of revolutionary America, one democratic and
hopeful, one imperial and tribal. Undeniably, the country in 1848 was stronger, more secure economically, and more culturally diverse, and the pace of
life had quickened. Nowadays, we may have a problem in understanding the
hypocrisy of those who agreed about the wickedness of the war, or who were
pacifists, or who acknowledged that the war violated our republican and our
revolutionary heritage yet supported it, if not as a "just," then certainly as a
necessary war. The reasons had less to do with "manliness" or even "Manifest
Destiny" and more to do with what the *Democratic Review* called a nation's
"social duties" and the obligations of being a member of the "great family of

the civilized nations," which may require interference in the affairs of "other members of the community" who have a "disorderly house."[46]

As had Mexico, the United States had dispatched its regular army and particularly its volunteers off to war with reminders that they must not only act in the service of their country but also serve as models of a new type of citizen-soldier who protected women and honor and refrained from such vices as drunkenness, promiscuity, gambling, and idleness. There were, of course, alternative versions of male masculinity in which these and related vices formed the essence of male identity. Mexico's army, particularly its officers, came under similar pressure to achieve a standard of behavior for the citizen-soldier. Although most of its army was composed of conscripts, the army Mexico sent into the field was more inclusive of people of color and made up of individuals whom polite society wished to rid from the community or, as in the United States, to remold into more honorable and worthy males. In the end, those males who found an alternative identity to masculinity in their violent behavior in wartime or in the service of preserving white supremacy in the South might not qualify as model citizens, but they understood that in certain causes they were needed.[47]

As in the abolitionist movement, there was a transatlantic pattern in revolutionary change. In the first quarter of 1848, fifty revolutions sprang up in France, Austria, Prussia, and several of the German and Italian states. Everywhere the reasons were different: economic deprivation, nationalism, poor agricultural production, or a yearning for change by intellectuals. The war had hemispheric political reverberations. In *Democracy in America* Tocqueville (like Bolívar) had been dismissive of the revolutionary legacy in Latin America, especially in Mexico. By the 1850s, however, a new generation of Latin American leaders—some who looked to the United States as a model for modernity, but more who looked within their own societies—took their place alongside those in the United States to debate and to war over the future. A parallel to the northern Young America movement sprang up among a generation whose parents had liberated a continent and wished to make their mark. Social and political leaders now used the name "Latin America" (created in the aftermath of the Mexican-American War) to distinguish themselves from the Anglo-America of the North. They became more receptive to ideas of cultivating republican ideals of citizenship and accepting the mingling of different ethnicities toward the goal of creating modern nations.[48]

In the aftermath of the war, U.S. political leaders presumed that, as in past domestic crises, they could find a means of dealing with the long-recognized imperfections of a political system if people were willing to compromise. The settling up of affairs presented them with a variety of challenges, some reaching back to the Revolution itself. In July 1848 women delegates gathered at Seneca Falls, New York, and drafted the Declaration of Sentiments, which invoked the Declaration of Independence's call for equality as a powerful statement on behalf of women's rights. As if to validate Abigail Adams's "Remember the Ladies" letter to John Adams in April 1776, the Declaration of Sentiments served as an indictment of men for denying to women rights that "are given to the most ignorant and degraded men" and, in language as severe as that leveled against George III, insisted on women's "admission to all the rights and privileges which belong to them as citizens of these United States." Every resolution save the right to vote, which some believed might discourage support for other issues, passed unanimously.[49]

Of more immediate concern to political leaders of both major parties was the future of the war's territorial bounty and how it would affect what some perceived as a deepening sectional crisis over slavery in the territories and the parallel issue of racial and gender equality as issues inherited from the American Revolution, both requiring resolution. To others, the obverse was more compelling. These questions and the divisive debates they generated were not moral issues but something more important: power and the preservation of the Union. Victory in what was a war supported by Democrats brought new challenges to a political system that had achieved success in building a North-South political coalition while preserving slavery and dismantling Henry Clay's American System of internal improvements, a national bank, and a protective tariff. War had contained if not eliminated the British challenge in North America. The abolitionist movement and the parallel threat of slave insurrection appeared less threatening.

The festering issue of the expansion of slavery had become more complicated. In 1846 a Pennsylvania Democratic congressman, David Wilmot, with particular concern for white settlers, added a proviso to an appropriations bill prohibiting slavery in any territories acquired in the war. (The Wilmot Proviso made it through the House but was struck down by the Senate.) Support for free soil was a political goal of the Liberty Party, made up of antislave Democrats and so-called Conscience Whigs. In the election of 1848, Van Buren (with Charles Francis Adams as his running mate) ran for president as the nominee of the Free Soil Party, a political splinter group born with the walkout of New York antislavery delegates from the Democratic Convention. Van Buren believed slavery was incompatible with the Revolution, and the platform on which he ran condemned slavery "as a great moral, social, and political evil—a relic of barbarism which must necessarily be swept away in the progress of Christian civilization."[50]

Polk condemned the Free Soil movement as a threat as serious as the Hartford Convention, but the deeper concern among many northerners lay in a fear that in some real and even intangible way the future of the country and the revolutionary promise had been hijacked by a political force that could not be contained—unless, of course, there could be a reprise of what had been achieved three decades before: a political compromise. What emerged from months of confusing politicking and proposals from the fall of 1849 and into 1850 about what to do with slavery in the Mexican cession was called the Compromise of 1850, but the final settlement was less a compromise than a list of distinct agreements that, save for the admission of California as a free state, decided the question of slavery in the other territories by popular sovereignty. As had those in 1776 and again in 1787, those framing this iconic political meeting of the minds deferred the question of slavery for later consideration to permit a focus on slavery in the territories, only to move cautiously on that issue.

THE YEARS FOLLOWING the war were made neither for the cautious nor, as the decade wore on, for those who believed that the political system inherited from the early republic was sufficient to reconcile the growing and increasingly more acrimonious debate over slavery, both its power and its grip on the national psyche. Democrats had expanded the national domain by one-third and elevated the common man in the political arena. National Republicans and Whigs had promoted economic development and a stronger federal government. Christianity retained its strength and role in national life. In the debates over slavery in the territories, southerners demanded enforcement of the 1850 Fugitive Slave Law. Despite apprehensions about the intimidating power of the slave states, abolitionists did not relent in their determination to continue their battle in the Upper South, where the economic vitality of slave labor continued to wane. Proslavery advocates took notice of the activities of the American Missionary Association in assisting antislavery evangelicals in the Upper South and the links between abolitionist groups and emigrant aid companies dedicated to establishing free labor colonies in Virginia and Kentucky.[51]

The effect was to reshape the debate over slavery and heighten proslavery concerns about the waning of a slave labor economy in the Upper South. Other proslavery advocates looked southward to Spanish Cuba and Brazil in charting the South's future. As industrialization, imperial competition, migration, and rapid capitalist growth transformed economies, slave-based economies from the Upper South to Cuba and Brazil adapted technology to forge a cohesive and efficient network of common interests to confront challenges. A combination of fears about the "Africanization" of labor, the belief of some Cuban slaveholders that U.S. annexation would lead to statehood, and a parallel fantasy of tropical empire would inspire a few prominent southerners to support three invasions of the island by Narciso López from 1849 to 1851. The South had a special relationship with Cuba that resonated with white slaveholders in both places—two profitable slaveholding societies where whites shared similar social and political views. Spanish Cuba as a territory would not only strengthen the "arc of slave empire" but also provide an outlet for reducing the slave and even the manumitted population. Cuba under U.S. control would preserve slave Cuba and ease the common fears of slaveholders in both societies. "A living death or tormented life is that of the Cuban and American slaveholder," wrote the black abolitionist and nationalist Manuel Dulaney. "For them there is no safety."[52] In the end, López's invasion ended ignominiously, as did the 1854 Ostend Manifesto, a recommendation of the three U.S. ministers to Spain, France, and Great Britain that if the Spanish refused to sell the island, the United States would be justified in seizing it.[53]

The European revolutions of 1848 and a devastating potato blight in Ireland combined to unleash another migratory wave of mostly young men from Ireland, Britain, and Continental Europe who arrived in the United States in a decade when momentous political and social issues were at stake. Often described in textbooks as failures, these revolutions provided a meaningful experience of participation in politics and enjoyment of civil liberties for millions of Europeans. The state intruded more into their lives at the expense of the landed nobility and its grip on the downtrodden. Their presence in the United States, unwelcome to some, would precipitate the first great anti-immigrant, anti-Catholic movement in the country. Along with the native-born, some would find their way to the gold fields of California, perhaps by the route across New Granada's Panamanian isthmus or Nicaragua, where the U.S. and British governments vied for influence, and a generation of commercial entrepreneurs, filibusters, sailors, diplomats, and even travel writers encountered people they considered inferior.[54]

Like the last colonial migration to British America, these newcomers arrived in time to be onlookers and participants in a decade-long crisis that would sorely test the power of the old political system to preserve the Union inherited from the Revolution and witness the creation of another. Lincoln, an astute politician who matured in the first and joined the second, would articulate the central issue in his iconic question of whether the country could survive half-slave and half-free. Although many of Tocqueville's observations in *Democracy in America* still resonate in our thinking, he could not have foreseen just how deeply the Mexican-American War would divide Americans. And he retained perhaps too much faith that they would instinctively reject revolution because they would see how much they could lose by the disorder every revolution brings.[55]

Tocqueville acknowledged that race and slavery and their symbiotic linkage to the Declaration of Independence, not to states' rights, lay at center stage in what the country was facing. Few who warned of a day of reckoning could be convinced that the kind of war that some said was coming or *should* come anticipated that it would be as devastating as the war that did.

CHAPTER 7

The American War and Peace

THE CIVIL WAR (1861–65) AND the years of Reconstruction, which I have extended beyond the traditional benchmark date of 1877 to the end of the nineteenth century, continues to be an ambivalent and contested era in the long American Revolution. In his first inaugural, Lincoln framed the issues in the context of the Constitution, the Union, and the rule of law. In the Emancipation Proclamation and in the Gettysburg Address, he focused on the meaning of the American Revolution and on the survival of democracy. The Union victory unambiguously settled only two issues. It invalidated the right of a state to secede and the right of one person to hold another human being in bondage. The war unleashed a slave revolt but not the vengeful, destructive uprising successive generations had feared. What was not anticipated was the latent anger of poor white males, who constituted the core of both armies, and the psychological and economic impact of the struggle on women.

The war and the postwar era changed the relationship not only between the central government and the states but also between government at every level and people, between men and women, and between black and white. What Lincoln called a "fiery ordeal" became a struggle of extraordinary interest to European governments still uncertain about the future of republican government and a test case for other hemispheric countries—especially Mexico and Canada—experiencing political struggles over issues not settled in the wars of independence.

In unparalleled ways, the war and the Radical Reconstruction that followed—often described as a time of political failure and anarchy—brought revolutionary changes in constitutional law and in the process not only defined national citizenship but also invoked federal law in the protection of the person, particularly the former slave. Both sides staked the legitimacy of their causes on the law and on scripture; both employed lawyers to buttress policies and decisions; both, as Lincoln reminded them in his second inaugural, prayed to the same God. Yet passion, fear, and appeals to honor often won out over appeals to the law. In the postwar era, as the idealism of the war withered from diminished northern commitment and southern obstruction and violence, lawyers remained committed to the ideal of equality and its power to sustain the rule of law.[1]

Prelude to Armageddon

By 1850 the republic was an impressive entity. In the fifty years since Jefferson's election, the population had doubled twice, and the country had quadrupled in size by purchase, settlement, annexation, or conquest at the expense of Indians, Britain, France, Spain, and Mexico. In the same period, the economy grew sevenfold, fueled by an industrial, commercial, and transportation revolution. Despite such impressive growth and in part because of it, the political system dominated by the Whig and Democratic Parties had begun to unravel in the debate over slavery's expansion and slavery itself.[2]

Demographic and cultural changes arising from immigration explained some of this change. From 1840 to 1860, 4.5 million immigrants came to the United States from Europe or fell under its jurisdiction when the country increased by one-third with the Treaty of Guadalupe Hidalgo. Two-thirds of these newcomers were German and Irish and predominantly Catholic. In a country experiencing another wave of evangelical fervor (including spiritualism) and reform focused on the moral debilities associated with alcoholism, inequalities of wealth, and rising discord and violence in the cities, these immigrants inspired nativist condemnation and sustained the appeal of a splinter antinativist party, the "Know Nothings," or American Party, which nominated former president Millard Fillmore as a presidential candidate in the 1856 election. Their hostility to the foreign presence in the country became a problem for the new Republican Party, which had been founded by Whigs in Michigan in 1854 in opposition to the Kansas-Nebraska Bill, which permitted the issue of slavery in that territory to be decided by popular sovereignty, effectively overturning the Missouri Compromise. For some Republicans, identifying with the Know Nothings created a dilemma. As Lincoln, a former Whig, explained, "I do not perceive how anyone professing to be sensitive to the wrongs of the negroes can join in a league to degrade white men."[3]

This was both a moral and a politically calculated statement, and the conflict between pro- and antislavery groups in Kansas would provide Lincoln yet another opportunity to demonstrate his political skills. Frustrated in their bid for statehood, the proslavers chose to settle matters by sacking the free-state stronghold of Lawrence in May 1856. As if he were God's chosen instrument of retaliation, John Brown led his four sons and several antislavers on a killing spree, which in turn led to even more bloodshed, which continued into the summer. A chase ensued for Brown, who eluded his pursuers and re-surfaced in the fall in New York, where he spoke to abolitionist sympathizers. "You know what I have done in Kansas," he reminded them. "I have no other purpose but to serve the cause of liberty."[4]

In his failed 1858 campaign to unseat Senator Stephen A. Douglas, the architect of popular sovereignty, Lincoln had to confront the explosive issue of Negro equality and popular sovereignty. In the landmark decision of *Dred Scott v. Sandford*, the Supreme Court declared that Congress had no authority to ban slavery in territories acquired after 1787 and stated that the Fifth Amendment to the Constitution prohibited the federal government from freeing slaves brought into the territories. Lincoln had already begun remaking himself from the politician who had difficulty in adjusting to the unraveling of the American Democracy after the Mexican War. His calculated political moves involved appealing not only to the Declaration of Independence and to the Constitution but also to the moral degradation of distorting the meaning of these sacred documents the framers had bequeathed to the nation. Less than two weeks after Senator Charles Sumner of Massachusetts came near death after a caning by an irate South Carolina congressman, Preston Brooks, over perceived insults to Brooks's older cousin in Sumner's "Crime against Kansas" speech (May 19, 1956), Lincoln announced the founding of the Illinois Republican Party. In his speeches, he began to go beyond the moral high ground of the pulpit in condemning the degradation of the slaveholder and assumed the view of the slave looking for freedom. Of course, he still needed "wiggle room" not to press too hard on abolition or black equality but to speak in memorable parables. Lincoln did not perceive popular sovereignty as a solution to the sectional crisis, and he voiced his fears in spiritual and moral terms in one of his most powerful public statements on the issue of slavery, its central message drawn from scripture: "A house divided against itself cannot stand."[5]

Popular sovereignty, Lincoln believed, served southern interests. Equality for the black man posed a different problem. For Douglas and many Illinois voters in the 1850s, the universal phrases about equality in the Declaration of

Independence did not apply to African Americans. Lincoln argued that it was wrong to hold that the Declaration's principles applied only to whites and on one occasion expressed his belief that the equality of black and white people should be a goal. He began to back away from that position, in part because Republican strategists believed it would cost him votes and, more likely, because he recognized the perils of taking such a stand. Pushed by Douglas on the matter, Lincoln declared that he was "not, nor ever [had] been in favor of bringing about in any way the social and political equality of the white and black races," but he did not believe that "because the white man is to have the superior position the negro should be denied anything."[6]

Among southern slave owners and industrialists there was an even more ominous concern: the weakening grip of the southern slaveholding power on the loyalty and commitment of poor whites to a society in which they had become increasingly marginalized, socially and especially economically. Unlike what Tocqueville had described in *Democracy in America*, southern white males did not believe themselves the equal of every other white man in the hierarchical society of the ruling slaveholder. In the economic downturns following the Panic of 1837, as their labor became more superfluous and land more expensive, poor whites grew more resentful. Increasingly, southern elites looked upon them as lazy and indolent, persons who would never own a slave and would always remain propertyless, surviving by taking on occasional jobs, by hunting, or by criminal activity. In the 1850s, as their conditions worsened, they became increasingly militant, taking advantage of the drain of black labor to the Gulf "inland empire," forming labor unions, and posing a threat to slavery. The reaction of slaveholders was a propaganda war of appeasement in defense of the industrial plantation economy. Poor whites, slaveholders affirmed, had much to lose with the end of slavery and the liberation of the slaves, who stood to become their new masters. In the circumstances, wrote one southern industrial leader, the only realistic choice was jobs for poor whites. That failing, he predicted, "it is this great upheaval of our masses that we have to fear, so far as our institutions are concerned."[7]

The two sections were going in different directions not only over slavery in the territories but also over the rights of *free* blacks. All but the five New England states denied free blacks the right to vote on an equal basis with whites, and New York imposed a $250 property qualification on black but not white voters. In the northern states, a free black person *was* free to move from state to state without special permission, to testify in court, to sue, to place his children in school, to own firearms, and to enter the professions. Few of these freedoms applied in the South. Indeed, in the *Dred Scott* decision, Chief Justice Roger Brooke Taney made clear a sentiment about the inferiority of peoples of African descent that reflected prevailing views in Confederate constitutional thought. "Our new government," wrote Confederate vice president Alexander H. Stephens, "is founded . . . upon the great truth that the negro is not equal to the white man; that slavery . . . is his natural and normal condition."[8]

For several generations, southern defenders of slavery had looked to the Haitian and Spanish American experiences as useful "case studies" about the dangers in extending greater rights to free blacks and colored. By the 1850s, however, a new generation of Latin American intellectuals and political leaders—most of them liberals—had come of age, and in discussions about modernity, slavery, and especially race and social conditions, they looked within the nation and not to Europe or even the United States for guidance. (Throughout Latin America, Liberal and Conservative parties sprang up after independence, often dividing on the issue of the influence of the Catholic Church.) In Brazil, liberal emperor Dom Pedro II kept order by persuading both liberal and conservative constituencies to incorporate peoples from different races and social groups. Often, poor people and even illiterates would gather in public places to listen to readings of newspapers or opinions of political leaders. Reactions to political and social change were not uniform, however. In Colombia and Venezuela, the combined impact of ending slavery, expanding the electorate, and improving the condition of the poor and colored precipitated a conservative backlash, growing racial tensions, and in Venezuela in 1858 the five-year Federal War.

In Mexico, liberals pushed through reformist laws that struck directly at the power and property of the Catholic Church and the military and were enshrined in the Constitution of 1857. When conservatives drove the moderate Mexican president from power and made the liberal Benito Juárez an interim president, the three-year War of the Reform ensued. As it raged, Mexico's powerful clerics and social conservatives plotted with foreign governments and bankers, their efforts inspired in part by a need for funds but also by the conviction that only a restored monarch could save the nation from liberal depredation.[9]

In some ways, the Cuban experience seemed more relevant for understanding the dynamics of slavery, race, and equality and their implications for the United States. White Cubans and Spaniards had put down the 1844 Escalera slave revolt and in the process weakened the island's free colored population. In the aftermath, the victors continued their persecution of the Afro-Cuban middle and upper classes, who had advanced economically but continued to experience social and political discrimination. Since the days of the early republic, white Cuban Creoles had fancied U.S. annexation, but that hope was predicated on territoriality and then statehood, the only sure way of relieving their anxieties about Spanish capabilities in defending them. In the 1850s they were beginning to express some apprehension about annexation, as Richard Henry Dana recorded in his tour of the island, largely out of "fear that the Anglo-Saxon race would swallow up the power and property of the island, as they have done in California and Texas, and that the Creoles will go to the wall."[10]

The Confederate Counterrevolution

The southern slaveholding elite held similar apprehensions about the shifting political winds in the country. On the eve of the Civil War, the South had more free colored persons than the North, and southern ideologues and political leaders harbored their own fears about preserving their status and place in the republic. By the 1850s proslavery southerners had begun to dismiss Jefferson's reliance on the Declaration of Independence and its "self-evident truths" about human equality deduced from nature. Empirical evidence and history, they believed, affirmed human inequality and, by flawed deductive reasoning, its racist corollary of Negro inferiority. Slavery sustained agriculture and a plantation system led by an educated elite born to rule and lead in public affairs. As the conservative Virginian Abel P. Upshur had confirmed when Jackson became president, "Only a few are necessary for the wise ordering of public affairs and for the safety and prosperity of the nation."[11]

Under fire, some proslavers supported expansion in the Caribbean. Frustrated in Kansas, rebuffed in their efforts to acquire Cuba, they turned their sights on Nicaragua. In 1855 a band of filibusters (or mercenaries) led by William Walker, a charismatic, well-educated Tennessean, had arrived in the country at the invitation of business enemies of Cornelius Vanderbilt, who had created a profitable transit company ferrying people headed for the gold fields of California across the isthmus, and of liberals needing Walker's help to regain power. Within a year, Walker had made an enemy of Vanderbilt and had pushed out the weak Nicaraguan president. Pierre Soulé, one of the authors of the notorious 1854 Ostend Manifesto, which called for Cuban annexation, persuaded Walker that by restoring slavery in Nicaragua he could gain U.S. recognition and that Nicaragua would perhaps become the next slave state. The "Grey-Eyed Man of Destiny" understood the perils of a Republican strategy to contain slavery. In 1857 Walker described the Nicaraguan war he provoked as a struggle for "whiteness" and implored southerners not to be "hemmed in on the South [i.e., in the Caribbean and Central America] as you already are on the North and West."[12]

Walker considered himself an inheritor of the revolutionary tradition and representative of Young America. In a recent biography, Walker and his men (most of them northerners) are portrayed as allies of those Nicaraguans fighting ruling social elites and whose efforts at nation building collapsed. The Central Americans who united to bring him down have a different view of the man, as Walker's promise of liberation and U.S.-style democracy turned into a reign of oppression. Nicaragua's liberals believed in isthmian unity, countering British influence, and making Nicaragua a modern, progressive state. Their conservative enemies managed to mobilize allies in Guatemala and Costa Rica, leaders who believed in protecting their Catholic homelands from Protestant invaders. With the help of the U.S. Navy, Walker got out of Nicaragua in 1857 and returned to the United States, where he was lionized by the public but became an irritant for the Buchanan administration. He launched his third invasion in 1860 from New Orleans, ostensibly on behalf of Bay Islanders resisting Honduran control. When the invasion collapsed, Walker surrendered to the British, who turned him over to Honduran officials, who tried and executed him. Central Americans wrote his epitaph: "God will condemn his arrogance and protect our cause."[13]

John Brown also perceived himself as a liberator, as God's warrior against slavery. In October 1859 he and twenty-one followers seized the U.S. armory in Harpers Ferry, Virginia, with the intent of launching a slave rebellion to rid the country of slavery. Brown tried but failed to enlist former slave Frederick Douglass in his cause. In the end, only five slaves joined him. After a thirty-six-hour siege, Brown surrendered, was quickly tried, and was promptly executed. His final words—an invocation of biblical justice in the cause of slave freedom—drove a wedge between the sections. Once considered a fanatic vowing to purge the land with blood, Brown in death became for many northerners a martyr in a holy cause. In the South, contrastingly, alarm and disgust over the outpouring of praise for Brown prompted calls for disunion coupled with increased vigilance over not only free blacks and slaves but also white men and women. At the turn of the twentieth century, W. E. B. Du Bois stressed Brown's advocacy of violent change as the necessary antidote to abolitionist pacifism.[14]

As the 1860 political campaigning got underway, southern rhetoric and editorial commentary became increasingly militant in slavery's defense, with accompanying warnings of what would befall the nation if the federal government fell into the grip of the "Black Republicans." In 1860 unity of place and circumstance proved more powerful than Union because the latter had lost some of its mythical qualities. Secession in the defense of slavery and property rights could be wrapped in the defiant language of the Declaration of Independence or, conversely, a hollow threat. Those abolitionists ambivalent about remaining in the Union welcomed the idea of letting the South go its own way. Republicans dismissed as nonsense southern threats of disunion, and Lincoln, the nominee, refused to issue conciliatory statements. Southern slave owners knew that secession put at risk the constitutional guarantees of their property, but if they were denied the right to take their property into the territories, then a hostile federal government would fail to enforce the fugitive slave laws, and slaves would flee to the west. Republican strategists reasoned that the South did not dare risk a war.[15]

Lincoln had a political mandate dependent on those with strong moral convictions about slavery and their symbiotic alliance with those hostile to the slave power but with ambivalent feelings about slaves and free Negroes. In a campaign notorious for its political corruption, Lincoln's sectional strength in the North (and California and Oregon) made the difference. When his political adversary, William H. Seward, warmed to a compromise proposal extending the Missouri Compromise line all the way to the Pacific, Lincoln refused to go along. On slavery's expansion there could be no compromising. Charles Francis Adams, Van Buren's running mate in 1848, a Republican representative from Massachusetts in the U.S. Congress in 1860, and a grandson of a president who had suffered defeat because of the slave power, summed up the victory in triumphalist words: "The great revolution has actually taken place. . . . The country has once and for all thrown off the domination of the slaveholder."[16]

When Lincoln took the oath of office on March 4, 1861, conventions in seven states—South Carolina, Mississippi, Florida, Alabama, Georgia, Louisiana, and Texas, in that order—had approved ordinances of secession by an average majority of 80 percent. But these reflected the views of wealthy slave-holders, who dominated the conventions. For Lincoln, secession not only was unconstitutional but meant anarchy. Secession as an exercise of the right of revolution was a different matter. The principle of "liberty" implanted in the French Revolution appealed to many secessionists; its companion beliefs in "fraternity" to fewer and "equality" to almost none. In the charged rhetoric of the secession crisis, southerners found reassurance in the debates leading up to the Declaration of Independence and the categories of charges leveled at the king and particularly at Parliament about arbitrary and unjust exercise of power from a central government. They were neither discouraged by Lincoln's inaugural warning—"In your hands . . . and not in mine is the momentous issue of civil war"—nor persuaded by his reassurance that "we are not enemies but friends."[17]

Slavery and the parallel belief in white supremacy were subsumed but undeniably relevant issues in the Revolution, at the Constitutional Convention, and in the early republic. In the heated political climate of 1860, they played a central and dynamic role in the ideological battle underlying the case for secession and the founding of the Confederate nation. Slavery became the cornerstone of southern life despite the tensions within the institution and the parallel fears of slave revolt. In the Constitution, a slave was a person; in the mind of Chief Justice Taney or Jefferson Davis, president of the Confederacy, a slave was a thing, a piece of property. Hinton Rowan Helper's contention in *The Impending Crisis of the South* that slavery doomed the region because, among other things, it permitted three hundred thousand large slaveholders to keep six million whites poor and backward withered under the unifying belief among southern whites that abolition of slavery would unleash four million blacks to claim their place as equals to poor whites. That was the revolution that menaced the social system of the South and required preemptive action—a counterrevolution. Davis put the matter bluntly: the South had seceded "to save ourselves from a revolution."[18]

The Soul of Battle

The four remaining states of the Confederacy—North Carolina, Tennessee, Arkansas, and the critical state of Virginia—did not secede until after the firing on Fort Sumter on April 12, 1861, thus providing Lincoln with a constitutional mandate to respond. The war soon drew the interest of all nations. Confederate leaders recognized early on that to prevail and to gain recognition from other governments they had to appeal to European monarchs and conservative political leaders that the cause of the South was not about the preservation of slavery but a war of independence against a mighty industrial North that sought conquest. At the same time, the Union had to dispel any notion that its purpose lay in "wholesale abolition" or in precipitating racial turmoil.

Napoleon III of France vowed to unify the "Latin race" and halt the march of Anglo-Saxon Protestant democracy in the Americas. As protector of Italian monarch Victor Emmanuel II, he had to worry about the Italian republican leader Giuseppe Garibaldi, who threatened to mobilize his legion in the cause of liberating forty-two million slaves in the Americas. In Great Britain and Continental Europe, a traditional order under assault from radicals and republicans found reassurance in the symbol of a Confederate South that understood these perils and offered an alternative to the robust, socially diverse, and more democratic republic of the North.[19]

Despite their antislave tradition, Canadians showed little sympathy for their republican neighbors. There was an opportunistic feeling among some Canadians, including the conservative Sir John A. Macdonald of Upper Canada (modern Ontario), who would become Canada's first prime minister in 1867, that the failure of republican government was at hand, thus offering an opportunity to create a great North American nation—in Canada. Others were more fearful that a militarized republic posed a threat, and one contemporary observer warned that the "people of Canada should sleep no more, except on their arms, unless in their sleep they desire to be overtaken and subjugated."[20]

To make matters worse, the Benito Juárez government in Mexico, overwhelmed by debt after reclaiming power in January 1861 and unable to obtain moneys from the United States, announced a two-year moratorium on its international obligations. In late October, the British, French, and Spanish governments signed a tripartite agreement to intervene, and in early December the European forces landed in Veracruz. Juárez called for resistance, but his conservative enemies were already plotting with the French to push on into the interior. The British and Spanish withdrew, and the Spanish consoled themselves by occupying the Dominican Republic at the invitation of President Pedro Santana. The French pushed on. In May 1862 a ragtag Mexican force defeated the French invaders at Puebla, but the loss only galvanized Napoleon III's determination to revenge the loss. In 1864 he installed a Hapsburg prince, Maximilian, archduke of Austria, on the Mexican throne as Emperor Maximilian I. For three more years, Juárez and his makeshift government survived by fighting a guerrilla war and desperately hoping for a Union victory. Emboldened, Secretary of State Seward recommended that Lincoln adopt a more aggressive policy against the European threat in the hemisphere and seize Santo Domingo. Lincoln did not reply.[21]

By then the administration had weathered another crisis. In late 1861 southern leaders were heartened when they learned about the stern British response to an unauthorized and illegal seizure of two southern agents, James Mason and John Slidell, and their secretaries from a British mail steamer, the *Trent*, by Captain Charles Wilkes of the U.S. steamer *San Jacinto*. The incident precipitated a war scare fueled by congressional firebrands calling for the invasion of Canada. Its weak defense of only 5,000 regulars prompted the British to send another 11,550 troops to the Maritime Provinces and from there to Lower Canada and, if necessary, to call on the 100,000-man Canadian militia for a defense of the line from the Great Lakes to the Saint Lawrence River. The Royal Navy considered a preemptive strike against Maine and bombardment of coastal cities from Boston to Long Island. Some in Congress and even in Lincoln's cabinet called for war but were silenced by reminders that such an act meant they could not defeat the rebellion. British sympathy for the South remained, and British supplies of rifles, saltpeter, and lead proved crucial to the Confederate army. The British considered themselves blameless in the *Trent* Affair, but Union Brigadier General George Meade expressed northern anger in a letter to his wife: "If ever this domestic war of ours is settled, it will require but the slightest pretext to bring about a war with England."[22]

Public sentiment in the North about the war indicated something stronger than a determination to deny state secession, yet Lincoln hesitated in going much beyond the reasoning of his inaugural. In a succession of battles, Union troops had not fared well. Despite the logic of "King Cotton diplomacy," the Confederacy had failed to gain recognition from any European government (the notable failure was Great Britain), but Britain and seven other governments had acknowledged that the South was entitled to belligerent rights. Frustrated southern diplomats turned their attention to promoting their cause with Napoleon III and the pope, both fearful of a radical republican tide in the Atlantic world. Yet despite the French adoration of Confederate envoy John Slidell and Jefferson Davis's publicity campaign to promote the South as a Latin compatriot, the effort failed to bring about recognition. The Confederacy was a nation—indeed, the first created out of the American Revolution and War of Independence—but it was not going to be accepted into the community of nations. The Confederacy's leaders confronted a wartime dilemma: how to reconcile their antebellum beliefs in evangelism's rationale of hierarchy and control with the egalitarian and humanitarian ideals of Christianity and mobilize the people with appeals to unity and nation. In the war, Drew Faust writes, the Old South caught a glimpse of the New, revealing the promise and paradoxes of change the Confederate cause was determined to prevent.[23]

Both Lincoln and Davis expressed surprise at the militant spirit exhibited by ordinary people. Undeniably, the identification of the southern cause with slavery damaged the Confederate appeal among some Europeans, but Lincoln's reluctance to move more forthrightly on the issue struck some liberals at home and abroad as a sign that the North had a military but not a moral mission in the struggle. Horace Greeley, editor of the influential *New York Daily Tribune*, addressed the matter in an August 1862 letter—the "prayer of twenty millions"—to Lincoln. Greeley objected particularly to the practice of some Union generals who refused to enforce a confiscation law granting freedom to slaves who surrendered to Union armies. In his cautious reply, Lincoln wrote, "My paramount object in this struggle is to save the Union, and it is not either to save or to destroy slavery."[24]

Such a disingenuous acknowledgment had the effect of satisfying the differing views prevailing among contemporaries, but it reinforces modern beliefs that the abolition of slavery was secondary to Lincoln's intentions. On the contrary, his opposition to slavery was deeply felt, but he was a politically astute strategist. Greeley had pleaded for a moral statement about the war's purpose; Lincoln had responded in the words of a political leader and wartime commander. For him, the infuriatingly complicated issues surrounding the war—slavery, race, union, democracy—were knotted together. When Greeley's letter appeared, Lincoln had already decided to issue a statement that would evolve by year's end into the Emancipation Proclamation, a declaration that *in time* profoundly changed the meaning of the war and served as a reminder of the revolutionary promises of liberty, freedom, and equality. Despite the lack of any reference to slavery or emancipation-related directives in the Prussian-born American lawyer Francis Lieber's 1863 "Instructions for the Government of Armies of the United States in the Field," a guide to proper conduct for Union armies, Lincoln remained adamant about the elimination of slavery as central to wartime policy, as he made clear to the South toward the end of the war.[25]

The Preliminary Emancipation Proclamation, issued a month after Greeley's letter and a week after the grisly Battle of Antietam in Maryland on September 17, 1862—six thousand killed and seventeen thousand wounded—was a wartime measure from Lincoln the commander in chief and a president apprehensive about legal challenges, particularly to a Supreme Court still presided over by Roger Brooke Taney. Lincoln needed more soldiers, and the border slave states (Maryland, Delaware, Kentucky, and Missouri) needed reassurance of their exclusion from the proclamation's provisions. Lincoln had failed in his appeal to the governors of these states to accept his proposal of compensated emancipation. (Slave owners in the District of Columbia had participated in such a plan.) Five days after the battle and the departure of Confederate troops out of Maryland, Lincoln called his cabinet together and told the group that victory at Antietam represented the will of God, who "had decided this question in favor of the slaves" and of emancipation. He intended to warn the rebellious states that if by January they had not returned to the Union, he would declare their slaves emancipated. The proclamation incensed Democrats (notably General George B. McClellan, whose friends urged him to seize power with a military takeover) and southern whites. The *Times* of London denounced Lincoln for rousing "the black blood of the African."[26]

Lincoln removed McClellan from command in November. There was no military coup, as McClellan retired gracefully, and Lincoln continued to pursue plans for the colonization of freed slaves in Central America or Colombia, although he was already confronted with the anomaly of dealing with the contradiction of black slaves willing to fight for their freedom only to be told they should emigrate from the country. In his December 1, 1862, annual message, he proposed gradual (thirty-seven years) and compensated emancipation paid for by bonds issued to the states. By his reckoning, it was both practical and moral, and it was far more economical than the cost of the war. He presumed that many of those liberated blacks who did not emigrate would remain in the South and receive wages for their labors. Slave states could decide at what pace they would proceed with emancipation. At the same time, he warned that the war would go on and that the September Preliminary Emancipation Proclamation would become effective on January 1.[27]

Although the limits of the Emancipation Proclamation of January 1, 1863, displeased some dedicated abolitionists, its impact was far-reaching. It excluded the border states, where the president had no power to enforce it, and applied principally to those areas in the South that had to be subdued for its enforcement. In Union-controlled areas in the South, however, fifty thousand slaves did gain their freedom. On the Continent and in Great Britain, conservatives had mocked Lincoln's words, and the liberal chancellor of the exchequer, William Gladstone, warned of the dangers inherent in mobilizing the African. Yet the outpouring of popular support among the British, particularly from the London Emancipation Society and its branches and from Baptist ministers, indicated British awareness that by a stroke of the pen, Lincoln had altered the meaning of the war. Freedom now followed the flag, and the powerful nation-state had embraced the cause of liberty. As Karl Marx observed, "Up to now, we have witnessed only the first act of the Civil War—the constitutional waging of war. The second act, the revolutionary waging of war, is at hand."[28]

In the border slave states, Maryland, Delaware, West Virginia (admitted to statehood in June 1863), Missouri, and Kentucky, the course of the war was not so much revolutionary as taking a calculated political risk. The loss of the Border South undeniably hurt the Confederate cause, but the traditional argument that a southern victory in the Battle of Gettysburg in early July 1863 might have prompted these states to secede underestimates the real concerns of people in the region. Despite their almost visceral hatred of emancipation and even Lincoln, white people in these states were persuaded that they stood a better chance of preserving slavery and white supremacy by remaining in the Union and having federal protection. In the wartime western theater (Kentucky, Missouri, and the southern halves of Ohio, Indiana, and Illinois), a region that experienced shared migration patterns from the mid-Atlantic states and exhibited common racial antipathies and views about slavery, Lincoln's election and the parallel secession crisis probably weakened Republican support. The experience of war, particularly the suppression of dissent and military occupation, sharpened the divide among peoples living on opposite sides of the Ohio. North of the river, slavery equated with disunion, and at the end of the war veterans and civic leaders expressed little interest in intersectional reconciliation. In Saint Louis, slave and free African American women used the provost marshal's office in a variety of ways to improve their lives and protect themselves from abuse from their masters.[29]

What occurred over the next twenty-six months was a people's war that sometimes ill-fitted the traditional Marxian analysis of class struggle, if for no other reason than because both sides persistently invoked God's blessing on their respective causes. Southern ideology inscribed in the Confederate Constitution had proclaimed the institution of slavery and white supremacy as the cornerstone of a civilization ruled by a master class that stood in stark contrast to the North, the Caribbean, and mainland Latin America. In the early months of 1863, Confederate agents fanned out into the border slave states, warning that the emancipation of the slaves would unleash a blood-letting comparable to what had happened in Haiti and replace "God's truth of racial slavery" with the false doctrines of egalitarianism and racial equality. The Emancipation Proclamation enabled Lincoln to speak over the heads of British and French leaders to their people. Quite likely, it may have persuaded the British that they were correct in not intervening, but it may also have encouraged the reckless Napoleon III to pursue his Mexican venture.[30]

But the shifting fortunes in the war eroded southern notions about the utility of trying to sustain slavery and prompted Confederate leaders to accept the arming of slaves in defense of the cause. While Union losses in battle mounted and significant pockets of northern opposition to the war persisted—antiwar and anti-Negro sentiment was particularly strong in New York City—the Emancipation Proclamation had the effect of transforming the Union army into a powerful liberating force. In July 1863 came the Confederate setbacks at Gettysburg and Vicksburg. In November Lincoln used the occasion of the dedication of the battlefield cemetery at Gettysburg to proclaim the universality of the war's purpose in a brief but stirring address: "This nation, under God, shall have a new birth of freedom, and that government of the people, by the people, for the people, shall not perish from the earth."[31]

In this terse but powerful address, Lincoln made no mention of saving the Union, nor did he speak about slavery or democracy, but each sentiment was implied in his words and intent. His fusion of nationalism and equality was more problematical, because for women, people of color, and immigrants, equality presumed inclusivity in the civic order, but those who defined the nation in racial or ethnic measures could twist his words into a justification for limiting the basic rights of citizenship to immigrants or those considered inferior or backward. For political as well as moral reasons, Lincoln had opposed the anti-immigrant political movements of the day.

One of the officers at Gettysburg, Carl Schurz, who became a successful immigrant politician, had reminded Lincoln of the large numbers of immigrant troops—a quarter of the 2.2 million soldiers in the Union army, including 190,000 Germans and 144,000 Irish, and more than 40 percent of the Union navy. Union agents in Europe invoked the Homestead Act as a recruiting tool. Certainly, the president considered these immigrant soldiers deserving of the equal rights enjoyed by others, yet his vagueness about the granting of those rights struck some as ominous for the future of the republic, implying that immigrants, like free colored people and women, would be marginal players in the country's future.[32]

Lincoln had not yet fully resolved how to deal with the place of the liberated slave in the postwar republic. The utility of the African American as soldier had already been established, and the initial skepticism of white officers about African Americans' capability and commitment diminished after several key battles, notably the assault on Fort Wagner off Charleston by the Fifty-Fourth Massachusetts Infantry on July 18, 1863. The valor of the troops in this losing battle sparked recruitment among blacks in the Union army. By the end of the war their numbers in uniform had reached 180,000. Lincoln praised their contribution to the war, and northern feelings toward African Americans improved. Acceptance of black equality was a different matter. Despite the intensity of feelings among Union soldiers about slavery and the Union and Lincoln's acknowledgment of the impracticability of colonization, white nationalism remained a reality. Its explicit endorsement came in the 1862 House report by the Select Committee on Emancipation and Colonization: "The highest interests of the white race" call for the possession of "every acre of our present domain."[33]

In defiant response, black abolitionists and soldiers sometimes invoked the Haitian cause, but the egalitarian phrases of the Declaration of Independence and the promise of the Emancipation Proclamation proved far more powerful. Despite the harsh and brutal treatment of captured black soldiers by Confederate forces, black Union soldiers did not retaliate in kind, as had happened in the savage final years of the Haitian upheaval. Both French Saint-Domingue and the South in the Civil War years experienced slave rebellion inspired by political and social conflict between powerful groups in a society dominated by whites. Further, in both societies free people of color would play a part in setting postwar goals; in both, slaves disrupted plantation life and order either by flight or by demands; in both, a rebellion brought on a political as well as a social revolution, the military defeat of slaveholders, the abolition of slavery, and the creation of a political order greatly different from its predecessor. In both, slave and free colored agency proved to be critical in the outcome of the struggle; and in both, those who wielded power in the aftermath of the fighting had to confront often corrosive racial hatreds and fears. When the Union government authorized the creation of black regiments, some northern newspapers interpreted the move as a way for whites to avoid the draft or as a way to give the president more power. A former slave who had become a mariner, James Henry Gooding, recognized a higher purpose in the decision. The end of slavery, he wrote, depended not only on white men fighting and dying but also on the willingness of black soldiers to die as well in order to avoid the "indignity, the scorn, and perhaps violence, that will be heaped on [them]" if they did not.[34]

Haiti remained a powerful psychological reference in discussions among southerners about the coming and course of the war. At the same time, Republican proponents of Haitian recognition, which finally came in 1862, argued that Haiti could be a valuable ally in resisting European imperial ambitions in the hemisphere, as well as a home for freedmen who could help to civilize the black nation. Theodore Holly, an Episcopalian minister skeptical about the future of African Americans in the United States, believed that their Protestant faith and agricultural skills could profoundly alter Haiti's Afro-Latin culture. Others pointed to Dominican president Pedro Santana's encouragement of Spanish reoccupation of the republic in 1861—undertaken with Queen Isabella II's insistence that Santana maintain "racial purity"—as something that might very well have been prevented had Haitian recognition come earlier. Spanish discrimination against Dominicans brought on a guerrilla war in 1863.[35]

For contemporaries, particularly northerners, perhaps the most nagging issue surrounding emancipation and the mobilization of black soldiers had to do not only with fears about their behavior in wartime but also with the unsettling prospect of a vast influx of freedmen into the North. Although black soldiers fought ferociously, they did so as soldiers rather than as avenging warriors bent on destruction of the slave society and as free men deserving of the full rights of persons and citizens. Their restraint persuaded contemporaries, as well as several generations of historians, that there was no slave revolt during the war. As W. E. B. Du Bois's classic 1935 study, *Black Reconstruction in America, 1860–1880*, documented, southern slaves waited until they were certain the invading Union armies would not return them to servitude before they began deserting the plantations and joining the cause. The behavior of white soldiers on both sides became a matter of concern, and there was no single definition of "manliness" for the Confederate or Union soldier. Southern notions of manhood reflected more so the hierarchical values identified with a slave society and dueling, but even in Union ranks a sense of honor depended on one's public reputation and respect. Ordinary Union soldiers sometimes behaved violently, and their officers knew how to use brute force to keep the "lesser sorts" and "roughs" in line.[36]

Slave agency in the U.S. Civil War, although not as crucial to the outcome as in the Haitian and Spanish American wars of independence, did alter northern and even southern thinking about the country's racial future. One reason for the failure of colonizing schemes lay in the political decision made by the Lincoln administration to keep the freedmen in the South and out of the Midwest, which experienced a severe labor shortage during the war. Such a policy was, undeniably, a form of racial containment, but it helped to ease northern anxieties about the freedmen. Orestes A. Brownson, a conservative publicist who had accepted emancipation but had once favored colonization, acknowledged that a black soldier should be permitted to live in a country he was willing to fight for. As Union troops penetrated ever deeper into Confederate territory, black soldiers departed from the tradition of their white comrades by celebrating the Fourth of July with reaffirmations of their faith in God and the Declaration of Independence. Treatment of white and black soldiers in captivity differed. When Confederate soldiers violated the rules of war by killing white Union captives, there was reprisal, but despite the pleas of Frederick Douglass, after the killing of three hundred soldiers, most of whom were black, who had surrendered with the fall of Fort Pillow (forty miles north of Memphis) in April 1864, Lincoln gave no order to retaliate, telling Douglass, "Once begun, I do not know where such measures would stop."[37]

The last realistic opportunity for the Confederacy to reverse the course of the war came in the spring of 1864, when Grant's Overland Campaign against Lee's army in Virginia resulted in such heavy causes to both sides that some northern editorialists called for peace negotiations. In June came heartening news when the Hapsburg Ferdinand Maximilian Joseph Maria was crowned emperor of Mexico with the blessing of the country's conservatives and the military support of a French army that pushed Juárez's government as far north as the border, across the river from El Paso in the city that bears his name. The Confederacy did obtain European arms and munitions via that area of the Mexican North controlled by Juárez's political enemy, Santiago Vidaurri. But the Juaristas obtained Union financial aid, military assistance, and soldiers of fortune. In these years, U.S. investors commenced to invest in communications, mining, petroleum, and agriculture and thus laid the foundation for the rapid rise of the U.S. presence in Mexico after the war.[38]

The most devastating blow to the already weakened South came in the late fall of 1864 in the aftermath of the fall of Atlanta in September. Lincoln personally achieved an unexpected victory in the presidential election (212 to 21 electoral votes) two months later over former general George B. McClellan. Democrats had nominated the former general with the belief he would negotiate a peace. A soldier by training and instinct, McClellan scrapped the peace platform and vowed to fight the war more efficiently than Lincoln. Correctly sensing what was at stake, Lincoln dropped his popular vice president, Hannibal Hamlin, from the ticket and selected a war Democrat from Tennessee, Andrew Johnson, as his running mate in the hopes of wooing Democratic voters. In the end, what made the difference was the support Lincoln received from those soldiers who voted. Their commitment to the Emancipation Proclamation may have been doubtful, yet they became a liberating army.[39]

The victory required reaffirmation on the battlefield, a campaign without the high numbers of wounded and killed that had numbed the moral sensibilities of both northerners and southerners and changed the way ordinary people looked at death. In Major General William Tecumseh Sherman, the Union cause had the perfect commander to wage a different kind of war. Two weeks after the election, Sherman led an army of sixty-two thousand men in the forty-two-day "March to the Sea" from Atlanta to Savannah in a campaign of liberation and destruction. A man of reputedly volatile temperament, Sherman pledged to destroy southern morale and had at his service officers and soldiers made up of roughhewn midwesterners with an instinctive hatred for a society of plantation lords and serfs. Grant's troops killed men in battle. Sherman's troops liberated slaves; burned and destroyed farms, railroads, crops, and plantations; and, though ordered not to do so, sometimes plundered. In Georgia and elsewhere in the South, slaves helped escaping Union prisoners find their way to Union armies, further weakening the institution of slavery, as well as the morale of southern civilians.[40]

After the fall of Savannah, this army of liberation invaded South Carolina, whose defiant leaders had begun the war five years before. There, Sherman's reputation for tough discipline failed to prevent his troops from burning Columbia. In Virginia the battles between Grant's and Lee's armies were about killing; Sherman's devastating march through Georgia and into South Carolina and the accompanying Confederate retreat were about bringing down an entire society, destroying its will to fight, and demonstrating that white soldiers, not "black savages," were the ones culpable for the mindless destruction. In justifying the destructive behavior of his soldiers, Sherman invoked the Roman concept of usufruct. By his reasoning, southern planters were federal "tenants" whose treasonous behavior justified seizure of their land and slaves.[41]

Southerners were already exhausted by the experience of war when Sherman's army swept through Georgia. In the spring of 1862, when it became apparent that hortatory appeals to honor in the face of northern aggression or the presumed economic logic of "King Cotton" would not be sufficient to sustain public morale, Confederate leaders consciously began to promote industrial expansion and national organization over states' rights, agriculture, and decentralization. In the next two years, when the Union effort appeared to falter, the traditional slaveholder aristocracy confronted the challenge of proving its leadership not only in governance but also on the battlefield. The two warring sections began to resemble one another in their affirmation of a nationalist spirit and their creation of a centralized state in the cause of the struggle: higher taxes, draft laws, impressment, suspension of habeas corpus laws, and unprecedented intrusion into the lives of individuals. Ironically, despite their social and economic condition in the antebellum South, many poor whites supported what they fervently believed was a slaveholders' war. They had denounced secession as a conspiracy, but once the war began they took up arms to protect their families and their honor.[42]

In the victorious North, the transformation had a more dramatic and lasting impact: the creation of a national banking act, the Homestead Act, land-grant universities, and a pension system, as well as the authorization for a transcontinental railroad. Perhaps the most consequential commonality of the wartime experience lay in the human toll of the war—now estimated at 750,000, more than all the combined wars of the nation's history from the Revolution to Korea—which exerted a traumatic impact on the way ordinary people looked at death, social relationships, and community. Anti-Jacobin rhetoric and French revolutionary imagery provided powerful tropes to both sides in the war, particularly in the North, where once deeply pacifist abolitionists heeded the call for violence to destroy the evil of slavery and accepted the loss of life as a fair price to pay. This was the militarization of the long American Revolution. As some Christian leaders professed, the nation found a new "civil religion" and sense of a "messianic destiny" in the war's legacy.[43]

Despite these sweeping changes, there remained uncertainties that ending slavery would not be sufficient to sustain the "new birth of freedom" Lincoln alluded to at Gettysburg. Lincoln spoke to these issues as the political man and wartime commander committed to the abolition of slavery, the restoration of the Union, and the means to achieve both. In commenting on Jefferson Davis's call for negotiation with a plan to end slavery but with the South's departure from the Union, Lincoln was terse and direct in his denial of such an approach, but he coupled it with the alternative proposal of an appeal to the southern people to organize loyal state governments that would demonstrate their commitment to the Union by approving the proposed Thirteenth Amendment, which abolished slavery. His remarks during his last public address of April 11, 1865, spoke to the problem of dealing with "disorganized and discordant elements" in the South and the need to restore "the proper practical relations between those States" without belaboring the issue of status in the Union. Noting that in Louisiana twelve thousand voters had professed allegiance to the Union and committed to a free-state constitution, schools open to black and white, and suffrage for voters of both races, Lincoln said, "If we reject, and spurn them, we . . . in effect say to the white men, 'You are worthless' and to the blacks, we say 'This cup of liberty which these, your old masters, hold to your lips, we will dash from you.'" John Wilkes Booth was in the audience at that address. According to an oft-repeated story, he was overheard to say, "That is the last speech he will make."[44]

In his brief second inaugural on March 4, Lincoln had offered a different view about the meaning of the war. Its biblical allusions reminded Frederick Douglass of a sermon, and the editor of the *Spectator*, published in London, called it "sacred" and "prophetic." Lincoln used the occasion to remind his listeners of the spiritual bonds between North and South and their prayer that "his mighty scourge of war may speedily pass away." In words that evoked a New Testament forgiveness, he concluded with an appeal for "malice toward none" and "charity for all" and for a "just and lasting peace." Those reassuring phrases came after a warning that John Brown himself could have written: "Yet, if God wills that it continue, until all the wealth piled up by the bond-man's two hundred and fifty years of unrequited toil shall be sunk, and until every drop of blood drawn with the lash, shall be paid by another drawn with the sword, as was said three thousand years ago, so still it must be said, 'the judgments of the Lord are true and righteous altogether.'"[45]

Prominent northern theologians interpreted the Union victory as God's will, thus validating their belief that the United States was truly divine and had a unique destiny and that the American people were his chosen instrument for leading humans to perfection. Privately if not in his public professions, Lincoln came to an obverse judgment about the war: its horrors and savagery made doubtful the country's claim to an exceptional destiny. His words offered hope to those searching for a meaning in a war that the world had been watching. He understood the transformative power of struggle and that the nation must remake itself by adopting new models of citizenship and equality. "The dogmas of the quiet past," he had reminded Congress in December 1862, "are inadequate to the stormy present. . . . In *giving* freedom to the *slave*, we *assure* freedom to the *free*. . . . We shall nobly save, or meanly lose, the last best hope of earth."[46]

Revolutions may not be transformative, but a war can be. A nagging question remained: Would successive generations of white Americans imbued with the belief that their freedom depended on the enslavement of others accept Lincoln's reasoning about what freedom for the slave would mean? Probably not. Few contemporary theologians (among them Henry Ward Beecher, the Billy Graham of his day) could match Lincoln's profundity (or his ambiguity) about the war. Early in the war he wrote in "Moderation on the Divine Will" that "God's purpose is something different" and "He could give the final victory to either side any day." In the religious as in the social sphere, as Lincoln sensed and Frederick Douglass knew, few in the North would defend slavery even from biblical exegesis save for the intertwining of the institution with race.[47]

The magnanimity of Lincoln's words in his second inaugural appeals to our modern consciences. Some contemporaries and most of his cabinet were befuddled by his affirmation of divine will rather than the legal achievement of the rule of law as embodied in the Thirteenth Amendment. Lincoln was probably thinking about a more peaceful route to reconciliation of both sides. Preserving the republic and guaranteeing the freedom promised to the slaves required the use of power to advance positive liberty, a striking contrast to the negative liberty and its denial of government interference that slaveholders had invoked to justify their enslavement of other people. The militant rhetoric may strike us as unbefitting for what Lincoln had in mind, but it reflected the emancipatory spirit of the day and what more prudent observers believed was necessary in the face of persistent southern behavior.

One problem was the election of some former Confederate officials and military officers to office and the parallel enactment of "Black Codes" to control the activities and movements of former slaves. A second issue was the militancy of African Americans in their demands for land, civil rights, and the vote as President Johnson systematically began returning lands seized by some Union military officers to their former owners.

Despite these setbacks, there remained hope for a new day. With the wartime Homestead Act and the 1866 Southern Homestead Act, which opened 46 million acres of public lands in five southern states, both freedmen (and, after 1867, former Confederate soldiers) could realize what was called a "dual emancipation," thus validating Lincoln's prophecy that the liberation of the slave would mean the liberation of the poor southern white as well. Poor whites did improve their lot in the postwar years: they could now compete more effectively in the labor market, their social standing improved, and they could leave the South and find land and presumably a better life in the West.

As if to validate Marx's prediction about the meaning of the war, some postwar analyses framed it as a class struggle between the people and a slave aristocracy. On the eve of the war, Johnson had expressed similar sentiments. In 1865, when the First International, or International Working Men's Association, was founded for the purpose of altering the relationship between labor and industry, Marx remained convinced that the struggle for African American emancipation would continue. He incorporated his views about the meaning of the Civil War as he wrote his iconic *Capital*.[48]

THE DREAM NEVER worked out, neither for the former slave nor for the poor white. Like the poor white Virginians who incurred Abigail Adams's criticism in 1776, those of the postwar South resisted forming a common cause with the freedmen and joined in the war against them. In the escalating violence by whites against blacks—murders, whippings, and the burning of schools and churches—President Johnson began to ally himself with a planter class he had once detested and by implication accepted their apparent condoning of such action. This atmosphere of violence and growing southern white intransigence to accept the new order of affairs threw the country into a postwar crisis about unsettled questions, including the need for new laws to shield the freedmen and perhaps the equally vexing problem of dealing with an insurgency by southern whites.[49]

Generations of Americans from the Revolution to the Civil War had attributed their liberties to the barriers and restraints placed by states on the excess of power by a federal government. Southerners had justified slavery and secession by invoking negative liberty, but during the war many in the North began to look at these justifications as treason and anarchy and the Union army as the vindicators of the cause of freedom. Of the first twelve amendments to the Constitution, eleven limited the power of the federal government; six of the first seven passed after the Civil War expanded that power. Three of these—the Thirteenth, Fourteenth, and Fifteenth—constituted the legal underpinnings of what came to be known as Radical Reconstruction and were aimed directly at the power of the rebellious South. As then congressman James A. Garfield affirmed in 1867, "We must lay the heavy hand of military authority upon these rebel communities, and ... plant liberty on the ruins of slavery."[50]

His words bespoke a different future from the one Lincoln had called for in his second inaugural address. The long American Revolution had not run its course, and the United States had not become a nation.

CHAPTER 8

The End of the Long
American Revolution

IN LESS THAN A DECADE after Congressman Garfield's call in 1867 to "lay the heavy hand of the military" on defiant southerners, the commitment to equality for the freedman began to weaken. By the end of the century it would collapse in the harsh racial climate of Jim and Jane Crow America. The racism manifested in the violence against African Americans found expression and even validation from legislation in state laws and pseudoscientific studies of racial hierarchy to cultural exhibitions such as the "Great White City" at the 1893 World's Columbian Exposition in Chicago.

In the last quarter of the nineteenth century, the country experienced unparalleled economic and industrial growth, the nurturing of a middle-class society, and the building of a modern business and corporate bureaucracy. As if to confirm Marxian predictions for a capitalist economy, these accomplishments came at the expense of two major depressions, labor strife, Indian wars, a farmers' revolt that fueled a political movement (the Populist Party), and a pessimism that pacification and expansion rather than enforced reforms might be the answer to achieving national unity. The brief war with Spain in 1898 and the insular empire that followed exacerbated rather than resolved domestic social and political tensions.

In the first two decades of the twentieth century, the Progressive movement sought to address the challenge posed by corporate and industrial power through political, economic, and social reforms that could be achieved without the violence and extreme economic solutions the middle class identified with Populism. In their endeavors, the Progressives reconfigured the revolutionary agendas of the Founders and of Lincoln. They largely accepted the imperial role undertaken by the country after the war with Spain, found a following in both major parties, and with ex-president Theodore Roosevelt as candidate, launched their own party. By 1914, when Europe collapsed in a war that would destroy a generation's faith in progress, the industrial might of the United States exceeded that of three European industrial powers—Great Britain, France, and Germany—yet none of the three accepted the United States as a great power by European standards.

That would change with U.S. entry into the Great War of 1914–18 and the efforts of President Woodrow Wilson to use the power and example of the United States to make the world "safe for democracy" and create an international organization, the League of Nations, to prevent another world war. The failure of the United States to join the league in 1919 is often cited as critical for the course of world history over the next three decades. The Great War, not the Civil War, gave birth to the nation.

Race, Reconstruction, and Nation

That nation was not the one Lincoln had conceived nor what a militant group of congressional Republicans believed possible after his death. In their political battles with President Andrew Johnson, they resolved to fulfill the war's emancipatory commitment and at the same time pacify the defeated. In the reformist impulses of what became known as Radical Reconstruction, the freedman acquired a status and legal recognition in defiance of the racial practices and discriminatory laws of Jacksonian America.[1]

In that spirit, the Republican majority instituted a new round of loyalty oaths that disenfranchised southern white leaders and led to what southerners called "Black Republican" rule. Their battle with a recalcitrant Johnson ended with his impeachment in the House but no conviction in the Senate. For the most dedicated Republican leaders, the fulfillment of the revolutionary aspiration of equality defined in the Declaration of Independence and presumably validated as a promise by the war lay at the center of this crisis. This commitment to the freedman and the parallel hostility to Johnson explained their insistence that Congress must move beyond the Thirteenth Amendment, which abolished slavery, to guarantee *national* citizenship and equal protection of the law for persons born or naturalized in the United States (the future Fourteenth Amendment, ratified in 1868) and African American men's right to vote (the future Fifteenth Amendment, ratified in 1870).

Collectively, these three amendments constituted striking departures from the vision of the Founders and a challenge to seventy years of racial discrimination, limited federal power, and the ingrained faith in local autonomy. There were limits to this break with the past. Despite their entry into the workforce and critical role in the war effort, women gained little from the Fourteenth and Fifteenth Amendments. Women suffered a setback, as the benefits of the Fourteenth Amendment effectively narrowed the identity of the political community to male family members. Indirectly, some women's antislavery activists were to blame, as some in their numbers believed that linking women's voting rights to their cause would jeopardize black enfranchisement. Asian immigrants in the western states did not gain citizenship, but their children born in the United States did. Much depended, of course, on the willingness of the states to accept the laws and the parallel commitment of federal enforcement. Compared with the postemancipation laws and practices elsewhere in the Americas, these amendments were more progressive.[2]

In some respects, the Fifteenth Amendment proved as controversial as the Fourteenth. Before 1866 few in the North favored citizenship for the freedman, some for frankly racist beliefs, and still others perceived a fundamental difference between the right to own property or be treated equally in the courts and the right to vote. After the rejection of Presidential Reconstruction and the creation of Republican regimes in the South, party leaders recognized the need to sustain them against a rising Democratic electorate. Southern white males had an easier path to regaining suffrage. The issue was complicated by the numbers of women, free blacks, and Indians making their appeal to voting rights on the grounds of loyalty to the Union and in the spirit of the Declaration of Independence rather than using the historic measure of "active citizenship."

Frederick Douglass and the members of the Equal Rights Association, who favored suffrage for blacks and women, failed in their efforts to make the Fifteenth Amendment a truly national document. In the early 1870s a generation of southern "Redeemers" (political leaders who opposed Reconstruction and curried white voters, thus "redeeming" southern rights) acquired greater influence in southern politics, and the combination of economic depression and a Democratic majority in Congress served to weaken the North's commitment to protect the freedman. As Congressman Garfield remarked, "The Fifteenth Amendment cast upon the African race the care of its own destiny."[3]

The tragic implication of his words meant that the freedman in the South could not rely on federal enforcement of his right to vote. Even as Garfield spoke, white vigilantes continued to murder and terrorize blacks and intimidate their white allies. The support given to supporting the freedmen had rapidly withered. In his inaugural address of March 4, 1869, President Ulysses S. Grant pledged the "security of person, property, and free religious and political opinion in every part of our common country." Responding to the urgent pleas of southern governors, Grant declared a virtual war against the vigilantes and the Ku Klux Klan and finally succeeded in smashing it by 1872. Despite obstacles, in the first year after Appomattox the Freedmen's Bureau built 975 schools with fourteen hundred teachers educating ninety thousand students in fifteen southern states. By 1880, three years after President Rutherford B. Hayes pledged that federal troops would no longer interfere in local political disputes, 20 percent of southern black farmers owned land. And in small but significant ways, former slaves continued to hold office and play a role in the civic life of the South.[4]

A traditional view identifies the undermining of Reconstruction legislation as representative of a latent racist element running throughout the history of the republic from independence to the Civil War and beyond despite the intensity of growing hostility toward slavery. Laura F. Edwards, a legal and constitutional historian, points to another, more pertinent way of looking at the Civil War and Reconstruction—as a struggle in which both Union and Confederate leaders had to deal with the legal consequences of ending slavery and coming up with a different legal system to deal with such thorny issues as citizenship, legal authority, and especially the role of government in guaranteeing fundamental rights of citizens and persons. What occurred in the late nineteenth century, according to Edwards, was a focus on individual rights mandated by the Reconstruction Amendments that lamentably distracted the courts and political leaders from what she believes was the public's desire for a more active role for government and the legal system to assure human rights and economic justice. Such a course "disaggregated the American people into a nation of individuals, each one connected to the federal government through his or her own rights," which resulted in a "legal order at odds . . . [with] the aspirations of so many Americans."[5]

Over the next quarter century, the road to reunion would be pockmarked by persistent strife and localized violence, and the brief postwar interlude of reconciliation between North and South and even black and white would deteriorate. The promise of liberty, equality, inclusivity, and racial uplift withered in the making of a white republic and changing views among liberals about African Americans. The Liberal Republican Party, a splinter group that formed in 1872, drew on such sentiments. After the Prussian victory over France in 1871 and the creation of a unified German state, German immigrants who had once espoused liberal beliefs of cultural pluralism and antislavery became noticeably more dismissive of the capabilities of the former slaves to meet the qualifications of full citizenship. One German immigrant, the Liberal Republican Carl Schurz, who served in the Union army and afterward became a senator from Missouri, urged reconciliation between North and South. For Schurz and other German Americans, the Franco-Prussian War of 1870–71 became the turning point for changing views of the African American, as the nationalist and illiberal views inspired by the war resonated among German Americans, drawing them "away from liberal nationalism."[6]

In the process, the centrality of slavery and freedom diminished in the meaning of the war, and by the end of the century the conflict was one of states' rights versus union. This was not the outcome Ulysses S. Grant had wanted. He committed his presidency to equal rights for the freedman, smashed the Klan, and gave up notions of annexing Canada. He became an enthusiastic advocate of the annexation of the Dominican Republic as a place for colonizing freedmen and as a beacon of freedom for Brazilian and Cuban slaves, favored purchase of Cuba at a time when Secretary of State Hamilton Fish labored to settle the civil war on the island, and declared a policy of peace and assimilation with Indians.

All these fell victim to more violent solutions, political opposition, or a diplomatic crisis. The one undeniably important political achievement that can be attributed in part to Grant's involvement was settlement of the *Alabama* claims in the favor of the United States. The *Alabama* was a cruiser built in Liverpool for the Confederate navy and allowed to launch in 1862 despite British neutrality laws and after protests by U.S. officials. For two years the warship terrorized the Union merchant marine until it was sunk by a Union warship. In 1872 a special tribunal in Geneva awarded the United States $15.5 million for the damage to Union shipping done by the *Alabama* and other Confederate raiders constructed in British ports. Grant had been enraged about the issue of British laxity in enforcing its neutrality laws, but he restrained from making absurd demands for settlement, such as the cession of Canada. In the aftermath of the settlement, the British removed their troops from the North American continent.[7]

That was important to those who remained apprehensive about the monarchical dominion on the republic's northern border. So, too, was another symbol of the era, the Statue of Liberty. In its original design, the resplendent lady represented by the statue—conceived in the mind of a French liberal opponent of Napoleon III, Édouard de Laboulaye, as a gift to the United States—held broken chains to symbolize slave emancipation. Twenty years after Lee's surrender, when the statue was erected in New York harbor, the chains lay at Liberty's feet, and Liberty now symbolized America welcoming European immigrants, implying that the nation wanted white immigrants but not people of color.[8]

Progress, Empire, and the Color Line

The long war against dismantling slavery in the Americas, coupled with the commitment to whitening the population and labor force, continued. Except for Haiti and the United States, where armed struggle decided the outcome, other countries in the Americas settled the end of slavery but not racial discrimination through negotiation. In one form or another, the slaveholders were compensated. Haiti survived economically by paying an enormous subsidy of 150 million francs (later reduced to 90) to France, a debt that was not fully settled until after World War II. In the United States (except for slaveholders in the District of Columbia), the compensation came in the form of Jim and Jane Crow laws and segregation in the 1890s. In often subtle ways, black freedmen continued to play a role in southern political and civic life for a generation after the nominal end of Reconstruction. As did Argentina and Brazil, the United States pursued a policy of "whitening" its population through immigrant labor from Europe, and with Canada all four countries remade their labor forces with European migrants. Brazil mobilized freedmen of African descent during the War of the Triple Alliance (1864–70) with neighboring Paraguay, and the experience had a lasting social impact on Brazilian slaves.[9]

Some Latin American social commentators, particularly the Argentine Domingo Sarmiento, admired Lincoln and believed the United States served as a model to emulate. Others, such as the Chilean Francisco Bilbao (1823–65), a proponent of romantic nationalism and of the theory of positivism, tried to come down on both sides of the persistent question about the worthiness of the U.S. and even the Mexican example for a modern state. In the year he died, Bilbao wanted Latin America to "be the United States," perhaps because he sensed that the Civil War was about inclusivity of blacks, Indians, and the socially dispossessed and the evils done in the name of race—a theme articulated by the Cuban essayist and revolutionary José Martí (1853–95) that contrasted with Bilbao's views after the Mexican-American War and during William Walker's occupation of Nicaragua.[10]

Technology and industrial progress were central themes at the Centennial International Exhibition of 1876, held in Philadelphia against a disturbing backdrop of political, labor, and racial strife. At the World's Columbian Exposition in Chicago in 1893, where the historian Frederick Jackson Turner spoke of the significance of the frontier in shaping the American character, the dominating symbols were about whiteness and progress, a theme that figured in the Cotton States and International Exposition in Atlanta in 1895, where Booker T. Washington expressed thoughts about segregation that pleased his white audience even as some black women who were permitted a booth at the event urged black men to fight for women's rights. Black Protestant ministers of the era preached about "end times" and how African Americans dealt with the racism of the era by finding their place in the account of the Hebrews in the book of Exodus, as well as in the Acts of the Apostles and its reminder that "God hath made one blood all nations of men" (12:26).[11]

Military intervention in southern political and civic affairs diminished with the reduction of federal troops in the South—fewer than three thousand in 1877, a force woefully insufficient for policing the countryside, where vigilantes operated. In the last third of the nineteenth century, the U.S. West was incorporated into the national economy by violent means. In troubling ways, its history paralleled that of the South—a defiant region of "stockade states" where a more powerful federal government attempted to exert its power and in the process encountered resistance and defiance from competing groups and individuals, leading to the militarization of society.

Commencing with the wartime campaign against the Sioux in Minnesota in 1862 and continuing with Custer's defeat at the Little Big Horn in Montana in 1876, the U.S. Army would fight more than a thousand engagements in its campaign of pacification of the Indian West in a war that persisted until the slaughter at Wounded Knee in 1890, in which 147 Sioux died for practicing the Ghost Dance. Their deaths came in the aftermath of the killing of Sitting Bull, the famous Indian chief who had inspired the war against the reservation system, and the failure of the 1887 Dawes Act, Congress's efforts to find an alternative to the reservation system by turning Indians into farmers with the offer of land grants. Senator Henry Teller of Colorado had predicted the act would make the Indian a vagabond. Theodore Roosevelt, who had experienced life in the Dakotas, was blunter: any Indian who declined the offer should "perish from the face of the earth," as had the white hunters and trappers who had killed the game of the West. In the half century after the Dawes Act, Indians lost two-thirds of their 138 million acres of tribal lands. At the same time, in some of the states, particularly in the Northeast, racial animosities toward Indians had lessened, and Indians received citizenship or were offered citizenship under certain restrictions. These changes were progressive measures, but they also permitted the states to reinforce their sovereignty, enabling the conversion of communal lands and resources to private ownership and into a broader market and, it was argued, to assimilate Indians into white culture. In practice, the granting of citizenship to Indians increased white access to Indian lands and resources.[12]

The Canadian experience in this era is instructive by comparison. In 1867 Canadians created a confederation of four disparate provinces. In the years after Britain's withdrawal of troops in 1872, the Dominion of Canada expanded to the Pacific following an Indian policy similar to that of its southern neighbor at the cost of only seven military engagements. Fears about the republican neighbor to their south persisted among Canadians. Despite acceptance of ethnic and religious minorities, Canada lost a million of its people to migration to the United States in the late nineteenth century. Goldwin Smith, the Toronto writer who prophesied that Canada would become a "Scotland" in a North American union, wryly observed, "The Americans may say with truth that if they do not annex Canada they are annexing the Canadians."[13]

By some accounts, most of the physical destruction of the era came not from Indian "savages" but from white males, and the army often tried to keep the peace between both groups. In these years, too, economic depressions, which occurred in each of the three decades of the late nineteenth century (and most devastatingly in the last), brought with them labor strikes, often brutal repression, and a farmers' revolt. In the 1890s the country was plunged into a political and social conflict that is remembered with the birth of the Populist Party and the "Battle of the Standards," symbolically represented by the debate over the gold standard, the tariff, and especially the mobilization of labor and farmers against the East and its banking and commercial interests. In his spirited "Cross of Gold" speech at the 1896 Democratic Convention, William Jennings Bryan warned: "It is the issue of 1776 over again."[14]

An arrogant but remarkable generation of political leaders, businessmen, and economic thinkers believed the solution to the recurring social and political strife that came in the wake of economic downturns lay in the creation of a modern industrial and business enterprise at home and the opening of new global markets, particularly in the western Pacific and East Asia, and an even more ambitious plan for a hemispheric economic consortium to counter British competition. Its advocate was Secretary of State James G. Blaine; its slogan, "America for the Americans," which belied what some Latin American leaders considered a mechanism for expanding U.S. hegemony. A more optimistic vision of liberalism took hold, one extolling liberty, individualism, a reduction of the role of government in the private economy, progress measured by technology, industrial power, material accumulation, and a free labor system. For those who thought in strategic as well as economic terms, such a grand design called for a central government dedicated to a "New Empire." Secretary of State William H. Seward had anticipated the benefits of the project before the war began and expressed his vision of the nation's future: "command [of] the empire of the seas, which is real empire," and advancement of the country's place in the "commerce of the world, which is the empire of the world."[15]

Although Lincoln was no enemy of empire, this was the obverse face of the revolutionary mission he had invoked at Gettysburg, an ideological derivative of Jefferson's continental empire of liberty and Manifest Destiny. That ambition had fired the war hawks in 1812 and led to war with Mexico and, by a narrow but credible reasoning, to civil war in 1861. Acquiring influence and expanding power beyond national boundaries in what has been called "social imperialism" would mitigate social conflict within the country. Competition with European powers would be largely economic and commercial in East Asia and the Pacific and more aggressive in Latin America and the Caribbean, a region already viewed as of both strategic and economic importance. As Secretary of State Hamilton Fish explained in a message to Congress in 1870, "By the priority of their independence, . . . stability, . . . respect for the law, . . . resources, . . . wealth, naval power, [and] attractions to European immigrants, these United States occupy of necessity a prominent position on this continent which they neither can nor should abdicate."[16]

Undertaking such a role divided a generation about the meaning of the Revolution and the republic it had created and set the country on a collision course with other countries and other revolutions. As John Quincy Adams had predicted in 1825, Spanish Cuba remained prominent on the U.S. list of "problem places" for both strategic and political reasons. José Martí, who died in 1895 in the long war for Cuban independence, anticipated what would happen to the Afro-Cuban struggle for equality if the United States intervened and the island passed from one imperial master to another. He rightly feared that possibility, as well as the militarization of Cuba Libre, whose goal was an independent Cuba free of the debilitating scar of racial division. Martí believed that race did not exist. White Cuban slaveholders had precipitated the Ten Years' War in 1868 to claim their independence from Spain, yet, unlike defiant U.S. southern slaveholders of 1861, they had mobilized Afro-Cubans and slaves in their commitment to the Cuban nation. In the mid-1890s, when the war of independence erupted again, Martí remained convinced that Spanish agents would be unable to stoke the fears of a race war because black and white Cubans had "suffered for one another."[17]

With the resumption of the war in 1895, the old racial divisions and fears resurfaced in both Cuba and Puerto Rico. In the devastation of the campaign, as Antonio Maceo's liberating army of predominantly Afro-Cuban soldiers swept westward, destroying sugar plantations, white Cubans and Spaniards living on the island despaired at the inability of the Spanish government to protect them. Some revived the idea of U.S. annexation, believing that it might lead to statehood. The grant of autonomy to both Cuba and Puerto Rico had momentarily appeased Puerto Ricans, but the U.S. invasion of both islands in the summer of 1898 altered the future. Although African Americans formed a portion of the invading U.S. military force in Cuba, both in the course of the war and in the occupation that followed, American officers and officials drew a color line, denying Cuban leaders any meaningful participation in the Spanish surrender.

In accepting President William McKinley's call for intervention, Congress had insisted that Cuba would not be annexed and that the island would be readied for independence. The U.S. occupiers made clear that Cuban independence depended on the renunciation of all Cuban professions of a raceless nation and the willingness of Cuban leaders to pass a test of their worthiness to govern. Some Cuban nationalists acquiesced because there was no alternative other than a resumption of the war, which became the choice of

Philippine insurgents in 1899; others because they accepted U.S. judgments about the capacity of their compatriots.[18]

Race was a critical but not the singular driving force in explaining the character of U.S. insular empire. Imperialism's advocates did not like to play the "race card" in their arguments for expansion, although race persistently intruded into the discourse, particularly for those who insisted that acquiring territory meant that permanent possessions, such as Hawai'i, would be "safe for white people." Cubans would gain a qualified and humiliating independence in 1902 as a de facto U.S. protectorate, and within a decade two Cuban governments would crush the Afro-Cuban political movement's goal of equality. Puerto Rico would get a civilian government as a U.S. unincorporated territory but with the understanding that the benefits of the U.S. Constitution did not follow the flag. W. E. B. Du Bois, who wrote later that the war marked for the United States the triumph of white supremacy, argued that it could best be understood in the context of the worldwide struggle of people of color against their colonial rulers. Martí privileged the struggle for nationhood over race. For Du Bois, the battle of people of color for democracy superseded that for national unity. As a proponent of pan-Africanism, Du Bois was harsh in his indictment of the small numbers of African American missionaries sent by white Protestant religious organizations to Africa, as they were often politically and religiously conservative in their views about race. In the early twentieth century, some black churches began to send missionaries to Africa, and on their return they spread pan-Africanist ideas in the United States.[19]

Imperial and Transnational America

In his justification for intervention in Cuba and annexation of the Philippines, McKinley emphasized religious and humanitarian concerns to explain his actions. In the Philippines, the harsh suppression of a native guerrilla movement had roused the anti-annexationist camp. In gaining the support of evangelical Protestants, some of whom demonized Catholic Spain as "non-Christian," McKinley ran the risk of offending the sensibilities of U.S. Catholics, whose political clout in northeastern and northern cities had made a difference in the 1896 election. The reformist agenda of evangelical Protestants—opposing oppressive regimes, striving for moral uplift, and demonstrating the superiority of the U.S. model of imperial rule to that of the Europeans—sometimes put them at odds with political leaders and military officers whose central concerns involved pacification, preserving political stability, and winning over indigenous converts to their agenda. The vision of Protestant moral reform groups was global. Their organizations and missionaries perceived their work as the creation of a "moral empire" that rose above nation, as lobbyists for changes in the U.S. relationship in its insular empire and in the world.[20]

At the turn of the twentieth century—the twilight years of the long revolutionary age—race and religion remained powerful influences, and socialism and nationalism, not classical republicanism or liberalism, would be the driving ideologies. The acerbic and prophetic Edwin L. Godkin of *The Nation*, a classical liberal and dedicated opponent of imperialism, predicted in 1900 what was coming: "We hear no more of natural rights, but of inferior races, whose part it is to submit to the government of those whom God has made their superiors. The old fallacy of divine right has once more asserted its ruinous power, and before it is again repudiated there must be international struggles on a terrific scale."[21]

With some modification, Godkin's judgment turned out to be tragically on the mark. The war with Spain and especially the annexation of the Philippines, which triggered a guerrilla war in the islands, convinced Godkin that the world he had known had forever changed and for the worse. The liberal and republican ideals he believed would sustain a society of learning, peace, and commerce had been weakened by the jingoism, protectionism, and plunder that had brought on the war. In the years that followed, the challenges and opportunities that came with the victory over Spain would precipitate a seminal debate about what to do with an insular empire stretching across the Pacific from Hawai'i to the Philippines and in the Caribbean and Central America from Puerto Rico to the Panama Canal, an empire of unincorporated territories and protectorates populated mostly by people of color.

As had the Louisiana Purchase, the Mexican-American War, and the pacification and conquest of the West, this insular empire both shaped and distorted the modern nation that came in its wake, changing perceptions about not only what kind of country we wanted to be but also what role we would play in the world. Its militarist fantasies of regeneration through war and its racial nationalism distorted the reformist and religious endeavors of a country still recovering from the violence identified with late nineteenth-century industrialization, the parallel economic and social challenge from socialism, and the final years of the age of revolution. Those who believed that wartime heroism or the martial idea would inspire a moral reformation in the individual or move the wealthy to commit their lives to the public good, Jackson Lears notes in his sometimes harsh cultural critique of the half-century before the Great War, paled in numbers to those who recognized how easily such passions could be turned into repression or even slaughter in the name of promoting commerce, protecting property, or creating empire.[22]

In the years after the war with Spain, the United States took its place in the international imperial order. In the fifteen years between the decision to annex the Philippines in 1899 and the onset of the Great War in 1914, it built a modern navy, a workable alliance with corporate capitalism, and a bureaucracy committed to the service of its empire. The country's strategists visualized moving British political geographer Halford Mackinder's Central Asian "pivot of history" to the Caribbean, where the Panama Canal (which opened in 1915) served as the centerpiece of the nation's empire of unincorporated territories and protectorates.

There was no retreat from Asia, however, as in 1899 and 1900 Secretary of State John Hay sent a series of "Open Door Notes" to European powers opposing the creation of economic "spheres of influence" along the Chinese coast. In 1900 the United States joined with European governments in suppressing the antiforeign Boxer Rebellion in China. The march of empire enhanced the power of the state, but the transformation was neither spontaneous nor unchallenged by the European powers. Congress and the public were concerned about the costs or fears of "contaminating" the white republic and had apprehensions about competition from its colonial charges.[23]

In an era when industrialists had become more dependent on controlling the sources of raw materials and markets, the U.S. model offered a challenge to Europe. In the production of steel, wheat, railroads, and textiles, especially, the United States moved rapidly to the forefront. In 1914 its manufacturing capacity exceeded that of the United Kingdom, France, and Germany combined, and European leaders considered it an economic threat. The United States could feed its labor force and industrialize. Continental expansionism—the economic "plank" in the Founders' revolutionary platform—had paid off, but the task of pacifying the labor force and farmers or reconciling old grievances remained.[24]

A generation of Progressives—Populism's presumptive successors—believed themselves up to the task. They identified as heirs of the revolutionary legacy even as they reconfigured some of the basic tenets of the revolutionary canon. Most were middle class, with a stake in preserving the capitalist system, but not at the price of dismantling it or yielding power to corporations and their allies or in abandoning an imperial mission. Their concerns ranged from the impact of industrialization, labor strife, and growing economic inequality on the perceived withering of community life to addressing the problems associated with a national economy dominated by corporate power or state political governments that varied from reformist to those run by political mossbacks who blended an economic reformism into their racist agenda.[25]

Then, as now, immigration was a divisive issue. From 1880 to 1914 and the onset of the Great War in Europe, 23 million immigrants entered the country, 70 percent of them from southern and eastern Europe, most of them Catholic and coming to an America whose ruling social and political hierarchy remained Protestant. To these should be added a domestic migration of 1.5 million African Americans from the South, most of them to northern industrial cities. In what Felipe Fernández-Armesto identifies as the second Hispanic colonization, which commenced around 1900, more than 2 million Mexicans joined them, some lured as far north as Kansas City or even Chicago, beginning the reversal of a long decline in Hispanic culture in the territories acquired from the Mexican-American War. In California and especially in Texas, they suffered not only from racial and religious prejudices but also from an aggressive Anglo justice system in which they were victimized, lost their land, denied their basic rights, and killed. As industrialists readily pursued immigrant labor power, they became conscious not only of their role in enhancing the power of the state but also of the growing support for anti-immigrant legislation. After the turn of the twentieth century, when the number of immigrants from southern and eastern Europe began to surpass that from northern Europe, some political leaders began to call for changes in immigration law, particularly the use of literacy tests. In 1911 the United States Joint Immigration Commission (known as the Dillingham Commission) recommended that immigration from southern and eastern Europe be sharply reduced on the grounds that it posed a threat. The secretary of the Immigration Restriction League, Prescott Hall, stated the problem in stark terms: Did the people of the United States want "British, German, and Scandinavian stock, historically free, energetic, progressive, or Slav, Latin, and Asiatic races, historically downtrodden, atavistic, and stagnant?"[26]

Progressive leaders sensed a public willingness to break with the past but without the violence such ruptures often bring. The majority believed themselves both radical and utopian in their vision of the United States as a truly modern nation, one capable of changing not only the immigrant but also the individualistic Victorian into a prosperous middle-class citizen. With an activist government and involved citizenry, the power of big business would be brought under control, class conflict would be mitigated, and neither the hallowed individualism of tradition nor even segregation would be an impediment. Like revolutionary ideologues, Progressives had a different way of looking at things. Progressive legal scholars challenged a legal tradition based on contract and property rights and called for expanding the meaning of "freedom" to include "economic freedom," giving the word a moral and social equivalent. John Dewey advocated an education system that prepared an active student for a modern age. Charles A. Beard did a merciless vivisection of the Founders and their economic motives in writing the Constitution that fell out of favor in the Cold War but had a powerful impact on the historiography of the era. Proponents of the sociological school of jurisprudence, cofounded by Roscoe Pound, emphasized social as opposed to private and public interests as a guide to addressing the problem of social instability.[27]

This was their dream for the republic bequeathed by the long American Revolution, and it had to be squared with some realities if that republic could be transformed into a nation. Unlike those who clung to the nineteenth-century view of the individual and individualism as fundamental to sustaining the nation's institutions, freedoms, and rights, Progressives believed that the most effective way of addressing social unrest in a political economy dominated by corporations lay in creating or reviving a sense of community—a commonwealth—without destroying the corporation or undercutting private property. They retained the belief that they could accomplish this goal in a country where people clung to the notion that their prosperity depended on expansionism and a surplus of private property.

To counter such ideas, the Progressives drew on those revolutionary beliefs in the common or public good as paramount over individual wants and a parallel conviction that ownership of property carried with it an obligation to serve society. Some were influenced by the Social Gospel, which endorsed a Christian solution for bringing order and balance to society and the economy; others by syndicalist thought and its emphasis on trade organization and confederation. Such views sometimes conflicted with what business and political leaders came to recognize in the 1890s and Frederick Jackson Turner hinted at in his iconic essay on the end of the frontier: the frontier may have nourished democracy, but Turner warned that its encouragement of "selfishness and individualism" and its intolerance of "administrative experience and education" posed a danger to society.[28]

The Progressive agenda called for a more activist state, as well as a statement of the nation's purpose. Herbert Croly provided both in *The Promise of American Life* (1909), which became the secular bible of the New Nationalism. Croly took dead aim at the confidence that previous generations had placed in unfettered individual freedom, the cumulative effect of which was a society of inequality and corruption and an economic system that starved the community. The state had to assume a role in assuring the moral and equitable distribution of wealth. For Croly and other liberals, the compelling inspiration of the New Nationalism meant a symbiotic union of the Hamiltonian vision of a more powerful central government with the Jeffersonian insistence on shielding the person from the debilitating power of corporate America. In the seminal 1912 presidential campaign, the sweep of reformist and even radical ideas ranged from those of the Socialist Party candidate, Eugene Victor Debs, to the incumbent Republican, William Howard Taft, with the alienated Republican and now Progressive "Bull Moose" candidate, Theodore Roosevelt, and the Democratic nominee, Woodrow Wilson, between them. In their comparative rhetorical appeals, Roosevelt sounded more like Debs than either Taft or Wilson, who won the election.[29]

Wilson's victory slowed the reformist pace that Croly and Roosevelt were calling for by offering a variation of Progressivism, which in the end did not stop the movement for woman suffrage or upend Prohibition, what some called an anti-immigrant, anti-Catholic measure. Undeniably, the income tax, direct election of senators, and especially woman suffrage constituted important achievements, but one consequence of Progressive political reforms, which focused on fitness for citizenship, was to restrict political participation by moving away from universal manhood suffrage. In exalting the role of the regulatory welfare state, Progressives' increasingly secular vision of a Protestant Christian commonwealth struck a generation of Catholic, Jewish, Orthodox Christians, and even Evangelicals as a departure from what religious belief called for in the state.

Progressives provided women with greater protection in the workplace, and women took a notable role in settlement houses and in improving public health, but the nineteenth-century view that women would be corrupted by participation in politics and required protection from its harmful effects remained implanted in the male psyche. Progressives expressed less concern with civil liberties, free expression of ideas, pluralism, and the rights of ethnic minorities. They could be intolerant of deviant behavior. In the South, prohibitionists united women, evangelical preachers, and even white supremacists in a common cause to outlaw liquor on the grounds that drink was the bane of civilization. Freedom to consume alcohol called for punitive action by the state to make war on the saloon, and political leaders who favored it recognized they could invoke the Progressive referendum to take action.[30]

In the spirit of molding a "new person," Progressives advocated social engineering despite its distasteful theories about backward people, implicitly underwriting eugenics, which the Catholic Church opposed. Intelligence testing by the army during the Great War revealed that the mean intelligence of recruits was that of a moron or a thirteen-year-old boy. Poor white and black recruits from the South, a region lacking in public funding in education, stood at the bottom. Observers were quick to cite these tests to reinforce the belief that white men were dragging down the country. Radical essayist Randolph Bourne's 1916 essay on the social and ethnic variety of transnational America and the celebration of its diversity coincided with Madison Grant's racist indictment of the melting pot in *The Passing of the Great Race*. Adolf Hitler praised U.S. race and antimiscegenation laws in *Mein Kampf*, and the infamous Nuremberg Laws of Nazi Germany, especially the Citizenship and Blood Laws, referenced American practices.[31]

The more arrogant proudly claimed that the United States was taking "Britain's place," particularly in the Americas. (The goal of union with Britain would persist in the Atlantic Union movement of the late 1930s.) Others— among them the Social Darwinist William Graham Sumner—argued in a speech to Yale's Phi Beta Kappa Society in January 1899 that the country was assuming the role Spain had played in its empire and that we believed that our presence and our guidance would be welcomed by the people in our insular empire. The consequence of victory over Spain, Sumner warned, was that the United States, like Spain and other European nations before it, had succumbed to the illusion that imperialism and expansion brought prosperity. In its imperial ventures, the nation had taken its "domestic dogma" about the equality of all men, which in practice had been violated at home, and replaced it with the "Spanish doctrine" of repressing people "who resist our beneficence.... What is that but the policy of Spain?"[32]

The Spanish comparison was apt, if not always accurate in the details, particularly in the methods the United States employed to suppress insurrections and guerrilla wars, initially in the Philippines following the vote on annexation and in its Caribbean interventions. After the suppression of the insurrection, the Philippines became a territory governed by an American-run commission with a promise of independence in 1916 that became a reality after World War II. In suppressing the insurrection of 1899, the invading U.S. military used derogatory racist terms to justify its conduct in the war. After peace was declared in 1903, such metaphors as "little brown brother" and "calibrated assimilation" entered the discourse. At the Saint Louis World's Fair of 1904, the Philippines exhibit and its display of "savages in their native villages," designed in the belief that it would promote more understanding and acceptance, as well as promote loyalty and assimilation, had the obverse effect. At the 1915 Panama-Pacific International Exposition in San Francisco, the Philippines display conveyed an image of elite Filipino men as capable "representative men," but the hostility to Filipino immigration remained. Although the postwar U.S. tutelage of the Philippines and Puerto Rico conveyed different meanings to the local population, the cultural elites in both places were able to draw on their past experiences under Spanish rule to give them confidence that "unconscious masses" would continue to follow their counsel despite the arrogance of their occupiers.[33]

Puerto Ricans, unlike Cubans, never had a chance to experience the facade of independence, although with U.S. entry into the war islanders did acquire statutory citizenship in 1917. (The autonomist Luís Muñoz Rivera supported the measure because he believed it would lead to independence for the island. His son, Luís Muñoz Marín, played a critical role in pushing for the commonwealth after World War II in the belief that economic development would settle or at least distract from arguments over the "status question.") For those who expected equal treatment in coming under U.S. tutelage, the Supreme Court, in a series of thirty-five decisions (the "Insular Cases") early in the century, made clear that the rights of the Constitution did not follow the flag and that people in some territories were not as equal as those in others. That judgment conformed to the view of the British editorialist W. T. Stead, who called for a union of the English-speaking world—code for a unity of white people—as Britain's best hope for survival as a world power.[34]

Croly envisioned the promise of a new order in hemispheric terms, where the more stable and advanced larger states of South America and Mexico would join with the United States in a hemispheric international system as a shield against Europe. Despite his reputation as hemispheric bully, Roosevelt—with Secretary of State Elihu Root's invaluable assistance—had found a receptive audience for containing revolution and promoting hemispheric trade among the leaders of several mainland Latin American nations. The creation of a special commission of jurists at the Third International Conference of American States in 1906 in Rio de Janeiro to develop a hemispheric public law signaled a promising future for peaceful settlement of disputes in the Americas.

International lawyers, who largely supported the decision for war with Spain, served as advisors to policy makers with the purpose of turning the country's "informal" empire in the Caribbean and the Philippines into a "legalist" one in the belief that their efforts were consistent with their notions of American exceptionalism and U.S. national interest. Even missionaries would be enlisted in that endeavor. Like the international lawyers, they may have been heartened by the proverbial "better angels" of Roosevelt's nature without dwelling on his comment that "unless we keep the barbarian virtues, gaining the civilized ones will be of little avail."[35]

The most consequential flaw in the Progressives' agenda was their acquiescence in segregation and a parallel belief that it was not an impediment to the political and social reforms they championed. Segregation was pervasive everywhere in the country, and the boundary lines excluded not only blacks but also Indians, workers, and immigrants. Although Progressives believed in changing the social environment by mitigating class divisions, they looked at segregation as an opportunity to preserve and to protect the weak. Certainly, their purpose was not to unify whites but to prevent conflict as a way of lessening the tensions and violence of an industrial nation undergoing rapid social and economic change. A conciliation between North and South had gotten underway, but it was couched in the language and memory that veterans of the Civil War had of the battlefield and the dead or in the antebellum debate over nationalism rather than the radical ideals many of those in the North were told they were fighting for. In this discourse, the country the revolutionary generation had imagined in the aftermath of slavery would become the "republic of suffering," in which memories of sacrifice and death served to unify white northerner and white southerner not in the spirit of emancipation—as much for whites as for blacks—but in the imperative of racial hierarchy and the segregated society of the era. Booker T. Washington had acquiesced in that prescription, but not W. E. B. Du Bois, founder of the National Association for the Advancement of Colored People, who made the battle for equality for African Americans a universal cause. Du Bois himself confronted a formidable rival in the Jamaican Marcus Garvey, leader of the Universal Negro Improvement Association, who preached a militant anticolonialism and called on Africans to reclaim their homeland from European imperialism. To that end, Garvey enjoyed support from the reborn Ku Klux Klan.[36]

The racial character of America's revolutionary legacy also conformed to that of other hemispheric countries. In an era when the United States was pursuing racial nationalism, Latin America's writers, politicians, and leaders were subscribing to their own forms of racial determinism in their efforts to modernize their societies and labor forces. Earlier in the nineteenth century, Latin American leaders needed the support of ex-slaves and free blacks, but with the transition to export economies and closer ties to Europe and North America, the commitment of the region's oligarchs to egalitarianism diminished in the goal of transforming "backward" nations into "civilized republics." Even in Mexico, where the concept of *mestizaje* took hold during the revolution and became enshrined with the ideal of a "cosmic race," political leaders and intellectuals could not escape racial discourses.[37]

In the racial climate of the age, the issue of incorporating people of color from newly acquired territories such as Puerto Rico revived older debates about the character of the republic "deformed" by assimilation of people of color. Americanization became an obsession with Roosevelt, who fumed about the hyphenate with divided loyalties and who resisted assimilation, although he insisted in his prepresidential years that Americanism was a matter of "spirit, conviction, and purpose, not of creed or birthplace." Bourne confronted the issue in his essay "Trans-National America," in which he castigated the domination of the country by a dogmatic "British stock" insisting on telling the immigrant how to assimilate or the "melting pot," in which one's identity was lost. As if to anticipate the contemporary quarrels over diversity, he fused both into a paean for America as a "unique sociological fabric."[38]

Liberals and even more radical Progressives were disturbed by Bourne's positive vision of transnational America as the bulwark of the nation that had emerged from the long American Revolution. It was one thing to fashion a reformist political agenda that checked the power of the corporations or addressed the complaints of labor or woman suffrage, but in the political and social climate of the age, there were unsettling challenges from anarchists and socialists and a form of revolution that would commence as a war in the name of liberal democracy but would collapse in civil war and prove both destructive and transformative. It would erupt first in Mexico and then in Russia, and the United States would become ensnared in both.

The Great War

In his second inaugural, Woodrow Wilson proudly declared that this generation of Americans were no longer "provincials." In his war message of April 1917, he called for a declaration of war against the German government, not the German people, according to the principles of rightness and justice and in the spirit of the Declaration of Independence. The war would reveal ever more clearly the differing legacies of the age of revolution for Europeans and the peoples of the Americas.

For Europe, the outbreak of war in August 1914 had been a shock, a sharp break with the past and after a century in which Europeans had avoided a major war among themselves. In 1914 everything changed. A conflict that had begun within European Christendom would become a global struggle involving all the major powers and troops from overseas going far from home to fight. Within a year, the conflict on the western front had settled into a ghastly human massacre stretching from Belgium to the Swiss frontier. Unlike the previous wars in Europe, the Great War was a war without limits, to the death, leaving in its wake a devastated, broken, antiwar generation with neither the will nor a powerful international body to prevent a sequel, a Second Thirty Years' War.[39]

For the United States, the significance of the war went beyond concerns about cultural and economic ties to Great Britain or Germany's violations of neutral rights and challenge to U.S. interests. Civilization itself was in peril, and the liberal economic project threatened, particularly in the Americas. Wilson had begun his presidency committed to a reversal of his Republican predecessors' opportunistic policies in Latin America with a political and economic agenda that he believed would address the threat to liberal capitalism from the left and the right and counter European and especially German intrusion. In 1914 and especially in 1915 Wilson's pledge of neutrality in the war masked his acknowledgment that Germany was an economic rival and an enemy of Progressive reforms. The deeply religious secretary of state, Robert Lansing, believed a German victory in the war would spell the end of democracy and reverse human progress. Despite concerns over immigrant loyalties, public opinion may have been ahead of Wilson in singling out a militaristic German government as the cause of the war in defiance of the interests of the German people.[40]

From the turn of the century, the United States viewed Germany as an adversary in the hemisphere, particularly in the Caribbean and in Mexico. Wilson's interference in Mexican affairs would put the country on a collision course with a civil war that became a revolution in defiance of the United States. The convulsion on the border would lead to a race war in 1915 with the call for an uprising by Tejanos (the Plan of San Diego) and their allies in a war of independence for the border states in retaliation for Anglo disenfranchisement and atrocities against Mexicans, particularly in Texas. In 1914 and again in 1916 the Wilson administration undertook military interventions in Mexico.

The Mexican Revolution brought to power a government that was determined to pacify both the country peasant and the urban laborer, problems that reached back to the 1810 Hidalgo revolt. President Venustiano Carranza pursued an anti-U.S. policy in hemispheric affairs, but he was not so foolish as to be duped by the German proposal of an alliance (outlined in the intercepted Zimmermann Telegram) and the German promise of Mexico's recovery of the lands lost in the Mexican-American War. Carranza misread the zigzagging, chaotic course of the long revolution in Mexico as a defiant group drew up a new Mexican constitution in 1917 that contained clauses relating to land, labor, women, and subsoil rights that directly challenged U.S. economic interests.

In the 1920s the Mexican government undertook another war against the Catholic Church and in national politics created the Institutional Revolutionary Party (PRI is its acronym), which exercised virtually one-party rule in the country until 2000, when a candidate of the National Action Party won the presidential election. The Bolshevik Revolution in Russia may have ended the long nineteenth century in Europe, but the Mexican Revolution marked its culmination in the Americas, creating for the first time an ideological and economic, if not a military, alternative to the U.S. model of capitalism and governance. Ironically but not unexpectedly, the economic power of the United States in Mexico after the heroic phase of the Revolution ended in 1923 was greater than what it had been during the thirty-five-year reign of the dictator Porfirio Díaz. That was not the case with the Soviet Union.[41]

U.S. entry into the war came late and would be decisive in the German surrender in November 1918 on the basis of Wilson's peace plan, codified as the Fourteen Points and its critical proposal for a League of Nations. The manner in which Wilson dealt with his allies at the Peace Conference, coupled with his disastrous handling of the settlement when he returned home, it is generally argued, condemned Europeans to a reprise of their civil war two decades later.

The war broke up four empires—the German, the Austro-Hungarian, the Russian, and the Ottoman—with consequences that would plague later generations. Wilson's insistence on self-determination of subject peoples led to a drawing of boundaries or the creation of ethnic enclaves that would culminate in the disastrous war in the Balkans in the 1990s. Save for the British promise to provide a homeland for the Jews in Palestine, the territorial bounty of the collapsed Ottoman Empire was divided between the French and the British. Wilson persisted in the belief that the United States was impartial—it entered the war not as an ally but as an associate power—and he could never reconcile his ideals about what was fair and equitable with the reality that the peace settlement would be a victor's accord. Wilson staked everything on U.S. approval of the League of Nations and fought off all efforts to amend its twenty-six articles. Although unintended, the U.S. intervention enabled French prime minister Georges Clemenceau's humiliating and severe demands for punishing Germany and directly influenced German motives for launching its blitzkrieg attack two decades later.[42]

The war dealt a severe blow to the cause of international liberalism and a federation of governments able to prevent another world war. In Russia the revolutionary government that toppled Tsar Nicholas II was in turn overthrown by the Bolsheviks under the leadership of Vladimir Lenin (originally Vladimir Ilyich Ulyanov), who took Russia out of the war with Germany, a decision that plunged the country into a civil war. After their victory, the Bolsheviks created a federation of Russian and non-Russian republics as the Union of Soviet Socialist Republics. It was the brutal antithesis of Wilsonian liberal state modeling.

Ironically, it was Lenin who achieved the saintlike devotion as a figure of deliverance that Wilson aspired to, but he did so by employing ruthless, uncompromising means. In some ways, the two men were alike—self-righteous millennials who visualized a fallen world that dedicated men were capable of redeeming. Both were revolutionaries. Lenin would have agreed with Wilson's goal of making men free, but by Wilson's moral standards, Lenin's ideology and government enslaved rather than liberated Russians, and for that reason, Wilson chose to act. In September 1918 the United States dispatched five thousand troops to join the Allied intervention in North Russia, which fought the Red Army during the Bolsheviks' war with the White Russians. Wilson doggedly turned away those who predicted that U.S. refusal to deal with the Bolsheviks would have disastrous consequences for the future.[43]

The war expanded the power of the federal government and initiated a spirit of Americanism at home, but the methods employed to achieve these goals ranged from coercion, vigilantism, and denial of fundamental liberties to an official propaganda campaign coupled with humanitarian and religious outreach programs arrayed against an antiwar coalition as formidable as that which opposed the Vietnam War half a century later. In the end, believers in civil rights, Irish and German Americans, labor unions, women's movements, and socialists had to make a choice: protest the war, which was risky, or follow along in the belief that war would advance their cause.

As Bourne warned, the war expanded the power of the state, and in the hysteria of the times, the state proved more interested in punishment than in protection of the citizenry. Twenty-five U.S. cities experienced the most horrific racial violence since the Civil War in the summer of 1919. In the hysteria of the Red Scare, the Justice Department began deportations of socialists. At the same time, the American Relief Administration, headed by Herbert Hoover, had commenced its task of feeding the people of Europe, and in 1921, following the failure of mass collectivization of agriculture, it extended its program to Russia. From that role, Hoover took his considerable skills as a thinker and a doer into the Commerce Department and from there to the presidency. Hoover, not Wilson, was the liberal the country wanted for the postwar era—a Quaker, not a Presbyterian, a pacifist and philanthropist, not a crusader for international liberalism, someone who, like Wilson, knew where and when to draw a color line in defining America.[44]

THE PROGRESSIVES ADDRESSED more fundamentally the call for the creation of a political and economic system—ideally, a commonwealth or utopia—as a means of satisfying both the community needs and the individual aspirations and desires that have been the goals of democratic socialists. But the trick lay in accomplishing this without giving way to governments that were either national socialist or fascist or Bolshevist (from the right or from the left) or suffered from a stifling rabbit warren of bureaucracies. As had earlier generations of social reformers, they had tried and failed to mold an American appropriate to their definition of the model citizen and in that endeavor to unite the country in a common cause. In spite of their illiberal and oppressive wartime measures to achieve unity, the Progressives succeeded in bringing to bay a group more dangerous and destructive than nineteenth-century slaves or Indians: white males. And their methods of pacification were also a reminder that the Left stood much less a chance of gaining power in this country than the Right.[45]

The price of nationhood in the Great War was high: the validation of white supremacy and domination of people of color at home and in the nation's insular empire, and condemnations of world government and affirmation by Wilson's successor, Warren G. Harding, that the republic had experienced only one "ambiguity" (the Civil War) in fulfilling the design of the Founders. In words Jefferson might have approved, Harding believed the country should be an example to the world, avoid entanglements, and remain alert to dangers from within and from without. "If revolution insists upon overturning established order," he confirmed in his inaugural, "there is no place for it in America."[46]

That comment is not Jeffersonian. In the end, the Progressive Era and the wartime experience complicated more than settled the fundamental questions raised by the long American Revolution. In the wartime-forced alliance between a dominant white Protestant America and the diverse and polyglot America described by Bourne in "Trans-National America," the Progressives and a few liberal and socialist ideologues brought forth the second nation wrought by the Revolution—the United States. Europeans perceived the Great War as the end of a century of no major wars and the beginning of another Thirty Years' War.

For some if not all Americans, the war confirmed the end of the long American Revolution and a yet unacknowledged "Third Hundred Years' War" in North America that also shaped two very different nations whose long passage to nationhood remained intimately linked to the expansive dynamic of the American Revolution: Mexico and Canada.[47]

EPILOGUE

IN WAYS SOME AMERICANS PRAISE and others regret and disavow, the generation that came into its own in the early years of the twentieth century accomplished the long-sought ideal of nationhood by incorporating contemporary racial doctrines with a presumably scientific confirmation of the inferiority of both African Americans and poor whites. We must still confront the contradictions of that era in the visible scars of racism, white supremacy, social and economic inequities, and male narcissism, clothed in the rhetoric of liberation, nation building, and moral improvement identified with those years.

The New Deal in the 1930s offered liberals and Progressives an opportunity to use federal power to address the revolutionary aspiration of equality and address economic inequity, but federal programs, particularly those in housing, reinforced racial priorities, and the New Dealers proved more interested in expanding federal power with a secular approach to welfare and regulations rather than the Progressives' moral or Protestant vision of placing the common good over personal ambition. World War II offered a "second chance" to fulfill the Wilsonian liberal goal of creating an international body to safeguard the peace with the creation of the United Nations. African Americans fought not only for victory over the Axis but for equality at home, and women looked to translate the vital role they played in winning the war into advances in their status in peacetime, but their success proved disappointing. The confrontation with the Soviet Union and the resurgence of the civil rights movement in the 1950s and 1960s, among other issues, revived the national debate and questioning over the aspirations and legacy of the long American Revolution. Our history since then has given us no clear answer to that question.[1]

John Adams and Thomas Jefferson—two figures from central casting in the revolutionary band of brothers—confronted the same problem. Predictably, they had strikingly different judgments about the legacy of the Revolution and what it portended for the future. Both responded to requests to give their thoughts about the Revolution and Declaration of Independence for the

July 4, 1826, fiftieth anniversary of its signing. As befitted his style, Jefferson saw the Revolution as "a signal of arousing men . . . to assume the blessings and security of self-government." Adams conveyed his contingent feelings and his doubts about the Revolution's power to take root on foreign soil. Pressed by friends to amplify after a brief remark ("I will give you INDEPENDENCE FOREVER"), he warned that the United States was "destined in future history to form the brightest or blackest page, according to the role or the abuse of those political institutions by which they shall in time come to be shaped by the *human mind*."[2]

Adams is not memorialized on Mount Rushmore, but he proved a more prescient commentator on the future than Jefferson, who is. With the warnings about the dangers in our "civil religion"—the mission of nation building through sustaining democratic movements and institutions abroad while undermining them at home—have come even more disturbing predictions that restoring "America's greatness" is code for reversing or undermining the benefits of social capital we have invested in fulfilling the revolutionary promise. There's a world of difference between what restoration meant in 1776 and what some believe it means today. For example, we can't restore the imputed "originalism" of the Constitution by leaving out the Bill of Rights. A judge may be guided by Christian beliefs, but when the late conservative and Catholic associate justice of the Supreme Court Antonin Scalia dissented in a 2015 same-sex union case (*Obergefell v. Hodges*) that the practice was "contrary to the beliefs of many of our citizens," Richard Posner, a U.S. Appeals Court judge, commented that such a political ideal "verges on majoritarian democracy."[3]

Historians, social scientists, and journalists sometimes refer to this kind of thinking as an example of the contradictions and biases in our thinking about our laws and how we apply them. In advertising, it's called the "permissible lie"; in some churches, the hypocrisy that might be condoned if one is doing God's work. The point here is that the republic and its laws that the American Revolution created may be secular, but the American Revolution bonded the secular and the spiritual. Our revolution may not have motivated us to address the proverbial "social question," but our hypocrisy is world-class.

In other words, we may understand ourselves better than we believe we do, even if our thinking is out of sync with rational thought. We may need that dialogue with the Founders to reconfirm our priorities. Despite their political battles over the consequences of the American Revolution, both Adams and Jefferson formed an alliance of a kind in bringing it about and in sustaining it. They also realized that what was at stake then and still is today is the American Revolution—not the one encumbered with the appendages of material improvement, or expansionism, or the search for markets, or psychic crises about masculinity, or ingrained beliefs about white supremacy, or the slavery/freedom binary and its deceptive simplicity that one person's freedom depends on another's bondage, or the pitfalls of taking on the role of nation building in a turbulent world, but the revolution that made a radical turn without giving the impression that it was indeed radical.

Jefferson and Adams rarely agreed on anything, but, as did most of the Founders, they became more pessimistic about the revolutionary legacy as they aged. In three areas—slavery and African Americans, Indians, and women—they failed to give subsequent generations a clear sense of direction about fulfilling the Revolution's promise, but they did leave three unambiguous legacies. The first was the creation of a republican national state, if not a modern nation, that they deemed a model for the modern liberal state. Certainly not Adams and not even Jefferson believed that it could be "cloned" elsewhere. Second, and just as important, was their creation of a *secular* state and its parallel code of separation of church and state, at least at the federal level, which evangelicals and non-Anglicans favored. Third, they rejected the notion that political sovereignty must be lodged in one place by creating overlapping entities with authority—the federal government and even some federal agencies and the states—that blurred jurisdiction, required compromises, and in some major disputes—the Civil War was the most serious—provided no peaceful option for solution. Even in those issues we identify as failures, they left just enough legal or "moral space"—such as the denial of the right of property in persons in the Constitution—to sustain those movements engaged in the long war for the abolition of slavery or the struggle for women's rights.[4]

What Adams and Jefferson argued about was not the "social question" but the use of power—when and where and how it must be used. They disagreed on a common enemy—for Adams, it was France; for Jefferson, Great Britain—and despite his lofty visions about the Revolution's universal impact, not even Jefferson would have seconded our modern idea of American exceptionalism or nation building. They never underestimated the dangers of the reversal of the revolution and the republic from a foreign foe. Both brooded over the possibility that the republic, and with it the revolutionary aspirations, might collapse not from the "ruthlessness of the foe" but, as the philosopher/ theologian Reinhold Niebuhr wrote in the early 1950s, the failure of leaders "too blind to see all the hazards of the struggle, [a] blindness . . . induced not by some accident of nature or history but by hatred and vainglory."[5]

BUT FEW OF the Founders could have anticipated how the dynamic forces at work on the Revolution from the onset—such as immigration; the impact of other revolutions; religion, especially evangelical Protestantism; and words and phrases of the Declaration of Independence, notably "equality"—have shaped in our minds and laws how we value the worth and place of the person in this country and our role in the world. These forces and these words have been on a collision course with every one of our embedded prejudices and biases about race, religion, and gender since 1776 and our relationship with other nations.

What I have offered in this book is a suggestion rather than a conclusion—that the American Revolution played out differently from the French, Haitian, and Latin American Revolutions not because it was "scripted" from the beginning but because the American Revolution took a long time to play out, and the script kept changing. We became a republic more than a century before we became a nation, and we kept men, especially white males, at center stage. Our definition of what citizenship and the rights that go with it mean is not that of the Founders but that of the three constitutional amendments added during Reconstruction. But the Civil War generation understood its bond with the past more than we do today. Today, the American Revolution is still in play, endangered, but as relevant as it was in 1776. The essence of its appeal to the identity and rights of a person remains, and so does the implied but equally strong conviction of the need to preserve unity if the republic is to survive. This country remains a work in progress, and the American Revolution is the only war in our history we cannot afford to lose. The unity we identify with victory on the battlefield will neither resolve our differences nor confirm our nationhood. Something more is needed.[6]

I concede that the current mood in the country belies what I am expressing: a bias for hope in the face of seemingly incontrovertible evidence that the task of reconciling individual liberties with the equally compelling demands for social justice and human rights remains unfulfilled. But I retain the bias nonetheless when something happens in a particularly divisive and dangerous situation: I hear an outpouring of voices saying "This is a moral issue" accompanied by "do something." Historians and sociologists may continue to argue about the dynamics of race or class or gender and the relationship between all three, but I am equally persuaded about the persistence of religion, particularly Protestantism and its equally troublesome adjustment to Catholicism after the Great War and, nowadays, to Islam.[7]

We have incorporated something into the American Revolution that the Founders rarely dwelt on because they were of necessity preoccupied with resisting the power of a monarch and containing the revolution from below—democracy—symbolized in Tom Paine's America. The American Revolution has always had more seductive than transformative power. We have made it a morality play about diversity and inclusivity—and rightly so—or, if you like, *Hamilton*, the musical in which the only white cast member plays George III. The anger over that image is palpable and violent.

If this country is on a collision course with another civil war, as some predict, it may well revolve around persistent and nagging issues encompassing race and class, but I believe it will be about something more dangerous: a civil war in which the two leading combatants are Texas and California, two economic and political powerhouses, each vying for domination of the country. Ironically, these were the two political entities in the Jacksonian age whose passages to inclusion in the Union posed differences as striking then as they are today. Though nowadays their demographic identities may mirror one another, what each stands for offers a strikingly different vision of the future for the rest of the country.[8]

Such a war might throw Greater North America and perhaps both the Atlantic and Pacific worlds into an apocalyptic struggle to determine an outcome that might have been prevented if the American Revolution had found closure or if we had chosen an alternative revolution, one that did not give centrality to slavery and race, or expansionism, or the search for markets, or the encouragement of the communal instead of the acquisitive instincts of the individual, or not looking at every political or social issue as negotiable. For those who believe in single-issue counterfactuals as a determining force in explaining revolutions or retain a linear perspective on understanding their course, the American variation may offer a more persuasive answer than the one I've provided.

But revolutions do not follow a linear, predictable course, and the American Revolution is no exception. With the Enlightenment came the belief that liberalism, with its secular arguments reinforced by evidence, science, and facts, would win out over superstition and the tyranny of monarchs. Despite Benedetto Croce's affirmation of the liberal tenet that history is the triumph of liberty and the parallel belief that the public good and individual self-interest are compatible, the modern condition of humankind points to a different conclusion. It was the French, not the American Revolution, that rejected the notion of compatibility between individual self-interest and the public good. For a twentieth-century world, if not always for that of the eighteenth or nineteenth century, the French, if not the American, Revolution may have provided the model for those who look to revolution for its transformative power. But the French model is a troubling fit for those who find revolutionary ideas compatible with God's word.[9]

The resistance to closure points to the essence of the long American Revolution, which may help to explain, if not satisfy, those who believe that the revolutionary promise or aspiration has been subverted, that choices made to achieve one purpose have too often led to the obverse or morally repugnant outcome. Ours is the infuriating, if not unique or exceptional, contradiction of a revolution that professes one ideal or mission only to devour or divert those who unwittingly follow or serve it. I am heartened by those who subscribe to democratic socialism but am apprehensive that in this culture such a government would fall prey to dictatorship either via the ballot box or with public approval or a military coup. It can happen here. I am impressed with the strides in law, if not the behavior of people, toward bringing about a society dedicated to human rights—what the revolutionary generation identified as natural rights—even as I acknowledge that the age-old prescription of "white supremacy in a white republic" remains and may never go away, but I believe that is not the America we want to be and indeed we can never be, if that is what we desire to be. I concede the simplicity and appeal of race or what is expressed as "playing the race card" in politics or social policy, but the United States will never get to be "America" by doing so.

That may not be satisfactory for those who insist that we have yet to confront our revolutionary past. The literature on the subject is brilliant, tendentious, celebratory, riddled with gender and racial biases, and complicated by the persistent intrusion or "trap" of "American exceptionalism." What I have suggested is a framework for looking at the Revolution over a long period of time, viewing it from different angles (east–west as well as north–south), and keeping in mind the "lag time" between the creation of the republic and the moment when the nation assumed for us its problematical identity in the

Great War. For Europeans, the Great War began as a war between empires and a war within Christendom that ended with the destruction of four empires and with Christendom in the dock. For the United States, the war was about economic and cultural ties, and it was a war we entered for the presumed higher purpose of making the world safe for democracy. It was for us, if not for Europeans, the last war of the Protestant Reformation. At the end of that war the country had at last achieved the revolutionary goal of equality as a nation among nations. It was also a nation of nations. It still is.

I FOUND REMINDERS of that cultural and political anomaly in my zig-zagging trip in the mid-1980s across MexAmerica—one of several of the "nations" of North America—from Chicago to Mexico City interviewing persons for a book with the same title. (MexAmerica is usually described as a broad swath of territory straddling the two-thousand-mile U.S.-Mexican border. My definition is broader and more encompassing.)[10] Each person I spoke with could lay claim to what is called "identity politics," but each did so in a manner that validated the lasting influence of the American Revolution without the accompanying outrage about its failures to address the "social question." In Chicago I listened to a Latina (or Latinx, which is becoming the preferred choice) professor, Louise Kerr, speak painfully about her unpleasant experiences with immigration officials when she worked in the California orchards and her career in academia and in the role of social activist. In Kansas City I interviewed another Mexican American woman, Catherine Rocha, then the highest-ranking unelected person in the city government. She rejected the militancy of some Chicano leaders but reminded me that there was no color barrier she would tolerate with her phrase, "I'm just as white as you."[11]

In another interview for a proposed but not written book on Hispanic families, I learned what America can mean from the late Lucía Rede Madrid, a Mexican woman from the Big Bend region of Texas whose family had been settled in the area by the Texas government in the late nineteenth century as a barrier against the Indians. She told me stories of living near the Rio Grande during the Mexican Revolution, describing how U.S. soldiers would shoot at young Mexican boys watering their horses in the river. She married a storekeeper in Redford, only a few hundred yards from the river, and began lending donated books from a makeshift library to persons from either side of the border. From that modest beginning of transnational social and cultural endeavors, she attracted national and even international acclaim. "I believe in one America," she told me.

The experiences of these three women and others I interviewed in my north–south trek from Chicago to Mexico City in the mid-1980s were reminders of the contested legacy of the American Revolution as it played out for Mexicans and Mexican Americans in this country. In meeting them and listening to them, I sensed that they, better than I, grasped something about the American Revolution and its long history I had missed—its enticement or seduction or appeal to those who had reason to doubt its every promise. They had overcome adversity; they did not consider themselves victims; they had achieved. I felt as if they and I were kindred spirits. It was only years later that I realized the difference between them and me, and it had nothing to do with ethnicity or gender or socioeconomic circumstances. In becoming successes, they had retained a spiritual compass. In my relentless determination to succeed, I had lost my soul.

I DIDN'T COMPREHEND the damage until a few years later, when both my parents were in a nursing home but in separate rooms. In July 1994 I was in Mexico City, preparing to participate in a discussion on the Spanish-language edition of *MexAmerica: Two Countries, One Future*, and I received a call from my wife that my father had died. Such was my enduring dislike of the man that I tried to make excuses for not going to the funeral, but she reminded me that my family would be there, so I needed to be there. During the long flight back, I tried to think of my feelings about the man and what I believed was my mother's lifelong refusal to forgive him because she could not change him, which was my reason for not forgiving him.

I found at least a partial closure by remembering the last time I saw him, which was usually no more than once a year, and then after his senile dementia made it difficult for him to recognize me. On that final visit, when I approached the table where he was sitting, he turned to one of his friends and said, "This is my son. He writes books." In retrospect, I believe that he sensed I understood why he and many men are driven to behave in ways they know can be destructive, physically and spiritually. We are what we do, and too often we don't get it until it's too late. As much as others I have incorporated into this account, he, too, was a child of the long American Revolution. But his religious faith, unlike my mother's, was grounded in Masonry.

In February 1996 my mother died. I learned later that she had been choking on some food, and the attendant who performed the Heimlich maneuver had in the process broken some of her ribs. There was nothing the doctors could do, so she stopped eating and drinking. Surely God would never call that suicide.

She may have been right about looking at life and history as a morality play. I am certain she had never read Marx's comment that people make their own history, but it may not be the history they want to make. Social scientists can invoke theory or data to explain the course of events or the evil that men do, but the historian must grapple with intangibles as well. It's not the social question that befuddles those who study revolution, it's the moral consequences of those who act in the cause of revolution. If you understand that, you'll never have to ask, "What difference does a revolution make?" Just keep in mind that such a judgment is of limited use for those who are making policy and of no consequence for those who have no conscience.

That didn't matter as I gazed at her face for the last time. It was that of someone at peace, content in her faith in God, unconcerned if her husband would be awaiting her in heaven, and certain that she remained the moral compass of her last child and that one day he would regain the soul he believed he lost. He did.

Now you may better understand the dedication of this book and my relationship with those persons and groups and theirs with the long American Revolution—from a brother who defied authority yet served country, community, and family, to the Canadian who acknowledges the symbiotic bond his nation has with its North American neighbor. You may see why I have chosen a circular rather than a linear approach to looking at the long American Revolution and its legacy and have begun and ended this book from a personal perspective. There are children of the American Revolution who put God and scripture before ideas or self-interest or in obverse order in explaining their thoughts and deeds. I believe also that most of them would acknowledge, as depressing as it sounds, that there are persons for whom none of these inspirational or pecuniary motivations mean very much yet who are willing to serve and even die for those who do because each wanted to be "somebody." Actually, that was as true in 1776 as it is today.

A revolution, like a person, does have roots, and both are about a return to the beginning and about being and belonging.

TIME LINES

Chapter 1. A War of Consequence

1754	Beginning of French and Indian War in the Ohio Country
1756	Beginning of Seven Years' War in Europe, North America, West Africa, India, and the Caribbean
1759	British victory over French in Quebec leads to surrender of Montreal and New France a year later
	Carlos III becomes king of Spain
1760	George III becomes king of Great Britain
1761	Spain signs the Family Compact and enters the war on the French side
1762	British occupation of Havana
1763	Peace of Paris ends French and Indian War and Seven Years' War
	Pontiac's Indian rebellion in the Ohio Valley
	Proclamation of 1763 prohibits further settlement west of the Appalachian Mountains
1765	Parliament passes the Stamp Act
	Carlos III decrees a broadening of trade between Spanish ports and Spanish American cities and appoints a *visitador* to modernize the Mexican economy with new measures
	Increasing white resentment of free coloreds in Saint-Domingue results in new laws restricting their access to certain professions and political activities
1766	Parliament repeals the Stamp Act but affirms its right to legislate for the colonies in the Declaratory Act
1767	Parliament passes the Townshend Acts, levying indirect taxes, and

begins withdrawal of troops from the western country and stationing them in colonial cities under the Quartering Act of 1765

1770   Boston Massacre and repeal of Townshend duties except for the tax on tea

Lord North becomes prime minister

1773   Boston Tea Party

1774   Parliament passes the Coercive Acts, closing the port of Boston and re-organizing the Massachusetts government, and the Quebec Act, transferring the Indian trade and the land between the Ohio and Mississippi Rivers to Quebec

First Continental Congress meets in Philadelphia

1775   Battles of Lexington and Concord

Benjamin Franklin calls for a "United Colonies of North America," which included Quebec, St. Johns, Nova Scotia, East and West Florida, and appeals for support to the British West Indies, Bermuda, and even Ireland

London Common Council affirms right of colonial resistance

George Washington appointed commander of Continental Army

With sixty thousand Londoners cheering, George III goes to Parliament to address issue of rebellion in the colonies

Two invasions of Quebec end in failure in December

Lord Dunmore of Virginia declares freedom for any slave or indentured servant who takes up arms against the rebellion

1776   Thomas Paine publishes *Common Sense*

British Prime Minister Lord North offers plan of reconciliation

Declaration of Independence

British take command in New York City

Chapter 2. The Beginning of the Long American Revolution

1777   Patriot victory at Saratoga strengthens argument for obtaining foreign aid

1778	French sign treaties of amity and commerce and alliance with American delegates
	British peace proposal (Carlisle Commission) offers American Patriots a return to pre-1763 imperial status
1779	Spain declares war on Great Britain
1780	Empress Catherine II of Russia creates League of Armed Neutrality to safeguard neutral commerce
	British capture Charleston, South Carolina, and commence southern campaign
1781	Articles of Confederation ratified
	Lord Cornwallis surrenders at Yorktown
1783	Treaty of Paris formally ending the War of Independence
1786	Shay's Rebellion in Massachusetts
1787	Constitutional Convention meets in Philadelphia (May 27–September 17) ostensibly to revise the Articles of Confederation and ends up writing a constitution that creates a republic with three branches of government

Chapter 3. The Revolutionary Equation

1789	George Washington takes the oath of office as president and is both criticized and praised for showing "monarchical" or "kingly" airs, thus his appellation as a "republican monarch"
	Storming of the Bastille in Paris
	National Assembly in France approves the Declaration of Rights of Man and of the Citizen
1790	Free colored revolt against white rule in Saint-Domingue
1791	Slave revolt in North Province of Saint-Domingue
1793	Execution of Louis XVI
	British and Spanish governments declare war on France
	President George Washington declares U.S. neutrality

Razing of Cap-Français (Cap-Haïtien) by rebel slaves leads to French National Convention emancipation decree and declaration of slavery as a violation of human rights

White planters in Saint-Domingue call on British troops (already occupying French Martinique and Guadeloupe) to protect them

Toussaint Louverture emerges as leader of the Haitian slave revolt

1794   Treaty of Amity and Commerce with Britain (Jay Treaty)

1795   Treaty of San Lorenzo with Spain (Pinckney's Treaty)

Spain cedes eastern portion of Hispaniola to France

Washington issues his farewell address

France breaks the First Coalition, forces Spain to cede eastern two-thirds of Hispaniola

1798   Toussaint Louverture compels the British to withdraw from Saint-Domingue

Undeclared naval war (Quasi War) between the United States and France on the high seas

Federalist Congress passes Alien and Sedition Acts, extending time period for citizenship and punishing editors for harsh criticism of government

1799   Napoleon Bonaparte topples French government in November coup to prevent Jacobin resurgence

Official end of the French Revolution

1800   End of Quasi War with France and the Revolutionary War Alliance

Napoleon abruptly compels Spanish to cede Louisiana to France

1801   Jefferson inaugurated president after bitterly fought election; he affirms that "we are all Federalists [and] Republicans"

Toussaint ends slavery in Saint-Domingue but preserves the plantation economy with a severe labor code

Following Louverture's takeover of all Hispaniola, Napoleon plans to reestablish French control over the island

1802–1804   French invasion of Saint-Domingue and a two-year war with blacks and mulattos fighting on both sides

Louverture betrayed by his generals and sent to France in chains

Black-mulatto alliance against the French precipitates a racial war, with heavy French losses from battle and yellow fever

In 1803 the Peace of Amiens abruptly breaks, and Napoleon elects to sell Louisiana to the United States

In January 1804 Haiti becomes the second independent state of the hemisphere

Chapter 4. The Republic in Peril

1805–1807   France's Grand Empire in Europe begins to take shape

Napoleon creates the Continental System to control neutral trade and punish the British, who retaliate with Orders in Council, requiring neutrals to pay duties in British ports and permitting the searching of U.S. merchant vessels for mostly British subjects who have taken on U.S. citizenship to escape service in the Royal Navy

Jefferson retaliates with the embargo, which paralyzes the New England economy

1807–1810   Spanish crisis, with Napoleon forcing the abdication of Spanish monarch Carlos IV and Prince Fernando, which precipitates rebellion in Spain

In 1810 the political crisis in Spain precipitates a civil war in Spanish America between those who want the restoration of the Spanish monarch Fernando, those who want autonomy, and those who want independence; the most violent uprising occurs in Mexico, led by the priest Miguel Hidalgo, who loses control of his followers, most of them Indians and mestizos, and the countryside collapses in a race war

1812   Congress declares war on Great Britain and the United States plans invasion of Lower Canada

Napoleon, frustrated by Peninsular War in Spain, invades Russia

Following congressional passage of the "No-Transfer Resolution" of Florida from Spain to another European power, the Madison administration supports the efforts of the patriot army from Georgia and Alabama to seize East Florida

Creation of the Spanish parliament, the Cortes; the liberal Constitution of Cádiz establishes representative government for the Spanish nation in Europe and America and declares all free men regardless of color or status to be Spaniards

1813   Andrew Jackson leads militia in the Creek War campaign in Alabama

Simón Bolívar becomes dictator in Venezuelan second republic

U.S. invasion of Upper Canada and burning of York (Toronto)

Battle of Lake Erie

1814   Fernando restored to throne in Spain, abolishes the 1812 liberal constitution, and vows to crush independence movements in Spanish America

Napoleon is defeated in battle and sent into exile on Elba

Peace of Paris

Collapse of the Second Venezuelan Republic

Bolívar flees to Cartagena and then to Jamaica

British invasion of Chesapeake area and burning of public buildings in Washington, D.C., in retaliation for looting and burning by U.S. troops in Upper Canada

Congress of Vienna convenes to restore monarchical rule and create an international system to prevent another French revolution

Jackson takes his army to the Isle of Orleans for the defense of the city

Christmas Eve signing of the Treaty of Ghent ends the War of 1812

1815   Battle of New Orleans

News of Ghent settlement arrives in the United States

Napoleon lands in France, rebuilds his army, and triumphantly enters Paris on March 20

Battle of Waterloo

Napoleon abdicates and attempts to flee to the New World but is captured and sent to Saint Helena in the South Atlantic

Chapter 5. The Western Question

1815	Spanish Army of Pacification under Pablo Morillo lands at Santa Marta (in modern Colombia)

Bolívar writes the famous Jamaica Letter, setting out the reasons for the war, and appeals for British aid

Morelos revolt defeated in Mexico; Morelos is executed; Mexico plunged into five-year guerrilla war

1816   Denied aid from the British, Bolívar appeals to Alexandre Pétion of republican Haiti for assistance; Pétion grants the assistance in return for a pledge that slaves who join the fight will be given their freedom

American Colonization Movement founded to promote relocation of manumitted slaves outside the United States

1817–1819   Conflict in Venezuela and New Granada becomes a war of independence and a racial conflict

Bolívar becomes a popular figure in Congress and in the United States, but Secretary of State John Quincy Adams is suspicious about the use of African troops and is hesitant to pursue recognition while carrying out negotiations over the transfer of Florida and southwestern border issues

Andrew Jackson leads another invasion of Florida, warning of a war with Spain

In March 1818 Henry Clay makes the case for recognition of the new republics

In February 1819 Bolívar delivers his Angostura Address, which lays the foundation for the creation of Colombia (Gran Colombia), the union of Venezuela, New Granada, and Quito

1820–1822   Missouri statehood crisis plays out against the backdrop of the Spanish American wars of independence

Problems with the Spanish over the 1819 Transcontinental Treaty providing for Florida acquisition

Denmark Vesey slave revolt in South Carolina

Debate over U.S. policy in the Western Hemisphere about a joint U.S.-British or a unilateral approach to deal with the independence of former Spanish colonies

1822–1824   Defeat of liberal regime in Spain and fears of European aid to Spain to recover its empire in America

Russian expansion in the Pacific Northwest, and suggestions of British-U.S. cooperation in Latin America precipitate debate within Monroe's cabinet about U.S. choices, leading to the 1823 statement that became known as the Monroe Doctrine

Bolívar and the Argentine Juan de San Martín have a meeting in the independent city of Guayaquil

San Martín withdraws from royalist-held Peru, and Bolívar and his generals end Spanish rule

Bolívar becomes a transatlantic hero, oversees the creation of the new state of Bolivia in Upper Peru, and is recognized as the Spanish American "George Washington"

Jackson wins the popular vote in the presidential election but lacks an electoral majority, which throws the choice into the House of Representatives, where John Quincy Adams is chosen; Jacksonians blame Henry Clay, whom Adams names as secretary of state, as the culprit in this "Corrupt Bargain"

1825–1830   Adams leads the last presidency of the Old Republic, calling for U.S. participation in a meeting of former Spanish colonies to forge a defensive alliance

Adams promotes federal support and encouragement of economic development

Southern defenders of slavery and promoters of states' rights become more outspoken in their criticism of the revolutionary precepts of freedom and equality

Collapse of Bolívar's plan for a union of the Andean states, yet the example of Spanish America as a place where slaves and people of color could play a meaningful role in public affairs and civic life is identified as an example for African Americans in the United States

1828   Jackson wins the presidential election

Chapter 6. The American Democracy

1829   Andrew Jackson inaugurated president, promises fair treatment of Indians

Mexico abolishes slavery throughout the republic, but U.S. immigrants in Texas ignore the decree

Mexico expels Spaniards and defeats Spanish invaders

As proslavery and abolitionist elements become more outspoken, David Walker advocates armed struggle in *Appeal to the Coloured Citizens of the World*

1830   Indian Removal Act calls on Jackson to pursue ownership of all Indian lands east of the Mississippi River

Overthrow of Charles X in France

Louis-Philippe of the House of Orléans becomes constitutional monarch in France

Belgium secedes from the Netherlands

1830–1835   Mexico attempts to halt U.S. immigration into Texas

Antonio López de Santa Anna becomes president of Mexico; adoption of a centralist constitution precipitates a federalist revolt in Zacatecas and Texas

William Lloyd Garrison founds abolitionist newspaper *The Liberator*

Nat Turner slave revolt in Virginia precipitates fears of race war

Christmas slave revolt in Jamaica accelerates emancipation movement in the British West Indies in 1834

1835   Volume 1 of Alexis de Tocqueville's *Democracy in America* is published to acclaim in France and the United States

Onset of seven-year-long Second Seminole War in Florida

1835–1837   Texas revolution and war of independence revive debate over expansion of slavery

Santa Anna's victory at the Alamo and the massacre of Texans at Goliad prompt outcries in the United States

Sam Houston defeats Santa Anna at the Battle of San Jacinto and compels the Mexican leader to recognize Texas independence

Jackson decides to avoid a crisis by opposing Texas's appeal for statehood; in his last act as president he recognizes Texas independence

1837–1838   Rebellions in Lower and Upper Canada influenced in part by Jacksonian democracy lead to a border crisis and peaceful settlement with the union of the two provinces into Canada East and Canada West

In the 1842 Webster-Ashburton Treaty, the United States and Britain clarify disputes over the border demarcation from Maine to the Lake of the Woods

1839–1842   John Quincy Adams (elected representative from Massachusetts in 1830) wins victory in the *Amistad* case, involving African slaves sold in Cuba who rebel aboard the transport vessel but end up in U.S. jurisdiction; in the ensuing trial Adams invokes the American revolutionary principle of self-determination in arguing they had a right to be returned to Africa

1842   Two unsuccessful Texan military encounters with Mexican forces revive the issues of slave expansion and U.S. fears of French and especially British efforts to contain U.S. continental expansion in North America

1844   Narrow victory of Democrat James K. Polk in the presidential election precipitates twin crises, one with Great Britain over U.S. claims in the Oregon Territory and U.S. efforts to acquire California, the second with Mexico over California and especially the decision of the outgoing John Tyler administration to approve Texas statehood

1846   Skirmish between Mexican and U.S. troops near present-day Brownsville prompts Polk to declare that Mexico "has shed American blood on American soil." One month later, the United States and Britain agree to a peaceful settlement of the Oregon boundary at the forty-ninth parallel

1846–1848   Three-pronged assault on Mexico, the first by General Zachary Taylor into northern Mexico in May 1846, and the second into New Mexico and California in July and August 1846

When Mexico refuses to sue for peace, Polk orders General Winfield Scott's army into the interior of Mexico in March 1847

The invasion of Central Mexico precipitates criticism of Polk from Whig congressmen and in the press for waging an offensive and "wicked" war

1848   In February 1848 Polk reluctantly accepts a peace treaty negotiated by a diplomat he has disowned, even though the treaty gives the United States virtually everything it wants

Convention of women delegates at Seneca Falls, New York, draft the Declaration of Sentiments, modeled on the Declaration of Independence

Democratic Party splits over slavery in the territories

Martin Van Buren runs as candidate of the Free Soil Party

Fifty revolutionary uprisings in Europe fail to overturn monarchical rule but succeed in deposing Louis-Philippe in France and sending Klemens von Metternich of Austria into exile

The uprisings and the Irish potato famine send another wave of European migration to the United States

1849–1851   Southern slaveholders give aid to Narciso López's efforts to overturn Spanish rule in Cuba

White Cuban slaveholders favor U.S. annexation and eventual statehood

1850   Compromise of 1850 settles Texas boundaries, provides for California statehood as a free state, ends the slave trade in the District of Columbia, alters the Fugitive Slave Law, establishes a territorial government for Utah and New Mexico, and sets the U.S.-Mexican boundary

1854   "Ostend Manifesto" crisis resulting from publicity over recommendation of three U.S. diplomats to seize Cuba if the Spanish refuse to sell the island

Fighting commences between pro- and antislave groups in Kansas territory

Republican Party formed in Michigan in opposition to the proposal to allow slavery to be decided by popular sovereignty in Kansas-Nebraska Territory

Chapter 7. The American War and Peace

1856	Sacking of Lawrence, Kansas (a free-state stronghold), by proslavers leads to bloody retaliation by John Brown and his sons
	Proslavery Democratic candidate James Buchanan wins the presidential election over Republican James Fremont and former president Millard Fillmore, who is running as the anti-immigration American Party candidate
1857	Supreme Court decides in *Dred Scott v. Sandford* that a former slave (Scott) who had been taken to free territory had no right as a citizen to sue in federal court and that the Missouri Compromise of 1820 was unconstitutional
1857–1861	Liberal-Conservative clashes in Venezuela, Colombia, Nicaragua, and Mexico precipitate conflicts in which slavery and race, along with the power of the central government, are major issues
	In Mexico the civil war is complicated by a religious struggle; in Nicaragua, by the invasion of William Walker, who gains power, institutes slavery, becomes a popular figure in the United States, and is finally defeated by a Central American coalition
1858	Abraham Lincoln's debates with Stephen A. Douglas for an Illinois senatorial seat reveal Lincoln's hesitant views about African American equality
1859	John Brown and his band seize the U.S. armory in Harpers Ferry, Virginia, but fail to incite a slave insurrection
1860	Lincoln wins the presidency, precipitating the secession of seven southern states before his March 4, 1861, inauguration

1861   Firing on Fort Sumter and Lincoln's response prompt four more southern states (including Virginia) to secede

Canadians anticipate the end of the republican government in North America and fear a U.S. invasion

Liberal government of Benito Juárez in Mexico faces threatened Spanish-British-French intervention over Mexico's debt; Spanish and British withdraw, but Napoleon III of France elects to move his forces into the interior

At the invitation of President Pedro Santana, the Spanish occupy the Dominican Republic; Secretary of State William H. Seward calls for an aggressive response

Seizure of two Confederate agents from the British ship *Trent* creates a crisis with the British government

1862   Horace Greeley, editor of the *New York Daily Tribune,* calls for a moral purpose to the war in his "Prayer of Twenty Million"

After the Battle of Antietam and despite skepticism in his cabinet, Lincoln issues the Preliminary Emancipation Proclamation

At the end of the year, the president proposes a plan for gradual and compensated emancipation

Passage of the Homestead Act

Recognition of Haiti in the belief it would inhibit European imperialism in the hemisphere and serve as a place to relocate African Americans

Spanish occupy the Dominican Republic, precipitating a guerrilla war

1863   Emancipation Proclamation becomes policy on January 1, excluding four border slave states but transforming the Union army into a liberating force and making the war a test case for the survival of republican government and democracy

Battles of Gettysburg and Vicksburg point to Union victory, but draft riots in New York City reveal the deep racial fissures in the North

In dedication of Gettysburg Cemetery, Lincoln invokes the Revolution in his call for a new birth of freedom

1864   French invaders drive Juárez and his government from Mexico City

                  With strong clerical support, Mexican conservatives place Ferdinand
                  Maximilian Joseph of Austria, a Hapsburg, in power

                  The fall of Atlanta, Lincoln's victory in November, and the ensuing
                  march of Sherman's army to the sea raise hopes of a Union victory

1865   In his March 4 inaugural message, Lincoln invokes warnings of Old
                  Testament justice and follows with conciliatory words; in his last public
                  speech, he calls for equality in the right to vote for African Americans

                  Onset of Reconstruction with passage of Thirteenth Amendment,
                  which bans slavery

                  President Andrew Johnson faces rising criticism by Republicans and
                  African Americans by returning land seized by the Union army to its
                  former owners

1866   Birth of the Ku Klux Klan

                  Civil Rights Act of 1866 establishes national citizenship for males

                  Republicans sweep congressional elections

Chapter 8. The End of the Long American Revolution

1867   First and Second Radical Republican Reconstruction Acts

                  Escalating violence against African Americans

                  Defeat and execution of Maximilian in Mexico

                  Seward oversees Alaska purchase

                  Creation of the Canadian Confederation

1868   Passage of the Fourteenth Amendment, defining national citizenship
                  and equal protection of the law for males in the political community

                  Impeachment of President Andrew Johnson; Senate fails to convict him

                  Ulysses S. Grant wins the presidential election; in his inaugural message
                  he pledges security of person and property, but resistance to Radical
                  Reconstruction persists

1870–1871   Proposed annexation of Dominican Republic fails despite President Grant's argument that U.S. annexation will transform the island as a beacon of liberty between Cuba and Brazil, where slavery still exists

Ratification of the Fifteenth Amendment, guaranteeing the right to vote to African American male citizens

Prussian victory over France in Franco-Prussian War, ending the Third Empire of Napoleon III

Paris Commune uprising and suppression

1876–1877   Centennial year exhibition displays country's industrial and technological achievements against the disturbing backdrop of a divisive presidential campaign, an Indian war in the West, and labor violence

Railroad strike in the East and Custer's defeat at the Little Big Horn

Rutherford B. Hayes becomes president following a Senate inquiry into disputed electoral votes from three southern states

1877–1900   Canada, the United States, Brazil, and Argentina rely on immigration to modernize and "whiten" their labor forces

Settlement and pacification of the West, coupled with labor and rural unrest, illustrate differences in U.S. and Canadian experiences

Mexico modernizes under long dictatorship of Porfirio Díaz (1877–1910) and U.S. investment, fueling cultural resentments and rural unrest

Depressions in the 1870s and 1890s precipitate labor strikes and rural discontent, leading to the rise of the Populist Party and the pivotal presidential election of 1896, in which Republican William McKinley defeats Democrat/Populist William Jennings Bryan

U.S. political and business leaders fashion plans for a "new empire" dedicated to expanding U.S. markets in Latin America, the western Pacific, and China

War with Spain in 1898 fulfills that goal, as well as the strategic plan to modernize the U.S. Navy, but the postwar creation of insular empire and protectorates in the Caribbean and the western Pacific precipitates a bitter debate over imperialism and the threat of empire to a "white" republic

1900–1920 U.S. economic and industrial growth and the country's political and
military role in the Caribbean and Central America sustain its claim to
world power

Progressive political movement addresses political, economic, social,
and cultural challenges brought on by rapid immigration, industrial
unrest, and the rise of militant socialist movements

African Americans struggling under segregation are confronted with
differing political and social strategies advanced by the accommoda-
tionist Booker T. Washington; the more radical approaches of W. E. B.
Du Bois, founder of the NAACP; and the Jamaican Marcus Garvey

After three problematic years of neutrality, President Woodrow Wilson
calls for a U.S. declaration of war with Germany in April 1917, invoking
the spirit of the Declaration of Independence and the right of subject
peoples to self-determination; the United States becomes an "associated
power" of the British, the French, and the Russians in the Great War

Civil war and revolution in Mexico (1910–19) lead to two U.S. military interventions, a race war on the border, and a new Mexican
Constitution that directly conflicts with U.S. interests

Wilson's peace plan—embodied in the Fourteen Points and a proposal
for a League of Nations—encounters opposition and ultimate defeat in
the U.S. Senate after the president refuses to compromise

Despite military assistance from the United States and other Allied
governments, the White Russians lose their civil war with the
Bolsheviks in Russia. In the aftermath, the victors create the Union of
Soviet Socialist Republics

NOTES

Introduction

1. Honor Sachs, *Home Rule: Households, Manhood, and National Expansion on the Eighteenth-Century Kentucky Frontier* (New Haven, Conn., 2015), 2, 9–12, 46, 63, 73, 81.

2. John F. Kennedy, inaugural address, January 20, 1961, Inaugural Addresses of the Presidents of the United States, https://www.bartleby.com/124/pres56.html. For more precise definitions of American exceptionalism, see the classic work by the sociologist Seymour Martin Lipset, *American Exceptionalism: A Double-Edged Sword* (New York, 1997); and Ian Tyrrell, "American Exceptionalism, from Stalin with Love," Aeon, https://aeon.co/ideas/american-exceptionalism-from-stalin-with-love.

3. See the foreword by Anthony Barnett in *The Long Revolution*, by Raymond Williams (Cardigan, Wales, 2011; orig. pub., 1961), viii–xi. Williams believed that communists were not revolutionaries, which got him into trouble with the Left. Liberals get into trouble because they never understand that they cannot get to the left of the Left.

4. Hannah Arendt, "Introduction: War and Revolution," in *On Revolution* (New York, 1963), 11–20. Arendt emphasized that until the French Revolution, "revolution" meant "a return to first principles," so my answer was satisfactory. At least, the committee had to move on.

5. John Patrick Diggins, *The Lost Soul of American Politics: Virtue, Self-Interest, and the Foundations of Liberalism* (New York, 1984), 5.

6. Haitians had to pay a horrific indemnity of 150 million francs to France (which was later reduced to 90 million) to guarantee Haiti's survival. In the United States (except for the District of Columbia), the indemnity was indirect but just as costly—Jim and Jane Crow laws. Haiti did not pay off its debt to French bankers until after World War II. The United States, it is sometimes argued, settled accounts with the civil rights laws of the 1960s and with affirmative action laws. But reparations—to whom and for whom—are a different matter.

7. Some Canadian students of the issue would put Canadian nationhood either at 1931, when the Statute of Westminster gave the dominion self-governing autonomy, or with World War II. A popular but also controversial definition of "nation"—an "imagined community"—and of "nationalism" appears in Benedict Anderson, *Imagined Communities: Reflections on the Origin and Spread of Nationalism* (London, 2006; orig. pub., 1983).

Chapter 1. A War of Consequence

1. D. W. Meinig, *The Shaping of America: A Geographical Perspective on 500 Years of History*, vol. 1, *Atlantic America, 1492–1800* (New Haven, Conn., 1986), 267. Fred Anderson articulates the case for the significance of the Seven Years' War in the coming of the American Revolution in *Crucible of Empire: The Seven Years' War and the Fate of Empire in British North America* (New York, 2000). See also Matt Schumann and Karl Schweizer, *The Seven Years' War: A Transatlantic History* (New York, 2008). English-speaking Canadians refer to the war as the Seven Years' War; French-speaking Canadians as the War of Conquest.

2. Robert W. Tucker and David C. Hendrickson, *The Fall of the First British Empire: Origins of the War of American Independence* (Baltimore, Md., 1982).

3. Quoted in Russell Shorto, *Revolution Song: A Story of American Freedom* (New York, 2018), 93. See also David L. Preston, *Braddock's Defeat: The Battle of the Monongahela and the Road to Revolution* (New York, 2015).

4. See D. Peter MacLeod, *Northern Armageddon: The Battle of the Plains of Abraham and the Making of the American Revolution* (New York, 2016).

5. Quoted in Trevor Burnard, "The British Atlantic," in *Atlantic History: A Critical Appraisal*, ed. Jack P. Greene and Philip D. Morgan (New York, 2009), 113.

6. Thomas L. Purvis, "The Seven Years' War and Its Political Legacy," in *A Companion to the American Revolution*, ed. Jack P. Greene and J. R. Pole (Malden, Mass., 2004), 112–17. Virginia, Massachusetts, and New York contributed the most in moneys and troops raised for the war effort and indebtedness incurred.

7. Peter Silver, *Our Savage Neighbors: How Indian War Transformed Early America* (New York, 2008), xviii–xxi. Robert M. Owens, *Red Dreams, White Nightmares: Pan Indian Alliances in the Anglo-American Mind, 1763–1815* (Norman, Okla., 2015), also details how U.S. military and political leaders in the early republic tried to placate Indians by restraining settler retaliation or, alternately, carrying out preemptive strikes to prevent pan-Indian alliances.

8. Jack P. Greene, "The Origins of the New Colonial Policy, 1748–1763," in Greene and Pole, *Companion*, 101–11.

9. For Washington's ambivalent relationship to Indians and their place in the coming of the Revolution and in the early republic, see Colin G. Calloway, *The Indian World of George Washington: The First President, the First Americans, and the Birth of the Nation* (New York, 2018).

10. S. Max Edelson, *The New Map of Empire: How Britain Imagined America before Independence* (Cambridge, Mass., 2017), 21; P. J. Marshall, *The Making and Unmaking of Empires: Britain, India, and America, 1750–1783* (Oxford, 2005), 378. See also Michael Witgen, *An Infinity of Nations: How the Native New World Shaped Early America* (Philadelphia, 2012).

11. Claudio Saunt, *West of the Revolution: An Uncommon History of 1776* (New York, 2014), 192–93.

12. Quoted in Joseph J. Ellis, *His Excellency, George Washington* (New York, 2005), 26.

13. Gregory Evans Dowd, *War under Heaven: Pontiac, the Indian Nations, and the British Empire* (Baltimore, Md., 2002), 2. Pontiac's remarks are quoted in Alan Taylor, *American Colonies* (New York, 2001), 437.

14. Quoted in Saunt, *West of the Revolution*, 167. One of the most egregious violations of the Proclamation of 1763 occurred in 1775, when Richard Henderson, a land speculator, purchased twenty-two *million* acres (most of Kentucky and part of Tennessee) for approximately £2,700. Although two state legislatures later nullified the transaction, Henderson received two hundred thousand acres for his troubles (ibid., 17–28).

15. Mike Rapport, *The Unruly City: Paris, London, and New York in the Age of Revolution* (New York, 2017), xxvii–xxxiv. For a succinct assessment of the Stamp Act crisis in the context of the constitutional debate over direct and virtual representation, see Jack Rakove, *Revolutionaries: A New History of the Invention of America* (Boston, 2010), 20–23. The classic statement of its significance is Edmund S. Morgan and Helen M. Morgan, *The Stamp Act Crisis: Prologue to Revolution* (Chapel Hill, 1995; orig. pub., 1953).

16. Carl B. Cone, "America's Unknown King," in *The American Revolution and a "Candid World,"* ed. Lawrence Kaplan (Kent, Ohio, 1977), 4–5, 10–11; Gordon S. Wood, *The American Revolution: A History* (New York, 2003), 42; Jack P. Greene, *Peripheries and Center: Constitutional Development in the Extended Polities of the British Empire and the United States* (New York, 1990; orig. pub., Athens, Ga., 1986), 103.

17. David Brion Davis, *Inhuman Bondage: The Rise and Fall of Slavery in the New World* (New York, 2006), 124–26.

18. Seymour Drescher, *Abolition: A History of Slavery and Antislavery* (New York, 2009) offers a sweeping account of the subject from the Middle Ages to World War II. In the eighteenth century, notes Ralph Bauer, "race" referred less to skin color or related biological factors and more to cultural factors such as nationality, family, and religion. As the chroniclers and Enlightenment thinkers began to draw sharper distinctions between Europeans and New World peoples, descendants of European settlers in the Americas began to use "whiteness" or "race" to affirm their equality with Europeans. Ralph Bauer, "The Hemispheric Genealogies of 'Race': Creolization and the Cultural Geography of Colonial Differences across the Eighteenth-Century Americas," in *Hemispheric American Studies*, ed. Caroline F. Levander and Robert S. Levine (New Brunswick, N.J., 2008), 36–56.

19. Taylor, *American Colonies*, xiii.

20. Quoted in Barry Alain Shain, *The Myth of American Individualism: The Prot-*

estant Origins of American Political Thought (Princeton, N.J., 1994), 79. See also Eric Foner, *The Story of American Freedom* (New York, 1994), 6–9.

21. Quoted in Ambrogio Caiani, "The Enlightenment: Who, When, and Where," in *Understanding and Teaching the Age of Revolutions*, ed. Ben Marsh and Mike Rapport (Madison, Wis., 2017), 68. There are almost as many biographies of Martin Luther as there are of Jesus Christ. Eric Metaxas, *Martin Luther: The Man Who Discovered God and Changed the World* (New York, 2017), portrays Luther as one who made the modern ideas of the individual, as well as religious liberty, self-government, and pluralism, possible. Yet some German scholars attribute the roots of the Holocaust to his anti-Semitic passages.

22. J. C. D. Clark, *The Language of Liberty, 1660–1832: Political Discourse and Social Dynamics in the Anglo-American World* (Cambridge, 1993), xii–xiii, 296–97, 305.

23. Justin Du Rivage, *Revolution against Empire: Taxes, Politics, and the Origins of American Independence* (New Haven, Conn., 2017), 120.

24. T. H. Breen, *American Insurgents, American Patriots: The Revolution of the People* (New York, 2010), 10.

25. Rapport, *Unruly City*, 42–52.

26. Stephen Conway, "Britain and the Revolutionary Crisis," in *The Oxford History of the British Empire*, vol. 2, *The Eighteenth Century*, ed. P. J. Marshall (New York, 1998), 336. Others, including some of North's supporters, alleged that his plan was to divide defiant Massachusetts and all New England from the other colonies.

27. Edward Larkin, "Thomas Paine and the *Common Sense* of Revolutions," in Marsh and Rapport, *Understanding and Teaching*, 145–60.

28. Quoted in Wood, *American Revolution*, 30, who places the number of troops at four thousand.

29. Quoted in Jack P. Greene, "Empire and Identity from the Glorious Revolution to the American Revolution," in Marshall, *The Eighteenth Century*, 225.

30. Quoted in Pauline Maier, *American Scripture: Making the Declaration of Independence* (New York, 1997), 36; Edward Countryman, "Social Protest and the Revolutionary Movement, 1765–1776," in Greene and Pole, *Companion*, 184–85.

31. Chris Tudda, "'A Messiah That Will Never Come': A New Look at Saratoga, Independence, and Revolutionary War Diplomacy," *Diplomatic History* 32 (November 2008): 783; Anthony Pagden, *Lords of All the World: Ideologies of Empire in Spain, Britain, and France c. 1500–c. 1800* (New Haven, Conn., 1998), 197. See also John Brewer, "Ben Franklin: Caught between Worlds," *New York Review of Books*, November 2016, 42–43, a review of Carla J. Mulford, *Benjamin Franklin and the Ends of Empire*, and George Goodwin, *Benjamin Franklin in London*.

32. Quoted in David Armitage, *Civil Wars: A History in Ideas* (New York, 2017), 140.

33. Quoted in James K. Martin and Mark Lender, *A Respectable Army: The Military Origins of the Republic, 1763–1789* (Arlington Heights, Ill., 1982), 45.

34. Wendy Warren, *New England Bound: Slavery and Colonization in Early America* (New York, 2016), 2–3, 8–9, 250–51.

35. Sylvia Frey, *Water from the Rock: Black Resistance in a Revolutionary Age* (Princeton, N.J., 1991), 55.

36. Quoted in Gary B. Nash, *The Unknown American Revolution: The Unruly Birth of Democracy and the Struggle to Create America* (New York, 2005), 147.

37. Ira Berlin, *Many Thousands Gone: The First Two Centuries of Slavery in North America* (Cambridge, Mass., 2000), 138–41.

38. James Sidbury, *Ploughshares into Swords: Race, Rebellion, and Identity in Gabriel's Virginia, 1730–1830* (New York, 1997), 11–12, 48–49.

39. Mark R. Anderson, *The Battle for the Fourteenth Colony: America's War of Liberation in Canada, 1774–1776* (Lebanon, N.H., 2013). The author is a veteran of "wars of liberation" in Iraq and Afghanistan.

40. Thomas Paine, *Common Sense* (Mount Vernon, N.Y., 1976; orig. pub., 1776), 31.

41. Eric Foner, *Tom Paine and Revolutionary America* (New York, 1976), xii–xiii, 78–79, 80–81. On the use of the word "revolution" by contemporaries, see Ilan Rachum, "From 'American Independence' to the 'American Revolution,'" *Journal of American Studies* 27, no. 1 (1993): 73–92.

42. Abigail Adams to John Adams, March 31–April 5, 1776, *Adams Family Papers: An Electronic Archive*, Massachusetts Historical Society, http://www.masshist.org /digitaladams.

43. Ibid.

44. David Hackett Fischer and James C. Kelly, *Bound Away: Virginia and the Westward Movement* (Charlottesville, Va., 2000), xvi.

45. John Adams to Abigail Adams, April 14, 1776, is available in Founders Online, National Archives, http://founders.archives.gov/documents/Adams/04-01-02-0248.

Chapter 2. The Beginning of the Long American Revolution

1. Quoted in Joseph J. Ellis, *His Excellency, George Washington* (New York, 2005), 112. For insights into Washington's character, see Richard Brookhiser, *George Washington's Rules of Civility & Decent Behavior in Company and Conversation* (Boston, 1997).

2. Quoted in Jack N. Rakove, *The Beginnings of National Politics: An Interpretive History of the Continental Congress* (New York, 1979), 107. Deputies in the First Continental Congress confirmed their loyalty as "faithful subjects" of the king, but the Declaration of Independence, Pauline Maier notes, was treason, and the Congress did not send copies to the states until mid-January 1777 (*American Scripture: Making the Declaration of Independence* [New York, 1997], 152–53).

3. Quoted in Bernard Bailyn, *To Begin the World Anew: The Genius and Ambiguities of the American Founders* (New York, 2003), 34. Jack Rakove has appropriately described the delegates as "provincials before they became revolutionaries, revolutionaries before they became American nationalists, and nationalists who were always mindful of their provincial roots" (*Revolutionaries: A New History of the Invention of America* [Boston, 2010], 16).

4. Quoted in David Brion Davis, *Revolutions: Reflections on American Equality and Foreign Liberations* (Cambridge, Mass., 1990), 18. For some contemporaries, liberty constituted a privilege, not a right, and was largely reserved for those who occupied the upper rungs of the social order. See Michael Rozbicki, *Culture and Liberty in the Age of the American Revolution* (Charlottesville, Va., 2011).

5. Quoted in David Armitage, *Civil Wars: A History in Ideas* (New York, 2017), 127–28. See also Maier, *American Scripture*, 22–23, 30–31.

6. Robert Bothwell, *Your Country, My Country: A Unified History of the United States and Canada* (New York, 2015), 57. See also John M. Murrin, "The Great Inversion, or Court versus Country," in *Rethinking America: From Empire to Republic* (New York, 2018), 31–97; and Marc W. Kruman, *Between Authority and Liberty: State Constitution Making in Revolutionary America* (Chapel Hill, N.C., 1997).

7. Quoted in Maier, *American Scripture*, 79.

8. Claudio Saunt, *West of the Revolution: An Uncommon History of 1776* (New York, 2014), incorporates these events and happenings across North America into an "uncommon history of 1776."

9. Maier, *American Scripture*, 94–96, 167.

10. Don Higginbotham, "The War for Independence, after Saratoga," in *A Companion to the American Revolution*, ed. Jack P. Greene and J. R. Pole (Malden, Mass., 2004), 292.

11. Quoted in Maier, *American Scripture*, 41.

12. Stephen Conway, "'Founded in Lasting Interests': British Projects for European Collaboration in the Age of the American Revolution," *International History Review* 37, no. 1 (2015): 22–40; Jack Rakove, *Beginnings of National Politics*, xv–xvi.

13. Lawrence Kaplan, "Toward Isolationism: The Rise and Fall of the Franco-American Alliance, 1775–1801," in *The American Revolution and "A Candid World,"* ed. Lawrence Kaplan (Kent, Ohio, 1977), 134–57.

14. Jonathan Dull, "Diplomacy of the Revolution," in Greene and Pole, *Companion*, 352–61.

15. Larrie D. Ferreiro, *Brothers at Arms: American Independence and the Men of France and Spain Who Saved It* (New York, 2015), 334–36; Thomas E. Chávez, *Spain and the Independence of the United States: An Intrinsic Gift* (Albuquerque, N.M., 2002), 39.

16. Carl Lotus Becker, *The History of Political Parties in the Province of New York, 1760–1776* (Madison, Wis., 1960; orig. pub., New York, 1909).

17. Gary Nash, *The Unknown American Revolution: The Unruly Birth of Democracy and the Struggle to Create America* (New York, 2005), 453–55. See also Edward Countryman, *Enjoy the Same Liberty: Black Americans and the Revolutionary Era* (Lanham, Md., 2011).

18. Quoted in Ellis, *His Excellency*, 111.

19. Ibid., 114.

20. Quoted in John Patrick Diggins, *The Lost Soul of American Politics: Self-Interest, and the Foundations of Liberalism* (New York, 1984), 23. See also Ellis, *His Excellency*, 114–15.

21. David Brion Davis, *The Problem of Slavery in the Age of Revolution, 1770–1823* (Ithaca, N.Y., 1975), 76–80.

22. See Douglas R. Egerton, *Death or Liberty: African Americans and Revolutionary America* (New York, 2009), 65–92; and Judith Van Buskirk, *Standing in Their Own Light: African American Patriots in the American Revolution* (Norman, Okla., 2017).

23. Robert Parkinson, *The Common Cause: Creating Race and Nation in the American Revolution* (Chapel Hill, N.C., 2016), 4–7, 22–23.

24. Quoted in David Brion Davis, *Inhuman Bondage: The Rise and Fall of Slavery in the New World* (New York, 2006), 148. On the war as counterrevolution, see Gerald Horne, *The Counter-Revolution of 1776: Slave Resistance and the Origins of the United States of America* (New York, 2014).

25. Colin G. Calloway, *The American Revolution in Indian Country: Crisis and Diversity in Native American Communities* (New York, 1995), xii–xiii, 292–301. On how some reformers attempted to mitigate anti-Indian prejudices, see Peter Silver, *Our Savage Neighbors: How Indian War Transformed Early America* (New York, 2008), 294–97. See also Ellis, *His Excellency*, 123–24; Saunt, *West of the Revolution*, 27.

26. Maya Jasanoff, *Liberty's Exiles: American Loyalists in the Revolutionary War* (New York, 2011), 12–13. The statistics on the loyalist exiles are taken from Bothwell, *Your Country, My Country*, 60–61. See also Ruma Chapra, *Unnatural Rebellion: Loyalists in New York City during the Revolution* (Charlottesville, Va., 2011).

27. Mark A. Noll, *America's God: From Jonathan Edwards to Abraham Lincoln* (New York, 2002), 69, 141–52. See also Thomas S. Kidd, *God of Liberty: A Religious History of the American Revolution* (New York, 2010), 4–9, 75, 91. Bernard Bailyn offered a dissenting view that "religion as such, or any of its doctrinal elements, had a unique political role in the Revolutionary movement" ("Religion and Revolution: Three Biographical Studies," *Perspectives in American History* 4 [1970]: 85).

28. Quoted in Thomas Fleming, *The Strategy of Victory: How George Washington*

Won the American Revolution (New York, 2017), 48. See also Charles Royster, *A Revolutionary People at War: The Continental Army and the American Character, 1775–1783* (Chapel Hill, N.C., 1980), 62–63.

29. Andrew O'Shaughnessy, *The Men Who Lost America: British Leadership, the American Revolution and the Fate of the Empire* (New Haven, Conn., 2013), 10–14, 353–54; J. C. D. Clark, *The Language of Liberty, 1660–1832: Political Discourse and Social Dynamics in the Anglo-American World* (Cambridge, 1994), 300–303.

30. John Shy, *A People Numerous and Armed: Reflections on the Military Struggle for American Independence* (New York, 1976), 212–13.

31. Quoted in Ferreiro, *Brothers at Arms*, 304.

32. Mike Rapport, *The Unruly City: Paris, London, and New York in the Age of Revolution* (New York, 2017), 114–21. For the long fight for Catholic emancipation in England, see also Antonia Fraser, *The King and the Catholics: England, Ireland, and the Fight for Religious Freedom, 1780–1829* (New York, 2018).

33. Jack P. Greene, *Peripheries and Center: Constitutional Development in the Extended Polities of the British Empire and the United States* (New York, 1990; orig. pub., Athens, Ga., 1986), 155–56.

34. Quoted in Joseph J. Ellis, *The Quartet: Orchestrating the Second American Revolution, 1783–1789* (New York, 2015), 77–78. See also Jane G. Landers, "Rebellion and Royalism in Spanish Florida: The French Revolution on Spain's Northern Frontier," in *A Turbulent Time: The French Revolution and the Greater Caribbean,* ed. David Barry Gaspar and David Patrick Geggus (Bloomington, Ind., 1997), 156–77.

35. Quoted in Ellis, *The Quartet,* 58.

36. Quoted in Joseph J. Ellis, *American Dialogue: the Founders and Us* (New York, 2018), 176.

37. Quoted in Rakove, *Beginnings of National Politics,* 335. See Ellis, *The Quartet,* 63, for Alexander Hamilton's views of the postwar crisis.

38. David Szatmary, *Shay's Rebellion: The Making of an Agrarian Insurrection* (Amherst, Mass., 1980), 122–23.

39. James Sidbury, *Ploughshares into Swords: Race, Rebellion, and Identity in Gabriel's Virginia, 1730–1810* (New York, 1997), 34–37.

40. John A. Ragosta, *Wellspring of Liberty: How Virginia's Religious Dissenters Helped Win the American Revolution* (New York, 2010), 4, see also 5–13; Rhys Isaac, *The Transformation of Virginia, 1740–1790* (Chapel Hill, N.C., 1982), 292–95, 310. For Jefferson's views on the need for the act on religious freedom, see his pamphlet *Notes on the State of Virginia* (New York, 1964; orig. pub., 1861), 206–7.

41. Quoted in Gordon S. Wood, *The Idea of America: Reflections on the Birth of the United States* (New York, 2011), 132.

42. Andrew Jackson O'Shaugnessy, *An Empire Divided: The American Revolution and the British Caribbean* (Philadelphia, 2000), 242–47.

43. David Ramsay to Benjamin Rush, July 11, 1783, in Ramsay, *History of the American Revolution*, ed. Lester H. Cohen, 2 vols. (Indianapolis, 1990; orig. pub., Philadelphia, 1789), 1:xxiii. See also Jack P. Greene, "The Limits of the American Revolution," in *The American Revolution: Its Character and Limits*, ed. Jack P. Greene (New York, 1987), 10–12; Alan Taylor, "Crèvecoeur's 'Letters from an American Farmer': The Dark Side," *New Republic*, July 19, 2013, 5–12.

44. Frederick W. Marks III, *Independence on Trial: Foreign Affairs and the Making of the Constitution* (Baton Rouge, La., 1973), xii–xvi, 218–19.

45. Eliga H. Gould, *Among the Powers of the Earth: The American Revolution and the Making of a New World Empire* (Cambridge, Mass., 2017), 10–13.

46. Quoted in David O. Stewart, *Madison's Gift: Five Partnerships That Built America* (New York, 2005), 40.

47. Greene, *Peripheries and Center*, 213–15.

48. Quoted in Michael J. Klarman, *The Framers' Coup: The Making of the United States Constitution* (New York, 2016), 631.

49. Peter S. Onuf, *The Origins of the Federal Republic: Jurisdictional Controversies in the United States, 1775–1787* (Philadelphia, 1983), 321.

50. See the classic study by Edmund Morgan, *American Freedom, American Slavery: The Ordeal of Colonial Virginia* (New York, 1975), and what is now considered its sequel, Alan Taylor, *The Internal Enemy: Slavery and War in Virginia, 1772–1832* (New York, 2013).

51. Danielle Allen, *Our Declaration: A Reading of the Declaration of Independence in Defense of Equality* (New York, 2014), 21–23, 145, 267–69; Maier, *American Scripture*, 154–55. See also Gordon Wood, "A Different Idea of Our Declaration," *New York Review of Books*, August 24, 2014, 37–38.

52. Paul Finkelman, *Slavery and the Founders: Race and Liberty in the Age of Jefferson* (Armonk, N.Y., 1996), ix, 5, 22, 36, 71, 81. See also Gary Nash, *Race and Revolution* (Madison, Wis., 1990), 3–23, who makes the case for the widespread support for slavery's abolition in this era.

53. Sean Wilentz, *No Property in Man: Slavery and Antislavery at the Nation's Founding* (Cambridge, Mass., 2018), 22, see also 2, 11, 19, 41–42, 58–59, 118–21.

54. Quoted in Eric Nelson, *The Royalist Revolution: Monarchy and the American Founding* (Cambridge, Mass., 2014), 2.

55. Ellis, *The Quartet*, xvi–xvii; David M. Golove and Daniel J. Hulsebach, "A Civilized Nation: The Early American Constitution, the Law of Nations, and the Pursuit of International Recognition," *New York University Law Review* 85, no. 4 (October 2010): 226–27. For a markedly different view, see Alan Taylor, *American Revolutions: A Continental History, 1750–1804* (New York, 2016).

56. Quoted in Harry Ward, *The War for Independence and the Transformation of American Society* (London, 1999), 244.

57. Franklin's response came from the notes of Dr. James McHenry, a delegate from Maryland, which were published in the *American Historical Review* 11 (1906): 618.

Chapter 3. The Revolutionary Equation

1. William Maclay, "The Inauguration of George Washington," www .eyewitnesstohistory.com/washingtoninaug.htm. A year later, the seat of the federal government was moved to Philadelphia; ten years later, it was moved to its permanent location in the District of Columbia.

2. Quoted in Eric Nelson, *The Royalist Revolution: Monarchy and the Founding* (Cambridge, Mass., 2017), 229, see also 231.

3. Quoted in David O. Stewart, *Madison's Gift: Five Partnerships That Built America* (New York, 2005), 51–52. On Madison's political style, see Noah Feldman, *The Three Lives of James Madison* (New York, 2017).

4. Peter S. Onuf, "Imperialism and Nationalism in the Early Republic," in *Empire's Twin: U.S. Anti-imperialism from the Founding Era to the Age of Terrorism*, ed. Ian Tyrrell and Jay Sexton (Ithaca, N.Y., 2015), 34–37.

5. For contrasting views of the Revolution's impact on women, see Mary Beth Norton, *Liberty's Daughters: The Revolutionary Experience of American Women, 1750–1800* (Ithaca, N.Y., 1980); and Linda K. Kerber, *Women of the Republic: Intellect and Ideology in Revolutionary America* (Chapel Hill, N.C., 1980). On changes in African identity in this era, see James Sidbury, *Becoming African in America: Race and Nation in the Early Black Atlantic* (New York, 2007).

6. Kathleen DuVal, *Independence Lost: Lives on the Edge of the American Revolution* (New York, 2015), 338–39. See also Patrick Griffin, *American Leviathan: Empire, Nation, and Revolutionary Frontier* (New York, 2007).

7. Colin G. Calloway, *The Indian World of George Washington: First Americans, the First President, and the Birth of the Nation* (New York, 2018), 2–10. See also Timothy Shannon, review of *Revolutionary Negotiations: Indians, Empires, and Diplomats in the Founding of America*, by Leonard J. Sadosky, *Diplomatic History* 35, no. 5 (November 2011): 897–900.

8. Joseph J. Ellis, *American Dialogue: The Founders and Us* (New York, 2018), 188–91.

9. Quoted in ibid., 127.

10. Quoted in Thomas P. Slaughter, *The Whiskey Rebellion: Frontier Epilogue to the American Revolution* (New York, 1986), 221.

11. See the section "External Effects of the Revolution," in *A Companion to the American Revolution*, ed. Jack P. Greene and J. R. Pole (Malden, Mass., 2004), 495–

555; and Alan Taylor, *The Civil War of 1812: American Citizens, Irish Rebels, & Indian Allies* (New York, 2010), 15–16, 37–56. Upper Canada was the first British territory in the Americas to abolish slavery.

12. H. W. Brands, *Andrew Jackson: His Life and Times* (New York, 2006), 66–79.

13. Quoted in Susan Dunn, *Sister Revolutions: French Lightning, American Light* (New York, 2000; orig. pub., 1999), 5.

14. William Doyle, *The Oxford History of the French Revolution* (New York, 1990), 110–11.

15. On the similarities of language about human rights in the Virginia Bill of Rights and the Declaration of Independence with the French *Declaration of the Rights of Man and of the Citizen*, see Lynn Hunt's introduction in *The French Revolution and Human Rights: A Documentary History*, ed. Lynn Hunt (Boston, 1996), 13–15. In October 1791 the Legislative Assembly became the second government created by the French Revolution. In September 1792 it was replaced by the National Convention.

16. Quoted in David Andress, *1789: The Threshold of the Modern Age* (New York, 2008), 363.

17. Mike Rapport, *The Unruly City: Paris, London, and New York in the Age of Revolution* (New York, 2017), 215. On the transatlantic character of radicalism in the 1790s, see Seth Cotlar, *Tom Paine's America: The Rise and Fall of Transatlantic Radicalism in the Early Republic* (Charlottesville, Va., 2011).

18. Quoted in Joseph J. Ellis, *Founding Brothers: The Revolutionary Generation* (New York, 2000), 142.

19. Eric Foner, *Tom Paine and Revolutionary America* (New York, 1976), 90–91, 211–13. Paine fell out of favor with the more radical Jacobins, was arrested in December 1793, and spent a year in prison, narrowly escaping execution. Released in 1794, he lived another eight years in France, largely ignored. A radical intellectual, he was ideally suited for a generation that questioned monarchy but largely indifferent to governmental structure and day-to-day political affairs.

20. Rapport, *The Unruly City*, 199–202, 304–5; Diarmaid MacCulloch, *Christianity: The First Three Thousand Years* (New York, 2010), 806–8.

21. Quoted in David Brion Davis, *Revolutions: Reflections on American Equality and Foreign Liberations* (Cambridge, Mass., 1990), 41.

22. Lawrence Kaplan, *Jefferson and France: An Essay on Politics and Political Ideas* (New Haven, Conn., 1967), 30–33. Despite his harsh critique of Jefferson's Francophilia, Conor Cruise O'Brien confirms that Jefferson's approval of the French Revolution diminished after its "intrusion" into U.S. domestic politics in 1793 (*The Long Affair: Thomas Jefferson and the French Revolution* [Chicago, 1996], 36–37, 188–89). See also Joseph J. Ellis, *His Excellency, George Washington* (New York, 2005), 112, 218–19.

23. Quoted in Gordon S. Wood, *Empire of Liberty: A History of the Early Republic* (New York, 2009), 185–86. In contemporary documents there was no circumflex over the second *e* (Genêt).

24. Quoted in Mark A. Noll, *America's God: From Jonathan Edwards to Abraham Lincoln* (New York, 2005), 72. See also Rachel Hope Cleves, *The Reign of Terror in America: Visions of Violence from Anti-Jacobinism to Antislavery* (New York, 2009), 84–85.

25. Robespierre, Christmas speech, 1793, in Rapport, *Unruly City*, 252–53; James Jackson Aston, "Music in the Age of Revolutions: American Anthems," in *Understanding and Teaching the Age of Revolutions*, ed. Ben Marsh and Mike Rapport (Madison, Wis., 2017), 136–37. On the cult of the French Revolution and the cultural emphasis on the "new man," see Mark Carnes, "Deep Revolutions: Inculcating Rousseau's 'Unitary Self,'" in ibid., 96–99.

26. Quoted in Cleves, *Reign of Terror*, 89.

27. C. L. R. James, *The Black Jacobins: Toussaint L'Ouverture and the San Domingo Revolution* (New York, 1989; orig. pub., 1938), 82–84; David Patrick Geggus and Norman Fiering, eds., *The World of the Haitian Revolution* (Bloomington, Ind., 2009), 13–14, 59, 90–91, 108, 117; Jeremy D. Popkin, *You Are All Free: The Haitian Revolution and the Abolition of Slavery* (Cambridge, 2010), 18–19.

28. Quoted in Douglas Egerton, *Death or Liberty: African Americans and Revolutionary America* (New York, 2009), 265.

29. Ashli White, *Encountering Revolution: Haiti and the Making of the Early Republic* (Baltimore, Md., 2010), 133. In the 1790s, writes James Alexander Dun, the dual encounter with the French and Haitian Revolutions compelled Americans to reconsider their own Revolution and its limits, making the United States "representative, not exceptional" (*Dangerous Neighbors: Making the Haitian Revolution in Early America* [Philadelphia, 2016], 79).

30. Cleves, *Reign of Terror*, 106–7, 148–49.

31. George Washington, farewell address, 1796, Yale Law School, the Avalon Project: Documents in Law, History, and Diplomacy, avalon.law.yale.edu /18th_century/washing.asp. The address appeared in the Philadelphia newspaper, the *American Daily Advertiser*, on September 19, 1796.

32. In October 1795 Jackson wrote North Carolina congressman Nathaniel Macon, urging him to oppose the Jay Treaty and thus "have the insulting cringing, and ignominious child of aristocratic secrecy removed, erased, and obliterated from the archives of the grand republic of the United States" (quoted in H. W. Brands, *Andrew Jackson: His Life and Times* [New York, 2006], 76).

33. See Lester J. Cappon, ed., *The Adams-Jefferson Letters: The Complete Correspondence between Thomas Jefferson and Abigail and John Adams* (Chapel Hill, N.C., 1959).

34. Ashli White, "The Saint-Domingue Refugees and American Distinctiveness in the Early Years of the Haitian Revolution," in Geggus and Fiering, *World*, 248–56. On Gabriel's two revolts, see the exhaustive account by Douglas Egerton, *Gabriel's Rebellion: The Virginia Slave Conspiracies of 1800 and 1802* (Chapel Hill, N.C., 1993). After 1793 Toussaint began signing documents with "Louverture."

35. Cleves, *Reign of Terror*, 90–91.

36. Wood, *Empire of Liberty*, 263–65.

37. Quoted in Lester D. Langley, *The Americas in the Age of Revolution, 1750–1850* (New Haven, Conn., 1996), 129.

38. Quoted in Egerton, *Death or Liberty*, 266.

39. Madison Smartt Bell, *Toussaint Louverture: A Biography* (New York, 2007), 224–26, surmises that he probably never received the letter.

40. Quoted in Egerton, *Death or Liberty*, 269. Jefferson's first inaugural (March 4, 1801) is in Yale Law School, the Avalon Project: Documents in Law, History, and Diplomacy, avalon.law.yale.edu/19th_century/jefinau1.asp.

41. Robin Blackburn, epilogue in Geggus and Fiering, *World*, 398–401.

42. There were exceptions to the pledge. Haitians of the early years of independence considered control and even absorption of the eastern two-thirds of the island important for moral and strategic reasons, and in 1816 Pétion provided vital support to the flagging cause of Simón Bolívar. See Ada Ferrer, "Haiti, Free Soil, and Antislavery in the Revolutionary Atlantic," *American Historical Review* 117 (February 2012): 41.

43. Quoted in Eric Foner, *The Story of American Freedom* (New York, 1994), 44.

44. Ibid., 45. Black Virginians often criticized Jefferson's hypocrisy on matters of race, James Sidbury notes, yet they also laid claim to the Founders' ideas in their fight for racial equality (*Ploughshares into Swords: Race, Rebellion, and Identity in Gabriel's Virginia, 1730–1810* [New York, 1997], 257).

45. Franklin Knight, *The Caribbean: The Genesis of a Fragmented Nationalism*, 2nd ed. (New York, 1990), 215.

46. Ellis, *Founding Brothers*, 247–48. For a cogent explanation of the Adams-Jefferson relationship, see T. H. Breen, "Founding Frenemies," *New York Review of Books*, December 20, 2018, 68, 70–71, a review of Gordon S. Wood, *Friends Divided: John Adams and Thomas Jefferson* (New York, 2018).

47. Joyce Appleby, *Inheriting the Revolution: The First Generation of Americans* (Cambridge, Mass., 2000), 5, 6–15.

48. Larry E. Tise, *The American Counter Revolution: Retreat from Liberty, 1783–1800* (Mechanicsburg, Pa., 1998), 527–28. In *The Elusive Thomas Jefferson: Essays on the Man behind the Myths* (Jefferson, N.C., 2017), editors Mark Holowchak and Brian W. Dotts presume to provide a balanced approach to the image of Jefferson in the current scholarship they inaccurately describe as "reckless and shambolic" (1).

49. Quoted in Linda K. Kerber, *Women of the Republic: Intellect and Ideology in Revolutionary America* (Chapel Hill, N.C., 1980), 35; see also xi–xii, 284–85.

50. Mary Beth Norton, *Liberty's Daughters: The Revolutionary Experience of American Women, 1750–1800* (Boston, 1980), 299; see also 295–98.

51. Abigail Adams to John Adams, 21 February 1801, Adams Family Papers: An Electronic Archive, Massachusetts Historical Society, http://www.masshist.org /digitaladams/.

52. Jefferson, second inaugural (March 4, 1805), in Yale Law School, the Avalon Project: Documents in Law, History, and Diplomacy, avalon.law.yale.edu /19th_century/jefinau2.asp; Foner, *Story*, 50–51. See also Brian Steele, *Thomas Jefferson and American Nationhood* (New York, 2012); and William H. Bergmann, *The American National State and the Early West* (New York, 2012).

53. The classic statement of this change is Winthrop Jordan, *White over Black: American Attitudes toward the Negro, 1550–1812* (Chapel Hill, N.C., 1968).

54. David Brion Davis, *The Problem of Slavery in the Age of Revolution, 1770–1823* (Ithaca, N.Y., 1975), 184–95.

55. Leonard Levy, *Jefferson and Civil Liberties: The Darker Side* (Cambridge, Mass., 1963), 161.

56. Ellis, *American Dialogue*, 32–35.

Chapter 4. The Republic in Peril

1. Jefferson to Joseph Priestley (1802), quoted in *Empire of Liberty: The Statecraft of Thomas Jefferson*, by Robert W. Tucker and David Hendrickson (New York, 1990), 254. On Jefferson's conception of the role of the United States, see Peter S. Onuf, *Jefferson's Empire: The Language of American Nationhood* (Charlottesville, Va., 2000).

2. J. Hector St. John de Crèvecoeur, "What Is an American?," Letter III of *Letters from an American Farmer* (1782), in Yale Law School, the Avalon Project: Documents in Law, History, and Diplomacy, http://avalon.law.yale.edu/18th_century /letter_03.asp.

3. On these points, see David Waldstreicher, *In the Midst of Perpetual Fetes: The Making of American Nationalism, 1776–1820* (Chapel Hill, N.C., 1997); and Padraig Riley, *Slavery and the Democratic Conscience: Political Life in Jeffersonian America* (Philadelphia, 2016).

4. Joseph J. Ellis, *American Sphinx: The Character of Thomas Jefferson* (New York, 1997), 213. On federal land policy, see John R. Van Atta, *Securing the West: Politics, Public Lands, and the Fate of the Old Republic, 1785–1850* (Baltimore, Md., 2014).

5. D. W. Meinig, *The Shaping of America: A Geographical Perspective on 500 Years of History*, vol. 2, *Continental America* (New Haven, Conn., 1993), 17.

6. Peter S. Onuf, "'Empire for Liberty': Center and Peripheries in Postcolonial America," in *Negotiated Empires: Centers and Peripheries in the Americas, 1500–1820*, ed. Christine Daniels and Michael V. Kennedy (New York, 2002), 312–15. On the defection of the Old Republicans and their legacy, see Norman K. Risjord, *The Old Republicans: Southern Conservatism in the Age of Jefferson* (New York, 1965), 2–10.

7. Ira Berlin, *The Long Emancipation: The Demise of Slavery in the United States* (Cambridge, Mass., 2015), 43. See also Gary Nash, *Race and Revolution* (Lanham, Md., 1990), 48–50, 72–73, 80–83.

8. Response to "Query VIII, Population," in *Notes on the State of Virginia* (1785), in Yale Law School, the Avalon Project: Documents in Law, History, and Diplomacy, http://avalon.law.yale.edu/18th_century/jeffvir.asp.

9. George Dargo, *Jefferson's Louisiana: Politics and the Clash of Legal Traditions* (Cambridge, Mass., 1975), 172–73; Peter J. Kastor, *The Nation's Crucible: The Louisiana Purchase and the Creation of America* (New Haven, Conn., 2004), 4–5, 186–87. See also Adam Rothman, *Slave Country: American Expansion and the Origins of the Deep South* (Cambridge, Mass., 2005).

10. Quoted in R. Kent Newmyer, *The Treason Trial of Aaron Burr: Law, Politics, and the Character of the New Nation* (New York, 2012), 198. Leonard Levy devotes an entire chapter to the Burr trial in *Jefferson and Civil Liberties: The Darker Side* (Cambridge, Mass., 1963).

11. Quoted in R. R. Palmer, *The Age of Democratic Revolution: A Political History of Europe and America, 1760–1800* (Princeton, N.J., 1964), 2:214. See also George Rudé, *Revolutionary Europe, 1783–1815* (Malden, Mass., 2000; orig. pub., 1964), 199–200; Lawrence F. Kaplan, *Jefferson and France: An Essay on Politics and Political Ideas* (New Haven, Conn., 1961), 104.

12. Quoted in Alan Taylor, *The Civil War of 1812: American Citizens, British Subjects, Irish Rebels, and Indian Allies* (New York, 2010), 117. On the intensity of Republicans' commitment to free trade and the rights of sailors, see Paul Gilje, *Free Trade and Sailors' Rights in the War of 1812* (New York, 2013).

13. Kaplan, *Jefferson and France*, 105–7, 112–15, 124–29.

14. Garry Wills, *"Negro President": Jefferson and the Slave Power* (Boston, 2003), 147–49, 222–25. Leonard Levy devotes two chapters of *Jefferson and Civil Liberties* to indicting Jefferson's use of the Embargo Act to carry out unconstitutional violations of civil liberties.

15. Quoted in Frank Lawrence Owsley Jr. and Gene A. Smith, *Filibusters and Expansionists: Jeffersonian Manifest Destiny, 1800–1821* (Tuscaloosa, Ala., 1997), 16. See also Arthur Whitaker, *The Western Hemisphere Idea: Its Rise and Decline* (Ithaca, N.Y., 1954), 29; and Alf J. Mapp Jr., *Thomas Jefferson: America's Paradoxical Patriot* (Lanham, Md., 1987), 395–96.

16. Charles F. Walker, *The Túpac Amaru Rebellion* (Cambridge, Mass., 2014).

Historians disagree on the death toll of the uprising. Nicolas A. Robins, *Genocide and Millennialism in Upper Peru: The Great Rebellion of 1780–1782* (Westport, Conn., 2002), 70, estimates the number at one hundred thousand, 90 percent of whom were Indians.

17. Rafael Altamira, *Resumen histórico de la independencia de la América Española* (Buenos Aires, 1918), 18.

18. Quoted in Caitlin Fitz, *Our Sister Republics: The United States in an Age of American Revolutions* (New York, 2016), 42. For a succinct review of the major issues in Latin America's war of independence and revolution, see Marcela Echeverri, "Independence and Revolution in Latin America," in *Understanding and Teaching the Age of Revolutions*, ed. Ben Marsh and Mike Rapport (Madison, Wis., 2017), 262–79.

19. Fitz, *Our Sister Republics*, 25–26. See also Karen Racine, *Francisco de Miranda: A Transatlantic Life in the Age of Revolution* (Wilmington, Del., 2003), 142–47, 172.

20. Jeremy Adelman, *Sovereignty and Revolution in the Iberian Atlantic* (Princeton, N.J., 2006), 177–89.

21. Quoted in Lester D. Langley, *The Americas in the Age of Revolution, 1750–1850* (New Haven, Conn., 1996), 167. In his perceptive review (*American Historical Review* 122, no. 4 [October 2017]: 1273) of the collection of essays in *The Haitian Declaration of Independence: Creation, Context, and Legacy* (ed. Julia Gaffield, Charlottesville, Va., 2016), Roberto Breña of El Colegio de México takes issue with the statement that because the Haitian Revolution departed from both the American and French Revolutions as models, it could be identified as "the first of the Latin American Revolutions" (17).

22. Langley, *The Americas*, 179–85.

23. Arthur Preston Whitaker, *The United States and the Independence of Latin America, 1800–1830* (New York, 1962), 80–83.

24. Quoted in Fitz, *Our Sister Republics*, 41, see also 48–51.

25. Quoted in Gordon S. Wood, *Empire of Liberty: A History of the Early Republic* (New York, 2009), 669. Troy Bickham, *The Weight of Vengeance: The United States, the British Empire, and the War of 1812* (New York, 2012), emphasizes the importance of self-image in the coming of the war—a felt need to prove that the country belonged in the community of nations. The instinct was equally important for Britain.

26. Jefferson to Adams, June 11, 1812, in *The Adams-Jefferson Letters: The Complete Correspondence between Thomas Jefferson and Abigail and John Adams*, ed. Lester J. Cappon (Chapel Hill, N.C., 1959), 308. See also Taylor, *Civil War of 1812*, 134–37.

27. Quoted in Taylor, *Civil War of 1812*, 180, see also 177–79; and Rachel Hope Cleves, *The Reign of Terror in America: Visions of Violence from Anti-Jacobinism to Antislavery* (New York, 2009), 180–81, 230–31.

28. Quoted in Taylor, *Civil War of 1812*, 57. That was untrue. The newcomers lacked the commitment of the first generation of loyalist migrants, and within a few years

the British began restricting land grants for Americans to two hundred acres. What this later generation of American migrants possessed was a nostalgic sense for the colonial social tolerance of their differences in the cultural "mosaic" of Upper Canada. They did not have to melt in, and they wanted to be left alone.

29. Taylor, *Civil War of 1812*, 327, 351, 438–39.

30. Robert Bothwell, *Your Country, My Country: A Unified History of the United States and Canada* (New York, 2015), 85–86.

31. James G. Cusick, *The Other War of 1812: The Patriot War and the American Invasion of Spanish East Florida* (Gainesville, Fla., 2003).

32. Quoted in H. W. Brands, *Andrew Jackson: His Life and Times* (New York, 2006), 232.

33. Quoted in Robert Remini, *Andrew Jackson and the Course of American Empire, 1767–1821* (New York, 1977), 254.

34. Ashli White, *Encountering Revolution: Haiti and the Making of the Early Republic* (Baltimore, Md., 2010), 201. See also Robert L. Paquette, "Revolutionary Saint Domingue in the Making of Territorial Louisiana," in *A Turbulent Time: The French Revolution and the Greater Caribbean*, ed. David Patrick Geggus and Barry Gaspar (Bloomington, Ind., 1997), 204–25; and Daniel Rasmussen, *American Uprising: The Untold Story of America's Largest Slave Revolt* (New York, 2011).

35. Mark Jarrett, *The Congress of Vienna and Its Legacy: War and Great Power Diplomacy after Napoleon* (London, 2013).

36. Gene Allen Smith, *The Slaves' Gamble: Choosing Sides in the War of 1812* (New York, 2013), points out that for slaves choosing sides depended on circumstance and place.

37. In the end the United States won access to the fisheries, but the British did not gain access to navigation of the Mississippi. John Quincy Adams, "The Dispute within the American Delegation," in *John Quincy Adams and American Continental Empire: Letters, Papers, and Speeches*, ed. Walter LaFeber (Chicago, 1965), 64–67.

38. Quoted in Taylor, *The Civil War of 1812*, 417.

39. Quoted in ibid., 419.

40. James Madison, first inaugural, March 4, 1813, in Yale Law School, the Avalon Project: Documents in Law, History, and Diplomacy, http://avalon.law.yale.edu/19th_century/madison2.asp.

41. Charles Breuning and Matthew Levinger, *The Revolutionary Era, 1789–1850*, 3rd ed. (New York, 2002), 119–24.

42. Daniel Walker Howe, *What Hath God Wrought: The Transformation of America, 1815–1848* (New York, 2009), 1–18; Taylor, *The Civil War of 1812*, 458.

43. Quoted in H. W. Brands, *Andrew Jackson: His Life and Times* (New York, 2006), 230. Troy Bickham, *The Weight of Vengeance: the United States, the British Empire, and the War of 1812* (New York, 2012), 262–76, indicts the British for waging

a war to humble the United States and failing. Richard Buel, *America at the Brink: How the Political Struggle over the War of 1812 Almost Destroyed the Young Republic* (New York, 2005), 2–3, 237–44, identifies the Federalists as the culprits in bringing on the war by their efforts to subvert the government and policies of their Republican successors out of anxieties about French influence on Jefferson's policies.

44. David McCullough, *John Adams* (New York, 2001), 606–9.

45. On this religious frontier war, see Sam Haselby, *The Origins of American Religious Nationalism* (New York, 2015); and Nathan O. Hatch, *The Democratization of American Christianity* (New Haven, Conn., 1989).

46. On these themes, see Padraig Riley, *Slavery and the Democratic Conscience: Political Life in Jeffersonian America* (Philadelphia, 2015); and his "Slavery and the Problem of Democracy in Jeffersonian America," in *Contesting Slavery: The Politics of Bondage and Freedom in the New American Nation*, ed. John Craig Hammond and Matthew Mason (Charlottesville, Va., 2011).

Chapter 5. The Western Question

1. Eric Hobsbawm, *The Age of Revolution: Europe, 1789–1848* (New York, 1996; orig. pub., 1962), 100–101, 115–17.

2. John Quincy Adams to John Adams, August 1, 1816, from England, in *John Quincy Adams and American Continental Empire: Letters, Papers, and Speeches*, ed. Walter LaFeber (Chicago, 1965), 139–40.

3. Sean Wilentz, *The Rise of American Democracy: Jefferson to Lincoln* (New York, 2005), 162–64, 181; Gordon S. Wood, "Illusions and Disillusions in the American Revolution," in *The American Revolution: Its Character and Limits*, ed. Jack P. Greene (New York, 1987), 358–60.

4. Wilentz, *Rise of American Democracy*, 182–83.

5. David Patrick Geggus, "Slavery, War, and Revolution in the Greater Caribbean," in *A Turbulent Time: The French Revolution and the Greater Caribbean*, edited by David Barry Gaspar and David Patrick Geggus (Bloomington, Ind., 1997), 31.

6. In Cuba, grievances over social conditions had inspired a free person of color and captain in a black militia, José Antonio Aponte, to proclaim a Cuban war of liberation in 1812. Matthew D. Childs, *The 1812 Aponte Rebellion and the Struggle against Atlantic Slavery* (Chapel Hill, 2006); Ada Ferrer, *Freedom's Mirror: Cuba and Haiti in the Age of Revolution* (New York, 2014).

7. Caitlin Fitz, "The Hemispheric Dimensions of Early U.S. Nationalism: The War of 1812, Its Aftermath, and Spanish American Independence," *Journal of American History* 102, no. 2 (September 2015): 356–79.

8. On this theme, see Marixa Lasso, *Myths of Harmony: Race and Republicanism during the Age of Revolution, Colombia 1795–1831* (Pittsburgh, Pa., 2007).

9. Caitlin Fitz, *Our Sister Republics: The United States in an Age of American Revolutions* (New York, 2016), 114–15. On the reluctance of both the British and the U.S. governments to come to his aid, see David Bushnell, "The United States as Seen by Simón Bolívar," in *Simón Bolívar: Essays on the Life and Legacy of the Liberator*, ed. David Bushnell and Lester D. Langley (Lanham, Md., 2008), 136–37.

10. Adams to Alexander Hill Everett, December 29, 1817, in *The Writings of John Quincy Adams*, ed. Worthington C. Ford (New York, 1913–17), 6:282.

11. Marie Arana, *Bolívar: American Liberator* (New York, 2013), 164–67; John Lynch, *The Spanish American Revolutions, 1808–1826* (New York, 1973), 218–21.

12. March 28, 1818, in *The Papers of Henry Clay*, vol. 2, *The Rising Statesman, 1815–1820*, ed. James F. Hopkins (Lexington, Ky., 1961), 551. Jackson departed from his instructions as well as legal concepts in waging what for him was a war akin to the revolutionary years and the belief about what was necessary to fight Indians and "banditti." See Deborah A. Rosen, *Border Law: The First Seminole War and American Nationhood* (Cambridge, Mass., 2015).

13. Bolívar to Francisco Paula de Santander, April 20, 30, 1820, in *Selected Writings of Bolívar*, trans. Lewis Bertrand, ed. Harold A. Bierck Jr., and comp. Vicente Lecuna, 2 vols. (New York, 1951), 1:221–23; Lester D. Langley, *Simón Bolívar: Venezuelan Rebel, American Revolutionary* (Lanham, Md., 2009), 64; Peter Blanchard, *Under the Flags of Freedom: Slave Soldiers and the Wars of Independence in Spanish South America* (Pittsburgh, Pa., 2008), 66–67.

14. Henry Clay, "The Emancipation of South America," March 24, 1818, in the World's Famous Orations, America II (1818–1865), https://www.bartleby.com/268/9/5.html.

15. February 15, 1819, in *Selected Writings of Bolívar*, 1:191.

16. "Slavery and the Missouri Question," *North American Review* 10 (January 1820): 158. For Bolívar's complicated views on race, see Langley, *Simón Bolívar*, 114.

17. Quoted in Joseph J. Ellis, *American Dialogue: The Founders and Us* (New York, 2018), 36; Douglas R. Egerton, "Averting a Crisis: The Proslavery Critique of the American Colonization Society," *Civil War History* 43, no. 2 (1997): 142–47.

18. Adams, *Memoirs*, April 20, 1820, in LaFeber, *John Quincy Adams*, 86.

19. Quoted in Martin Öhman, "A Convergence of Crises: The Expansion of Slavery, Geopolitical Realignment, and Economic Depression in the Post-Napoleonic World," *Diplomatic History* 37, no. 3 (June 2013): 434. See also Stephen Hahn, *The Political World of Slavery and Freedom* (Cambridge, Mass., 2009), 7–13.

20. Wilentz, *Rise of American Democracy*, 201–3.

21. On the Missouri statehood debate in Congress, see ibid., 222–37.

22. Jefferson to Adams, January 22, 1821, in *The Adams-Jefferson Letters: The Complete Correspondence between Thomas Jefferson and Abigail and John Adams*, ed. Lester J. Cappon (Chapel Hill, N.C., 1959), 570. The "fire bell in the night" comment is in Jefferson to John Holmes, April 22, 1820, in *Thomas Jefferson: Writings*, ed. Merrill Peterson (New York, 1984), 1433–35. On its purpose, see Daniel Walker Howe, *What Hath God Wrought: The Transformation of America, 1815–1848* (New York, 2009), 157. On the two variants of freedom, see Major L. Wilson, *Space, Time, and Freedom: The Quest for Nationality and the Irrepressible Conflict, 1815–1861* (Westport, Conn., 1974), chap. 2.

23. March 3, 1820, in LaFeber, *John Quincy Adams*, 143.

24. Quoted in David Brion Davis, *Inhuman Bondage: The Rise and Fall of Slavery in the New World* (New York, 2006), 277.

25. Quoted in ibid., 276.

26. Douglas R. Egerton, *He Shall Go Out Free: The Lives of Denmark Vesey* (Madison, Wis., 1999), 130.

27. Both quotations are in Eugene Genovese, *From Rebellion to Revolution: Afro-American Slave Revolts in the Making of the Modern World* (Baton Rouge, La., 1992), 96.

28. Quoted in David Brion Davis, *The Problem of Slavery in the Age of Revolution, 1770–1823* (Ithaca, N.Y., 1975), 50. The statistics of apportionments for representation in the U.S. Congress reinforced Lundy's point. In the 1790 census, free states got 57 representatives, and the slave states got 48; by 1820 the difference was 123 to 90. The South had a great deal of political influence on the question of slavery, but it remained a minority. See Sean Wilentz, *No Property in Man: Slavery and Antislavery at the Nation's Founding* (Cambridge, Mass., 2018), 187.

29. Quoted in Arthur Preston Whitaker, *The United States and the Independence of Latin America, 1800–1830* (New York, 1962), 356.

30. Ibid.; "sound of the trumpet of Zion" is on 358.

31. Quoted in ibid., 336. Joseph Traub, *John Quincy Adams: Militant Spirit* (New York, 2016), based largely on Adams's exhaustive fourteen-thousand-page journal, is the most recent biography.

32. Whitaker, *The United States*, 178–85; Arthur P. Whitaker, *The Western Hemisphere Idea: Its Rise and Decline* (Ithaca, N.Y., 1954), 14–17.

33. Quoted in LaFeber, *John Quincy Adams*, 127. See also Louis A. Pérez Jr., *Cuba and the United States: Ties of Singular Intimacy*, 3rd ed. (Athens, Ga., 2003), 36–37; and Brenda Gayle Plummer, *Haiti and the United States: The Psychological Moment* (Athens, Ga., 1992), 28–31.

34. Whitaker, *The United States*, 254–56.

35. John Quincy Adams to Hugh Nelson, April 28, 1823, in Ford, *Writings of John*

Quincy Adams, 7:372–73; Judith Ewell, "Bolívar's Atlantic World Diplomacy," in Bushnell and Langley, *Simón Bolívar*, 46–47; Whitaker, *The United States*, 341.

36. Allan Nevins, ed., *Diary of John Quincy Adams, 1794–1845: American Diplomacy and Political, Social and Intellectual Life from Washington to Polk* (New York, 1951), 310–11; Ernest R. May, *The Making of the Monroe Doctrine* (Cambridge, Mass., 1975), 254–60, argues that political considerations best explain how the doctrine was crafted.

37. Nevins, *Diary*, 312–13; James Monroe, Seventh Annual Message, December 2, 1823, in Yale Law School, the Avalon Project: Documents in Law, History, and Diplomacy, http://avalon.law.yale.edu/subject_menus/inaug.asp.

38. Quoted in LaFeber, *John Quincy Adams*, 114.

39. Quoted in Fitz, *Our Sister Republics*, 102–3.

40. Everett to Secretary of State Henry Clay, January 27, 1827, quoted in Langley, *Simón Bolívar*, 96. See also Fitz, *Our Sister Republics*, 104–7, 148–51.

41. Quoted in Robert V. Remini, *Andrew Jackson: The Course of American Freedom, 1822–1832* (New York, 1984), 110. On the appeal of postmillennialist thought, see Howe, *What Hath God Wrought*, 286–89.

42. On the larger meaning of U.S. participation in the Congress of Panama, see James A. Field Jr., *The American Union and the Problem of Neighborhood: The United States and the Collapse of the Spanish Empire, 1783–1829* (Chapel Hill, N.C., 1998), 205–14.

43. Quoted in Fitz, *Our Sister Republics*, 208.

44. Sam W. Haynes, *Unfinished Revolution: The Early American Republic in a British World* (Charlottesville, Va., 2010), 2.

45. Bolívar's remark about the U.S. threat is taken from Bushnell, "The United States as Seen," 142. See also Tulio Halperin Donghi, *The Contemporary History of Latin America*, ed. and trans. John Charles Chasteen(Durham, N.C., 1993), 92–94. On the difficulties of creating modern entities in the aftermath of revolution in this era, see François-Xavier Guerra, *Modernidad e independencias: Ensayos sobre las revoluciones hispánicas* (Mexico City, 2014; orig. pub., 1992), 52–53.

46. Bushnell, "The United States as Seen," 139–43.

47. Caitlin Fitz, "The Black Bolívars: African Americans in an Inter-American World," paper delivered at Omohundro/SEA annual meeting, Chicago, 2015, 4–5.

48. Davis, *Inhuman Bondage*, 258–59.

49. Ibid., 142–45.

50. George Reid Andrews, *Afro-Latin America, 1800–1900* (New York, 2004), 53–67.

51. Robert J. Cottrol, *The Long, Lingering Shadow: Slavery, Race, and Law in the American Hemisphere* (Athens, Ga., 2013), 8–11.

52. Jeremy Adelman discusses these and related issues in "An Age of Imperial Revolutions," *American Historical Review* 113, no. 2 (April 2008): 319–40.

53. Gretchen Murphy, *Hemispheric Imaginings: The Monroe Doctrine and Narratives of U.S. Empire* (Durham, N.C., 2005), 6–7, 14, 32–39, 58–61.

54. Felipe Fernández Armesto, *The Americas: A Hemispheric History* (New York, 2006), 103; Tulio Halperín Donghi, *The Aftermath of Revolution in Latin America*, trans. Josephine de Bunsen (New York, 1973), 111–40. See also Jaime E. Rodríguez O, *The Independence of Spanish America* (New York, 2013), 244–46; and John Charles Chasteen, *Americanos: Latin America's Struggle for Independence* (New York, 2009), 184–87, who reaffirm what Spanish Americans were up against in both the timing and the character of their wars of independence and what was achieved despite the obstacles. On the anomaly of Louisiana's place in the early republic, see Peter J. Kastor, *The Nation's Crucible: The Louisiana Purchase and the Creation of America* (New Haven, Conn., 2004), 226–28.

55. Carl Lawrence Paulus, *The Slaveholding Crisis: Fear of Insurrection and the Coming of the Civil War* (Baton Rouge, La., 2017).

56. Richard H. Immerman, *Empire for Liberty: A History of American Imperialism from Benjamin Franklin to Paul Wolfowitz* (Princeton, N.J., 2010), 69; Langley, *Simón Bolívar*, 120–21. Bolívar was forty-seven when he died, en route to exile. In time, he would become a cult figure not only in his native Venezuela but also in Latin America. In the twentieth century, the Venezuelan government would sponsor the erection of statues of the Liberator in many countries, including the United States. One stands not far from the Washington Monument in the District of Columbia. With the election of the populist Hugo Chávez as president in 1999, the name of Venezuela became the Bolivarian Republic of Venezuela.

Chapter 6. The American Democracy

1. On utopian societies, see Christopher Bentley, "Building the American Dream," *New York Review of Books*, April 6, 2017, 18–20. See also David Reynolds, *Waking Giant: America in the Age of Jackson* (New York, 2008), 260–61, 382–84.

2. Robert V. Remini, *Andrew Jackson: The Course of American Freedom, 1822–1832* (New York, 1984), 155.

3. Quoted in Daniel Walker Howe, *What Hath God Wrought: The Transformation of America, 1815–1848* (New York, 2009), 410; Harry L. Watson, *Liberty and Power: The Politics of Jacksonian America* (rev. ed., New York, 2006; orig. pub., 1990), 47, 51, 252.

4. Watson, *Liberty and Power*, 93–94, 170–71, 179, 238–40; Nancy Isenberg, *White*

Trash: The 400-Year Untold History of Class in America (New York, 2016), 112–13; James R. Van Atta, *Securing the West: Politics, Public Lands, and the Fate of the Old Republic, 1785–1850* (Baltimore, Md., 2014), 225–28.

5. Quoted in Howe, *What Hath God Wrought*, 438–39.

6. Kevin Peraino, *Lincoln in the World: The Making of a Statesman and the Dawn of American Power* (New York, 2013), 46–47. On the Steamboat Empire, see Walter Johnson, *River of Dark Dreams: Slavery and Empire in the Cotton Kingdom* (Cambridge, Mass., 2013).

7. Quoted in Howe, *What Hath God Wrought*, 704. See also Robert V. Remini, *The Revolutionary Age of Jackson* (New York, 1976), 16–18.

8. Alexis de Tocqueville, *Democracy in America*, with an introduction by Alan Ryan, 2 vols. (New York, 1994), 1:349; Kevin Butterfield, *The Making of Tocqueville's America: Law and Association in the Early United States* (Chicago, 2015), 2–5, 230–31.

9. On Indians and their role in the Mexican War, see Pekka Hämäläinen, *The Comanche Empire* (New Haven, Conn., 2008), 2–3, 356–59; and especially Brian De-Lay, *War of a Thousand Deserts: Indian Raids and the U.S.-Mexican War* (New Haven, Conn., 2008), xiii–xxi.

10. Quoted in Felipe Fernández-Armesto, *Our America: A Hispanic History of the United States* (New York, 2014), 138.

11. Andrew J. Torget, *Seeds of Empire: Cotton, Slavery, and the Transformation of the Texas Borderlands, 1800–1850* (Chapel Hill, N.C., 2015), 140; Randolph B. Campbell, *An Empire for Slavery: The Peculiar Institution in Texas, 1821–1865* (Baton Rouge, La., 1989), 32–33, 256–59.

12. Quoted in Eugene C. Barker, *Mexico and Texas, 1821–1835* (Dallas, 1928), 21.

13. Quoted in Robert V. Remini, *Andrew Jackson: The Course of American Democracy, 1833–1845* (New York, 1984), 359.

14. The quotation from the Texas Declaration of Independence is from Christopher Conway, ed., and Gustave Pellón, trans., *The U.S.-Mexican War: A Binational Reader* (Indianapolis, 2010), 17; Adams's remarks are on page 34.

15. Tocqueville, *Democracy in America*, 1:431–32.

16. Ibid., 1:3, 263, 2:287–88. See also Kevin Butterfield, *The Making of Tocqueville's America: Law and Association in the Early United States* (Chicago, 2015).

17. Watson, *Liberty and Power*, 106–9.

18. Ibid., 355; Jackson, annual message, December 6, 1830, quoted in H. W. Brands, *Andrew Jackson: His Life and Times* (New York, 2006), 490. On the devastating social "demonization" of free African Americans and Seminoles as "outsiders" by white settlers and how the U.S. Army changed a "war of attrition" into a "war on women," see Laurel Clark Shire, *The Threshold of Manifest Destiny: Gender and National Expansion in Florida* (Philadelphia, 2016), 55–56, 130.

19. David Brion Davis, *Inhuman Bondage: The Rise and Fall of Slavery in the New World* (New York, 2006), 208–9, 258–59.

20. Ibid., 218–20. See also Eugene Genovese, *From Rebellion to Revolution: Afro-American Slave Revolts in the Making of the Modern World* (Baton Rouge, La., 1992), 100–103.

21. David Olusoga, "The History of British Slave Ownership Has Been Buried: Now Its Scale Can Be Revealed," *Manchester Guardian*, July 11, 2015, https://www .theguardian.com/world/2015/jul/12/british-history-slavery-buried-scale-revealed.

22. Davis, *Inhuman Bondage*, 260–64; Rachel Hope Cleves, *The Reign of Terror in America: Visions of Violence from Anti-Jacobinism to Antislavery* (New York, 2009), 266–67. On the abolitionists' connection with transatlantic reformers, see W. Caleb McDaniel, *The Problem of Democracy in the Age of Slavery: Garrisonian Abolitionists and Transatlantic Reform* (Baton Rouge, La., 2013).

23. Tocqueville, *Democracy in America*, 1:359, 378–79.

24. Davis, *Inhuman Bondage*, 12–26.

25. George Reid Andrews, *Afro-Latin America, 1800–2000* (New York, 2004), 85–100. See also Tulio Halperín-Donghi, *The Aftermath of Revolution in Latin America* (New York, 1973), 21–29.

26. David Sheinin, *Argentina and the United States: An Alliance Contained* (Athens, Ga., 2006), 14–16.

27. See Alan McPherson, Jeffrey Malanson, William Weeks, and Jay Sexton, "A Roundtable Discussion of Jay Sexton's *The Monroe Doctrine: Empire and Nation in Nineteenth Century America*," *Passport* 43, no. 1 (April 2012): 5–13; and William R. Weeks, *Building the Continental Empire: American Expansion from the Revolution to the Civil War* (Chicago, 1996).

28. Sam W. Haynes, *Unfinished Revolution: the Early American Republic in a British World* (Charlottesville, Va., 2010), 6–9, 280–83, 294–96; Peter S. Onuf, "Imperialism and Nationalism in the Early Republic," in *Empire's Twin: U.S. Anti-imperialism from the Founding Era to the Age of Terrorism*, ed. Ian Tyrrell and Jay Sexton (Ithaca, N.Y., 2015), 39–40.

29. Alan Taylor, *The Civil War of 1812: American Citizens, British Subjects, Irish Rebels, and Indian Allies* (New York, 2010), 452–54.

30. Ibid., 456–57.

31. Quoted in Sean Wilentz, *The Rise of American Democracy: Jefferson to Lincoln* (New York, 2005), 584.

32. David Montejano, *Anglos and Mexicans in the Making of Texas, 1836–1986* (Austin, Tex., 1987), 25–28.

33. Quoted in Howe, *What Hath God Wrought*, 706. See also Christopher Clark, *Social Change in America from the Revolution to the Civil War* (Chicago, 2006).

34. On the role of the American Board of Commissioners for Foreign Missions,

see Emily Conroy-Krutz, *Christian Imperialism: Converting the World in the Early American Republic* (Ithaca, N.Y., 2015).

35. Quoted in Allan Nevins, ed., *The Diary of John Quincy Adams, 1794–1845: American Diplomacy, and Political, Social, and Intellectual Life from Washington to Polk* (New York, 1928), 570–71; Polk, inaugural address, March 4, 1845, in Yale Law School, the Avalon Project: Documents in Law, History, and Diplomacy, http://avalon.law.yale.edu/subject_menus/inaug.asp. Cultural historians describe this more militant rhetoric as "martial manhood." See Amy Greenberg, *Manifest Manhood and the Antebellum American Empire* (New York, 2005).

36. James K. Polk, First Annual Message, December 2, 1845, in Yale Law School, the Avalon Project: Documents in Law, History, and Diplomacy, http://avalon.law.yale.edu/subject_menus/inaug.asp.

37. John Herd Thompson and Stephen J. Randall, *Canada and the United States: Ambivalent Allies*, 3rd ed. (Athens, Ga., 2002), 26–32. The southern portion of Vancouver Island, which fell below the forty-ninth parallel, remained Canadian.

38. The quotations are from Conway, *The U.S.-Mexican War*, 108–9.

39. Quoted in Robert W. Merry, *A Country of Vast Designs: James K. Polk, the Mexican War, and the Conquest of the American Continent* (New York, 2009), 414–15. See also Ted C. Hinckley, "American Anti-Catholicism during the Mexican War," *Pacific Historical Review* 31 (May 1962): 125–30.

40. U.S. Army Center of Military History, *The Occupation of Mexico, May 1846–July 1848*, 41–46, https://history.army.mil/brochures/Occupation/Occupation.htm. On Polk's civil-military relations during the war, see John C. Pinheiro, *Manifest Ambition: James K. Polk and Civil-Military Relations during the Mexican War* (Westport, Conn., 2007), 2–3, 150–51, 198–99.

41. Peter Guardino, *The Dead March: A History of the Mexican-American War* (Cambridge, Mass., 2017), 212–13, 218–19, 280–81, 324–25; John C. Pinheiro, *Missionaries of Republicanism: A Religious History of the Mexican-American War* (New York, 2014).

42. David A. Clary, *Eagles and Empire: The United States, Mexico, and the Struggle for a Continent* (New York, 2009), 201–2, 248–49, 379–80, 418–19.

43. Richard Griswold del Castillo, *The Treaty of Guadalupe Hidalgo: A Legacy of Conflict* (Norman, Okla., 1990), 174–75.

44. Quoted in Howe, *What Hath God Wrought*, 799, see also 808–9. On the Mexican-American War in memory and literature, see GoScott Van Wagenen, *Remembering the Forgotten War: The Enduring Legacies of the U.S.-Mexican War* (Amherst, Mass., 2012); and Jaime Javier Rodríguez, *The Literatures of the U.S.-Mexican War: Narrative, Time, and Identity* (Austin, Tex., 2010), 249–53.

45. Quoted in Wilentz, *Rise of American Democracy*, 562.

46. Quoted in Robert W. Johannsen, *To the Halls of the Montezumas: The Mexican War in the American Imagination* (New York, 1985), 286–87, see also 290–91, 310–12.

47. Brands, *Andrew Jackson*, 554–57; Peter Guardino, "Gender, Soldiering, and Citizenship in the Mexican-American War of 1846–1848," *American Historical Review* 119, no. 1 (February 2014): 23–46.

48. Michael Gobat, "The Invention of Latin America: A Transnational History of Anti-imperialism, Democracy, and Race," *American Historical Review* 118, no. 5 (December 2013): 1345–75. See also James E. Sanders, "The Vanguard of the Atlantic World: Contesting Modernity in Nineteenth-Century Latin America," *Latin American Research Review* 46, no. 2 (2011): 104–27.

49. Declaration of Sentiments and Resolutions, Women's Rights Convention, Seneca Falls, N.Y., July 19–20, 1848, in the Elizabeth Cady Stanton and Susan B. Anthony Papers Project, ecssba.rutgers.edu/docs/seneca.html.

50. Quoted in Wilentz, *Rise of American Democracy*, 618; Watson, *Liberty and Power*, 242–43.

51. Stanley Harrold, *The Abolitionists and the South, 1831–1861* (Lexington, Ky., 1995), challenges long-standing views about abolitionism's allegedly passive role in the antislavery movement in the Upper South.

52. Quoted in Matthew Pratt Guterl, *American Mediterranean: Southern Slaveholders in the Age of Emancipation* (Cambridge, Mass., 2008), 33. On U.S. expansion, slavery, and the development of the Deep South, see Adam Rothman, *American Expansion and the Origins of the Deep South* (Cambridge, Mass., 2005), 220–23. On the "second slavery" of the nineteenth century, see Daniel B. Rood, *The Reinvention of Atlantic Slavery: Technology, Labor, Race, and Capitalism in the Greater Caribbean* (New York, 2017), 1–2, 4–5, 12–13, 197–201.

53. Louis A. Pérez Jr., *Cuba and the United States: Ties of Singular Intimacy*, 3rd ed. (Athens, Ga., 2003), 42–44. For filibustering, see Robert E. May, *Manifest Destiny's Underworld: Filibustering in Antebellum America* (Chapel Hill, N.C., 2002).

54. Mike Rapport, *1848: Year of Revolution* (New York, 2008), 400.

55. Quoted in David Brion Davis, *Revolutions: Reflections on American Equality and Foreign Liberations* (Cambridge, Mass., 1990), 79. On Tocqueville's assimilation of English political values into his thinking, see Seymour Drescher, *Tocqueville and England* (Cambridge, Mass., 1964), 220–23.

Chapter 7. The American War and Peace

1. Peter Charles Hoffer, *Uncivil Warriors: The Lawyers' Civil War* (New York, 2018), 180–82.

2. The classic account of the prewar decade remains David Potter, *The Impending Crisis, 1848–1861* (New York, 1976).

3. Quoted in James M. McPherson, *Battle Cry of Freedom: The Civil War Era*

(New York, 1988), 137, see also 7–10, 22, 30–33, and 130–35. See also Jason H. Silverman, *Lincoln and the Immigrant* (Urbana, Ill., 2015). As was common in the era, Lincoln did not capitalize "Negro."

4. Quoted in McPherson, *Battle Cry of Freedom*, 692.

5. Quoted in Eric Foner, *The Fiery Trial: Abraham Lincoln and American Slavery* (New York, 2010), 99–100. See also Sidney Blumenthal, *A Self-Made Man: The Political Life of Abraham Lincoln, 1809–1849* (New York, 2016), 450–51, 456–58.

6. Quoted in Foner, *The Fiery Trial*, 107.

7. Quoted in Keri Leigh Merritt, *Masterless Men: Poor Whites and Slavery in the Antebellum South* (New York, 2017), 113, see also 4–9, 18–19, 90–92.

8. Quoted in Robert J. Cottrol, *The Long, Lingering Shadow: Slavery, Race, and Law in the American Hemisphere* (Athens, Ga., 2013), 109.

9. On these changes, see James Sanders, "The Vanguard of the Atlantic World: Contesting Modernity in Nineteenth-Century Latin America," *Latin American Research Review* 46, no. 2 (2011): 104–27. See also George Reid Andrews, *Afro-Latin America, 1800–2000* (New York, 2004), 96–97, 100–101. President Buchanan tried and failed to get the Senate to approve an agreement giving the United States police powers over Mexico if it were attacked by a third power. See Brian Loveman, *No Higher Law: American Foreign Policy and the Western Hemisphere since 1776* (Chapel Hill, N.C., 2010), 115–16.

10. Quoted in Louis A. Pérez Jr., *Cuba and the United States: Ties of Singular Intimacy*, 3rd ed. (Athens, Ga., 2003), 52.

11. Quoted in Merrill Peterson, *The Jeffersonian Image in the American Mind* (New York, 1960), 167.

12. Quoted in David Brion Davis, *The Problem of Slavery in the Age of Emancipation* (New York, 2010), 326. The article appeared in *De Bow's Review* in 1857.

13. Quoted in *Comisión histórico de la campaña de 1856–1857*, in *Documentos relativos a la guerra contra los filibusteros* (San José, Costa Rica, 1956), 64. See also Michael Gobat, *Empire by Invitation: William Walker and Manifest Destiny in Central America* (Cambridge, Mass., 2018).

14. R. Blakeslee Gilpin, *John Brown Still Lives! America's Long Reckoning with Violence, Equality and Change* (Chapel Hill, N.C., 2011).

15. James Oakes, *The Scorpion's Sting: Antislavery and the Coming of the Civil War* (New York, 2015).

16. Quoted in Eric Foner, *Free Soil, Free Labor, Free Men: The Ideology of the Republican Party before the Civil War* (New York, 1970), 223. See also Kevin Peraino, *Lincoln in the World: The Making of a Statesman and the Dawn of American Power* (New York, 2013), 93–95.

17. Abraham Lincoln, inaugural address, March 4, 1861, in the American Presidency Project, https://www.presidency.ucsb.edu/documents/inaugural-address-34; McPher-

son, *Battle Cry of Freedom*, 234–35. The issue of the war as a "civil war" or a "rebellion" is a thorny one. Both Lincoln and the legal scholar Francis Lieber used both words interchangeably, but unlike a civil war, in which two or more portions of the state fight for the control of the whole, only the Union intended to restore the entire territory of the United States under one government. The official U.S. title was "War of the Rebellion" until 1907, when Congress agreed on "Civil War" as the official name. See David Armitage, *Civil Wars: A History in Ideas* (New York, 2017), 188–93.

18. Quoted in McPherson, *Battle Cry of Freedom*, 245.

19. Don H. Doyle, *The Cause of All Nations: An International History of the American Civil War* (New York, 2015), 6–8, 25.

20. Quoted in John Herd Thompson and Stephen J. Randall, *Canada and the United States: Ambivalent Allies*, 3rd ed. (Athens, Ga., 2002), 35.

21. Kevin Peraino, *Lincoln in the World: The Making of a Statesman and the Dawn of American Power* (New York, 2013), 66–67.

22. Quoted in Amanda Foreman, *A World on Fire: Britain's Crucial Role in the American Civil War* (New York, 2011), 201, see also 175–98, 737–38. On Canadian defense preparations, see Robert Bothwell, *Your Country, My Country: A Unified History of the United States and Canada* (New York, 2015), 114–15.

23. Drew Gilpin Faust, *The Creation of Confederate Nationalism: Ideology and Identity in the Civil War South* (Baton Rouge, La., 1988), 82–85. On the roots of southern nationhood, see Emory Thomas, *The Confederate Nation, 1861–1865* (New York, 2011; orig. pub., 1979), esp. chap. 1. On the Union's advantages in recruitment of soldiers, especially from Europe, see Doyle, *The Cause of All Nations*, 166–69.

24. Quoted in Roy C. Basler, ed., *The Collected Works of Abraham Lincoln* (New Brunswick, N.J., 1952–55), 5:388–89.

25. On slavery's role in the conduct of the war, see D. H. Dilbeck, *A More Civil War: How the Union Waged a Just War* (Chapel Hill, N.C., 2016). On the making of the "political" Lincoln, see Sidney Blumenthal, *A Self-Made Man: The Political Life of Abraham Lincoln, 1809–1849* (New York, 2016). For Lieber's "Instructions," see http://avalon.law.yale.edu/19th_century/lieber.asp.

26. The quoted material is in James McPherson, "A Bombshell on the American Public," *New York Review of Books*, November 22, 2012, 18.

27. Abraham Lincoln, second annual message, December 1, 1862, in the American Presidency Project, https://www.presidency.ucsb.edu/documents/second-annual-message-9.

28. Quoted in Foner, *The Fiery Trial*, 247. See also Doyle, *The Cause of All Nations*, 234–36, 240–41, 246–47.

29. Stanley Harrold, *Border War: Fighting Over Slavery before the Civil War* (Chapel Hill, N.C., 2010), xii–xiii, 209–13. See also Christopher Phillips, *The Rivers Ran Backward: The Civil War and the Remaking of the American Middle Border* (New

York, 2016); Sharon Romeo, *Gender and the Jubilee: Black Freedom and the Reconstruction of Citizenship in Civil War Missouri* (Athens, Ga., 2016).

30. Matthew Pratt Guterl, *American Mediterranean: Southern Slaveholders in the Age of Emancipation* (Cambridge, Mass., 2013), 66–68; Peraino, *Lincoln and the World*, 222–23.

31. Sean Wilentz, "Democracy at Gettysburg," in *The Gettysburg Address: Perspectives on Lincoln's Greatest Speech*, ed. Sean Conant (New York, 2015), 51–53, 66–67. Doyle, *The Cause of All Nations*, 282–83, identifies Lincoln's words as the "language of international republicanism." In New York City the precipitating factor in the riot was the perceived unfairness of the Conscription Act, which permitted those who paid $300 to avoid service, but the largely Irish mobs soon turned their rage on the city's African American population after several Democratic political leaders predicted that freed slaves would be taking their jobs while the Irish would be fighting. See Richard Hofstadter and Michael Wallace, *American Violence: A Documentary History* (New York, 1971), 211–13.

32. Alison Clark Efford, "Immigration and the Gettysburg Address," in Conant, *The Gettysburg Address*, 211–13; Doyle, *The Cause of All Nations*, 173–76. See also Silverman, *Lincoln and the Immigrant*.

33. Quoted in George M. Fredrickson, *The Black Image in the White Mind: The Debate on Afro-American Character and Destiny, 1817–1914* (New York, 1971), 151, see also 168.

34. Quoted in Douglas R. Egerton, *Thunder at the Gates: The Black Civil Regiments That Redeemed America* (New York, 2016), 7. See also Steven Hahn, *The Political Worlds of Slavery and Freedom* (Cambridge, Mass., 2009), 70–71, 96–99.

35. Brenda Gayle Plummer, *Haiti and the United States: The Psychological Moment* (Athens, Ga., 1992), 45–48; G. Pope Atkins and Larman Curtis Wilson, *The Dominican Republic and the United States: From Imperialism to Transnationalism* (Athens, Ga., 1998), 18–20. Matthew J. Clavin makes the case for the centrality of the Haitian Revolution in bringing on the Civil War in *Toussaint Louverture and the American Civil War: The Promise and Peril of a Second Haitian Revolution* (Philadelphia, 2010).

36. Hahn, *Political Worlds*, 106–9; Loren Foote, *The Gentlemen and the Roughs: Manhood, Honor, and Violence in the Union Army* (New York, 2010), 2–3.

37. Quoted in George S. Burkhardt, *Confederate Rage, Yankee Wrath: No Quarter in the Civil War* (Carbondale, Ill., 2007), 2. See also Fredrickson, *Black Image*, 166–67; Eugene Genovese, *From Rebellion to Revolution: Afro-American Slave Revolts in the Making of the Modern World* (Baton Rouge, La., 1992), 135–36.

38. Thomas D. Schoonover, *Dollars over Dominion: The Triumph of Liberalism in United States–Mexican Relations, 1861–1867* (Baton Rouge, La., 1978), 251–53, 275–76.

39. Jonathan W. White, *Emancipation, the Union Army, and the Reelection of Abraham Lincoln* (Baton Rouge, La., 2014), 9.

40. Lorien Foote, *The Yankee Plague: Escaped Union Prisoners and the Collapse of the Confederacy* (Chapel Hill, N.C., 2016).

41. Victor Davis Hanson, introduction to *The Soul of Battle: From Ancient Times to the Present Day, How Three Great Leaders Vanquished Tyranny* (New York, 1999); Nancy Isenberg, *White Trash: A 400-Year Untold History of Class in America* (New York, 2016), 171–72.

42. Merritt, *Masterless Men*, 320–21; Emory Thomas, *The Confederacy as a Revolutionary Experience* (Englewood Cliffs, N.J., 1979), 134–37.

43. Harry S. Stout, *From the Altar of the Nation: A Moral History of the Civil War* (New York, 2006), xxi. On the traumatic impact of Civil War casualties on this generation, see Drew Gilpin Faust, *This Republic of Suffering: Death and the American Civil War* (New York, 2008).

44. Quoted in "Lincoln's Last Public Address, April 11, 1865," in Abraham Lincoln Online—Speeches and Writings, http://abrahamlincolnonline.org/lincoln/speeches/last.htm.

45. Lincoln, "Second Inaugural Address, March 4, 1865," in Abraham Lincoln Online—Speeches and Writings, abrahamlincolnonline.org/lincoln/speeches/inaug2.htm; Rachel Hope Cleves, *The Reign of Terror in America: Visions of Violence from Anti-Jacobinism to Antislavery* (New York, 2009), 278–81.

46. Abraham Lincoln, annual message to Congress, December 1, 1862, in the American Presidency Project, https://www.presidency.ucsb.edu/documents/second-annual-message-9. On the northern and southern theologians' view of the war, see Mark Noll, *America's God: From Jonathan Edwards to Abraham Lincoln* (New York, 2002), 432–36.

47. Quoted in Noll, *America's God*, 431, see also 416–17, 420–21, 424–25, 432.

48. Merritt, *Masterless Men*, 320–22, 324–31; Karl Marx and Friedrich Engels, *The Civil War in the United States*, ed. Andrew Zimmerman (New York, 2016).

49. Eric Foner, *Forever Free: The Story of Emancipation and Reconstruction* (New York, 2005), 108–11; Foner, *Reconstruction: America's Unfinished Revolution, 1863–1877* (New York, 1988), xxiv–xxvii.

50. Quoted in James M. McPherson, *Abraham Lincoln and the Second American Revolution* (New York, 1991), 138. See also Hoffer, *Uncivil Warriors*, 164–65.

Chapter 8. The End of the Long American Revolution

1. For a synthesis of a generation of revisionist scholarship on Reconstruction and its connection to the civil rights movement of the 1960s, see the classic study by Eric Foner, *Reconstruction: America's Unfinished Revolution, 1863–1877* (New York, 1988; updated edition, 2014), esp. 602–3, 609–12. See also the essays in Kate Masur

and Gregory P. Downs, eds., *The World the Civil War Made* (Chapel Hill, N.C., 2015).

2. Eric Foner, *Forever Free: Emancipation and Reconstruction* (New York, 2014), 122–25. See also Laura Free, *Suffrage Reconstructed: Gender, Race, and Voting Rights in the Civil War Era* (Ithaca, N.Y., 2015).

3. Quoted in Foner, *Forever Free*, 149. See also Susanne Michele Lee, *Claiming the Union: Citizenship in the Post–Civil War South* (New York, 2014). Douglass' views of Lincoln changed in the postwar decade. Speaking at the unveiling of a statue of Lincoln (the Freedmen's Monument) on Capitol Hill in April 1876, Douglass said, "Abraham Lincoln was not. . .either or man or our model. In his interests, in his associations, in his habits of thought, and in his prejudices, he was a white man. . . . [And] while Abraham Lincoln saved for you [white people] a country, he delivered us from a bondage" (quoted in Jon Meachem, *The Soul of America: The Battle Over Our Better Angels* [New York, 2018], 33–34.)

4. Ulysses S. Grant, first inaugural, March 4, 1869, in Inaugural Addresses of the Presidents of the United States, https://www.bartleby.com/124/pres33.html; Ron Chernow, *Grant* (New York, 2017), 701–9. On the accomplishments and violence of the Reconstruction era, see Douglas R. Egerton, *The Wars of Reconstruction: The Brief Violent History of America's Most Progressive Era* (New York, 2014).

5. Laura F. Edwards, *A Legal History of the Civil War and Reconstruction: A Nation of Rights* (Cambridge, 2015), 6.

6. Alison Clark Efford, *German Immigrants, Race, and Citizenship in the Civil War Era* (New York, 2013), 164.

7. Chernow, *Grant*, 655–67, 694–96, 701–27.

8. Tyler Stovall, "White Freedom and the Lady of Liberty," *American Historical Review*, February 2018, 13. On postwar celebrations, reconciliation, and memory, see David Blight, *Race and Reunion: The Civil War in American Memory* (Cambridge, Mass., 2005), 2-3, 210; and on the meaning of death for the Civil War generation, see Drew Gilpin Faust, *The Republic of Suffering: Death and the American Civil War* (New York, 2008), xii–xiii, 4–5, 270–71.

9. Vitor Izeckson, *Slavery and War in the Americas: Race, Citizenship, and State Building in the United States and Brazil, 1861–1870* (Charlottesville, Va., 2014).

10. Mauricio Tenorio Trillo, *Latin America: The Allure and Power of an Idea* (Chicago, 2017), 5–8.

11. On the critical importance of religion in this era, see Matthew Harper, *African American Religion and Politics in the Age of Emancipation* (Chapel Hill, N.C., 2016); and Edward J. Blum, *Reforging the White Republic: Race, Religion, and American Nationalism, 1865–1898* (Baton Rouge, La., 2005).

12. Roosevelt's comment on the Dawes Act is from Lester D. Langley, *The Americas in the Modern Age* (New Haven, Conn., 2002), 18. On the role of the states in

Indian policy after the Civil War, see Deborah A. Rosen, *American Indians and State Law: Sovereignty, Race, and Citizenship, 1790–1880* (Lincoln, Neb., 2009), 202–5.

13. Quoted in John Herd Thompson and Stephen J. Randall, *Canada and the United States: Ambivalent Allies*, 3rd ed. (Athens, Ga., 2002), 52.

14. William Jennings Bryan, speech, Democratic National Convention, Chicago, July 9, 1896, historymatters.gmu.edu/d/5354.

15. Quoted in Thomas Schoonover, *Uncle Sam's War of 1898 and the War with Spain* (Lexington, Ky., 2013), 56. See also Walter LaFeber, *The New Empire: An Interpretation of American Expansion, 1860–1898* (Ithaca, N.Y., 1998; orig. pub., 1963).

16. Quoted in Brian Loveman, *No Higher Law: American Foreign Policy and the Western Hemisphere since 1776* (Chapel Hill, N.C., 2010), 128.

17. Quoted in Ada Ferrer, *Insurgent Cuba: Race, Nation, and Revolution, 1868–1898* (Chapel Hill, N.C., 1999), 122. Martí's belief that "there can be no racial animosity, because there are no races," appeared in "Our America," *La Revista Ilustrada* (New York), January 1, 1891.

18. Ferrer, *Insurgent Cuba*, 200–203.

19. David Luis-Brown, *Waves of Decolonization: Discourses of Race and Hemispheric Citizenship in Cuba, Mexico, and the United States* (Durham, N.C., 2008), 68–71. See also David A. Hollinger, *Protestants Abroad: How Missionaries Tried to Change the World but Changed America* (Princeton, N.J., 2017), 13.

20. On the role of U.S. Protestant reformist groups in the late nineteenth and early twentieth centuries, see Ian Tyrrell, *Reforming the World: The Creation of America's Moral Empire* (Princeton, N.J., 2010), 4–7; and Matthew McCullough, *The Cross of War: Christian Nationalism and U.S. Expansionism in the Spanish-American War* (Madison, Wis., 2014).

21. Edwin L. Godkin, "The Eclipse of Liberalism," *Nation*, August 9, 1900, 105.

22. Myles Beaupre, "'What Are the Philippines Going to Do to Us?': E. L. Godkin on Democracy, Empire, and Anti-imperialism," *Journal of American Studies* 46, no. 3 (August 2012): 711–27. For a cultural critique of the era, see Jackson Lears, *Rebirth of a Nation, 1877–1920* (New York, 2009), 30–33.

23. Colin D. Moore, *American Imperialism and the State, 1893–1921* (New York, 2017).

24. Sven Beckert, "'American Danger': United States Empire, Eurafrica, and the Territorialization of Industrial Capitalism, 1870–1950," *American Historical Review* 122, no. 4 (October 2017): 1137–70.

25. Michael McGerr, *A Fierce Discontent: The Rise and Fall of the Progressive Movement in America* (New York, 2003), xiii–xvi.

26. Quoted in Desmond King, *Making Americans: Immigration, Race, and the Origins of the Diverse Democracy* (Cambridge, Mass., 2000), 53; Felipe Fernández-Armesto, *Our America: A Hispanic History of the United States* (New York,

2014), 248–49; Paul A. Kramer, "The Geopolitics of Mobility: Immigration Policy and American Global Power in the Long Twentieth Century," *American Historical Review* 123, no. 2 (April 2018): 406–7, 424–25.

27. Eric Foner, *The Story of American Freedom* (New York, 1998), 140–41. See also Charles A. Beard, *An Economic Interpretation of the Constitution of the United States* (New York, 1913); and John Dewey, *The School and Society* (Chicago, 1900).

28. Frederick Jackson Turner, "The Significance of the Frontier in American History, 1893," address delivered at the World's Columbian Exposition, July 12, 1893. See also William Appleman Williams, *The Contours of American History* (London, 2011; orig. pub., 1961), 356–57, 363–64, 374; and Barry Shain, *The Myth of American Individualism: The Protestant Origins of American Political Thought* (Princeton, N.J., 1994).

29. Herbert Croly, *The Promise of American Life* (New York, 1909), 300–305.

30. Thomas C. Leonard, *Illiberal Reformers: Race, Eugenics, and American Economics in the Progressive Era* (Princeton, N.J., 2016), 15–16. On the effectiveness of evangelical prohibitionists in the South in the Progressive Era, see Gregory P. Downs, *Declarations of Dependence: The Long Reconstruction of Popular Politics in the South, 1861–1908* (Chapel Hill, N.C., 2011), 208–11.

31. Nancy Isenberg, *White Trash: A 400-Year Untold Story of Class in America* (New York, 2016), 198. On the influence of Progressive Era race laws on Nazi Germany, see James G. Whitman, *Hitler's American Model: The United States and the Making of Nazi Race Law* (Princeton, N.J., 2017).

32. William Graham Sumner, "The Conquest of the United States by Spain," January 16, 1899, in Mises Daily Articles, https://mises.org/library/conquest-united -states-spain.

33. Julian Go, *American Empire and the Politics of Meaning: Elite Political Cultures in the Philippines and Puerto Rico during U.S. Colonialism* (Durham, N.C., 2008), 141. See also Paul A. Kramer, *The Blood of Government: Race, Empire, the United States, and the Philippines* (Chapel Hill, N.C., 2006).

34. W. T. Stead, *The Americanisation of the World; or, the Trend of the Twentieth Century* (London, 1902). On the Insular Cases, see Bartholomew H. Sparrow, *The Insular Cases and the Emergence of American Empire* (Lawrence, Kans., 2006). Although Hawai'i was put on a path toward statehood, the racial and ethnic makeup of the islands' population remained controversial even after statehood was granted in 1959.

35. Quoted in Walter A. McDougall, *Promised Land, Crusader State: The American Encounter with the World since 1776* (New York, 1997), 105. See also Benjamin Allen Coates, *Legalist Empire: International Law and American Foreign Relations in the Early Twentieth Century* (New York, 2016).

36. McGerr, *A Fierce Discontent*, 182–83. See also Susan Grant, "Americans Forging a New Nation, 1860–1916," in *Nationalism in the New World*, ed. Don H. Doyle and Marco Antonio Pamplona (Athens, Ga., 2006), 82–85, 94–96.

37. Gretchen Murphy, *Hemispheric Imaginings: The Monroe Doctrine and Narratives of U.S. Empire* (Durham, N.C., 2005), 7. See also Gary Gerstle, "Race and Nation in the United States, Mexico, and Cuba, 1880–1940," in Doyle and Pamplona, *Nationalism*, 272–303; and George Reid Andrews, *Afro-Latin America: 1800–2000* (New York, 2004), 112–13, 118–19.

38. Randolph Bourne Jr., "Trans-National America," in *The Radical Will: Selected Writings, 1911–1918* (New York, 1977), 255; Theodore Roosevelt, *American Ideals, and Other Essays, Social and Political* (New York, 1897), 23.

39. Eric Hobsbawm, *The Age of Extremes: A History of the World, 1914–1991* (New York, 1991), 22–30.

40. Williams, *Contours*, 420–21. Michael S. Neiberg, *The Path to War: How the First World War Created Modern America* (New York, 1916), emphasizes that the war offered immigrants and African Americans an opportunity to prove their commitment to joining mainstream society and their "Americanization."

41. W. Dirk Raat, *Mexico and the United States: Ambivalent Vistas* (Athens, Ga., 1992), 115, 124–25. The first socialist government in the Americas in the twentieth century was not that created by the Mexican Constitution of 1917 but the U.S. Panama Canal Zone, where there was no private property and all enterprises were government operated.

42. Robert H. Wiebe, *The Search for Order, 1877–1920* (New York, 1967), 277–78; Christopher Hitchens, "The Pacifists and the Trenches," a review of Adam Hochschild, *To End All Wars: A Story of Loyalty and Rebellion, 1914–1918* (New York, 2011), in the *New York Times*, May 13, 2011.

43. One was a former aide, William C. Bullitt, who proved especially prophetic, yet even his insights sometimes overlooked or underestimated critical contexts. See the review of his biography (Alexander Etkind, *Roads Not Taken: An Intellectual Biography of William C. Bullitt* [Pittsburgh, 2017]) by David S. Foglesong in H-Diplo Review Essay No. 157, https://networks.h-net.org/node/28443/discussions /1934361/h-diplo-review-essay-157-roads-not-taken-intellectual-biography. See also Cara Lea Burnidge, *A Peaceful Conquest: Woodrow Wilson, Religion, and the New World Order* (Chicago, 2016), 52; Arthur Herman, *1917: Lenin, Wilson, and the Birth of the New World Disorder* (New York, 2017), 397, see also 381–98, 422–23; and John Morrow Jr., *The Great War: An Imperial History* (New York, 2010; orig. pub., 2004), 320–23.

44. Herman, *1917*, 413; Hobsbawm, *The Age of Extremes*, 31–32, 55; Randolph Bourne Jr., *The State* (1918). Bourne died in the flu epidemic of 1918, and the manuscript of *The State* was published posthumously.

45. See the essay review "It Can Happen Here," *New York Review of Books*, June 28, 2018, 64–65; McGerr, *A Fierce Discontent*, 310–11.

46. Warren G. Harding, inaugural address, March 4, 1921, in the American Presidency Project, https://www.presidency.ucsb.edu/documents/inaugural-address-49.

47. As Robert Bothwell points out, Canada's experience in the war had inspired a latent nationalist sentiment, which meant that it would remain in the empire but had "earned the right to be treated as a separate entity" (*Your Country, My Country: A Unified History of the United States and Canada* [New York, 2017], 177).

Epilogue

1. Comparison of JFK's inaugural with that of President Donald Trump reveals strikingly different perspectives over national goals and problems and their solution. See also Michael McGerr, *A Fierce Discontent: The Rise and Fall of the Progressive Movement in America, 1870–1920* (New York, 2003), 316–19; and Jackson Lears, *Rebirth of a Nation: The Making of Modern America, 1877–1920* (New York, 2009), 352–53.

2. Quoted in Joseph J. Ellis, *Founding Brothers: The Revolutionary Generation* (New York, 2000), 246–47.

3. Transcript of Antonin Scalia interview with Tom Gjelten, February 14, 2016, on the PBS program *All Things Considered.* On the consequences of such contradictions, anomalies, and inconsistences in our history, see Walter A. McDougall, *The Tragedy of U.S. Foreign Policy: How America's Civil Religion Betrayed the National Interest* (New York, 2016); Jon Meacham, *The Soul of America: The Battle for Our Better Angels* (New York, 2018); and new editions of classic works: Reinhold Niebuhr, *The Irony of American History*, introduction by Andrew Bacevich (Chicago, 2008; orig. pub., 1952); and William Appleman Williams, *Empire as a Way of Life: An Essay on the Causes and Character of America's Past Predicament along with a Few Thoughts on the Causes and Character of America's Present Predicament, along with a Few Thoughts about an Alternative* (Brooklyn, N.Y., 2007; orig. pub., 1980).

4. Joseph J. Ellis, *American Dialogue: The Founders and Us* (New York, 2018), 225–26.

5. Niebuhr, *The Irony*, 174.

6. The number of and differences in North America's "nations" keeps growing. See Joel Garreau, *The Nine Nations of North America* (New York, 1981); and Colin Woodward, *American Nations: A History of the Eleven Rival Regional Cultures of North America* (New York, 2014).

7. Two strikingly different examples convey what I am getting at here. The first is Peter Marshall, *1517: Martin Luther and the Invention of the Reformation* (New York, 2017), who argues that Luther's act of nailing the "Ninety-Five Theses" on the Castle Church door in Wittenberg on October 31, 1517, may have been a myth, but

the act has endured as a symbol of protest against abusive power. The second comes from a multibook review by Jackson Lears—"Aquarius Rising," *New York Review of Books*, September 27, 2018, 8–14—in which Lears points to the radicalism of the 1960s in the United States as a manifestation of the antinomian Protestant tradition and Christian existentialism and a call for the country to be a "moral example to the world."

8. See Lawrence Wright, *God Save Texas: A Journey into the Soul of the Lone Star State* (New York, 2018); and Manuel Pastor, *State of Resistance: What California's Dizzying Descent and Remarkable Resurgence Mean for America's Future* (New York, 2018).

9. See Michael Ignatieff, "Making Room for God," and David Bell, "Pity Is Treason," in the *New York Review of Books*, June 28, 2018, 59–60 and 75–76, respectively. Although I would never have used the comparison in an academic discussion, if you want to know the difference between the American and French Revolutions, compare the lyrics of the French national anthem, "La Marseillaise," with those of the unofficial anthem of the Civil War, the "Battle Hymn of the Republic." God is nowhere to be found in the first; he is in every stanza of the latter.

10. Lester D. Langley, *MexAmerica: Two Countries, One Future* (New York, 1988).

11. Ibid., 62–78.

BIBLIOGRAPHICAL ESSAY

THIS ESSAY DEALS PRINCIPALLY WITH broad and interpretive books on revolution; the age of revolution, especially in the Atlantic world; slavery, abolition, and race; and U.S. history, especially the American Revolution, from both comparative and traditional national perspectives. The endnotes identify works and sources that pertain to more specific issues.

As the title promises, Jack Goldstone, *Revolutions: A Very Short Introduction* (New York, 2014), provides a succinct introduction to a controversial topic but offers precise comparisons between revolts and revolutions. In the tradition of those who follow the structuralist approach, he identifies critical factors that can trigger a revolution. A marked contrast is Eric Selbin, *Revolution, Rebellion, Resistance: The Power of Story* (London, 2010), which departs from traditional political science methods to illustrate how stories can be more helpful in telling us why revolutions—assessed thematically—occur in one place but not another. Graduate students in the early 1960s were still reading Crane Brinton's classic *Anatomy of Revolution* (New York, 1965; orig. pub., 1938), which deals with four revolutions—the English Revolution of the 1640s, the American Revolution, the French Revolution, and the 1917 Russian Revolution—and the patterns of moderation, the reign of terror, and then the dictatorship that occurred in their development. Predictably, the American Revolution was not a "neat fit" in Brinton's comparisons. Those frustrated by the differences between a sociological and a historical approach to revolution will profit from Keith Michael Baker and Dan Edelstein, eds., *Scripting Revolution: A Historical Approach to the Comparative Study of Revolutions* (Stanford, Calif., 2015), a volume of essays on how revolutionary participants "script" their actions by relating them to examples from the past. The essays in Joanna Innes and Mark Philp, eds., *Re-imagining Democracy in the Age of Revolutions: America, France, Britain, Ireland, 1750–1850* (New York, 2013), show how revolutionary experiences in four different places transformed the meaning of "democracy" from its meaning of anarchy or mob rule into a positive ideal for government.

More germane to what I am doing in this book is the classic account by Hannah Arendt, *On Revolution* (New York, 1963), which inspired my "when a wheel goes around once" definition that proved so useful in getting through my doctoral prelims in October 1964. Arendt commences with a probing comparison between the French and American Revolutions, arguing that the French were preoccupied with scarcity and inequality and the Americans with political freedom. From that beginning she skillfully moves to a thematic and philosophical probing of the revolutionary tradition. Although more critical of the French model, Arendt was no fan of the British antidemocratic example extolled by Edmund Burke in his acerbic 1790 "Reflections on the Revolution in France." Equally compelling, although neglectful of the Haitian and Spanish American revolutions, is the sweeping Marxist interpretation by Eric Hobsbawm, *The Age of Revolution, 1789–1848* (New York, 1996; orig. pub., 1962), which is presented as world history but emphasizes the suggestive theme of a dual revolution—industrial (the British) and political (the French). To these I would append a third: Raymond Williams, *The Long Revolution*, 3rd ed. (Cardigan, Wales, 2011; orig. pub., 1961). Williams objects to any deterministic or reductionist view of revolution.

In contrast to the perspectives of Williams, Hobsbawm, and Arendt and a great many revisionist or anticelebratory students of the American Revolution, Jonathan Israel, *The Expanding Blaze: How the American Revolution Ignited the World, 1775–1848* (Princeton, N.J., 2017), places the American Revolution at center stage in the age of revolution both as exemplar of the modern revolution and as defender of universal human rights, freedom of expression, and republican liberty. Early American historians will benefit from the collection of John M. Murrin's essays in *Rethinking America: From Empire to Republic* (New York, 2018). The collection of essays edited by David Armitage and Sanjay Subrahmanyam, *The Age of Revolutions in Global Context, c. 1760–1840* (London, 2010), provides interpretations and assessments by well-known historians of the major revolutions of the era and their impact in North and South America, the Caribbean, Africa, Europe, the Middle East, South Asia, Southeast Asia, and China.

Robert R. Palmer, *The Age of the Democratic Revolution: A Political History of Europe and America, 1760–1800*, 2 vols. (Princeton, N.J., 1959, 1964), has become a classic account, although very much influenced by the Cold War and its political tensions. Much to the displeasure of the French, Palmer identified the American Revolution as the lodestar for those who grasped Tom Paine's idea of the American Revolution as the cause of all humanity and especially for those Europeans seeking to overthrow monarchy and make their world anew. Contrastingly, Lester D. Langley, *The Americas in the Age of Revolution, 1750–1850* (New Haven, Conn., 1996), turns Palmer's east–west perspective on a north–south axis and brings the Haitian and Latin American revolutions into a detailed account that suggests the American Revolution can better be understood in the context of the other revolutions in the western hemisphere. Wim Klooster, *Revolutions in the Atlantic World: A Comparative History* (New York, 2009), neatly packages the four major revolutions in the Atlantic world—the American, French, Haitian, and Spanish American— and offers tidy comparisons of their causes, character, and legacy. Janet Polasky,

Revolutions without Borders: The Call to Liberty in the Atlantic World (New Haven, Conn., 2015), skillfully blends biographical sketches in a sweeping account of the successes and failures of revolutions in places both familiar and sometimes forgotten. With an understandable acknowledgment to Tom Paine and the pamphleteers of the era, the author reminds us that the American Revolution was not the first assault against European monarchy, but it became a model for the power of ideas in fermenting revolutionary change. The second edition of George Rudé, *Revolutionary Europe, 1783–1815* (Malden, Mass., 2000; orig. pub., 1964), provides a social and economic assessment of Europe in the revolutionary era from the eve of the French Revolution to the end of the Napoleonic wars. James H. Billington, *Fire in the Minds of Men: Origins of the Revolutionary Faith* (New York, 1980), provides an assessment of the messianic faith driving revolutionaries from the French to the Russian Revolution.

An important element in evaluating revolutions is nationalism. Perhaps the most successful and provocative book on nationhood and nationalism is Benedict Anderson's *Imagined Communities: Reflections on the Origin and Spread of Nationalism* (London, 1983; rev. eds., 1991, 2006), which redirected attention away from ideology, elites, and socioeconomic forces and toward the link between our imagination or cognitive processes and people we've never met as members of our "imagined community." Mark Bergholz, "Thinking the Nation," *American Historical Review* 123, no. 2 (April 2018): 518–28, assesses Anderson's thesis, and the essays in Don H. Doyle and Marco Antonio Pamplona, eds., *Nationalism in the New World* (Athens, Ga., 2006), address its utility in studying nationalism in several hemispheric countries. Thomas Bender, *A Nation among Nations: America's Place in World History* (New York, 2006), skillfully and effectively frames U.S. history in a global context. In a massive and eloquently written narrative, *These Truths: A History of the United States* (New York, 2018), Jill Lepore explains how we must look to the transcendent ideals and truths of our past to confront an uncertain and perilous future.

Ernst Renan in "Qu'est-ce qu'une nation?" (What is a nation?), a paper delivered at a conference at the Sorbonne on March 11, 1882, defined "nation" as "a soul, a spiritual principle" and excluded "race, language, interests, religious affinity, geography, [and] military necessities." Renan elaborated by referring to a nation as a people who share a "glorious heritage" and a "great solidarity" because of their sacrifices and the consent to a program they desire (ucparis.fr/files/9313/6549/9943/What_is_a_Nation.pdf). Ernest Gellner, *Nations and Nationalism* (Ithaca, N.Y., 1993; orig. pub., 1983), defines nationalism in essence as a political principle and locates its social roots in industrial social organization. E. J. Hobsbawm, *Nations and Nationalism since 1780: Programme, Myth, Reality*, 2nd ed. (New York, 2012; orig. pub., 1990), agrees with Gellner that nationalism requires a congruency between the political and national entity, but, contrastingly, he argues that those who lead nations must take into account ordinary people's needs and interests, which may not be national.

The Founders—those dead white males who continue to dominate the historiographical landscape—and their intrusive role in revolutionary history continue to absorb our attention. In *The Radicalism of the American Revolution* (New York, 1990), Gordon Wood rescued this band of often contentious brothers from a persistent charge of unbending conservatives who tried to shackle the democratic forces unleashed by the Revolution by portraying them as victims, men who grew fearful of the very success of their endeavors—a democratic society that passed them by. In *Founding Brothers: The Revolutionary Generation* (New York, 2000), Joseph J. Ellis artfully details how the success of the early republic depended less on institutions than on the intersection and cooperation of personalities. And with *American Dialogue: The Founders and Us* (New York, 2018), Ellis explores such issues as race, income inequality, jurisprudence, and foreign policy to confirm the adage that the present must always engage the past. Jack Rakove, *Revolutionaries: A New History of the Invention of America* (New York, 2010), takes another perspective in a collective biography of persons who found themselves thrust into the revolutionary whirlwind and shaped by its impact on them, a judgment that Abraham Lincoln himself confirmed during the Civil War. Tom Cutterham offers a more compelling interpretation of the Founders and their motives in *Gentlemen Revolutionaries: Power and Justice in the New American Republic* (Princeton, N.J., 2017) by exploring how they identified themselves by their work and their belief that property should be paramount in the pursuit of justice. As Richard D. Brown details in *Self-Evident Truths: Contesting Equal Rights from the Revolution to the Civil War* (New Haven, Conn., 2017), such views contrasted with the Declaration's political and social contract and commitment to equality, particularly where property, patriarchy, coverture, religious disestablishment, and the pursuit of happiness were at risk. In *Revolution against Empire: Taxes, Politics, and the Origins of American Independence* (New Haven, Conn., 2017), Justin Du Rivage reconsiders the traditional scholarship on the reasons for independence by focusing on taxation and how key groups in the transatlantic British imperial community perceived the colonial relationship with the mother country.

By the measure of achievement toward democracy, the American Revolution rates favorably in James T. Kloppenberg's *Toward Democracy: The Struggle for Self-Rule in European and American Thought* (New York, 2016). Kloppenberg focuses on function rather than ideology and slights the French and Haitian Revolutions. In a similar fashion, Max M. Edling, *A Hercules in the Cradle: War, Money, and the American State* (Chicago, 2014), details how the self-proclaimed Jeffersonian and Jacksonian enemies of central government used war and the threat of war to expand federal spending. In *Republican Empire: Alexander Hamilton on War and Free*

Government (Lawrence, Kans., 1999), Karl-Friedrich Walling emphasizes how the United States exploited Alexander Hamilton's financial planning to demonstrate its exception to the axiom that war is destructive of free government.

Fitting the American Revolution into the transatlantic or the global age of revolution can be difficult, especially for those who are focused on the question of American exceptionalism. So, too, is the obverse approach of understanding the myriad ways the transatlantic or global revolution has fitted into the long American Revolution. The historiography of the American Revolution is both rich and controversial, varying from the hagiographic literature of the nineteenth century to the more critical and sophisticated scholarship of the twentieth and twenty-first centuries. Successive generations of historians have supplemented a once-dominating but still-relevant political approach with social, cultural, military, imperial, biographical, and gendered perspectives, among others. Eliga H. Gould and Peter S. Onuf have assembled a useful collection of essays in *Empire and Nation: The American Revolution in the Atlantic World* (Baltimore, Md., 2005), although it is less comparative and focuses largely on the British Atlantic. More detailed is Jack P. Greene and J. R. Pole, eds., *A Companion to the American Revolution* (Malden, Mass., 2000), which offers brief and authoritative essays on the major issues. After an introduction discussing the impact of J. Franklin Jameson's *The American Revolution Considered as a Social Movement* (Princeton, N.J., 1926), Alfred Young and Gregory Nobles, *Whose American Revolution Was It? Historians Interpret the Founding* (New York, 2011), identify distinctive eras in revolutionary historiography and interpretation. From the 1930s to the 1970s, a generation of Progressive historians (such as Curtis Nettels, Merle Curti, Merrill Jensen, and Jackson Turner Main) followed Jameson's urging to look at outcomes and emphasized economic approaches to flesh out Jameson's narrative. With *No Property in Man: Slavery and Antislavery at the Nation's Founding* (Cambridge, Mass., 2018), Sean Wilentz skillfully makes the case that the Founders may have indirectly abetted slavery in the Constitution, but in denying any constitutional right to hold a person as property, they sustained the antislavery movement in its long struggle against the institution.

In the 1950s they were challenged by a Cold War generation, sometimes labeled as Counter-Progressive (such as Daniel Boorstin, Louis B. Hartz, and Robert Brown), who viewed the Revolution as an extension of processes already underway. Jack P. Greene, Bernard Bailyn, and Gordon Wood are sometimes lumped into this group, although their collective imprint on revolutionary historiography and the distinctiveness of their individual contributions set them apart from each other. Their work in turn inspired naysayers in their thinking and scholarship (among them, Staughton Lynd, Jesse Lemisch, Edward Countrymen, Gary Nash, and Alfred Young) who looked more closely at "history from the bottom up" and studied the small community or the urban crucible. Edward Countryman, *The American*

Revolution (New York, 1985), provides a balanced view of the myriad groups that participated in and were changed by the Revolution. In a perceptive review of another book in this genre (Ray Raphael, Alfred Young, and Gary Nash, eds., *Revolutionary Founders: Rebels, Radicals, and Reformers in the Making of the Nation* [New York, 2012]), Mary Beth Norton (*New York Times*, May 20, 2011) astutely points out that the preoccupation with "white men" in such studies distracts from the role of women, African Americans, Indians, and even loyalists. In *Fighting Over the Founders: How We Remember the American Revolution* (New York, 2015), Andrew M. Schocket tries to untangle the continuing battles over the meaning of the Revolution by dividing the contentious groups into two broad and suggestive categories: "essentialists" and "organicists," or, respectively, those who believe in fixed truths and those who agree but who argue that the work of the Revolution remains unfinished. In a seminal article, "A Different Kind of Independence: The Postwar Restructuring of the Historical Study of Early America," *William and Mary Quarterly*, 3rd ser., vol. 50 (April 1993): 245–67, Joyce Appleby demonstrates how a post–World War II generation of historians broke from the "exceptionalist model" of studying the revolutionary era.

The collection of essays in Jeffrey L. Parsley, Andrew W. Robertson, and David Waldstreicher, eds., *Beyond the Frontier: New Approaches to the Political History of the Early Republic* (Chapel Hill, N.C., 2004), describes the myriad ways in which African Americans, women, Indians, and entrepreneurs shaped the politics of the early republic. In different ways, Kathleen Duval, *Independence Lost: Lives on the Edge of the American Revolution* (New York, 2015), and Claudio Saunt, *West of the Revolution: An Uncommon History of 1776* (New York, 2014), remind us how much a narrow focus on the Atlantic seaboard colonies can distort the meaning of the Revolution. Holgar Hoock, *Scars of Independence: America's Violent Birth* (New York, 2017), is absorbed by the visceral and random violence that accompanied the Revolution, while Andrew Jackson O'Shaughnessy, *The Men Who Lost America: British Leadership, the American Revolution, and the Fate of Empire* (New York, 2013), fleshes out a much-needed story about why British misreading of the war as a rebellion cost the empire so dearly. From a parallel military perspective, Larrie D. Ferreiro, *American Independence and the Men of France and Spain Who Saved It* (New York, 2016), joins the increasing number of modern scholars who have engaged the lingering debate over the importance of French and Spanish assistance in the winning of independence. In *The Declaration of Independence: A Global History* (Cambridge, Mass., 2007), David Armitage stresses the international appeal of the claims of the document about the rights of states and individuals in spite of the challenges and legal rebuttals it received.

Contemporaries, particularly white males, often looked at the Revolution in ways our generation would disapprove of. In *Inheriting the Revolution: The First*

Generation of Americans (Cambridge, Mass., 2000), Joyce Appleby describes the legacy of the Revolution for society as individualistic, egalitarian, and liberal, a departure from the elitist, republican order the Founders had hoped to bring about. This visionary world proved alien to the South, to millenarians who preached doom about the growing materialism of the era, and of course to enslaved minorities. This was a sharply contrasting vision to the one that Seth Cotlar describes in *Tom Paine's America: The Rise and Fall of Transatlantic Radicalism in the Early Republic* (Charlottesville, Va., 2011). He details a vigorous democratic nation of the 1790s that frightened even the Jeffersonians. In power after 1800, they erected a bipartisan political system to curtail the radical movement against the liberal capitalist order that evolved in the early nineteenth century and the contested democracy described in Sean Wilentz's massive *The Rise of American Democracy: Jefferson to Lincoln* (New York, 2005). For a briefer account surveying similar themes, see Harry L. Watson, *Liberty and Power: The Politics of Jacksonian America* (New York, 2006; orig. pub., 1990), which contains a superb afterword on the historiographical controversies about the economic and ideological legacies of the American Revolution for Jacksonian America.

THESE AND SIMILAR works have prompted criticism from Atlantic world historians about the nationalist focus of early Americanists and the parallel and more controversial question of American exceptionalism. These issues are explored in detail in Ian Tyrrell, "American Exceptionalism in an Age of International History," *American Historical Review* 96, no. 4 (October 1991): 1031–55, and in Michael McGerr, "The Price of the 'New Transnational History,'" in the same issue, 1056–67. Godfrey Hodgson is both angry and skeptical about American exceptionalism in *The Myth of American Exceptionalism* (New Haven, Conn., 2009). In *Imagined Communities: Reflections on the Origin and Spread of Nationalism* (London, 1991; orig. pub., 1983), Benedict Anderson addresses the relationship between revolutions and the rise of nationalism. In Don H. Doyle and Marco Antonio Pamplona, eds., *Nationalism in the New World* (Athens, Ga., 2006), scholars from the Americas and Europe address the question of nationalism and national identity in the Americas. In *American Revolutions: A Continental History* (New York, 2016), Alan Taylor frames the Revolution in the context of imperial rivalries and the efforts of national leaders to "tame" the democratic insurgency of the 1790s. As do other historians, Taylor sees continental expansion as reinforcing white supremacy and black slavery. Robert Bothwell, *Your Country, My Country: A Unified History of the United States and Canada* (New York, 2015), is both witty and perceptive; the book lives up to its subtitle.

Susan Dunn's gracefully written comparison of the American and French Revolutions, *Sister Revolutions: French Lightning, American Light* (New York, 1999), is less concerned with American exceptionalism as offering a guide to understanding why these two upheavals that shaped our modern world followed such different paths. Yet she is pessimistic about the character of both societies at the end of the twentieth century, when consumerism replaced an engaged citizen politics. Rachel Hope Cleves, *The Reign of Terror: Visions of Violence from Anti-Jacobinism to Antislavery* (New York, 2009), is less restrained about the impact of the French Revolution on U.S. political culture and society, particularly on the fear of violence associated with Jacobinism among Federalists and abolitionists.

Simon Schama, *Rough Crossings: Britain, the Slaves, and the American Revolution* (London, 2005), places slavery as the principal cause of the American Revolution. In *Death or Liberty: African Americans and Revolutionary America* (New York, 2009), Douglas Egerton details how whites retreated from the revolutionary promise to liberate enslaved Americans and thus "doomed" the nation to civil war. As Edmund Morgan boldly concluded in *American Slavery, American Freedom: The Ordeal of Colonial Virginia* (New York, 1975), the notion that slavery was the exception to the achievement of liberty and equality in U.S. history distorted the truth about how the Founders had persuaded white males that their liberty and equality rested on the existence of slavery. In *The Empire of Necessity: Slavery, Freedom, and Deception in the New World* (New York, 2014), Greg Grandin skillfully employs the fiction of Herman Melville, who was at his height in the turbulent 1850s, to illustrate the contradictions of slavery and freedom and a country trapped by its biases. In a broad survey, *The Story of American Freedom* (New York, 1990), Eric Foner, known principally for his stimulating studies on the Civil War era, focuses particularly on three complicated characteristics of freedom since the Revolution: the untidy relationship between political and economic freedom; civil liberties; and the expansion of white freedom at the expense of African Americans.

The essays in María Teresa Calderón and Clément Thibaud, eds., *Revoluciones en el mundo atlántico* (Bogotá, Colombia, 2006), offer little on Europe but are particularly useful in identifying the differences between the American and Spanish American revolutions. The essays by Jack Greene, whose work has set a standard in early American and revolutionary history, and by Anthony McFarlane, his distinguished British counterpart, stand out in this superb collection. Those in Christine Daniels and Michael V. Kennedy, eds., *Negotiated Empires: Centers and Peripheries in the Americas, 1500–1820* (New York, 2002), address the European encounter with the Americas over a 350-year period. No one has done more to change historians' ways of looking at the wars of independence in Spanish America than Jaime Rodríguez O, whose *The Independence of Spanish America* (New York, 1998) frames the conflict in the context of a civil war in the Hispanic world. Unlike their U.S. counterparts, historians of the Spanish American revolutions do not suffer from the constraints of defending or disproving American exceptionalism, but they do have to deal with the burden of revolutionary hagiography and the legacy of a fragmented past. Much more accessible is John Charles Chasteen, *Americanos: Latin America's Struggle for Independence* (New York, 2008). He skillfully utilizes biography to frame his story about Latin Americans' efforts to expand Western political values of self-determination and popular sovereignty and how their examples differed from that of the United States.

In *Sovereignty and Revolution in the Iberian Atlantic* (Princeton, N.J., 2006), Jeremy Adelman cautions against facile explanations about the collapse of Spanish and Portuguese rule with reminders about the centrality of the struggle over sovereignty within far-flung empires under stress. Similarly, Brian Hamnett, *The End of Iberian Rule on the American Continent, 1770–1830* (New York, 2017), points to the slow decline of Spanish and Portuguese authority and influence rather than such cataclysmic events as the Napoleonic invasions of Iberia in 1807 and 1808 and indigenous insurrections that explained the disaffection of Creole elites to the monarchy after 1814 and the collapse of Iberian rule a decade later. In a brief but suggestive review essay ("What's in a Revolution," *Latin American Research Review* 47, no. 1 [February 2012]: 186–95), Jeremy Adelman notes that modern scholarship on the Latin American revolutions and wars of independence may have shifted away from nation building to other issues, such as the rights of subject peoples and localism and federalism. As in the nineteenth century, fascination with the individual leader, notably the Venezuelan Simón Bolívar, whose role as a liberator, statesman and state builder, and thinker, offers an insight into the complexities and consequences of the revolutions in Latin America and their impact on U.S. foreign policy and domestic politics.

The wars of independence in Latin, principally Spanish, America coincided with a long political crisis within the United States, ranging from the efforts of the Jeffersonians to justify their claim as the inheritors of the revolutionary tradition and steer a perilous course toward European powers at war from 1800 to 1815 to a deeply divisive national debate over slavery and the posture of the United States toward the newly emerging independent states in the hemisphere. The best introduction to the era remains Arthur Whitaker, *The United States and the Independence of Latin America, 1800–1830* (New York, 1962; orig. pub., 1941). James E. Lewis Jr., *The American Union and the Problem of Neighborhood: The United States and the Collapse of the Spanish Empire, 1783–1829* (Chapel Hill, N.C., 1998), emphasizes how the domestic political crisis posed by the Florida acquisition and the Missouri crisis of 1820–21, coupled with the appeal of Jacksonian democracy, ultimately doomed efforts to promote hemispheric unity. Caitlin Fitz, *Our Sister Republics: The United States in an Age of American Revolutions* (New York, 2016), provides a parallel story about a generation of Americans, black and white, pro- and antislavery, united in their struggle against the presumed common enemy of European monarchy and tyranny. As the contentious debate over slavery and the role of people of color intruded into the discussion, the bonds of neighborhood weakened under the strain of American exceptionalism and the parallel belief of white supremacy. The North American element of the hemispheric crisis is superbly detailed in Alan Taylor, *The Civil War of 1812: American Citizens, British Subjects, Irish Rebels, and Indian Allies* (New York, 2010), which unravels the complicated strands of the American Revolution and the continuing civil war between monarchical and republican Americans on the northern frontier.

AS MORE THAN one student of the age of revolution has pointed out, we may sometimes exaggerate the impact of the American Revolution in the Atlantic world because of its presumed ideological reach; because of the complications in distinguishing between the U.S. War of Independence, which involved power politics and security issues, and the American Revolution, which is identified with the contradictory symbols and legacies of white supremacy and slavery, on the one hand, and freedom, equality, and liberty, on the other; and because it got there first among the "big four." (Of course, as I suggest here, it got there first and last.) At one time, the Haitian Revolution merited perhaps a paragraph in a U.S. history survey text. Since the mid-1990s, scholarship on the upheaval on the island has grown exponentially, revealing not only the impact of the French Revolution in triggering the colored and then the slave revolt but also the countervailing power of the revolution on the course of the French and Spanish American Revolutions and on the early U.S. republic. Nevertheless, one should always begin with the classic account of C. L. R. James, *The Black Jacobins: Toussaint L'Ouverture and the San Domingo Revolution* (New York, 1989; orig. pub., 1938), then move on to other works and themes relating to the Revolution in David Geggus, ed., *The Impact of the Haitian Revolution in the Atlantic World* (Columbia, S.C., 2001) or in David Geggus and Norman Fiering, eds., *The World of the Haitian Revolution* (Bloomington, Ind., 2009). Laurent Dubois ably retells the heroic struggle of the slaves for their freedom in *Avengers of the New World: The Story of the Haitian Revolution* (Cambridge, Mass., 2005) while showing how the Revolution interacted with and influenced events in the United States, Great Britain, France, Spain, and Cuba. Ashli White, *Encountering Revolution: Haiti and the Making of the Early Republic* (Baltimore, Md., 2010), offers a nuanced explanation on how the Haitian Revolution intruded into Federalist and Jeffersonian America. Julia Gaffield, *Haitian Connections in the Atlantic World* (Chapel Hill, N.C., 2015), explores the tangled legal and maritime ties by which an unrecognized Haiti insinuated itself in the early nineteenth-century Atlantic world.

For a broader perspective on slavery, emancipation, and slave revolts in the age of revolution, three works by David Brion Davis are essential reading: *The Problem of Slavery in the Age of Revolution, 1770–1823* (Ithaca, N.Y., 1975); *The Problem of Slavery in the Age of Emancipation* (New York, 2014); and *Inhuman Bondage: The Rise and Fall of Slavery in the New World* (New York, 2006). The first follows the course of antislavery from an abstraction in 1770 to detailing how Haitian revolutionaries made it a cause that challenged the most powerful. The second reminds us how strongly black leaders resisted colonization movements and fought to achieve a truly integrated society. The third draws upon a lifetime of the study of slavery by exploring its impact in both Western and New World contexts. All should be supplemented by the hemispheric perspective by Eugene Genovese, *From Rebellion to Revolution: Afro-American Slave Revolts in the Making of the Modern World* (Baton Rouge, La., 1979). Wendy Warren, *New England Bound: Slavery and Colonization in Early America* (New York, 2016), shows how New England, which never became a slave society, was nonetheless economically bound to the Caribbean and its sugar islands and how slavery through law, practice, and ideas about freedom reached deeply into New England society.

A "long view" prevails in several key works on slavery, antislavery, and emancipation. In *Abolition: A History of Slavery and Antislavery* (New York, 2009), Seymour Drescher commences his global narrative in the Middle Ages and ends in the post–World War II era. James Walvin, *Sugar: The World Corrupted; From Slavery to Obesity* (New York, 2018), and Sven Beckert, *Empire of Cotton: A Global History* (New York, 2014), frame the intertwined narratives of slavery, capitalism, and globalization in their respective accounts of two commodities and their role in shaping the modern world. In a comprehensive history, *The Slave's Cause: A History of Abolition* (New Haven, Conn., 2015), Manisha Sinha surveys the struggle against slavery from the late colonial era to the end of the Civil War, with the early 1830s as a critical turning point. Robert J. Cottrol, *The Long, Lingering Shadow: Slavery, Race, and Law in the American Hemisphere* (Athens, Ga., 2013), brings a legal perspective to a variety of topics—slavery, emancipation, scientific racism, immigration, and racial classification—to emphasize how the impact and legacy of slavery on the United States differed from that of other hemispheric societies. In a deft analysis, *The Political Worlds of Slavery and Freedom* (Cambridge, Mass., 2009), Steven Hahn reminds us that there was one long emancipation process from 1777 to 1865 and that even free Negroes outside the South endured a conditional and provisional status not unlike that of the Maroons in the Caribbean and Brazil. A protracted struggle dominated by the agency of slaves, former slaves, and their descendants is a dominant theme in Ira Berlin, *Long Emancipation: The Demise of Slavery in the United States* (Cambridge, Mass., 2015). George Reid Andrews, *Afro-Latin America: Black Lives, 1600–2000* (Cambridge, Mass., 2016), provides a comparative perspective on

Africans in the revolutionary struggle and the late nineteenth-century policy of "whiteness" in political culture. The classic account of the symbiotic union of race and the working class is David R. Roediger, *The Wages of Whiteness: Race and the Making of the American Working Class* (London, 1999).

Matthew Pratt Guterl, *American Mediterranean: Southern Slaveholders in the Age of Emancipation* (Cambridge, Mass., 2008), shifts attention away from the national North–South trajectory and looks at the slavery diaspora into the Americas and how southerners perceived their place in that world before and after the Civil War. Matthew Karp offers a parallel history in *This Vast Southern Empire: Slaveholders at the Helm of American Foreign Policy* (Cambridge, Mass., 2016), an account of how southern leaders set aside their apprehensions about central power and used it to advance and extend the slave power beyond national boundaries. Keri Leigh Merritt, *Masterless Men: Poor Whites and Slavery in the Antebellum South* (New York, 2017), skillfully uses land policy, legal records, and labor history to show how slaveholders exploited poor whites. With *The Cause of All Nations* (New York, 2013), Don Doyle joins the list of modern historians who have pushed Civil War history beyond national boundaries.

Scholarship on the transnational trajectory of the long American Revolution has further undermined celebratory accounts. As David Armitage details in *Civil Wars: A History in Ideas* (New York, 2017), the age of revolution held out the promise but largely failed in civilizing those brutal and senseless contests. His book is an apt introduction to an equally ambitious narrative by Steven Hahn, *A Nation without Borders: The United States and Its World in the Age of Civil Wars, 1830–1910* (New York, 2016). Hahn begins his account of the transformation of an agrarian republic into an industrial imperial power with the Texas rebellion and ends it with the Mexican and Bolshevik Revolutions and their challenge to the liberal economic order imposed by the United States. In that eighty-year epoch, nation building was a harsh and often violent experience for Indians, African Americans, laborers, and women, among others, who in the name of revolutionary ideas such as human dignity and rights retaliated by various means of resistance.

With the publication of Amy Kaplan and Donald Pease, eds., *Cultures of United States Imperialism* (Durham, N.C., 1994), American studies scholars and cultural historians began looking more closely at the cultural landscape of U.S. expansion. A decade later, Gretchen Murphy's nuanced study, *Hemispheric Imaginings: The Monroe Doctrine and Narratives of U.S. Empire* (Durham, N.C., 2005), showed how a political statement about the U.S. role in the hemisphere blended with cultural norms, such as the joining of Manifest Destiny with domestic virtue. In *The Anarchy of Empire in the Making of U.S. Culture* (Cambridge, Mass., 2005), Amy Kaplan explores the national belief that wants the rest of the world to be like us but insists that we are different or exceptional. Fredrick B. Pike, *The United States and Latin America: Myths and Stereotypes of Civilization and Nature* (Austin, Tex., 1992), is less didactic and more persuasive than either in conveying the critical importance of how different perspectives on nature have shaped often sharply divergent views among white Europeans and Latin Americans about development and character.

These are muted critiques of American exceptionalism compared to Carol Smith-Rosenberg's indictment in *This Violent Empire: The Birth of an American National Identity* (Chapel Hill, N.C., 2010), which describes the legacy of the American Revolution as a relentless assault by antidemocratic elites against those who challenged their authority. In *Building the Continental Empire: American Expansion from the Revolution to the Civil War* (Chicago, 1996), William Earl Weeks reinforces the argument that the singular purpose of the American Revolution was continental empire and nation building. Although less attentive to cultural forces than Smith-Rosenberg, Brian Loveman, *No Higher Law: American Foreign Policy and the Western Hemisphere since 1776* (Chapel Hill, N.C., 2010), focuses on the U.S. role in the western hemisphere in his dissection of the inconsistencies between U.S. professions of democratic mission and the violence carried out in that quest. As Walter Hixson insists in *The Myth of American Diplomacy: National Identity and U.S. Foreign Policy* (New Haven, Conn., 2008), the legacy of the Revolution has been relentless violence against those who oppose us. He pursues a similar theme in *American Settler Colonialism: A History* (New York, 2013), in which the Anglo-American colonial project uses a violent, militaristic style of warfare to push aside or eliminate indigenous peoples in its quest. The provocative essays in Richard Immerman, *Empire for Liberty: A History of American Imperialism from Benjamin Franklin to Paul Wolfowitz* (Princeton, N.J., 2010), takes the lives and thought of six influential men to explain how Jefferson's presumably inclusive "empire of liberty" became an "empire for liberty," thus justifying a more aggressive role for the nation in North America and in the world by those who insist the United States is not imperialistic! Two handy works on the British and American Empires are David Cannadine, *Victorious Century: The United Kingdom, 1800–1906* (New York, 2018), and the more analytical and comparative study, Julian Go, *Patterns of Empire: The British and American Empires, 1688 to the Present* (New York, 2011).

Another contested issue of the age of revolution, particularly the American Revolution, revolves around the dynamic interplay of race and class. Jacqueline Jones, *A Dreadful Deceit: The Myth of Race in America from the Colonial Era to Obama's America* (New York, 2013), is insistent that race is a distraction in assessing power and the control of one person by another or by a system. Nancy Isenberg focuses almost exclusively on poor whites in *White Trash: The 400-Year Untold History of Class in America* (New York, 2016) in a sweeping history of the persistent and often cruel denigration they have suffered from the early colonial era to the present. In *The Wages of Whiteness: Race and the Making of the American Working Class* (London, 1991), David Roediger makes a more subtle argument about the impact of whiteness on the psyche of the working class from the Revolution to the Civil War.

Religion, even more than class, played a critical role in the long American Revolution and in our political culture and role in the world, as several works acknowledge. Eran Shalev, *American Zion: The Old Testament as Political Text from the Revolution to the Civil War* (New Haven, Conn., 2013), explores the intersection of theology and political culture and the perception of the republic as a reborn Israel. Sam Haselby, *The Origins of American Religious Nationalism* (New York, 2015), challenges those studies that frame discussions of nationalism around the discourse of race or whiteness or civic humanism rather than tie them more closely to religion. Emily Conroy-Krutz, *Christian Imperialism: Converting the World in the Early American Republic* (Ithaca, N.Y., 2015), looks at how U.S. missionaries advanced the cause of national expansion after the Revolution. Nathan Hatch, *The Democratization of American Christianity* (New Haven, Conn., 1989), stresses the role of churches in nourishing democratic idealism and the spirit of independence. In *Religion in America: A Political History* (New York, 2011), Denis Lacorne identifies the competing narratives of national identity as secular, which called for separation of church and state, and religious, which posited an alternative vision that called for blending Protestant and republican values. J. C. D. Clark identifies the American Revolution as the last war of religion in *The Language of Liberty, 1660–1832: Political Discourse and Social Dynamics in the Anglo-American World* (New York, 1993). Mark A. Noll, *America's God: From Jonathan Edwards to Abraham Lincoln* (New York, 2002), provides an exhaustive contextual history of Christian theology and the changes in Christian doctrine from the 1730s to the 1860s.

For a critique of the role of civil religion in the nation's foreign relations, see Walter A. McDougall, *The Tragedy of U.S. Foreign Policy: How America's Civil Religion Betrayed the National Interest* (New Haven, Conn., 2016). Edward J. Blum, *Reforging the White Republic: Race, Religion, and American Nationalism* (Baton Rouge, La., 2005), takes issue with those historians who minimize the role of religion and religious leaders in the shaping of the nation's identity and the rise of ethnic nationalism. On the role of U.S. Protestant reformist groups in the late nineteenth and early twentieth centuries, see Ian Tyrrell, *Reforming the World: The Creation of America's Moral Empire* (Princeton, N.J., 2010), and Matthew McCullough, *The Cross of War: Christian Nationalism and U.S. Expansionism in the Spanish-American War* (Madison, Wis., 2014). Despite its age, Robert Kelley's account of nineteenth-century liberalism, *The Transatlantic Persuasion: The Liberal-Democratic Mind in the Age of Gladstone* (New York, 1969), remains essential reading.

THE LAST FORTY years of the age of revolution—from about 1880 to the end of the Great War and the collapse of Wilsonian liberalism at Versailles—also serve as a coda for the long American Revolution, as well as the initial years of the long twentieth century. Depression, war, rapid industrial growth, massive immigration, labor strikes, demands for reform, the creation of an insular empire that precipitated guerrilla war, and a divisive political debate at home tested a generation. In *Standing at Armageddon: The United States, 1877–1919* (New York, 1987; revised edition published in 2008 as *Standing at Armageddon: A Grassroots History of the Progressive Era*), Nell Irvin Painter captures the turmoil of the age and the shift from an agrarian and rural society to an industrial one. Contrastingly, Jackson Lears, *Rebirth of a Nation: The Making of Modern America, 1877–1920* (New York, 2010), surveys the same era through a cultural lens and sees a generation bent on confronting modernity and rebuilding the nation through war and racism. Stephen Kinzer, *The True Flag: Theodore Roosevelt, Mark Twain, and the Birth of American Empire* (New York, 2016), is similarly critical of the course of empire.

In the early 1960s graduate students in U.S. history and informed citizens were reading Richard Hofstadter's *The Age of Reform: From Bryan to FDR* (New York, 1955), which was less reliable in providing lasting explanations than in providing a guide to a controversial era set against the backdrop of Populism, Progressivism, and war. Those dissatisfied with the views of "consensus" historians could look to William Appleman Williams, whose *The Tragedy of American Diplomacy* (Cleveland, Ohio, 1957) and *The Contours of American History* (New York, 1961) shook both liberals and conservatives alike with their unflinching assault on what he perceived as territorial and especially market expansion as a tool to ease class and racial tensions at home. A sense of moral outrage permeates Williams's books, and in the heated Cold War politics of the times, he endured harsh criticism, yet what he had to say about the course of U.S. history remains relevant even today.

One of his students, Walter LaFeber, demonstrated in *The New Empire: An Interpretation of American Expansion, 1860–1898* (Ithaca, N.Y., 1963; thirty-fifth-anniversary edition, 1998) that it was possible to understand why political and business leaders in the late nineteenth century looked to market expansion as a means of easing the impact of depression and that economic forces were the driving forces in explaining the nation's quest for world power. More important, LaFeber provided a long-overdue corrective to the persistent notion that the war with Spain was an "aberration." In a similar fashion, Thomas Schoonover, *Uncle Sam's War of 1898 and the Origins of Globalization* (Lexington, Ky., 2003), provides a sweeping account of the "long history" of the nation's rise to globalism through commercial expansion southward into the Caribbean and westward across the Pacific. Ian Tyrrell, *Reforming the World: The Creation of America's Moral Empire* (Princeton, N.J., 2010), surveys the role of Protestant reformist elements in the late nineteenth and early twentieth centuries and identifies their intention as nonterritorial. Andrew Preston, *Sword of the Spirit, Shield of Faith: Religion in American War and Diplomacy* (New York, 2012), discusses how religion played a critical role in explaining the U.S. role in World War I as a moral endeavor. Woodrow Wilson was a historian, a social scientist, and a Calvinist Presbyterian, and he perceived the U.S. role in the world as a covenant. In *Waves of Decolonization: Discourses of Race and Hemispheric Citizenship in Cuba, Mexico, and the United States* (Durham, N.C., 2008), David Luis-Brown provides a transnational assessment of people challenging the racial and imperial ideologies of the era and calling for something akin to "hemispheric citizenship." As the title suggests, David Hollinger, *Protestants Abroad: How Missionaries Tried to Change the World but Changed America* (Princeton, N.J., 2017), shows how American and European Protestant missionaries indirectly supported imperial and racist projects but also established schools and institutes that survived. Transformed by their experience, many returned to the United States as advocates for reform about the role of missions in Asia, Africa, and the Seven Seas.

Emily S. Rosenberg, *Spreading the American Dream: American Economic and Cultural Expansion, 1890–1945* (New York, 1982), eschews "imperialism" in favor of "expansion" in order to capture the spirit of U.S. liberal developmentalism in the world—the diffusion of U.S. trade and investment coincidental with the promotion of U.S. interests and ideas. Herbert Croly's *The Promise of American Life* (New York, 1910), which flattered Theodore Roosevelt and was incorporated into his New Nationalism platform, remains relevant, although Croly, one of the founders of the *New Republic*, became disillusioned with Roosevelt and Wilson too after U.S. entry into the war. Randolph Bourne Jr., "Trans-national America," *Atlantic Monthly*, July 1916, 86–97, which decried the celebratory history and "Americanization" in defense of the immigrant, describes a nation that persists to this day. Thomas C. Leonard, *Illiberal Reformers: Race, Eugenics, and American Economics in the Progressive Era* (Princeton, N.J., 2016), is a devastating critique of a generation. Michael McGerr, *A Fierce Discontent: The Rise and Fall of the Progressive Movement* (New York, 2003), shows that the movement was both middle class and radical. David Kennedy, *Over Here: The First World War and American Society* (New York, 2004; orig. pub., 1980), details how deeply the war divided the nation, the measures taken to suppress dissent, and the growth of government during the war. Two essential volumes on the coming and course of the war—Eric Hobsbawm, *The Age of Empire, 1875–1914* (London, 1987), and John H. Morrow Jr., *The Great War: An Imperial History* (New York, 2005)—explain in unsettling detail how capitalism and the pursuit of empire brought on a war that destroyed empires and in its mindless carnage battered a generation's faith in progress and human improvement. For the antiwar movement and its dilemmas, see Michael Kazin, *War against War: The American*

Fight for Peace, 1914–1918 (New York, 2017), and especially Adam Hochschild, *To End All Wars: A Story of Loyalty and Disloyalty* (New York, 2011), which demolishes Woodrow Wilson's claim about the democratic purposes of the war. The essays in Thomas W. Zeiler, David K. Ekbladh, and Benjamin C. Montoya, eds., *Beyond 1917: The United States and the Global Legacies of the Great War* (New York, 2017), address the long-term consequences of the war. Jon Meachem evaluates the contemporary populist assault on liberalism in *The Soul of America: The Battle for Our Better Angels* (New York, 2018).

INDEX